就这 *900* 句

玩转口语

英语口语900句 ● 最精典

主编 【美】艾瑞克(Eric Wayne Fink)　　方振宇　王玲

【美】杰西卡(Jessica Dawn Brosius)　【留美】王雄

海豚出版社
DOLPHIN BOOKS
CIPG 中国国际出版集团

使用说明
Instructions

Like a long lonely stream, I keep running towards a dream.

就这 900 句 玩转口语

Clerk: The next available flight leaves at 9:00 a. m. this Tuesday. Shall I book you a seat?

职员：这周二上午九点有一班。要我为您订个座位吗？

Kevin: Er... it is a direct flight, isn't it?

凯文：是的……这是直达吗？

Clerk: Yes it is. You want to go first class or coach?

凯文：是的。您想订头等舱还是经济舱？

Kevin: I prefer first class, what's the fare?

凯文：我想订头等舱的机票。多少钱？

Clerk: One-way is $856.

职员：单程票是 856 美元。

Kevin: OK, I'll take one.

凯文：好的，我订一张。

◇alternative [ɔ]'tɜːnətɪv] *n.* 选择
◇coach [kotʃ] *n.* (普通) 旅客车厢，经济舱

---

4 情景配图

针对具体场景精选了美国本土拍摄的实景图片，让大家从图片中体会到话题的内容，同时也让大家多视角感受鲜活的美国。

文化穿越

在美国有很多种机票购买方式，最简单便捷的就是网上购买。网上购票需注意这几点：

第一，选择适合的网站。代理机票的网站很多，另外，还有航空公司自己的网站如 AA、United、Continental、Air China、Northwest 等。网上购票最好的办法是在大致浏览了一些网站后，锁定一两个网站做详细的比较，选定最适合自己的机票。

第二，在选定网站和适合自己的机票后，就可以在该网站进入购买程序。购买机票一定要有信用卡或银行卡，美国是国外申请的卡，美国之外的卡有时网站不能识别。网上买机票除了要填写护照姓名、住址、旅行时间、地点等之外，还可以在网上定座位和选择电话提醒服务。在提交购买确定后，网站会在 24 小时内向你的邮箱发出电子机票，在得到电子机票后，一定要仔细核对每项信息，确定无误。在指定日期到达机场后，在该航空公司的电脑上输入电子机票的号码，并按指令输入相应信息就可以，整个过程几分钟即可完成，非常方便。

第三，在美国可以提前几个月购买机票，而且预订的时间早，价格相应越低，比如，6 月份出行，2、3 月份就开始订机票了，如果在 4 月份以后才订，价格肯定会上来，而且有时价格每天都在变。通常网上订的机票不能或不方便退，如有变化如更改时同等，航空公司通常收取手续费，手续费最少在 150 美元以上，所以在订机票时一定要确定各项信息无误后才能提交。

---

5 文化穿越

补充每个话题涉及的美国本土文化，每一章节的文化穿越都让大家感受到美国本土的气息，在轻松活泼之余，也在扩充知识面，让大家跨文化交际不再有障碍。

图书在版编目（CIP）数据

就这 900 句 玩转口语 / 方振宇等主编 . —北京: 海豚出版社，2011.2

ISBN 978-7-5110-0432-1

Ⅰ . ①就… Ⅱ . ①方… Ⅲ . ①英语－口语 Ⅳ . ① H319.9

中国版本图书馆 CIP 数据核字（2011）第 024015 号

书 名：	JIUZHEJIUBAIJU WANZHUANKOUYU	
	就这 900 句 玩转口语	
主 编：	方振宇 等	
责任编辑：	董 锋	
出 版：	海豚出版社	
网 址：	http://www.dolphin-books.com.cn	
地 址：	北京市百万庄大街 24 号	
邮 编：	100037	
电 话：	010-68997480（销售）	
	010-68998879（总编室）	
传 真：	010-68994018	
印 刷：	北京世纪雨田印刷有限公司	
经 销：	新华书店	
开 本：	32 开（850 毫米 ×1168 毫米）	
印 张：	18.75	
字 数：	298 千字	
版 次：	2011 年 3 月第 1 版 2011 年 6 月第 3 次印刷	
标准书号：	ISBN 978-7-5110-0432-1	
定 价：	34.80 元	

Kevin

与你一路同行

Hello, everybody，我是 Kevin，很高兴认识大家，也很高兴有这个机会和大家在英语学习的路上一路同行。

我是一个 ABC，一直生活在美国，我在感受全方位美国文化的同时，也经常在爸爸妈妈思念祖国的情愫中领略到中华文明的博大精深。这次终于有机会回到祖国，看到日益开放的祖国在崛起的同时，也感慨大多数同胞的英语口语水平确实还需大大提升，因为，我们要和国际接轨，就必须要消除交流障碍，而语言就是我们的通行证。于是我有了一个伟大的想法，回到美国把美国人生活工作中经常说的话记录下来，然后把这一本活生生的语言送给国人，以此希望能为提高国人的英语水平，特别是口语水平助一臂之力。

有想法就立即付诸行动！因为 Kevin 深知"Activity is the only road to success.（行动是通往成功的唯一道路。）"其实这也是我想跟大家说的第一点，如果你想提高自己的英语口语，就必须要有实际行动。哪怕只是每天记一个单词、说一句英语，你也在一点一滴地进步！但如果你没有行动，那永远只能原地踏步，甚至倒退！

我想跟大家说的第二点是，不要心存疑虑，尽管大胆开口。美国总统罗斯福曾经说过："The only limit to our realization of tomorrow will be our doubts of today.（实现明天理想的唯一障碍是今天的疑虑。）"要想提升英语口语，就不要在开口之前担心自己说出的话是否符合语法，是否结构正确，只要你打破开口的尴尬，离成功也就不远了！

Kevin 想跟大家说的第三点是，很多人都报口语培训班，买各种各样的口语资料，但这不是最根本的，因为这些经验都是别人的，要想完全适合你自己，只有通过亲身体验。Kevin 提醒大家 "Experience is not what happens to a man; it is what a man does with what happens to him.（经验不会从天而降；经验只有通过实践才能获得。）"

所以选一本地地道道的口语书，加上自己坚持不懈地训练，这才是提升口语的关键。《就这900句，玩转口语》是美国人日常生活工作中的话语记录，是一本来自美国本土的新鲜语言！下面 Kevin 给大家介绍一下本书的内容和特色：

本书内容：

全书分为 15 大主题，129 个话题，涉及生活、交际、工作、学习、交通、态度、情感等老外从早到晚都在说的各方面内容。每一部分所包含的版块如下：

◆ 口语大放送

把同一个话题所需要用到的各种地道表达都说出来，且设置了各种场景的问答，让你说英语不再感觉枯燥！

◆ 交流面对面

把每一个话题以现场交流的方式直观表达出来，让你说英语不再觉得无聊！

◆ 文化穿越

用老外的话解释了每个话题涉及的美国本土文化，让你说英语不再有顾忌！

本书特色：

◆ **美国本土编写，语言地道鲜活**

本书全部内容都在美国本土编写，再现美国人生活、工作、学习的各个场景，语言纯正地道、风格时尚流行。有正式用语，也有街头巷语，让大家全方位感受地道美语！

◆ **人物主角串联，全书融为一体**

本书以 Kevin 为人物主角，通过 Kevin 的活动，把我们融入到日常生活工作学习的各个场景，环环相扣，节节相连。一个场景就是人物主角的一个生活舞台，一本书就是一个人物主角的生活历程，有喜怒哀乐，有笑语悲歌，让大家多场景感受地道美语！

◆ **精美实物图片，置身美国风情**

本书每个话题都配备了美国本土拍摄的精美实物图片，光看图片也能体会到话题的内容，话中显图，图中衬话，交并相容，让大家多视角感受地道美语！

◆ **精美双色印刷，愉悦视觉系统**

本书采用双色印刷，重点突出，有的放矢，让大家在学习的同时既能抓住重点，又能享受视觉感官带来的快乐，从而避免学习的疲劳，提高效率！

本书内容都是纯正的美语录音，让大家在感受美音氛围的同时，加深对句子的记忆和理解，从而做到脱口而出！

Kevin 最后提醒大家，英语口语不是背出来的，而是在实实在在的交流中说出来的，所以在提升口语的过程中，默默无闻地学习是不够的，只有说出来才是你自己的！亲爱的朋友们，和 Kevin 一起玩转英语口语，你会感受到英语其实很 EASY！不要再迟疑，只要大胆说，你的口语提升之路不会太遥远，Kevin 将一路伴你同行！

Kevin
振宇英语中心

Contents

就这 **900** 句 玩转口语

Chapter 1

纽约来客
New Yorker

Section 1 预订机票
Flight Ticket Reservation

我说过我要把美国人生活工作中经常说的话记录下来，把他们活生生的语言送给大家。我一旦有了这个想法，就迫不及待地想实现它，赶紧去预订机票，踏上回美国的征程。预订机票有好几种方式，比如你可以电话预订，还可以通过网上预订，现在Kevin把这些相关的英语口语奉送给大家。

 1

Excuse me, could I make a reservation for flight F8008 to America? 打扰一下，我可以预订去美国 F8008 号航班的机票吗？

> 直接点明了你的意图：
> - Hello, I'd like one seat for tomorrow's China Airlines Flight F8008 to America, please. 你好，我想买一张中国航空明天 F8008 次航班到美国的机票。
>
> 这时工作人员进一步询问：
> - Yes, which day do you want to book? 好的，你要订哪一天的票？
> ❖ make a reservation 预订（机票）

在这里，暂时先把这一对话搁下，我再告诉大家购买机票的一些其他表达。

2

Will you be traveling first class or economy? One-way or a round-trip ticket? 您要搭乘头等舱，还是经济舱？单程票还是双程票？

> 询问机票或航班类型：
> - What kind of ticket do you want, first class or economy? 您想要哪种票，头等舱，还是经济舱？
> - Would you like the morning flight, afternoon flight, or red-eye flight? 您是喜欢上午航班、下午航班还是夜间航班？
> ❖ a round-trip ticket 往返票，双程票
> ❖ red-eye flight 夜间航班

【补充】这句话中 red-eye flight 这个词很富有想象力，想一下夜晚坐飞机常常更易疲劳，睡不好会造成"红眼"。不过 red-eye flight 的票价会比白天的航班便宜很多哦。

这时你可以询问一下机票的价格。

3 What's the fare to America, economy class? 去美国的经济舱票价是多少？

询问经济舱的票价：

- How much is the economy class to America? 去美国的经济舱票价是多少？
- ❖ economy class 经济舱

如果你想进一步了解机票的价格，请接着看下面的内容。

4 Are there any discount tickets available? 我可以买到有折扣的票吗？

通常机票打折的情况比较多：

- Will you give me a discount? 有打折吗？
- Any tickets on discount? 有打折的票吗？

当然，如果没有这样的优惠活动，工作人员通常会这样回答你：

- Sorry, there are no discounts. 对不起，没有折扣。
- ❖ available [ə'veləbl] *adj.* 可得到的，可买到的
- ❖ discount ['dɪskaunt] *n.* 折扣，打折扣

5 I want to take a direct flight. 我想搭乘直航班机。

从中国飞往美国的班机有时候需要转机，如果你不想转机，就可以要求买直达航班的。

- ❖ direct flight 直航，直达班机

这时候如果你想知道飞机的起飞时间，请接着看下面的表达。

6 What's the departure time? 起飞时间是什么时候？

当然你也可以比较客气地询问：

- Could you tell me the departure time? 能告诉我起飞时间吗？
- Would you mind telling me the departure time? 能告诉我起飞时间吗？

询问下一次航班的时间：

- When's the next plane for America? 下一班去美国的飞机是什么时候？
- What time is the next plane for America? 下一班去美国的飞机是什么时候？

这时工作人员一般会很热心地告诉你：

- The departure time is 9:00 a. m. Monday. 起飞时间是周一上午九点。
- ❖ departure [dɪ'partʃə] n. 离开，出发，起程

 I'm sorry. I'd like to change my reservation. 对不起，我想更改一下我订的票。

想更换机票或取消航班：

- Could I change my reservation? 我能改一下我订的票吗？
- Excuse me, I'd like to change this ticket to first class. 不好意思，我想把这张票换成头等舱的。

别的航班还有票：

- Okay. Then tell me your new reservation. 好的，告诉我你想要的新时间。

头等舱的票已经卖完了：

- I'm sorry, they are already full. 抱歉，全都满了。
- ❖ reservation [ˌrɛzə'veʃən] n. 预订的房间（或座位）
- ❖ first class 头等舱

 I'd like to cancel my reservation to America. 我想取消我预订的去美国的航班机票。

相同意思的表达：

- What if I want to cancel my reservation to America? 我想取消我预订的去美国的航班机票可以吗？
- Could I cancel my reservation to America, please? 我能取消我预订的去美国的航班机票吗？

可以，但通常取消预订要扣除费用的哟：

- Okay. Tell me your name and your reservation number. 好的，请告诉我你的姓名和你的预订号码。
- ❖ cancel ['kænsl] vt. 取消，废除

预订后确认班机或取票。

9 Excuse me, I'd like to reconfirm my flight from Beijing to New York. 打扰一下，我要再确认一下我从北京到纽约的班机。

礼貌地询问航班号以便查询：

- OK. Please tell me your flight number. 好的，请把你的航班号告诉我。
- ❖ reconfirm [ˌriːkənˈfɜːm] *vt.* 再证实，再确认，再确定

10 Where do I pick up the ticket? 我要到哪里取机票？

更礼貌的说法：

- Do you mind telling me where I can get the ticket? 你能告诉我在哪里取机票吗？
- Could you tell me where I can pick up the ticket? 你能告诉我在哪里取机票吗？

通常对方会告诉你：

- You'll pick up the ticket at the airport counter. 你会在机场柜台拿机票。

交流面对面

Flight Ticket Reservation Conversation

Clerk: Good morning, the China Airlines. What can I do for you?

职员：早上好，中国航空公司。我能为您做些什么？

Kevin: Yes, I'd like to make a reservation to New York tomorrow.

凯文：我想订一张明天飞往纽约的机票。

Clerk: We have Flight F8008 tomorrow. Just a moment please. Let me check whether there're seats available. I'm sorry we are all booked up for Flight F8008.

职员：我们明天有 F8008 次航班。请稍等，我查一下是否有座。非常抱歉，F8008 次航班已经预定满了。

Kevin: Then, any alternatives?

凯文：那还有别的吗？

Clerk: The next available flight leaves at 9:00 a. m. this Tuesday. Shall I book you a seat?	职员：这周二上午九点有一班。要我为您订个座位吗？
Kevin: Er... it is a direct flight, isn't it?	凯文：哦……是直航对吗？
Clerk: Yes it is. You want to go first class or coach?	职员：是的。您想订头等舱还是经济舱？
Kevin: I prefer first class, what's the fare?	凯文：我想订头等舱的机票。多少钱？
Clerk: One-way is $856.	职员：单程票是 856 美元。
Kevin: OK, I'll take one.	凯文：好的，我订一张。

❖ alternative [ɔl'tɜː'nətɪv] *n.* 选择
❖ coach [kotʃ] *n.* (普通) 旅客车厢，经济舱

文 化 穿 越

在美国有很多种机票购买方式，最简单便捷的就是网上购买。网上购票需注意这几点：

第一，选择适合的网站。代理机票的网站很多，另外，还有航空公司自己的网站如 AA、United、Continental、Air China、Northwest 等。网上购票最好的办法是在大致浏览了一些网站后，锁定一两个网站作详细的比较，选定最适合自己的机票。

第二，在选定网站和适合自己的机票后，就可以在该网站进入购买程序。购买机票一定要有信用卡或银行卡，最好是在美国申请的卡，美国之外的卡有时网站不能识别。网上买机票除了要填写护照姓名、住址、旅行时间、地点等之外，还可以在网上定座位和选择电话提醒服务。在提交购买确定后，网站会在 24 小时内向你的邮箱发出电子机票，在得到电子机票后，一定要仔细核对每项信息，确定准确无误。在指定日期到达机场后，在该航空公司服务台的电脑上输入电子机票的号码，并按指令输入相应信息就可以，整个过程几分钟就可完成，非常方便。

第三，在美国可以提前几个月购买机票，而且预订的时间早，价格相应低一些，比如，6 月份想出行，2、3 月份就要开始订机票了，如果在 4 月份以后才订，价格肯定会上涨，而且有时价格每天都在变。通常网上订的机票不能或不方便退，遇有变化如更改时间等，航空公司通常收取手续费，手续费最少在 150 美元以上，所以在订机票时一定要确定各项信息无误后才能提交。

Section 2 检票登机
Check in and Board

在飞机起飞前两小时，我得到机场去检票登机了，这是一个比较繁琐的过程，在这里我提醒坐飞机的朋友们一定要早作准备。接下来我把在这一过程中可能要用到的英语和大家分享一下，一起跟着 Kevin 来吧！

① Where is the check-in? 在哪里办理登机手续？

还可以更礼貌些：
- Do you know where I can check in at? 你知道在哪里办理登机手续吗？

对方知道的话会告诉你：
- Yes, it's right down that hallway. 知道，就在那过道下面。
- ❖ check in 登机办理柜台
- ❖ hallway ['hɔl,we] n. 过道，门厅，走廊

② Here is my ticket and passport. 这是我的机票和护照。

同样的说法：
- This is my ticket and passport. 这是我的机票和护照。
- ❖ passport ['pæs,port] n. 护照，通行证

③ Where is security located? 在哪里安检？

以下的说法也表达同样的意思：
- Do you know where security is? 你知道安检在哪里吗？
- I need to get through security, where is it? 我需要过安检，在哪里呢？

对方会告诉你：

- It's right around the corner. 就在那角落里。
- ❖ security [sɪ'kjurətɪ] *n.* 安全，安检

4 Where is terminal A? A 号航站楼在哪里？

还可以请人帮忙找一下：

- I'm looking for my terminal, can you help? 我在找航站楼，你能帮我一下吗？
- Could you help me find my terminal? 你能帮我找到航站楼吗？

对方会很乐意帮忙：

- It's just down this way. 从这条道走下去就行。
- Sure, no problem. 好的，没问题。
- ❖ terminal ['tɜ·mənl] *n.* 航站楼

5 When is the plane boarding? 什么时候登机？

询问登机的时间：

- Do you know when the plane is boarding? 你知道什么时候登机吗？

告知确定的时间：

- It will board at 7:00 p. m. tonight. 今晚 7 点登机。

不确定时间：

- The plane has been delayed. I'm not sure. 飞机晚点了，我也不确定。
- ❖ delay [dɪ'le] *vt.* 耽搁，延误

Check In and Board Conversation

Kevin: Is this where I check in?	凯文：	这是检票的地方吗？
Clerk: Yes, it is, sir.	职员：	是的，先生。
Kevin: Alright, here's my ticket.	凯文：	好的，这是我的机票。

Clerk: Show me your passport too, please.	职员： 请把你的护照也给我看看。
Kevin: Here you go.	凯文： 给你。
Clerk: Thank you, sir. Do you need directions to your gate?	职员： 谢谢你，先生。你需要我给你指一下登机门的方向吗？
Kevin: No, thank you.	凯文： 不用了，谢谢你。
Clerk: Don't forget to show your ticket to security.	职员： 别忘了把你的机票给安检人员看看。
Kevin: I won't. Do I check my bags in over there?	凯文： 不会忘的。我要在那里安检我的包吗？
Clerk: Yes. Have a good day!	职员： 是的，祝你玩得愉快！

文化穿越

第一次坐国际航班需要注意以下几点。首先可以在网上提前订好自己的座位（走廊的位置比较方便上卫生间），还有一些对于食物的特殊要求。例如，有专门针对素食主义者的食物。建议在飞机起飞 24 小时前给机场打个电话确认下行程没有变更，因为有时飞机行程会有变更。之后确认自己的几个重要证件，护照、机票确认打印件（不一定需要，但有最好）。如果是留学生，还得带上 I-20（美国学校发给外国学生用来申请签证以便进入美国的通行证，上面载明了持该表学生就读的学校、系所、准予合法在美国居留的期限及应提出财力证明的金额等重要事项），还有一定要备用零钱，大概 200 元人民币和一定的美元，因为在机场的免税店里可以买两条烟和一些必需品。另外最重要的就是国际航班需要至少提前 3 个小时到机场，因为安检以及行李重量检查比较耗时间，如果行李超重还得重新打包。最后就是拿好自己换好的登机牌和行李牌准备登机了。

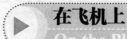
Section 3　▶ 在飞机上
On the Plane

　　现在我已经在飞机上了，窗外是蓝天白云，地上的一切都尽收眼底，我有一种高高在上一览无余的感觉。不过提醒大家在飞机上还是有许多事情需要注意的，特别是晕机的朋友。下面欢迎大家和 Kevin 一起来说在飞机上需要用到的英语。

1 What's the in-flight movie? 飞机上放映什么电影?

还可以这样询问:
- Do you know what the movie will be? 你知道要放什么电影吗?

乘务员会告诉你:
- We'll announce the movie at take-off. 我们会在起飞的时候播报电影的。
- ❖ in-flight ['in'flait] *adj.* 飞行中的, 飞行过程中的
- ❖ announce [ə'nauns] *vt.* 播报

2 Will food be served? 会提供食物吗?

还可以询问具体的食物:
- Will there be any food on the ride? 飞行途中有什么食物吗?

如果有食物提供:
- Yes, we'll have our menus ready soon. 有, 我们会很快把菜单准备好的。

如果没有食物提供:
- No, but we can give you peanuts. 没有, 但我们可以给你提供花生。
- ❖ peanut ['pi:nʌt] *n.* 花生, 花生果

3 I'm so afraid of flying. 我很害怕坐飞机。

表达害怕还可以说：

- I'm terrified of flying. 我害怕坐飞机。
- I hate flying. I'm terrified of it. 我讨厌坐飞机，我害怕。

有人会有同感：

- Me too! 我也是。
- ❖ terrified ['terɪfaɪd] *adj.* 受惊吓的，感到恐惧的

4 Could I get a pair of headphones? 我能要副耳机吗？

飞机上有时候会卖耳机：

- Could I purchase some headphones? 我能买副耳机吗？

买东西乘务员当然会高兴了：

- Sure, 5 dollars please. 好的，5 美元。
- ❖ headphone ['hed,fon] *n.* 头戴式耳机
- ❖ purchase ['pɝtʃəs] *vt.* 买，购买

5 Do you have any pillows? 你们有枕头吗？

还可以直接跟乘务员要：

- Could I get a pillow please? 我能要个枕头吗？
- ❖ pillow ['pɪlo] *n.* 枕头

6 Where is the bathroom? 卫生间在哪里？

同样的说法还有：

- Where's the bathroom located? 卫生间在哪里？

对方会告诉你：

- The bathroom is just down the hall. 卫生间就在门厅下面。

如果刚好遇上湍流：

- The bathroom is down the hall, but you must wait until after turbulence. 卫生间就在门厅下面，但你必须得等湍流过后才能用。
- ❖ turbulence ['tɝbjələns] *n.* 空气和水的湍流，紊流

7 What is turbulence? 什么是湍流？

万一遇到湍流该怎么办：

- What can I do if we have turbulence? 如果我们遇到湍流我该怎么办？

对方会告诉你怎么做：

- Just remain seated until the turbulence passes. 坐到座位上等湍流过去就行了。

On the Plane Conversation

Kevin: Do you mind if I trade you for the window seat?	凯 文：我和你换个靠窗户的座位行吗？
Passenger: No problem, man. Go ahead.	乘 客：没问题。换吧。
Kevin: Thanks.	凯 文：谢谢。
Stewardess: Would you like any refreshments before we take off?	乘务员：在飞机起飞前，你们想要什么点心吗？
Kevin: Yes please. Could I have a bottle of water and a bag of pretzels please?	凯 文：是的。能给我来瓶水和一包椒盐饼干吗？
Stewardess: Alright. Here you go.	乘务员：好的。给你，先生。
Kevin: Thank you very much.	凯 文：多谢你啊。
Stewardess: Enjoy your flight.	乘务员：旅途愉快。
Kevin: Thank you, ma'am. When will the meals be served?	凯 文：谢谢你，女士。什么时候供饭？
Stewardess: Around 4:30.	乘务员：大约 4:30 吧。

❖refreshment [rɪ'frɛʃmənt] *n.* 茶点，饮料

❖pretzel ['prɛtsl] *n.* 椒盐脆饼

文化穿越

　　在飞行途中，晕机的朋友可以向空姐要点药。一般长途飞行飞机都会提供食物，但食物的质量取决于航空公司，水一般可以无限次提供，理论上食物也可以，但空姐或许会微笑地告诉你食物已发光。另外就是飞机上的娱乐项目，这些是必须的，因为从中国飞到美国旅程确实有点长，且有点儿无聊。有的高级点的大型飞机每个座位后面都会有小屏幕，可以自己挑选电影或者听音乐。如果飞行超过 15 个小时，你会发现看电影和听音乐也是种煎熬，眼睛疼得不行。有些人的耳朵会有高压反应，听什么都不太清楚，甚至会有轻微的疼痛。除此之外，别指望在飞机上能过个舒服的夜晚，除非是公务舱。飞机的引擎会很吵。另外提醒大家，坐飞机时尽量穿长袖，因为即使是在夏季，飞机在高空时舱内温度仍然较低。

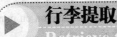
Section 4 ▶ 行李提取
Retrieve the Luggage

经过十几个小时的飞行，我又能踩在土地上了，这让我有一种很踏实的感觉。不过别着急，我还得去提取行李呢。这时候提醒大家要仔细检查自己的行李，千万别拿错了，万一行李有损伤的话，就赶紧和相关工作人员联系。

1 Where is the luggage pickup spot? 行李提取处在哪里？

还可以换种说法：
- Where do I have to go to pick up my luggage? 我该在哪里领取行李？
- I need my luggage, where can I find it? 我要领取行李，我在哪里能找到？

对方会告诉你：
- Right down the hallways. 就在那过道下面。
- ❖ spot [spɑt] *n.* 场所，地点

2 I lost a piece of luggage. 我丢失了一件行李。

也可以说：
- I seem to have lost my luggage. 我的行李好像丢了。

机场工作人员会跟你说：
- Let me attempt to assist you. 我尽力帮你找。
- ❖ attempt to 尝试，试图，尽力

3 I'm missing a carry-on. 我丢失了一件随身行李。

如果行李是在飞机上丢失的：
- It looks like I'm missing one of my carry-ons from the plane. 我好像在飞机上丢失了一件随身携带的行李。

- Could I check the plane for a carry-on on mine? 我能查查飞机上是否有我一件随身携带的行李吗？

工作人员会给你帮忙：

- Let me try and help find it. 我尽力帮你找。

但不会允许你再返回飞机：

- I'm sorry, but we can't admit anyone back on to the plane. 很抱歉，我们不允许任何人回到飞机上去。

❖ carry-on ['kærɪˌɑn] *n.* 手提行李，随身行李

4 When can I pick up my luggage? 我什么时候能领取行李？

以下两种说法都可以：

- Do you know when I can get my luggage? 你知道我什么时候能领取行李吗？
- Is my luggage ready yet? 我的行李准备好了吗？

如果一切准备妥当，工作人员会要求：

- Yes, can I have your name? 好的，我能知道你的名字吗？

5 What happens if I get the wrong luggage? 如果我领错行李了会怎么样？

同样的说法还有：

- What would happen if I picked out the wrong luggage? 如果我领错行李了会怎么样？

机场工作人员给你的官方答复：

- We will ask you to return it, and announce to those waiting we've found it. 我们会要求你归还它，然后通知那些等待取行李的人我们已经找到了他们的行李。

交流面对面

Retrieve Your Luggage Conversation

Clerk: Hi there. I hope you had a good flight. 职 员：你好，希望您飞行旅途愉快。

Kevin: I did, thank you. Which conveyor belt will my luggage be on?	凯　文：旅途不错，谢谢你。我的行李在哪条传送带上？
Clerk: It's right over there, sir.	职　员：就在那边，先生。
Kevin: Okay, thank you.	凯　文：好的，谢谢你。
Stranger: Be prepared for a wait. I've been standing here for 10 minutes.	陌生人：还是准备等一会儿吧，我都在这儿站了10分钟了。
Kevin: Really? That sucks. I have someone waiting for me.	凯　文：是吗？那太糟糕了。有人在等我了。
Stranger: Better call them and tell them you'll be late.	陌生人：最好给他们打个电话告诉他们你会晚一点。
Kevin: Alright. Thanks for the warning.	凯　文：好的，谢谢你的提醒。
Stranger: No problem. Oh, there's my bag. Good luck.	陌生人：没关系。哦，那是我的行李。祝你好运。
Kevin: Thanks.	凯　文：谢谢。

❖conveyor belt 传送带，输送带
❖be prepared for 为……作准备
❖No problem. 没关系。

文化穿越

　　取行李是件锻炼耐性的事儿。最先托运行李的人一般都是最后拿到行李，因为行李存储是有顺序的。在存储行李的时候有两件事需要记住，一是需要往自己的行李上系个醒目的布条或者胶带，取行李的时候比较容易找到；二是需要在你的行李外部和内部放个名字牌，名字牌需要用双语写清你的名字，住址，联系方式等，万一行李丢失，机场可以及时联系到行李主人。如果行李丢失，应马上与机场工作人员联系，有时候行李可能会比人晚到一些。买了保险的人，如果行李丢失，保险公司会给予一定的赔偿。

Section 5  通关检查
Security Check

拿到行李后，过了这最后一道关口，就真正踏上美国的土地了，这就是通关检查，也就是我们通常说的安检。美国的安检比较繁琐，检查的内容也非常细致，所以在这里，我把安检需要用的英语给大家一一列举出来，希望对出国的朋友们有所帮助。

1 Please remove all metal items. 请把所有的金属物件都拿开。

同样还可以说：
- Please remove everything that is metal from your person. 请把随身戴的金属物件全部拿开。

对方按要求做即可：
- Sure, one second. 好的，等一下啊。

2 Could I look through your bag? 我能查看一下你的包吗？

检查包里面的东西：
- We need to see inside of your bag, ma'am. 女士，我们需要看看你包里面的东西。

乘客会说：
- No problem. 没问题。

❖ look through 仔细查看

3 Place your items in the tray and send them through to me. 把你的物件放到托盘上传过来给我。

还可根据具体情况说：

- Place items in this box and put it on the conveyor belt. 把物件放到这个盒子里再把盒子放到传送带上。
- ❖ conveyor [kən'veəˌ] *n*. 输送带，传送带

4 Could you take your shoes off, please? 请你把鞋脱了，好吗?

或者可以说：

- Could we get you to take your shoes off, please? 请你把鞋脱了，好吗?

乘客会照做：

- No problem. 没问题。

5 Please step through the metal detector ahead of you. 请走过你前面的金属探测器。

类似的表达还有：

- Please take a step forward through the metal detector. 请向前迈一步通过金属探测器。

乘客会照做：

- Sure, no problem. 好的，没问题。
- ❖ step through 逐步通过，走路通过
- ❖ metal detector 金属探测器
- ❖ take a step forward 向前一步

6 You may retrieve your items after they've passed through our x-ray machine. 等通过我们的 X 光机后你就可以取回你的物件了。

这句表达也同样适用：

- You can pick up your items at the end of this conveyor belt. 你可以在这传送带的末端取回你的物件。

乘客表达感激之情：

- Thank you. 谢谢你。
- Have a good day. 祝你愉快。
- ❖ retrieve [rɪ'triv] *vt*. 取回，收回

Security Check Conversation

Kevin: Do I need to take my watch off?	凯 文：我需要把手表取下来吗？
Security: Yes. And put your bags on the table, please.	安检员：是的，请把包放在桌子上。
Kevin: Alright, here you go.	凯 文：好的，给你。
Security: Take off anything metal you have and step through the doorway.	安检员：请把随身戴的任何金属的东西都取下来，走过这个门口。
Kevin: Sure.	凯 文：好的。
Security: The alarm is going off. Are you sure you removed everything metal?	安检员：警报铃响了，你确定你把所有的金属物件都取下来了吗？
Kevin: Let me check…Oh, I'm sorry! I forgot about my luggage keys.	凯 文：让我看看……，哦，对不起！我忘了把行李钥匙取下来了。
Security: Alright, you're good to go.	安检员：好的，你可以放心走了。
Kevin: Thanks. Sorry about that.	凯 文：谢谢，刚才很抱歉啊。
Security: No problem, sir.	安检员：没关系，先生。

❖go off 突然响起

文化穿越

　　安检是个很烦人的步骤。尤其是美国的安检，裤腰带和鞋都需要脱，另外需要将电池从笔记本上拆下来一起放到盒子里进行扫描，还有相机、手机，一切金属物件全部要放在盒子里。当然，别把自己的护照和登机牌也一起扫描，因为安检门那儿的工作人员有时会查看你的登机牌和护照。扫描完毕后，要检查是否已带上自己的所有东西。有时候机场会有抽查小组，他们会将你带到一边，要求你打开行李箱。按要求做就可以了，一般都没问题。

Section 6　▶ 问路指路
Directions Inquiry

我一向是不分方向的，连平时逛街都有可能迷路，经过长时间的飞行后，我有点晕头转向就更分不清方向了，接机的家人和朋友还没有到，我打算去问路了。我相信大家都有过问路的经历，接下来我把自己的这一经历写下来，供大家用英语问路的时候参考。

① **I'm looking for the bus stop, can you help me?** 我在找公交车站，你能帮我个忙吗？

请人帮忙还可以说：

• Could you help me find the bus stop? 你能帮我找到公交车站吗？

如果对方知道的话会乐意给你指路：

• Sure, it's right down this way. 好的，沿着这条路走下去就行。

如果对方也是这里的陌生人：

• I'm sorry. I'm new around here, too. 对不起，我也不熟悉这儿。
• I don't know either. 我也不知道。

② **Where is the car rental company?** 租车公司在哪里？

如果想找停车位：

• I need to pick up my car, where is the rental place? 我要把车开出来，哪里有出租停车位的？

指出大致方向：

• I think it's a couple streets away, go left and then right. 我想有几条街远吧，往左走然后向右转。

❖ rental ['rentl] *adj.* 租赁（业）的；供出租的

3 Where's a good place to get some lunch? 有什么吃午餐的好地方吗?

问熟悉的人:

- I'm starving, where can I get lunch? 我饿了，有吃午餐的地方吗?

对方会就近给你建议:

- Try the sandwich shop across the street! 试试街对面的那家三明治店。
- ❖ starving ['stɑːvɪŋ] *adj.* 挨饿的，饥饿的

4 I need directions to Time Square. 我想知道去时代广场的方向。

还可以这样问路:

- Could you direct me to the Empire State Building? 你能告诉我帝国大厦怎么走吗?

对方对此很熟悉:

- Sure, just follow the signs that start down this street. 好的，只要循着这条街上的标志物走就行。
- ❖ Time Square 时代广场
- ❖ the Empire State Building 帝国大厦

5 Where is the cheapest parking around here? 这附近最便宜的停车场在哪里?

以下两种表达也不错哦:

- I'm looking for cheap parking, can you help me? 我在找便宜的停车场，你能帮帮我吗?
- Could you help me find a good place to park around here? 你能帮我在这附近找个停车的地方吗?

很模糊的回答:

- Yeah, there's a lot down the street. 好的，这条街有很多。
- ❖ parking ['pɑːkɪŋ] *n.* 停车处

6 Excuse me, but I'm lost. 对不起，我迷路了。

不知道自己所处的位置：
- I don't know where I am. 我不知道我在哪儿。
- Where am I? 我在哪儿呢？

如果在地图上找不到你的位置：
- Where am I on this map? 我在地图上的什么地方？

对方会在地图上给你指出来：
- You're right here, the Time Square. 你在这儿，时代广场附近。

7 Is it far? 到那儿远吗？

还可以具体点：
- Is it far from here? 离这儿远吗？
- Will it take long? 要多长时间？

可根据具体情况回答：
- Not far. 不远。
- It's not far. 不远。
- It's not far at all. 一点儿也不远。
- It's not that far. 不太远。

还可告知大约的时间：
- About five minutes. 差不多 5 分钟吧。

Directions Inquiry Conversation

Kevin: Excuse me. Do you know where Time Square is?

凯　文： 打扰一下，你知道时代广场在哪里吗？

Stranger: Oh yeah. It's five blocks from here going that way.

陌生人： 哦，知道，从那条路走，离这里有五个街区。

Kevin: Thanks. Sorry the flight got me feeling a little jet-lagged.

凯　文： 谢谢。抱歉，这飞机坐得我感觉有点儿时差综合症了。

Stranger: Oh it's no problem, happens to the best of us.	陌生人：哦，这不是什么问题，我们大家都会这样的。
Kevin: I'm sorry, but where's the bus station?	凯　文：抱歉，公交车站在哪儿？
Stranger: Right across the plaza, but the bus won't be here for another 30 minutes.	陌生人：就在广场对面，但是这公交车要再过半小时才能到这里。
Kevin: Oh okay. Maybe I'll see some sights. Is there anything nearby worth seeing?	凯　文：哦，好的。也许我会看看风景。这附近有什么可看的吗？
Stranger: Yeah, the Rockefeller Christmas tree is always worth a gander.	陌生人：有啊，洛克菲勒圣诞树一直都是值得看的。
Kevin: Cool, and where is that?	凯　文：太好了，那在哪儿呢？
Stranger: Right across the street behind the skating rink.	陌生人：就在街对面的滑冰场后面。

❖ block [blɑk] *n.* 街区
❖ jet-lagged [ˌdʒet'læɡd] *adj.* 飞行后感觉疲劳的
❖ happens to the best of us 我们大家都会这样的，我们大家都有这样的感觉
❖ plaza ['plæzə] *n.* 广场，购物中心
❖ gander ['ɡændə] *n.* 一眼，一瞥（口语）
❖ skating rink 滑冰场，溜冰场

文化穿越

　　一般情况下，不管在什么地方坐飞机，起程之前一定联系好接机的人，否则，下飞机后初到一个地方你会觉得分不清东南西北。当然，如果不是第一次出国，有美国驾照的话，可以自己租车回去。打车的话可能会比较贵，而且不一定安全。一般接机的人会像电影里面那样举个名字牌。不管怎样，建议在出国前一定先安排好接机的事情，尤其是晚上到达目的地的行程，坐了那么久的飞机已经很疲惫了，如果没有人接，可能会有危险。

Section 7

坐公交
Take a Bus

其实我在美国通常是不怎么坐公交的，倒不是因为别的，而是在美国乘坐公共汽车的人较少，所以每趟车之间的相隔时间也较长，等公交自然也是一件很费时的事儿。在这里为了内容的完整性，同时也为了方便大家的出行，我把相关交通的话题和大家一起聊一下。

1 How much is bus fare? 车费是多少?

询问车费还可以这样表达：

* How much do I owe you to ride the bus? 坐公交我该付你多少钱?
* How much is the fare to this station? 到这个站要多少钱?

对方会告诉你：

* It's $2.00 to ride. 2 美元。
* ❖ fare [fɛr] n. 票价，车费

2 Could I sit next to you? 我能坐在你旁边吗?

以下这些表达同样可以脱口而出：

* Is there any way I could sit here? 我能否坐在这儿?
* Do you mind if I sit next to you? 你介意我坐在你旁边吗?
* Can I sit here? 我可以坐这儿吗?
* Is this seat taken? 这儿有人坐吗?

如果该座位没人：

* No, go right ahead. 不介意，坐吧。

3 I hate traffic jams. 我讨厌堵车。

堵车确实是件挺烦人的事：

- I can't stand being in traffic. 我受不了堵车了。
- I hate driving in the rush hour. 我讨厌在交通高峰时间开车。

相信大家也都是这种感觉：

- Me either, I wish people would hurry up. 我也是，我希望大家能快点儿。

❖ traffic jams 塞车，交通堵塞，交通拥堵

❖ rush hour 交通拥挤时间，上下班高峰时间

4 Isn't the traffic heavy? 路上是不是很堵车?

堵车还可以换种说法：

- Isn't it crowded? 是不是很拥堵啊？
- Isn't the road congested? 这路堵吗？

堵车是经常的事：

- Yeah, especially in the rush hour. 是啊，尤其是在高峰期。

❖ crowded ['krauɖid] *adj.* 拥挤的

❖ congested [kən'dʒestɪd] *adj.* 堵塞的，拥挤的

5 Could I get off at the next stop? 我可不可以在下一站下车?

万一坐错车了，可以说：

- I need to get off the bus, please. 我要下车。

如果你对这路车的路线不熟悉：

- Could you tell me when to get off? 到站时您告诉我一声好吗？

司乘人员会很乐意帮忙的：

- Sure, no problem. 好的，没问题。

❖ get off 下车

6 Can I buy a bus pass? 我能买张公交卡吗?

询问公交卡的价格：

- How much is it to buy a bus pass? 买一张公交卡要多少钱？

可根据具体情况回答：

- Yeah, it's 5 dollars a month. 好的，一个月是 5 美元。
- Ten dollars for a year round bus pass. 公交年卡是 10 美元。

7 The bus has just left. 公交车刚走。

错过公交车了：

- The bus just left. 公交车刚走。
- We just missed our bus. 我们刚错过了公交车。

可以问一下旁人：

- How long do I have to wait for the next bus? 还得等多长时间才能有下趟公交车？

交流面对面

Take a Bus Conversation

Kevin: Oh good, the bus is here.	凯　文：哦，太好了，公交车来了。
Bus driver: Do you have a pass?	司　机：你有公交卡吗？
Kevin: No. How much is the fare?	凯　文：没有。车票多少钱？
Bus driver: $1. 50. Put it in the box.	司　机：1. 5 美元，放到盒子里吧。
Kevin: Alright. Excuse me…	凯　文：好的，打扰一下……
Stranger: Yeah?	陌生人：什么事？
Kevin: Could I sit here?	凯　文：我能坐在这里吗？
Stranger: Yeah, that's cool. Just let me move my bag.	陌生人：好的。我来把包挪一下。
Kevin: Thanks. Everywhere else looks full…	凯　文：谢谢，到处都好像很挤……
Stranger: It's always like this.	陌生人：一直都这样。

文化穿越

　　美国的公交系统没有中国那么发达。中国遍地都是公交车网络，美国有些直线的公交车最长可能两个小时才来一趟，一旦没赶上，恐怕就得耐下心来等了。大城市的公交系统也不是很发达。纽约的公交车相对好一些，但依然没有中国那么发达，而且也不可能有中国公交的价格。传说中的灰狗也挺贵的，而且搭乘它去旅游挺累的，因为时间较长。在美国坐公交，学生一般用学生证可以免费，学校里一般也会有专门为学生服务的车，不过仅是学校范围内。

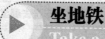
Section 8 ▶ 坐地铁
Take a Subway

> 在美国坐地铁是很方便的，因为地铁四通八达，不过这也让初到美国的人容易坐错路线，另外就是美国的地铁没有北京的那么便宜。在这里和大家分享一些坐地铁时用到的英语口语，希望大家能运用自如。

口语大放送

1 Which train should I take? 我该坐哪条地铁？

如果双方都知道目的地：
- Which train will get me to where I need to go? 哪条地铁能到我要去的地方呢？

对方会告诉你怎么坐车：
- You should take A, and then from there take C. 你应该坐 A 号地铁，然后到那里换乘 C 号地铁。

2 How long does it take to get to the next stop? 到达下一站要多长时间？

这样说也一样：
- How long is the ride to the next stop? 到达下一站要多长时间？

告知大约时间：
- It should take about 5 minutes. 应该 5 分钟吧。

3 How much is a ticket to ride? 一张票要多少钱？

可以换种说法：
- How much to ride the train? 坐地铁要多少钱？

坐地铁一天的花销：
- It's 5 dollars to ride per day. 一天 5 美元吧。

4 Where will this train take me? 这趟车是去哪里的?

这样坐车有点儿盲目哦:
- I'm curious, where does train A go? 我很想知道，A 号地铁是开往哪里的?
- Where will the train be stopping? 这车会在哪里停啊?

不过对方还是会告诉你:
- It will be stopping in Queens. 将在皇后区停。
- The train will stop at Time Square. 这趟列车将在时代广场停。
- ❖ curious ['kjuriəs] *adj.* 好奇的，渴望知道的

5 Is it safe to ride at night? 晚上坐地铁安全吗?

复杂点的表达:
- How safe are the subways at night time? 在夜间的时候坐地铁安全吗?

一般会比较安全的:
- They're all monitored, don't worry. 都是全程监控的，别担心。
- ❖ monitor ['manətər] *vt.* 监控，监视

6 How often do the trains come? 列车多长时间来一趟?

同样的说法:
- How frequently do the trains come? 列车多长时间来一趟?

告知明确的时间:
- The trains come every ten minutes. 列车 10 分钟一趟。

比较模糊的说法:
- The trains come very often. 列车一会儿一趟。
- ❖ frequently ['frikwəntlɪ] *adv.* 经常，频繁地

7 Which train should I take to Manhattan? 到曼哈顿，我该坐哪趟车?

可以用不同的动词变换说法:
- Which train goes to Manhattan? 哪趟车到曼哈顿?
- Which train stops at Manhattan? 哪趟车在曼哈顿停?
- Which train is going toward Manhattan? 哪趟车开往曼哈顿?

指明具体的车次：
- It's just right this train. 这趟车就是。

8　Where am I supposed to change? 我该在哪里换乘?

以下几种说法可以丰富你的口语哦：
- Where do I change trains? 我要在哪里换车?
- Where should I change trains? 我该在哪里换车?
- Where am I supposed to transfer? 我该在哪里换乘?
- At what station should I change? 我该在哪个站换乘?

简短的回答：
- At Manhattan. 在曼哈顿。
- ❖ be supposed to... 应该做……
- ❖ transfer [træns'fɜ] vi. 换车，转车

Take a Subway Conversation

Kevin: To get to Queens which train should I take, A or B?	凯文：去皇后区我该坐哪趟车，A号线还是B号线?
Woman: You need to take A, but you're going to need to transfer to the D train at the next stop.	女士：你该坐A号线，不过你得在下一站换乘D号线。
Kevin: How long is it before the next stop?	凯文：到达下一站要多长时间?
Woman: About 10 minutes. Would you like to purchase your ticket?	女士：大约10分钟吧。你要买票吗?
Kevin: Yes, how much is it?	凯文：是的，多少钱?
Woman: $3.50 for the one way, $5.00 for the two-way.	女士：单程票是3.5美元，双程票是5美元。
Kevin: I'll just take the one way please.	凯文：我要张单程票就行。
Woman: OK. Here you go. Your train will be arriving shortly.	女士：好的，给你。你的车马上就要到了。
Kevin: Thank you very much.	凯文：谢谢你。

Woman: No problem. Have a nice day!	女士：不客气，祝你愉快。

文化穿越

　　美国有些城市的地铁路线设计还是很经典的。有名的纽约地铁虽然由于年头久了，比较脏且陈旧，路线设计方面却四通八达，非常方便。华盛顿的地铁相比之下比较新，各方面设计也都比较漂亮。一般情况下，美国地铁大概有几种票可以买，一日通，一周通和一月通。票都是纸质的，不回收。不过无论是哪里的地铁，第一次坐都需要看清每种颜色线路的去向，免得坐错了车，耽误时间。

Section 9　▶ 坐出租车
Take a Taxi

在美国的城市中心和机场附近，出租车很多，招手即来。但其他大部分地区，坐出租车需要电话预约。出租车计价表一般都贴在车内，大多以里程计费，在这里提醒大家在美国坐出租车是要给小费的，费用为车费的百分之十到二十，或以行李件数计算，一般是一件行李一美元，所以在美国坐出租车是很贵的。

口 语 大 放 送

1 Excuse me, taxi! 你好，出租车！

还可以这样叫出租车：
- Hi, taxi! 嗨，出租车！
- Could I get a taxi please! 请给我叫辆出租车！

出租车司机会问你目的地：
- Sure, bud, where to go? 好的，哥们儿，去哪儿？
- Okay, where're you going? 好的，你要去哪儿？
- Where would you like to go? 您想去哪儿？
- ❖ bud [bʌd] *n.* 哥们儿，朋友

2 Can you take me up a few blocks to the mall? 你能载我去几个街区远的购物中心吗？

还可以这样直接指出地点：
- I need to go to the mall a few blocks away please. 我要去购物中心，大概有几个街区远吧。

或者给司机看便条上的地址：
- To this address, please. 请到这个地址。

司机会爽快地回答：
- Sure, no problem. 好的，没问题。

3 (Calling taxi service) Hello, could I get a taxi delivered to my hotel?（叫出租车服务）你好，我能叫辆出租车来我的酒店吗？

> 或者可以说：
> - I'm in need of a taxi, could I get one delivered? 我要叫辆出租车，可以派一辆过来吗？
>
> 还可以请人帮忙叫车：
> - Call me a taxi, please. 请帮我叫辆出租车。
>
> 服务人员会告诉你：
> - Sure, they'll be there shortly. 好的，马上到你那儿。

4 How much is the cab fare? 车费是多少？

> 还可以简单些：
> - What's the fare? 车费是多少？
> - What is the rate? 要多少钱啊？
>
> 司机会直接告诉你花费的金额：
> - This is gonna run you 5 dollars. 这要花你 5 美元。
> ❖ cab [kæb] *n.* 出租车

5 Here's a tip. Thank you! 这是小费，谢谢你！

> 也可以把找零的钱作为小费：
> - Keep the change on this one. 零钱不用找了。
>
> 对方会礼貌地说声：
> - Thanks bud! 谢谢你，伙计！

6 Where can I get a taxi? 我在哪儿可以打到车？

> 同样的说法：
> - Where can I catch a taxi? 我在哪儿可以打到车？
>
> 询问出租汽车站：
> - Do you know where I can get a taxi? 您知道哪儿有出租汽车站吗？
> - Where's a taxi stand around here? 这附近哪儿有出租汽车站？

对方知道的话会告诉你：

- There's a taxi stand up ahead. 前面就有出租汽车站。

如果不知道：

- Sorry, I don't know. 对不起，我不知道。

❖ taxi stand 出租车招呼站

Take a Taxi Conversation

Kevin: Hey, I need to get to 58th Broadway.	凯文：嘿，我要去百老汇58号。
Driver: OK, we'll be there in about 7 minutes.	司机：好的，到那儿大约要7分钟。
Kevin: Would you mind taking the parkway? I enjoy the view.	凯文：你介意走公园路那条道吗？我喜欢那景色。
Driver: Alright, but it'll cost you extra.	司机：好的，不过你需要多花钱了。
Kevin: It's okay. I just got back in the city and I kind of missed it.	凯文：没关系，我刚回到这城市，我有点儿想念它了。
Driver: I know what you mean. No place else like it in the world.	司机：我明白你的意思，这世上没有像这样的地方了。
Kevin: You're telling me.	凯文：你说对了。
Driver: Okay, we're here. That'll be $9. 37.	司机：好了，我们到了，总共是9. 37美元。
Kevin: Alright, here you go.	凯文：好的，给你。
Driver: Have a nice night, bub.	司机：晚上愉快，小伙子。

❖ bub [bʌb] *n.* 小伙子，小家伙

文化穿越

　　美国的出租车价格比其他交通方式贵很多，而且得给小费。不过如果四五个人一起的话，每个人摊下来就几美元，也还是可以接受的。一般出去旅游还是自己开车方便，当然如果是几个人一起去比较近的地方，打车也是个比较快捷的途径。纽约的出租车都是黄色的，这已经成了纽约的象征之一。美国有的州是大乡村，相比之下比较偏僻，打车的话得给出租车公司打电话才行，不像纽约那样可以随手打到。

Section 10 ▶ 自驾车
Drive a Car

开车是我出行的主要方式。其实在美国几乎家家都有汽车，成年人几乎没有不会开车的。居家附近的日常出行，美国人都是自己开车。较短距离的旅行，多数美国人也是自己开车。所以知道一些关于自驾车的英语也是想提高英语的朋友需要具备的。

1 Hello, I'd like to pick up my rental car please. 你好，我想来取我租的车。

更客气点的说法：

- I rented a car from you, could I pick it up please? 我从你们这里租了辆车，我能取了吗？

或者租车：

- I'd like to rent a car, please. 我想租辆车。

对方询问你的信息：

- Sure, no problem. Could I get your name? 好的，没问题。我能知道你的名字吗？

❖ rental ['rentl] *adj.* 租赁的

2 What do I need to do to rent a car? 我要怎么做才能租车呢？

直接请人帮忙租车：

- I would like to rent a car. Can you help me? 我想租辆车，你能帮我吗？

索要资料：

- Yes. Just give me your passport, or ID please. 好的，请把你的护照或身份证给我就行。

3 Is it faster to walk or drive? 是走路快还是开车快?

作一下比较:

- Will it take me longer to walk? 走路会花更长的时间吗?
- Should I just drive? 我该开车吗?

当然是开车了:

- It's quicker by car. 开车更快。
- I think it's faster to drive. 我觉得开车更快。

万一堵车的话,走路是更好的选择:

- I believe it'll take longer if you drive. 我想你开车的话会花更长的时间。

4 Where can I stop for gas? 我在哪里能停下来加油?

复杂点的表达:

- I need to stop for gas, where should I go? 我要停下来加油,该往哪里走?

踏破铁鞋无觅处:

- There's a place right down here... 这里就正好有个地方……

5 I got shotgun! 我坐副驾驶座!

进一步强调:

- I call shotgun! 我坐副驾驶座!

互不相让:

- You always get shotgun! 你总是坐副驾驶座!
- ❖ shotgun ['ʃɑt,gʌn] *n.* 副驾驶座(美国俚语)

6 No outlet! 禁行!

类似的说法:

- No passing! 禁止超车!
- No parking! 禁止停车!
- Can I park my car here? 这儿可以停车吗?

看看标志牌吧：

- No, this is a no-parking zone. 不行，这一带禁止停车。
- ❖ outlet ['aut,let] *n.* 出口
- ❖ no-parking zone 禁止停车地带

7 I'll drive you home. 我会开车送你回家。

主动讨好的说法：

- Let me drive you home. 让我开车送你回家吧。

表达谢意：

- Thank you very much. 多谢你了。

Drive a Car Conversation

Kevin: Hey guys, thanks for picking me up, I thought I'd be stranded out here all night.

凯文：嘿，哥们儿，谢谢你们来接我，我还以为我要在这里流浪一个晚上呢。

Friend: No problem. Sucks you missed your bus though.

朋友：不客气，不过你错过了公交车实在是太糟糕了。

Kevin: Yeah, that's $10. I won't be seeing again.

凯文：是啊，那是 10 美元呢。我再也见不到了。

Friend: Alright, hop in the back seat. Steve has shotgun.

朋友：好了，上车吧，坐后排的位置，史蒂夫坐在前面了。

Kevin: Alright. Hey, would you mind putting on some music?

凯文：好的。嘿，放点音乐好吗？

Friend: OK, as long as it's not rap. Steve, put some tunes on.

朋友：好的，只要不是说唱音乐就行。史蒂夫放点音乐吧。

Kevin: Steve, could you turn that up? I love this song!

凯文：史蒂夫，你能把那个开大点儿吗？我喜欢那首歌！

Friend: OK, but only if you buckle up. I don't need a ticket.

朋友：好啦，你只要系好安全带就行，我可不想来张罚款单。

Kevin: Nobody does. The economy is pretty bad.

Friend: It'll get better.

凯文：谁也不想。这经济情况太糟糕了。

朋友：会变好的。

❖ strand [strænd] *vi.* 搁浅，处于困境
❖ rap [ræp] *n.* 说唱音乐
❖ buckle up 系好安全带，把……扣紧

文化穿越

　　自己驾车出行是比较经济方便的。设计好路线，加满油，带上些必需品就可以起程了。不过一般超过 4 个小时的路程最好轮换开，不然容易出事儿。当然，如果是一个人开车，累了就停下来休息休息也没问题。除此之外，美国租车业很发达，但其实并不便宜，一辆普通的车，一天下来最便宜也要 30 美元左右。不过租车也是出门旅游的不错选择。

Section 11　▶ 骑自行车
Ride a Bicycle

　　其实在美国，自行车多为健身工具，而非交通工具。住在校内或学校附近的朋友，也可以用自行车作为交通工具。需要注意的是，美国学校一般要求骑自行车的学生向校内警察登记，以防车被盗窃，如不登记可能会被罚款哦。

1 I'm looking to buy a bike, let me know if you see any.　我想买辆自行车，你如果看到有就告诉我一声。

同样的表达还有：
* If you see any bikes for sale, let me know. 如果你看到有卖自行车的，就告诉我。

如果想征询建议：
* I want to buy a mountain bike. Could you give me some advice? 我想买辆山地车，你能给我些建议吗？

顺口回答：
* Alright, I will do. 好的，我会的。
* ❖ mountain bike 山地车

2 How much for this fixed gear? 这辆单速车多少钱？

大众说法：
* How much for this bike? 这辆自行车多少钱？

告知具体金额：
* It's $120. 120 美元。

如果为非卖品：
* That's not for sale, sorry. 抱歉，那辆车不卖的。
* ❖ fixed gear 单速车

就这 900 句 玩转口语

3 Biking is such good exercise! 骑自行车是如此好的运动！

骑自行车的好处：

- Biking is great for getting in shape. 骑自行车对保持身材大有好处。

骑自行车的好处还有：

- Yeah it is. You save money too! 是啊，还省钱了！
- ❖ get in shape 保持身材

4 It's so easy to get around on a bike. 骑自行车到处走走挺方便的。

自行车友的说法：

- I love biking. It makes things so much easier. 我喜欢骑自行车，它让事情变得更简便了。
- Biking is fantastic for the city. 在城市里骑自行车非常好。

这种说法可要因人而异哦：

- Yeah it is. No one likes to drive in the city. 是啊，没有人喜欢在城市里开车。
- ❖ get around 到处走走，四处逛逛
- ❖ fantastic [fæn'tæstɪk] *adj.* 极好的，很棒的

5 Do you know where I can get a good bike lock? 你知道我能在哪里买到一把好的自行车锁吗？

好的自行车要配好锁：

- I need a bike lock, could you help me find one? 我需要一把自行车锁，你能帮我找一把吗？
- Do you know who makes the best bike lock? 你知道谁的自行车锁做得最好吗？

商店里有卖：

- I think I saw a few good ones at the store. 我想我在商店里看到不少好锁。

问错人了哦：

- I'm not sure. I actually don't have a bike! 我不太确定，事实上我没有自行车！

6 I go to work by bicycle. 我骑自行车上班。

看看动词的用法：

- I bikes to work every day. 我每天骑自行车上班。

回答因人而异：

- Me too. 我也是。
- I go to work by bus. 我坐公交上班。

Ride a Bicycle Conversation

Stranger: Wow, that's a nice bike!	陌生人：哇，好漂亮的自行车！
Kevin: Thank you, I just bought it.	凯　文：谢谢你，我刚买的。
Stranger: Why did you get it?	陌生人：你干吗买辆自行车呢？
Kevin: It's easier than driving a car in this city.	凯　文：在这个城市骑自行车比开车更方便。
Stranger: That is a good point. How much was it?	陌生人：这倒是个好办法。这多少钱？
Kevin: $140. They are selling them two blocks down the street.	凯　文：140美元。沿着这条街走两个街区就有卖的。
Stranger: That's cool. It sounds like a good investment.	陌生人：太好了，看起来这是个不错的投资。
Kevin: It saves a lot of money on gas too!	凯　文：还可以省很多油钱。
Stranger: Wow that's great. Well, I have to go to work.	陌生人：哇，太棒了。哦，我得去上班了。
Kevin: Okay. See you later!	凯　文：好的，再见。

❖investment [ɪnˈvɛstmənt] *n.* 投资，投资项目

文化穿越

　　自行车在美国很便宜。一般前后带液压减震的山地车最便宜的也就70美元左右。因此，美国人一般出门骑车都不用锁车，因为贼偷了也没用，除非偷完自家用。另外，在美国的很多州根本没有自行车道，也就是说，骑自行车的人真的很少，除非是爱好这个，或者专业选手训练时才会骑车。除此之外，有的中国留学生比较习惯于骑车，会买辆自行车骑着玩儿，锻炼身体。这或许和美国人不穿秋裤是一个道理，人家出门就上车了，下车就到办公室或者家了，因此也不会冷。

Chapter 2

你好，buddy

Basic Communication

Section 1  见面问候 Greeting

在机场等了一会儿，终于看到来接我的家人和朋友了。离别了这么长时间，再次见到他们，感觉真是太好了。来，朋友们，跟着Kevin 一起和他们打声招呼，互相问候一下吧。

1 Hey! Thanks for picking me up from the airport. How are you doing? 嘿！谢谢你来机场接我。你还好吗?

见到来接机的朋友：

- What's up, man? Thanks for picking me up. 最近怎么样，哥们儿？谢谢你来接我。
- How have you been? Thanks for getting me. 最近怎么样? 谢谢你来接我。

好朋友之间不需客气：

- No problem, man! I've been good, how about you? 不用谢,哥们儿! 我挺好的，你呢?
- Don't worry about it. I've been great, how are you doing? 没事儿。我挺好的，你还好吧?
- You're welcome. I'm fine. What's up with you? 不客气。我挺好的,你怎么样?

2 (In response to "what's up") Nothing much. (回答 "what's up") 没什么事。

还是照旧：

- Same old, same old. 老样子，老样子。

有好多要说的话：

- I have a bunch of stuff to tell you! 我有好多事要跟你说!

46

再次见面要好好聚聚：

- We need to catch up after we get to your house! 我们到你家后得好好聚聚!

那是必须的：

- Sure thing. Let's get going. 那是当然的，咱们快走吧。

❖ a bunch of 一连串，一大堆

❖ stuff [stʌf] n. 事情，东西

❖ catch up 聚会，小聚

❖ sure thing 当然，一定，毫无疑问的事

③ How's everything? 怎么样，还好吧?

同样的问候还有：

- How's everything? 还好吧?
- How's everything going? 一切都还好吧?
- How's it going? 还好吗?
- How are things? 情况怎么样?

回答可根据自己的具体情况：

- Same as always. 和平常一样。
- So-so. 还凑合吧。
- Not bad. 还可以。
- It's going pretty well. 一切很顺利。
- Terrible. 很糟糕。

❖ so-so ['so‚so] adj. 总算过得去的，不好也不坏的

④ Did nothing exciting happen while I was gone? 我走的这段时间没发生过什么让人激动的事情吗?

还可以简短些：

- What happened while I was away? 我不在的时候发生什么事了吗?
- How has your life been since I left? 我走后你的生活怎么样啊?

没什么事：

- Nothing too crazy happened. 没发生什么太疯狂的事。

有点儿遗憾：

- You missed a ton of stuff. 你错过了很多事情哦。

这里不太方便：

- We can talk all about it in the car. 我们在车上谈吧。
- ❖ a ton of 大量的，许多的

5 It's great to see you. 见到你真是太好了。

再次见面的喜悦：

- Seeing you again is great. 再见到你真是太好了。
- I'm glad we can hang out again. 我很高兴我们又能聚聚了。
- It's good seeing you again. 再见到你挺好的。

久别重逢大家的感觉都是一样的：

- Yeah. 是啊。
- It's great to see you too. 我也很高兴再见到你。
- ❖ hang out 闲逛，待在一起，聚会

6 Long time no see. 好久没见了。

稍微正式点的说法：

- I haven't seen you for a long time. 我已经很久没见你了。
- I haven't seen you for ages. 我已经很久没见你了。

常见的回答：

- Yeah, it's been so long. 是啊，好久没见。
- Yeah, too long. 是啊，是挺长时间了。
- Yeah, how have you been? 是呀，你还好吗？

7 It's a nice day, isn't it? 天气多好啊，不是吗？

与陌生人搭讪，还可以这么说：

- A lovely day, isn't it? 多好的天气啊，不是吗？
- It's a fine day today, isn't it? 今天天气不错，不是吗？

回答展开话题：

- Yeah, it really is. 是啊，确实不错。

8 Where did you park? 你把车停哪儿了？

朋友见面后找车：

- Do you remember where you parked? 你还记得把车停哪儿了吗？
- These airport parking lots are so confusing. Where is your car? 机场的这些停车场真是太混乱了。你的车在哪儿？

有点儿惊讶：

- I parked right over there. 我就停在那儿啊。

胸有成竹：

- Don't worry, I remember! 别担心，我记得的！

❖ confusing [kən'fjuːzɪŋ] adj. 混乱的，无秩序的，令人困惑的

Greeting Conversation

Kevin: Hey! It's good to see you again!	**凯　文：** 嘿！再见到你真是太好了！
Steve: You too, man. What's up?	**史蒂夫：** 我也是，哥们儿。最近怎么样？
Kevin: I have a ton of stuff to tell you.	**凯　文：** 我有好多事要跟你说。
Steve: Save it for the ride home. I want to get going!	**史蒂夫：** 在回家的路上还是省省吧，我想快点儿走！
Kevin: Yeah? Why in such a hurry?	**凯　文：** 是吗？干吗这么急？
Steve: I have some other friends I want you to meet. They're waiting in the car.	**史蒂夫：** 我想让你见见我其他的朋友。他们在车里等着呢。
Kevin: Oh, okay. Cool. I can't wait to meet them.	**凯　文：** 哦，好吧。太好了，我都等不及要见他们了。
Steve: Yeah. Don't worry, they're really nice.	**史蒂夫：** 是啊，别担心，他们真的挺好的。
Kevin: Well, that's good. I'm glad you didn't make any jerk friends while I was away. (laughs)	**凯　文：** 哦，那太好了。我很高兴我不在的时候你没有交什么混蛋朋友。（笑）
Steve: Of course not! Come on, let's go.	**史蒂夫：** 当然没有了！快点，咱们走吧。

Kevin: Sure.	凯　文：好的。

文化穿越

美国人打招呼的方式与我们平时在课本上学到的不太一样。一般情况下有这么几种：How are you doing / How are you? 是最常见的两种，回答一般就是 Good/ Not bad 等。What's up/ What up? 一般黑人用的频率比白人多，另外以男性之间的问候居多。回答是 Not much，或者同样问候一句 what's up。另外还有 How have you been，可以回答一下你最近的一些状况，相当于 How are you。除此之外，在美国，陌生人之间也是要互相打招呼问候的，尤其是当和别人有眼神交流时，可以简单问好。

Section 2

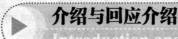

介绍与回应介绍
Introduction and Reply

在这些熟悉的面孔中，我意外地发现了几个新面孔。原来我的这些哥们儿姐们儿都带着自己的 MM 和 GG 呢。几个月不见，变化还真大啊。赶紧介绍一下哦，朋友们，一起来吧，也让我们大家都互相认识一下。

1 My name is Kevin. 我的名字叫凯文。

或者可以直接说：
- I'm Kevin. 我叫凯文。

对方也会自报家门：
- Hey, Kevin. I'm Sam. 嘿，凯文，我是山姆。

礼貌的客套语：
- Nice to meet you. 很高兴见到你。

2 It's a pleasure to meet you. 见到你是件很高兴的事。

同样的表达：
- It's nice to meet you. 很高兴见到你。
- Nice to meet you. 很高兴见到你。

客套的回应：
- Yeah, nice to meet you too. 是啊，我也很高兴见到你。

3 I've heard good things about you. 我听说过关于你的好话。

从侧面打听：
- My friends have told me a little about you. You seem cool. 我朋友跟我说过一些你的事情。你看起来好酷。

51

- You seem like a nice guy, judging by what my friends have said. 从我朋友说的话判断，你像是个不错的人。
- My friends told me you were a nice guy. 我朋友跟我说你是个不错的人。

有点儿自嘲了：

- Well, that's sweet of them. I hope I live up to my reputation. 哦，他们真是太好了，我希望是名不虚传。

❖ judging by 从……判断

❖ live up to 符合，不辜负，无愧于

❖ reputation [ˌrepjə'teʃən] n. 名誉，名声

4 Here is my number. 这是我的号码。

告知电话号码：

- I'll give you my number. 我把我的号码给你。

互换号码：

- Cool. Here's mine. 太好了，这是我的。
- Alright. I'll give you mine too. 好的，我也把我的给你。

5 You can have one of my business cards, in case you want to email me. 如果你想给我发电子邮件，我可以给你一张我的名片。

如果是商务人士：

- Here's my business card. It has my email address on it. 这是我的名片，上面有我的电子邮箱。
- Here's a copy of my business card, since it has my email on it. 这是我的一张名片，上面有我的电子邮箱。

表达谢意：

- Thanks. 谢谢。

❖ business card 名片，商务名片

6 It was nice meeting you. I'll see you around. 见到你很高兴，我们回头见。

见面完告别：

- It was a pleasure meeting you. I'll see you later. 见到你是件很高兴的事，我们稍后见。

- I hope I get to see you around. It was nice meeting you. 希望我们回头见，见到你很高兴。

对方也礼貌表达：

- You too. See you. 也很高兴见到你，再见。

7 May I have your name, please? 您贵姓？

询问对方的名字：

- What's your name, please? 请问您叫什么名字？
- May I ask who you are? 您是哪位？

告知自己的姓名：

- My name's Kevin. 我叫凯文。

Introductions and Reply Conversation

Kevin: Hey! You must be Sophie.	凯文：嘿！你一定是索菲了。
Sophie: Yeah. Nice to meet you.	索菲：是啊。很高兴见到你。
Kevin: It's nice to meet you too. My name's Kevin.	凯文：我也很高兴见到你。我叫凯文。
Sophie: Steve's told me all about you.	索菲：史蒂夫跟我说过你。
Kevin: I hope he said only good things.	凯文：我希望他说的都是好事。
Sophie: He talks about how awesome you are all the time.	索菲：他说你一直都挺棒的。
Kevin: (laughs) Well, that's a relief. We should hang out sometime.	凯文：（笑）哦，这我就放心了。我们什么时候该一起逛逛。
Sophie: Sounds good to me. Give me a call when you're free.	索菲：听起来不错。你有空的时候给我电话。
Kevin: Sure thing. Here's my number.	凯文：那是一定的，这是我的号码。
Sophie: Thanks, man. See you later!	索菲：谢谢，哥们儿。一会儿见。

❖ awesome ['ɔːsəm] *adj.* 了不起的，很棒的

❖ relief [rɪ'liːf] *n.* 轻松，宽心

文化穿越

　　自我介绍这一环节在美国课堂上经常会遇到。开学的第一堂课老师会让学生自告奋勇做自我介绍，尤其是研究生班学生较少的时候，每个人都逃不过这一环节。值得注意的是，国际学生往往是全课堂的焦点，尤其是来自亚洲的学生群体。亚洲学生普遍比较内向，没有美国学生那样外向能说，而且亚洲学生也不喜欢问老师问题，尤其是中国学生。中国学生喜欢聚在一起，不过这一点正是需要中国留学生注意的，因为到国外留学的目的之一是锻炼语言，要抓住所有锻炼语言的机会，包括每一个自我介绍、演讲的机会，另外多和美国同学在一起，尽量融入美国学生圈儿里去，彻底感受美国文化。

Section 3 ▶ 感谢与回谢
Gratitude and Reply

感谢是我们生活中一个经久不衰的话题，生活中确实也有很多我们需要感谢的人和事。就像现在一样，我非常感谢我的家人和朋友们来接我，让我感受到温暖，让我不再觉得孤独。我真诚地向你们说声：谢谢！

口 语 大 放 送

1 Thanks. 谢谢。

感激之情可逐渐递进：

- Thank you. 谢谢你。
- Thanks a lot. 多谢。
- Thank you so much. 非常感谢你。
- Thank you very much. 非常感谢你。
- I really appreciate it. 我真的非常感谢。

不用客气的：

- It's okay. You're welcome. 没事的，不客气。
- Don't mention it. 不值一提啦。
- ❖ appreciate [ə'priːʃɪeɪt] vt. 感谢，感激
- ❖ mention ['menʃən] vt. 提到，说起

2 I don't know how to thank you. 我不知道该怎么感谢你。

不知怎么表达谢意：

- I have no words to thank you. 我不知道说什么才能感谢您。
- I can't express how grateful I am. 我无法表达我是多么感激你。
- I can't thank you enough. 我无法表达对您的感谢。

- I really don't know how I can ever thank you. 我真不知道怎样才能感谢你。
- I really can't find a suitable word to express my sincere thanks to you. 我真的找不到合适的话语来表达我对您诚挚的谢意。

不用言谢的：

- Oh, you're welcome. I'm happy to be in help. 哦，别客气，我很高兴能帮上忙。
- ❖ have no words 无法用言语来表达
- ❖ grateful ['gretfəl] *adj.* 感谢的，感激的
- ❖ sincere [sɪn'sɪr] *adj.* 衷心的，真诚的

3 Thank you for your help. 谢谢你的帮助。

感谢对方的帮助：

- Thank you for helping me. 谢谢你帮我。
- I appreciate your help. 非常感谢你的帮助。

我乐意做的，不用客气：

- My pleasure. 我很乐意。

4 Thanks for everything. 谢谢你做的一切。

或者换种说法：

- Thanks for all you've done. 谢谢你所做的一切。
- Thank you for all of your kindness. 谢谢你所有的好意。

不必言谢：

- Not at all. 别客气。

5 You're welcome. 不客气。

语气可以更强烈些：

- You're very welcome. 你太客气了。

言谢的人总会客气一番：

- No really, thanks a lot. 没有啦，多谢。

Chapter 2 你好，buddy
Basic Communication

6 Don't worry about it. 别放在心上。

这种表达也很常用：

- No problem. 没关系的。

不说别的，还是感谢：

- Well, thanks again. 哦，再次感谢。

Gratitude and Reply Conversation

Kevin: Thanks, Steve.	凯 文：谢谢，史蒂夫。
Steve: For what?	史蒂夫：谢什么？
Kevin: For the ride home, of course!	凯 文：当然是谢你载我回家了！
Steve: Oh, no problem man. Any time.	史蒂夫：哦，没关系的，哥们儿。随时效劳。
Kevin: Thanks. If you ever need anything too, you can rely on me.	凯 文：谢谢。如果你需要什么东西，你可以找我。
Steve: Thanks, man. I really appreciate it.	史蒂夫：谢谢，哥们儿。真的很感谢了。
Kevin: You're welcome.	凯 文：不客气。
Steve: Well, I'll catch up with you later.	史蒂夫：哦，我回头再找你。
Kevin: Sure.	凯 文：好的。
Steve: See ya!	史蒂夫：再见！
Kevin: Bye.	凯 文：再见。

❖ ride home 骑车回家，开车回家
❖ rely on 依靠，依赖，指望
❖ ya ['jə] *pron.* 你（相当于 you，是美国口语中常见的说法）

文化穿越

　　中国人使用"谢谢你"远不及美国人那样频繁。中国人只有在别人提供了大量的帮助时，才说"谢谢"，而且是真正表示谢意。美国人无论是家庭成员之间，还是上下级之间、上下辈之间，为了一件小事，甚至是份内之事都需说"Thank you"。"Thank you"只是习惯性的用语，并不表示多大的谢意。例如：在给美国人上对外汉语课时，每次上完课后，英美学生习惯说"Thank you"。回答"Thank you"时，中国人往往说"这是我应该做的"。把这句话直译过来就是"It's my duty"，这会让美国学生听起来不那么愉快，因为"It's my duty"的含意是：我本不想做，但这是我的职责，所以不得不做。这与汉语表达的原意有很大出入，适当的回答应是"It's my pleasure."（我很乐意），"Don't mention it."（没什么）或"You're welcome."（不用谢）。

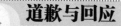

Section 4 　道歉与回应
Apology and Reply

　　这次回来，我本来都给大家带了礼物的，可打开包一看，礼物竟然不翼而飞，我有一种直觉，我丢东西了。大家的礼物可能都要落空了。I'm sorry，下次再给你们补上礼物吧。

 口 语 大 放 送

1 My mistake! 是我的错!

主动承认自己的错误：

- It's my fault. 这是我的错。
- I didn't mean to do that! 我不是故意那么做的！
- That was my fault. 那是我的错。
- I'm to blame. 全怪我。

对方会给予理解的：

- Yeah, but it's okay. 是啊，不过没关系。
- Don't stress about it. 别为此有压力。

❖ fault [fɔlt] *n.* 错误，责任
❖ blame [blem] *vt.* 责备，指责
❖ stress [strɛs] *vt.* 压力，紧张

2 I'm sorry. 对不起啊。

真诚道歉：

- Oh, sorry. 哦，对不起。
- I'm very sorry. 我很抱歉。
- I'm awfully sorry. 我非常抱歉。
- I'm sorry about that. 那件事真对不起。

对方也不会介意了：

- It's okay. 没事啦。
- Don't worry about it. 别太在意。

3 Forgive me. 原谅我。

请求对方原谅：

- Please forgive me. 请原谅我。

向对方道歉：

- My apologies. 我道歉。
- My sincerest apologies. 我真诚地道歉。

对方会原谅你的：

- It happens, don't worry. 碰巧的，别担心。

❖ apology [ə'pɒlədʒɪ] *n.* 道歉，赔罪（其动词是 apologize）

4 I don't know how to apologize to you. 我不知该怎样向您道歉。

还可以这样表达歉意：

- I can't express how sorry I am. 我无法表达我是多么抱歉。
- Any words can't express how sorry I am. 任何语言都无法表达我是多么抱歉。
- I have no words to apologize to you. 我不知道说什么才能对你表达我的歉意。

对方也不会追究了：

- It's no big deal. 不是什么大不了的事。

❖ apologize to... 向……道歉

5 I'm sorry to have kept you waiting. 抱歉，让您久等了。

类似的说法：

- I'm sorry to be late again. 对不起，我又来晚了。
- Sorry, I'm late again. 对不起，我又迟到了。

不介意等：

- It was nothing. 这没什么。

要再不来的话就走了：

- I was about to go home. 我正想要回家呢。

6 It's alright. 没关系。

同样还可以说：

- It's okay. 没关系。

都过去了：

- Alright. Good. 好了，没事了。

7 Don't worry about it. 别太在意。

不要放在心上：

- Never mind. 不必在意。
- It's not a big deal. 没什么大不了的。

你不介意，真是很感谢：

- Okay. Thank you. 好的，谢谢你。

交流面对面

Apologize and Reply Conversation

Kevin: I'm sorry for being such a hassle!	凯　文：我很抱歉,造成这样的麻烦。
Debra: Don't worry about it, it's no big deal.	黛布拉：别太在意，没什么大不了的。
Kevin: I can't believe I lost my bag at the airport…	凯　文：我不敢相信我竟然在机场把我的包给丢了。
Debra: Hey man, it happens. Don't be so hard on yourself.	黛布拉：嘿，伙计，是碰巧的。别这么为难自己。
Kevin: I guess so. Thanks.	凯　文：我想是吧。谢谢。
Debra: You're welcome. Sorry it took me a while to get here.	黛布拉：不客气。抱歉，到那里要花点儿时间。
Kevin: Nah, it's okay. I understand.	凯　文：没事的。我理解。
Debra: Cool. Let's go find your bag.	黛布拉：好的。咱们去找你的包吧。
Kevin: Okay. Thanks again.	凯　文：好的，再次感谢啊。

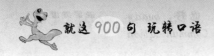

Debra: No problem, dude.	黛布拉：没关系，伙计。

❖hassle ['hæsl] *n.* 麻烦，困难
❖be hard on... 对……苛刻；对……要求严格
❖nah [nɑ:] *adj.* 没有，很少

文化穿越

　　美国人说"对不起"并不一定是做错了什么事，觉得理亏。比如请人让路，说声"对不起"，其实是叫你"Get out of my way, so I can come out."（你走开，我才过得去。），只是这种"命令"，有了"对不起"，让人容易接受罢了。所以严格说来，在不少场合"Excuse me"等于汉语的"借光"或"劳驾"。比较文明的中国人一般是以"请"开路，达到同样的效果。

Section 5 ▶ 邀请与回应
Invitation and Reply

　　离家一段时间后回来，自然就收到了很多朋友的邀请。给大家看看，聚会的邀请就有一大串呢。好吧，我也非常想见大家，我一一安排时间和大家见面聚聚。在这里，大家要注意了，发出邀请后你可能得到的是两种答复：一种是接受，一种就是拒绝了，所以大家得作好心理准备。

1 What are you doing tomorrow? 你明天要干什么?

邀请的前奏：
- Are you doing anything tomorrow? 你明天有什么事情要做吗?
- Are you busy tomorrow? 你明天忙吗?

根据自己的具体安排回答即可：
- I'm free tomorrow. 我明天有空。
- I'm not doing anything tomorrow. 我明天没什么事情要做。
- I'm busy tomorrow. 我明天比较忙。

2 Would you like to come over? 你想过来吗?

还可以这样发出邀请：
- Do you want to come over? 你想过来吗?
- Do you think you could come over? 你觉得你能过来吗?
- I'd like it if you came over. 如果你过来我会很高兴的。

接受：
- Okay, I can come over. 好的，我能过来。

模棱两可：
- I don't know if I want to. 我不知道我是不是想过来。

拒绝：

- I can't, I have work I need to get done. 我过不来了，我有工作得做。
- ❖ come over 过来，顺便来访

3 Can you come to my party? 你能来我的聚会吗?

类似的邀请：

- Can you go to the movies? 你能去看场电影吗？
- Would you honor me by coming to the party tonight? 请你赏光出席今晚的聚会好吗？
- Could I have the pleasure of dancing with you? 能请你跳支舞吗？

欣然接受邀请：

- Sure, I'd love to. 当然，我很愿意。

拒绝并说明理由：

- I'd very much like to, but I've already had plans for tonight. 我很愿意去，但我今晚已另有安排。
- I wish I could, but I've promised to show Tom around. 我希望能来，但我已答应带汤姆转转。

4 We can do something else instead. 我们可以做点其他的事情。

邀请方可以建议做些事情：

- We can go out if you want. 如果你想的话我们可以出去。
- We don't have to hang out at my place. We can go out. 我们不一定就在我这里待着，我们可以出去。
- We don't have to stay here if you want to go out instead. 我们不一定得在这儿待着，如果你想出去的话。

对方的意见：

- It's okay, we can just hang out at your place. 好的，我们就在你那里待一会儿吧。
- Alright, we can go out and do something. 好的，我们可以出去干点事情。

5 May we have the pleasure of your company at dinner? 我们可以请您一起共进晚餐吗？

邀请做其他的事情：

- Would you be free to come to a concert on Saturday? 你星期六有时间去音乐会吗？
- We should be delighted if you could spend an evening with us. 如果你能同我们一起度过一个晚上，我们将非常高兴。
- Shall we get together sometime? 咱们抽个时间聚聚怎样？

好啊，正中下怀：

- That would be a great idea. 那太好了。

❖ get together 聚会，聚集

6 I'd love to come over. 我很想过来。

接受别人的邀请：

- That sounds like fun. I'll be over soon. 听上去挺有意思，我一会儿过来。
- Sure, I'll come over. 好的，我会过来的。
- I'll head over soon. 我一会儿就过来。

对方会很高兴地说：

- Okay, see you soon. 好的，一会儿见。
- Talk to you soon. 一会儿聊。

7 I'm sorry, but I'm busy. 对不起，可是我很忙啊。

拒绝别人的邀请：

- I'm afraid I can't. 恐怕我不能来。
- I have things to do. 我有事情要做。
- I'm kind of busy. Maybe later. 我有点儿忙，也许以后吧。
- I'm busy right now. Sorry. 我现在很忙，抱歉。
- I can't come over right now. I'm busy. 我不能马上过来，我很忙。
- I can't come over. I'm sorry. 我过不来，对不起啊。

对方也许会遗憾：

- It's okay, maybe another time. 好吧，那下次吧。
- Don't worry; we can get together some other time. 没事儿，我们改天可以聚。
- Let's do it another time then. 那咱们就改天吧。

Invitation and Reply Conversation

Kevin: Hey, Debra. 凯　文：嘿，黛布拉。

Debra: Hey, I got your invite to the party. 黛布拉：嘿，我收到你的派对邀请了。

Kevin: Awesome! Did you RSVP? 凯　文：太好了！你回复了吗？

Debra: Yeah I did, it's in the mail. 黛布拉：回复了，在邮件里面。

Kevin: Cool, I'm glad you're coming. 凯　文：太好了，你要来我很高兴。

Debra: Yeah, I asked a few friends and I guess they're going to join me. 黛布拉：嗯，我叫了几个朋友，我想他们会和我一起来。

Kevin: Awesome. I can't wait to see how it turns out! 凯　文：好的，我都等不及想看看这派对会开得怎么样！

Debra: Me too. Who else did you invite? 黛布拉：我也是。你还邀请了谁？

Kevin: A few friends from high school I haven't seen in a while. 凯　文：高中的几个朋友，我们都有一段时间没见面了。

Debra: Did they reply? 黛布拉：他们都回复了吗？

Kevin: No, but I'm not too worried if they don't show up. 凯　文：没有，但如果他们不来的话我也不会太伤心的。

Debra: Yeah, well at least you invited them. 黛布拉：是啊，至少你邀请过他们了。

❖RSVP 回复，是法语 Répondez s'il vous plait. 的首字母缩写，相当于英语的 reply please。

❖turn out 结果是

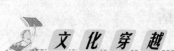

文 化 穿 越

　　邀请别人是种礼节。美国人的生活中离不开派对，他们经常喜欢借着派对聚在一起谈论最近的生活并一起娱乐。邀请别人的时候最好提前 3 天以上，因为别人需要查看自己的安排之后才能决定是否赴约。另外，如果是在自己的家里开派对，还需要注意要将家里的卫生打扫干净，当然还要准备些饮料。在美国，来开派对的朋友，一般每个人都会带一些食物或者饮料。另外，如果安排已满，需要拒绝别人的话，可以直接拒绝，不用拐弯抹角地解释。这是东西方文化的差异，美国人的方式一般比较直接，不需要很多借口。

Section 6 ▶ 接打电话
Answering the Phone

这次回美国，因为走得急，很多好朋友都来不及一一告知了。下了飞机后我才打电话告诉我在中国的朋友，Kevin 已经回到美国了。Steve 一路上听着我在打电话，也不由地惊呼："Kevin，你好像有胜利大逃亡的感觉啊，小心下次你的朋友们拖住你不让你走哦。"

1 Hello. This is Kevin. 你好，我是凯文。

打电话时先自报家门：
- Hello. Kevin speaking. 你好，我是凯文。
- Hi. This is Kevin speaking. 嗨，我是凯文。

如果对方知道你：
- Hi, Kevin. It's me. 嗨，凯文。是我。
- Hey Kevin! What's up? 嘿，凯文！什么事？

2 May I ask who's calling? 请问你是哪位？

对方不确定打电话的人是谁：
- Who is this? 你是哪位？
- May I ask who this is? 请问你是哪位？
- Who am I talking to? 你是哪位？

告知对方身份：
- It's Steve. 是史蒂夫。
- This is Steve. 我是史蒂夫。

3 May I speak to Kevin? 我能找一下凯文吗？

礼貌的说法：

- May I speak with Kevin? 我能找一下凯文吗？
- I'd like to speak to Kevin, please. 我想找凯文。
- Is Kevin there, please? 请问是凯文吗？

最简单的说法，但并不失礼：

- Kevin, please. 请找凯文。

对熟人可以这样说：

- Let me talk to Kevin, please. 我要找凯文。

如果找的人在：

- Okay, hold on please. 好的，请稍等啊。
- One moment, please. 请稍等。
- Just a second, please. 请稍等。

如果找的人不在：

- I'm afraid he isn't in right now. You've just missed him. 恐怕他这会不在。你刚好错过他了。
- I am sorry he's just stepped out. Would you like to call back in an hour? 对不起，他刚出去。你要不一个小时后再打过来？

❖ step out 走出去，暂时外出

---

4 (Would you like to hold? 你等会儿行吗？

同样的说法：

- Would you like to hold on? 你等会儿行吗？
- Would you like to stay on the line? 你等会儿行吗？
- Can you hold the line, please? 请等一会儿好吗？

用于朋友或熟人：

- Wanna hold? 能等会儿吗？

对方愿意等：

- Okay, thank you. 好的，谢谢你。

如果对方有事：

- No, I'll call back later. Thanks. 不用了，过会儿我再打吧。谢谢。

❖ stay on the line 不挂电话
❖ hold the line 不挂断电话
❖ wanna ['wɔnə] vt. 想要（相当于 want to）

5 He's not here right now. 他现在不在这里。

暂时没法来接电话：

- He can't come to the phone. 他没法来接电话。

比较忙而没法接电话：

- He's busy right now. 他现在很忙。
- He's too busy to talk. 他太忙了不能来接电话。

有点儿遗憾，但还是礼貌地回复对方：

- Alright, sorry for bothering you. 好吧，抱歉打扰你了。

确实有事要跟他说啊：

- Darn it, I really wanted to talk to him. 真讨厌，我确实需要和他谈谈。
- ❖ bother ['baðɚ] *vt.* 烦扰，打搅
- ❖ darn it 真讨厌

6 Can I take a message? 要我捎个口信吗?

对方要找的人不在：

- I can take a message if you'd like. 如果你愿意的话，我可以捎个口信。
- Do you want me to take a message? 你要我捎个口信吗?
- I'll take a message for you. 我会帮你留个口信的。

需要留口信：

- Sure. Do you have a pen and paper? 好的，你有笔和纸吗?

不需要留口信：

- No, I don't need to leave a message. Thank you. 不用，不需要留口信，谢谢你。
- ❖ take a message 捎口信，带口信
- ❖ leave a message 留言，留口信

7 I think you have the wrong number. 我想你打错电话了。

打错电话了：

- You dialed the wrong number. 你拨错号码了。
- I believe you dialed the wrong number. 我想你拨错号码了。

- You have the wrong number, sorry. 你拨错号码了，对不起。
- Sorry, you've dialed the wrong number. 对不起，你拨错号了。

因自己的过错给对方造成不便：

- I'm sorry. Have a nice day. 对不起，祝你愉快。
- Forgive me. I hope I didn't bother you. 请原谅，我希望没有打扰到你。
- Sorry! I hope you have a good day. 对不起！希望你愉快。
- ❖ have the wrong number 号码错了，打错电话，拨错号码
- ❖ dial ['daɪəl] vt. 拨（电话号码），打电话给

Answering the Phone Conversation

Kevin: Hello?	凯文：你好？
Katie: Hey!	卡蒂：嘿！
Kevin: Who is that?	凯文：你是哪位？
Katie: This is Katie. Is Alicia there?	卡蒂：我是卡蒂。是艾丽西娅吗？
Kevin: No, this is Kevin.	凯文：不是，我是凯文。
Katie: Who?	卡蒂：谁？
Kevin: I think you have the wrong number.	凯文：我想你打错电话了吧。
Katie: Oh gosh, I'm sorry!	卡蒂：哦，天哪，对不起！
Kevin: It's okay.	凯文：没关系。
Katie: Sorry. Bye.	卡蒂：对不起啊，再见。
Kevin: Bye.	凯文：再见。

文化穿越

刚到美国的中国人可能比较头疼于接美国人的电话，因为有的美国人语速较快，而且不同地区的口音也会不同，经常会听不懂。不过没关系，万一没听懂，可以请求人家再说一遍，如果确实听不懂，还有一招就是跟对方说，我的信号不好，能否发信息或者过一会儿回复过去。一般情况下，其实美国本地人说话还是相对清楚的。如果出去旅游，有时会遇到一些旅店的前台是印度人或者亚裔美国人，这时候和他们交流是件比较费劲的事，没办法，最好在把他弄急之前听懂他讲的话。

Section 7

天气
Weather

> 今天的阳光不是很好，如果在平时，我可能不太喜欢这样的天气。但今天不一样，马上就要到家了，我很激动，所以这天气在我看来也感觉特别亲切。不过在这里我要提醒大家，和英美人交流打开话匣子，天气这个话题永远都不会过时。

① The weather is beautiful. 天气很好。

天气好同样还可以这样表达：
- It's very nice out today. 今天外面的天气很好。
- The weather is nice out today. 今天外面的天气很好。
- It's sunny and warm today. 今天阳光灿烂、很暖和。

喜欢这种天气：
- Yeah, I love this kind of weather. 是啊，我喜欢这种天气。

有点儿挑剔了：
- It's a little too hot for my liking. 就我喜欢的天气来说，这还是有点儿太热了。

② It's really cold out. 外面真冷。

冷且恶劣的天气：
- It's freezing outside. 外面特别冷。
- The weather is nasty. 天气真恶劣。
- The weather outside is terrible. 外面的天气真糟糕。

天气确实糟糕：
- Yeah, this weather is awful. 是啊，这天气太糟了。

天冷了要多穿衣服：

- It's so cold; I'll need to get a new coat. 好冷啊，我得买件新外套了。

❖ nasty ['næstɪ] *adj.* （天气等）非常恶劣的

3 It's snowing today. 今天下雪了。

下雪啦：

- It's snowy outside. 外面下雪了。
- There's snow outside. 外面下雪了。
- It's cold and snowing today. 今天好冷，下雪了。

喜欢下雪的人：

- That's alright. I love the snow. 好啊，我喜欢雪。
- The snow is nice. 下雪挺好的。

不喜欢下雪的人：

- Snowy weather is dreadful. 下雪的天气真是糟透了。

❖ dreadful ['drɛdfəl] *adj.* 遭透的，非常讨厌的（口语）

4 It's rainy. 下雨了。

根据不同的时态表达下雨：

- It's raining outside. 外面正下雨呢。
- There's a lot of rain today. 今天下了很大的雨。
- It's going to rain. 要下雨了。

给予提醒：

- Don't forget your umbrella. 别忘了带伞啊。
- You probably shouldn't go outside today. 今天你或许不该出去。

❖ umbrella [ʌm'brɛlə] *n.* 伞，雨伞

5 The weather forecast said the storm would clear up tonight.
天气预报说暴风雨今晚就会停的。

随时注意天气预报：

- According to the forecast, the storm is going away later tonight. 根据天气预报，暴风雨今晚晚些时候就会过去的。
- The weatherman said it's supposed to stop storming tonight. 天气预报员说暴风雨今晚应该就会停止了。

- The storm should clear up tonight. I heard it on the daily forecast. 暴风雨今晚应该就停了，我在每日预报上听到的。

好的消息总是让人高兴的：

- That's good. I'm tired of this storm. 那太好了，我都烦死这暴风雨了。

天气预报有时候可能不准确，抱以希望吧：

- Hopefully the forecast will be right. 希望天气预报是对的。

❖　forecast ['fɔr,kæst] n. 预测，预报
❖　clear up（天）放晴
❖　according to 根据，按照，据……所说

6　There's a lot of thunder and lightning. 有很多电闪雷鸣。

这种天气很吓人的：

- The thunderstorm is really bad right now. 此刻这雷雨天气真糟糕。
- This lightning and thunder is crazy. 这闪电和雷声很疯狂。

这种天气对我们的影响：

- I know. It kept me up all night! 我知道，这让我整个晚上都没睡着。
- It's so loud. It's hard to concentrate with this weather. 声音太大了，这种天气很难集中精神。

❖　thunder and lightning 电闪雷鸣
❖　thunderstorm ['θʌndɚ,stɔrm] n. 雷暴，雷暴雨，大雷雨
❖　concentrate ['kɑnsɛn,tret] vi. 集中，聚集

7　It's supposed to be overcast tonight. 今晚应该是阴天。

在我们看来阴天和多云没多大区别：

- It's supposed to be cloudy today. 今天应该是多云的天气。
- It won't be very sunny. There are a lot of clouds. 天气不会很晴朗的，有好多云。
- The sky will be covered in clouds all day. 天空将一整天都被云层笼罩。

阴天总比下雨好啊：

- That's not too bad. At least it isn't raining anymore. 那还不是太糟糕，至少不再下雨了。

盼望太阳：

- I wish the sun would come out! 我希望太阳出来。

就有人喜欢阴天：

- I like this weather. The sun bothers me sometimes. 我喜欢这种天气。有时候太阳也很让我烦心的。

❖ overcast ['ovəˌkæst] *adj.* 多云的，阴的

8 The winds are very strong. 风好大啊。

有风的天气：

- It's really windy. 今天确实有风。
- It's windier than usual. 今天比平时风大。

能感觉到风吹：

- I agree. I feel like I'm going to fly away in it! 没错，我感觉就像要飞起来一样。
- Yeah, it pierces right through my coat. 是啊，风正穿过我的外套。

❖ fly away 飞走，飞行，起飞
❖ pierce [pɪrs] *vi.* 穿入，进入，透入

Weather Conversation

Kevin: Debra, it's getting cold.	凯　文：黛布拉，天气变冷了。
Debra: Yeah. It's a pretty rainy fall this year.	黛布拉：是啊，今年秋天的雨会特别多的。
Kevin: I wish it wasn't. I like dry autumns.	凯　文：我希望不是这样，我喜欢干爽的秋天。
Debra: I heard it was supposed to clear up for the weekend.	黛布拉：我听说这周末应当会天晴的。
Kevin: Well that's good. I'll have to go out and do something.	凯　文：哦，那太好了。那我要出去办点事。
Debra: Yup. Make some plans for the good weather!	黛布拉：是啊，要为好的天气作些计划！

Kevin: Is the rain returning after the weekend?	**凯　文：**周末过后又会下雨吗？
Debra: I think so. It will probably turn into snow soon, too.	**黛布拉：**我觉得是吧。也可能很快就会下雪。
Kevin: Oh man, it's winter already?	**凯　文：**哦，天啊，冬天已经来了吗？
Debra: There're always the spring and summer to look forward to.	**黛布拉：**我们总是盼望春天和夏天啊。

 ### 文化穿越

　　不同地区的气候差别很大。美国北部，尤其是加拿大边境附近地区冬天是很冷的，而且降雪量很大，可以埋掉汽车。因此，在冬天的时候，通常北边的人跑到南边避寒，佛罗里达和加利福尼亚都是不错的选择。北边大雪纷飞的时候，南边依然是阳光、沙滩、比基尼。不过，到了夏天，南边的人通常跑到北边去避暑，佛罗里达和加利福尼亚的夏天是很闷热的。另外，天气这个话题一般是比较安全的，陌生人之间或者朋友之间可以随时谈论天气，是个打破沉默的好话题。

Section 8 时间与日期
Time and Date

十几个小时飞行的劳顿，再加上时差的问题，我都分不清今天到底是几号了，再看看手表上的时间，还没调过来呢。朋友们，你们能告诉我今天的时间吗？呵呵，还是回家再说吧，反正现在是Steve在开车，一切都交给他了，我先靠在座位上打个盹儿休息一下。

1 What's the date today? 今天是几号?

还可以这样问日期：
- Could you please tell me the date? 你能告诉我日期吗？
- What day is it? 今天星期几？

看看日历才知道呢：
- Let me check my calendar. 让我看看日历啊。

想一想啊：
- Today? It's Sunday. 今天？是星期天啊。
- ❖ calendar ['kæləndə] n. 日历

2 Today is Sunday, October 3rd. 今天是星期天，10月3号。

以下几种说法有点儿像绕口令：
- The date is Sunday, October 3rd. 日期是星期天，10月3号。
- The date today is October 3rd, and it's a Sunday. 今天的日期是10月3号，还是星期天呢。
- It's Sunday, October 3rd today. 今天是星期天，10月3号。

别人告诉你了，该表达谢意：
- Okay, thank you. 好的，谢谢你。

3　What time is it? 现在几点了?

询问别人时间:
- Could I have the time? 能告诉我时间吗?
- Do you know what time it is? 你知道现在是几点了吗?
- Excuse me, what's the time? 打扰一下, 现在几点了?
- May I ask the time? 我可以问你现在几点吗?

对方会详细地告诉你:
- My watch says it's a little past 4. But it tends to be slow. 我手表上是四点多一点, 不过手表慢了。
- ❖　tend to 趋向, 有……的倾向

4　It's 4:15. 现在是四点一刻。

同一个时间的不同表达:
- The time is a quarter after 4. 时间是四点一刻。
- It's 15 minutes after 4. 现在是四点一刻。
- It's a little past 4 o'clock. 现在是四点过一点。

直接说声谢谢:
- Thank you very much. 多谢啦。
- ❖　quarter ['kwɔːtə] n. 一刻钟, 四分之一

5　The clock is three minutes slow. 这表慢了 3 分钟。

手表上的时间对不对:
- The clock is three minutes behind. 这表慢了 3 分钟。
- The clock is three minutes fast. 这表快了 3 分钟。
- My watch always keeps good time. 我的表一向很准的。

我还不知道呢, 多谢了:
- Thanks for telling me. 谢谢你告诉我。
- ❖　keep good time (钟、表) 走得准

6 I work at 5. 我五点上班。

言外之意就是让对方提醒你了：

- I have to go to work at 5 o'clock. 我五点钟就得去上班了。
- My shift starts at 5 today. 我今天是五点开始轮班。
- I need to be at work by 5. 我五点钟就要工作了。

给予建议：

- You should set an alarm on your phone so you can leave on time. 你应该在手机上定一下闹钟，这样你才能准时走。
- ❖ shift [ʃɪft] *n.* 轮班，轮班工作时间
- ❖ set an alarm 定闹钟

7 I have classes tomorrow, but they end at noon. 我明天有课，不过中午就结束了。

同样的表达：

- My classes end at noon tomorrow. 我明天的课中午就结束了。
- I have some classes tomorrow. They're over at noon, though. 我明天有课，不过中午就结束了。

那还有别的时间做其他的事：

- We should do something afterwards. 那之后我们该做些事情啊。

还有半天自由支配的时间，还不错：

- That doesn't sound too bad. 那听起来还不是太坏。

Time and Date Conversation

Debra: Where were you yesterday, man?	黛布拉：伙计，你昨天在哪儿呢？
Kevin: What do you mean?	凯　文：你什么意思？
Debra: I thought we were coming over at 4 o'clock.	黛布拉：我原以为我们 4 点钟就该过来了。
Kevin: Wait, what day is it? I thought it was Friday.	凯　文：等等，今天星期几啊？我还以为是星期五呢？

Debra: Nah, it's Saturday. Do you have your days mixed up?	黛布拉：不是，今天星期六。你把日期搞混了吧？
Kevin: Yeah, I guess so. I'm really sorry I never came over.	凯　文：哦，我想是的。真是对不起啊，我没有过来。
Debra: It's okay. We can always hang out some other time.	黛布拉：没关系啦，我们改天可以出去逛的。
Kevin: Sure. I just cancelled that doctor's appointment I had on the 5th. Do you want to hang out then?	凯　文：当然了，我刚取消了5号和医生的预约，到时候你想出去逛逛吗？
Debra: Sure, that works for me.	黛布拉：好啊，那个时间适合我。
Kevin: Alright. Sorry for not showing up yesterday.	凯　文：好的。不好意思啊，昨天没有露面。
Debra: Don't worry about it. See you later.	黛布拉：别放在心上。一会儿见。

❖come over 过来，顺便来访
❖mix up 混淆
❖some other time 改天，其他时间
❖appointment [ə'pɔɪntmənt] *n*. 约定，预约

文化穿越

在美国人看来，时间就好像一条奔腾不息的河流，时间一旦流逝便无法挽回，所以美国人格外珍惜时间。在美国大城市繁华的街道上，你很难看到悠闲自在行走的人。他们总是急匆匆地赶往某个地方办理某件事情，用 always on the run（总是不停地奔忙）来形容他们再确切不过了。由于美国人始终处于奔忙之中，结果也就养成了他们的时间紧张意识，而这种紧张意识带给他们的最大好处就是做事效率高。办事有计划是美国人又一个普遍的社会习惯。诸如 schedule（时间表）和 agenda（议事日程）这样的词语，在美国人的生活中用得很广泛。由于美国人办事喜欢计划，所以他们做任何事情都要严格遵守日程安排。守时是美国人另一个普遍的社会习惯。在美国人看来，准时赴约是理所应当的，姗姗来迟则是失礼的。无论是私人间的约会还是公众集会，都要明确几点几分开始，如果谁迟到了，便会被认为是懒散的不负责任的人，从而失去别人的信任。

Section 9  告别
Farewell

"Kevin，醒醒啦，到家了。"睁开蒙胧的眼睛，是 Steve 他们在叫我，"下车吧，你回家好好睡一觉，好好休息一会儿，我们先走了，改天再聚。Goodbye, Kevin!"

1 I have to go. 我得走了。

类似的表达：

- I've got to get going. 我得走了。
- I'm going to head out now. 我现在要出门了。
- I'm leaving now. 我要走了。
- I have some things I need to do. I have to leave. 我有些事情要做，我得走了。
- Time to shove off. 是该离开的时候了。

这就走太扫兴了：

- That sucks. Thanks for coming by, though. 太扫兴了，不过还是感谢你过来。

也不勉强留你了：

- Already? Well, I'll see you later I guess. 准备好了？好吧，那再见吧。
- ❖ head out 出门
- ❖ shove off 离开
- ❖ come by 拜访

2 It was nice seeing you. 见到你真是太好了。

见面之后好开心：

- It was good to see you. 见到你真好。
- It's been fun. 很开心哦。

我也一样：

- Yup. It was nice seeing you too. 是啊，也很高兴见到你。

❖ yup [jʌp] *adv.* 是的，对啊，不错

3 Let's hang out again sometime. 咱们什么时候再聚聚吧。

下次再聚吧：

- We should get together another time. 我们应该找时间聚聚。
- We can hang out some other time. 我们改天可以聚聚。
- We should hang out again sometime. 我们什么时候应该再聚聚。

好的，随时告诉就行：

- Sounds good to me. Just tell me when you're free. 我看不错，你有空的时候告诉我一声就行。
- Sure thing. Call me whenever you want to. 那是一定的事。你什么时候想聚就给我电话好了。

❖ hang out 和朋友在一起；闲逛

4 Come again. 再来啊。

一定要再来啊：

- Please come again. 请再来啊。
- I hope you can come over again. 希望你能再来。
- I'd be glad to have you over again. 你下次能来的话我会很高兴的。

一定会来的：

- I will. 我会来的。

5 See you later. 再见。

短期内还会见面的告别：

- Talk to you later. 回头聊。
- I'll catch you later. 我回头再找你。
- See you around. 回头见。

也说声再见：

- Yeah, see you. 好的，再见。

6 Goodbye. 再见。

通俗一点儿：

- Bye-bye. 再见。

白天的告别：

- Good day. 日安。

可能永不相见了：

- Farewell. 再见。

那就再见吧：

- Bye. 再见。

Farewell Conversation

Kevin: What time is it?	凯　文：现在几点了？
Debra: It's going on 5 o'clock.	黛布拉：快五点了。
Kevin: Oh, crap. I have to get home.	凯　文：哦，天哪。我得回家了。
Debra: Why so early?	黛布拉：干嘛那么早啊？
Kevin: My mom wanted me to make dinner tonight.	凯　文：我妈妈今晚上还想让我做饭呢。
Debra: Oh, alright. Well, it's been fun.	黛布拉：哦，好吧。和你在一起很高兴。
Kevin: Yeah. I'll get online later.	凯　文：是的。我一会儿上网。
Debra: Okay. Talk to you then.	黛布拉：好的，那到时候聊。
Kevin: Yeah. See you later!	凯　文：好的，再见。
Debra: See ya.	黛布拉：再见。

文 化 穿 越

　　美国有个基本礼节是见面时问候对方最近怎样，离开时要祝愿对方拥有美好的一天。例如，Have a nice day/ Good luck 等。另外，美国人经常说的 Talk to you later/ See you later，不是中文的"一会儿见"，而是"再见"的意思。另外，美国还有个礼节是在见面和分别的时候拥抱对方，当然，这事儿一般都是女方先主动才行。拥抱的时候，如果您是男性而对方如果是女性，别抱得太紧，点到为止，如果对方是男性，可以象征性地拥抱。但好友之间例外，为了表达想念和亲密，怎样拥抱都无所谓。

Chapter 3

想念温暖的家
Family

Section 1  家人团聚 Reunion

"Hey Kevin, welcome back!"看着爸爸妈妈张开双臂飞奔过来的样子，我不禁感慨这个欢迎仪式好隆重啊，我终于到家了。面对家人的声声问候，此刻，我不禁想问一下朋友们，你离家后回家的感觉是怎么样的？

 口语大放送

1 It's great to see you again! How are you? 再见到你真是太好了！你好吗？

同样可以这样表达：

- Hey, it's nice seeing you again! How have you been? 嘿，很高兴再见到你！你怎么样啊？

常见的回答有：

- Hey! I've been doing pretty well. How about yourself? 嘿！我挺好的。你自己呢？
- Hey, I'm alright. I hope you've been doing well. 嘿，我很好。我希望你也很不错。

2 Hey, what's up? 嘿，怎么了？

一般情况下的回答：

- Nothing much. How about you? 没什么事，你呢？

如果感觉不太好：

- I've not been better. 不太好。
- ❖ what's up? 怎么了？

3 What happened while I was away? 我走后发生什么事了？

或者可以这样问：

- Did something happen while I was gone? 我走后发生什么事了？

如果觉得对方有点儿异常，可以这样问：

- Are you okay? Tell me what happened. 你还好吗？告诉我发生什么事了。

回答可以根据实际情况：

- Nothing too exciting happened. 没发生什么令人激动的事。
- A bunch of stuff happened while you were gone. 你走后发生了一连串的事情。
- Don't worry about it; tell me how your flight went. 别担心这个，告诉我你的旅程怎么样。

❖ a bunch of 一连串，一大堆

4 The flight here was okay. 坐飞机到这里一路都挺好的。

坐飞机后需要休息：

- My flight was okay, but I need to get some sleep. 我的飞行挺好，但我需要睡会儿觉。

迫不及待想告诉家里人外面的见闻：

- I have a lot to tell you! Once I get settled in we can talk about it. 我有好多话要跟你说！我一安顿好咱们就好好说说。

听到一路平安，可以放心了：

- Alright, let's get you home. 好的，我们带你回家。
- Sounds good. If you need anything let me know. 听起来不错。如果你需要什么就告诉我。

❖ get settled 安顿好，安顿下来

5 Is anyone waiting at home to see me? 有人在家等着见我吗？

想知道是不是被人惦记还可以这样问：

- Will anyone be waiting for me when I get there? 我到了的时候有人会在等我吗？

家里人都等不及要见你了：

- Of course! Your father can't wait to see you again. 当然！你爸爸都等不及要见你了。
- Yes, your brother took the day off from school just so he could be there. 是啊，你弟弟从学校请了一天假，就为了能见你。

6 Mom, can you help me carry my luggage? 妈，你能帮我拿一下行李吗？

请求帮助还可以把情况说得更详细点：

- I'm tired. Could you carry some luggage for me? 我好累啊，你能帮我拿些行李吗？
- Can you help me put the luggage in the car? 你能帮我把行李放到车上吗？

对于你的请求，家人都会答应：

- Of course, give me the heavy one. 当然可以，把重的那个给我。
- Sure, let me take your bag. 当然可以，我来给你背包。

Reunion Conversation

Kevin: Mom! Hey!	凯文：妈妈！嗨！
Mom: Aw, Kevin, It's so good to see you safely back.	妈妈：哦，凯文，看到你安全回来真是太好了。
Kevin: It's good to be back, mom.	凯文：回来真好，妈妈。
Mom: Are you feeling alright from the flight?	妈妈：坐飞机感觉还好吗？
Kevin: I'm really freaking tired, but otherwise I'm okay. How's the rest of the family doing?	凯文：就是特别累，不过其他都还好。家里面其他人怎么样？
Mom: Oh, there's plenty of news to tell you, but let's get you home first.	妈妈：哦，有好多消息要告诉你，不过咱们还是先回家吧。
Kevin: Sounds good. Where did you park the car?	凯文：好的。你把车停哪儿了？

Mom:	Here. Let me take your bag and I'll walk us there.	妈妈：	在这儿。我给你拿包，咱们一起走过去。
Kevin:	Alright. Sorry if I fall asleep on the ride home.	凯文：	好的。如果坐车回家的路上我睡着了，对不起啊。
Mom:	Don't worry about it, sweetie.	妈妈：	别担心，宝贝儿。

❖ freaking [frikɪŋ] *adv.* 非常，十分，极其
❖ on the ride home 在坐车回家的路上

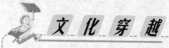

文 化 穿 越

　　美国家庭的团聚与中国类似，家庭主要成员甚至全家都会去迎接亲人从国外归来或长期在外工作休假回来。一直以为美国人独立性强，基本不怎么回家或者不怎么依靠父母，但其实美国大学生也有很多人每周末都回家，甚至把脏衣服攒齐了拿回家去洗。但有的美国家庭对于孩子在家居住是收费的，这一点在我们看来其实挺费解的，但从社会文化角度来看，它反映了父母照顾自己的孩子只是履行一种义务而已，但这种义务不是终身制，当孩子具备独立能力之后，这种义务自然消除。当然，美国父母也不求孩子的赡养和回报。

Section 2

家的模样
Home

回家的感觉真好！推开卧室的门，里面的摆设还是原来的样子，但干干净净的。我可以想象妈妈在想念我的时候，一遍遍地擦拭着我那些心爱的旧玩意儿。我爱我的家，我爱我的小卧室。

口语大放送

1 It's good to be back. 回家真好。

如果家门前静悄悄：
- Anybody home? 有人在家吗？

还是家的感觉好，赶紧抒一下情：
- Home, sweet home. 家，甜蜜的家啊。

家里人欢迎你：
- Kevin, welcome back! 凯文，欢迎回家！
- Hey buddy, good to see you again. 嘿，伙计，又见到你了真好。

2 This place is exactly the same. 这地方正是原来的样子。

这里永远是你的家：
- Of course it's the same. This place will always be your home. 当然还是原来的样子，这里永远都是你的家。

3 Wow, this place has changed a little. 哇，这地方有点儿改变哦。

给予解释：
- We did a little remodeling while you were gone. 你走后我们做了点儿翻修。
- Don't worry, it hasn't changed too much. 别担心，改变不大。
- ❖ remodel [ˌriːˈmɒdl] vt. 改建，翻修

④ Do I have any chores that need done? 有什么家务需要我做的吗?

或者简单一点问:

- Do I need to do any chores? 我需要做什么家务吗?

家里人也会体贴你的:

- You do have some chores, but get some sleep first. 你是有些家务活要做，但还是先睡会儿觉吧。

❖ chore [tʃɔr] n. 家庭杂务，家务琐事

⑤ I hope I don't have that many chores yet. I'm sleepy. 我真希望没有那么多家务活，我好困。

家里人也会尽力帮你做:

- I'll tell your brother to do some chores for you. 我让你弟弟帮你做些家务。
- I'll help you out with them in case you're too tired. 如果你太累的话我来帮你做吧。

但总是抱怨的话可不会有人来帮你哦:

- You just have a few chores. They're nothing to groan about. 你就那一点点家务活，没什么好抱怨的。

❖ groan [grəon] vi. 抱怨

⑥ I need a drink. I forget where the cups are… 我要喝杯水，我忘了杯子在哪里了……

如果忘了具体在什么地方:

- Are the cups in the right or left cabinet? I can't remember. 杯子是在右边的橱柜还是左边的呢? 我不记得了。

主动给人提供一个:

- I'll get a cup for you. 我给你拿个杯子。

很惊讶竟然忘了:

- You forgot?! They're right here. 你忘了? ! 就在这儿啊。

指明具体位置:

- They're in the left cabinet. 在左边的橱柜里。

❖ cabinet ['kæbənɪt] n. 橱柜

7 Can I just put my bags here? 我能把包放在这儿吗?

或者问一下别的地方:

- Should I put my bags somewhere else? 我该把包放在别的地方吗?

包可以随便放,只要记得就行:

- Sure, but don't forget about them there. 当然可以,但别忘了把它们放那儿了。
- You could take them up to your room if you want. 如果你想的话,也可以把包放到你自己的房间。

8 I can't wait to be in my room again. 我都等不及要进我的房间了。

还可以说:

- I missed my room. 我想念我的房间。

那可是你自己的天地:

- Go have some time to yourself, if you want. 如果你想的话就尽情享受吧。

9 Do you know where the remote to my TV is? 你知道我的电视遥控器在哪儿吗?

找不到遥控器:

- I can't find the remote. 我找不到遥控器了。

对方知道在哪儿:

- Yeah, I put it in the living room. 知道啊,我把它放在客厅了。
- It's in the living room with the other remotes. 和其他遥控器一样都在客厅里。

❖ remote [rɪ'mot] *n.* 遥控器

Home Conversation

Kevin: Hey, I'm home!	凯文:嘿,我回家了!
Dad: Welcome back, bud. Get something to drink and come over here!	爸爸:欢迎回来,伙计。拿点喝的东西到这儿来。

Kevin: I think I'm just going to head up to my room. Sorry, dad.	凯文：我就想去我的房间。抱歉，爸爸。
Dad: Why don't you come into the den and watch the football game with me?	爸爸：你干嘛不来小房间和我一起看足球比赛呢？
Kevin: Nah, I'm really tired. I want to take a quick nap first.	凯文：不，我真的累了。我想先小睡一会儿。
Dad: Fine, but I won't let you miss the whole thing!	爸爸：好吧，但我不会让你错过整个比赛的！
Kevin: When should I wake up?	凯文：我该什么时候醒呢？
Dad: Oh don't worry about that. I'll be sure to come pounding on your door before the game is over!	爸爸：哦，别担心这个。在比赛结束前我肯定会来敲你的门的。
Kevin: (laughs) Okay. Tell me what I miss when I wake up.	凯文：（笑）好吧。我醒来后告诉我错过的部分。
Dad: Will do.	爸爸：会的。

❖ head up 向……前进
❖ den [dɛn] *n.* 幽静小巧的私室（或书斋），活动场所
❖ take a quick nap 小睡一会儿
❖ pound [paund] *vi.* (连续) 猛击，(猛烈) 敲打

文化穿越

在这里聊一聊 home stay（家庭寄宿）的情况。一般情形下，无论你在哪个国家留学，首当其冲的问题有可能会是住在哪里。因为你得考虑住宿环境、离学校的距离、房租、合租或单住等一系列问题，因为房屋合同至少要签一个季度以上，另外还有保证金的问题。因此，找到一个性价比高的地方不是件容易的事儿，不过有一种情况是暂住在当地人的家里，有些家庭会给学生提供住宿，而且价格也比较低廉，甚至包括饭钱。不过，home stay 的时候，需要注意很多问题。其中主要的是安全问题，一定要确定这家人没有任何不正当企图。另外，就是自身需要注意的礼节，比如，在主人不在的情况下，不要随意进入人家的房间或者擅自使用人家的物品，还有要适当帮助人家做些家务以维持良好的人际关系，保持一颗感恩的心很重要。

Section 3

▶ 睡觉起床
Sleeping and Waking up

> 我确实很累了，我需要先睡会儿觉。妈妈，帮我定两个小时的闹钟哦。朋友们，你在非常困乏想睡觉的时候怎么用英语表达呢？在这一节里，我给大家分享一下我的"睡觉心得"。哈哈，也顺便帮喜欢赖床的朋友找个借口。

 口 语 大 放 送

1 I really need to relax and take a nap. 我真的需要休息睡一会儿。

同样还可以这样说：

- I'm gonna (going to) go and take a nap. 我要去睡一会儿。
- I think I'll take a nap. 我想我要睡一会儿。

对方可能会提醒你：

- You shouldn't sleep too long. You have to fix your schedule. 你不应该睡太长时间，你得安排你的日程。
- ❖ take a nap 小睡一下
- ❖ schedule ['skɛdʒul] n. 计划表，日程安排表

2 I'm exhausted. Wake me up in a bit. 我好累啊，一会儿叫醒我。

对方会回答：

- Alright, I'll wake you up in about an hour. 好的，一小时后我叫醒你。

老熟人之间还可以说：

- I'll make sure you don't sleep too long. 我保证你不会睡太长时间的。
- ❖ exhausted [ɪg'zɔːstɪd] adj. 精疲力竭的
- ❖ in a bit 一小会儿

3 My sleeping schedule is going to be so messed up for a while. 我的睡眠排程一时变得乱糟糟的。

远道而归，时差确实是令人头疼的事：

- This jetlag is going to kill me! 这时差综合症简直要我的命。
- I can't wait until this jetlag wears off... 我不能等到时差综合症消失了……

对方会给你建议，调整时差：

- Just set your alarm so you can fix it faster. 你定一下闹钟，这样你就能更快地调整了。
- ❖ mess up 搞糟，陷入困境
- ❖ for a while 暂时，一时
- ❖ jetlag ['dʒətlæg] n. 时差综合症
- ❖ wear off 磨损，逐渐消逝

4 I'm going to bed for the night. Goodnight! 我要上床睡觉去了，晚安！

还可以这样表达：

- I'm heading to bed. Night everyone. 我要上床睡觉了，各位晚安。
- Goodnight, I'm going to sleep. 晚安，我要去睡觉了。

对方也会同样祝你：

- Goodnight. 晚安。
- Sweet dreams. 做个好梦。

5 How early should I set my alarm? 我该把闹钟定多早呢？

还可以这样试探着问：

- Should I set my alarm early? 我该把闹钟定早点儿吗？
- I'm going to set my alarm. When do you think I should wake up? 我要定闹钟，你觉得我该什么时候醒？

还是尽量早一点儿起来吧：

- Try to wake up by 8 a.m. 尽量 8 点起来吧。
- Don't set it any later than 9. 不能定得晚于 9 点。

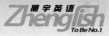
6 Ugh, I'm still tired. 啊，我还是很累。

还可以这样直截了当地表明想多睡一会儿：

• I want to sleep for a little longer. 我想再睡一会儿。
• I want to sleep some more. 我想再多睡一会儿。

Sleeping and Waking up Conversation

Kevin: Morning.	凯文：早上好。
Mom: Good morning, honey. Did you sleep well?	妈妈：早上好，宝贝。睡得还好吗？
Kevin: Yeah, but I'm still tired.	凯文：还好，但我还是很累。
Mom: Eat some breakfast.	妈妈：吃点早餐吧。
Kevin: I don't want to eat too early. It'll make me feel sick!	凯文：我不想吃得太早了，这会让我感觉恶心的！
Mom: And it'll give you more energy.	妈妈：这会给你更多的能量。
Kevin: Maybe in a bit. I just want some coffee first.	凯文：那就过会儿吃吧。我想先喝点儿咖啡。
Mom: Okay, I just made some. Help yourself. You have a long day today.	妈妈：好的，我刚好煮了点。你自己随便喝吧，今天可够你忙的。
Kevin: Thanks…Ugh, don't remind me.	凯文：谢谢……啊，别催我啊。
Mom: (laughs) Don't complain and just drink your coffee.	妈妈：（笑）别发牢骚了，喝你的咖啡吧。

文化穿越

　　时差是个有趣的话题。除了离中国较近的几个国家以外，欧洲、美洲的时差是比较大的。美国东部时间通常与北京的时间差在夏令时是 12 小时，当转入冬令时时，将会是 13 小时。其实，国外的生活就是基于这种与国内时差相反之上的，每天当你睁开双眼的时候，正是国内朋友们要睡觉的时候，而当你要睡觉的时候，国内的朋友们正在上班。依然拿美国东部举例，这边的时间比北京晚，也就是说美国东部时间 10 号晚上，相当于中国北京时间 11 号早晨。此外，倒时差也是因人而异的，一般年轻人大概 3 天就够了。一定记住倒时差时，如果白天犯困是一定不能睡的，不然生物钟会一直紊乱，时差会倒得很慢。最后需要记住的是，买机票的时候，一定要将时差计算好，因为很多机票的计时方式是以当地时间为准的。

Section 4　一日三餐
Meals

　　一觉醒来，都到吃晚饭的时间了。估计是妈妈看我睡得正香，闹钟响了都不忍心叫醒我。肚子也早已饿得咕咕叫了，开饭喽！哇，都是我最喜欢吃的耶！

1 I'm hungry. What's for dinner? 我饿了，晚餐吃什么？

还可以用 have 这个万能动词来表达：
- What are we having tonight? 我们今晚吃什么？

充满爱意的回答：
- I'm whipping up some of your favorites. 我在做你最喜欢吃的东西。

不浪费，要节俭：
- We're just having leftovers. 我们就吃点剩饭菜。

今天妈妈不在家：
- We just ordered a pizza, since your mom had to pick up your brother from soccer practice. 我就订了份比萨，因为你妈妈去接你那参加足球训练的弟弟了。

对于挑食浪费的孩子：
- Sorry bud, you'll have to scavenge tonight. 抱歉，孩子，今晚你得吃剩饭菜了。

❖　whip up 快速准备（非正式用法）
❖　leftover ['left,ovɚ] *n.* 吃剩的饭菜（常用复数）
❖　soccer practice 足球训练
❖　scavenge ['skævɪndʒ] *vi.* 清除污物（或垃圾）

2 Do you need any help with dinner? 你需要帮忙准备晚餐吗?

还可以这样随便问问:

- Got anything for me to do? 有什么事情需要我做吗?

你这样问正中下怀了:

- Aw, thanks. Can you peel the potatoes? 啊,谢谢。你能把这些土豆削了皮吗?
- Can you gather the ingredients for me? 你能帮我调一下调料吗?
- Sure, wash the vegetables for me. 好的,帮我把蔬菜洗了吧。

当然,也许真的不需要帮忙了:

- It's okay! You don't have to help. 没关系!不需要帮忙。
- ❖ ingredient [ɪn'ɡrɪdɪənt] n. (烹调的) 原料

3 When are we eating? 我们什么时候吃饭?

饿了的人还可以说:

- Are we eating soon? 我们一会儿就吃饭吗?

告知具体时间:

- It'll be about an hour. 大约一小时吧。
- In about five more minutes. 再有 5 分钟吧。

4 How long will it take for dinner to be ready? 晚餐需要多长时间准备好?

还可以简单一点说:

- How soon can you get it ready? 还要多久才能做好呀?

通常的回答:

- It's almost ready. 差不多准备好了。

5 I'll set the table. 我来摆餐具。

带有一点不满的说法:

- Should I set the table yet? 还该我来摆餐具吗?

对于你的帮忙表示感谢:

- Alright, thank you. 好的,谢谢你。

对你不满的回应：

- Yeah, set the table please. Dinner will be ready in a bit. 是的，摆餐具吧。晚餐一会儿就准备好了。

❖ set the table 摆餐具

6 Should I say grace tonight? 今晚上该我做饭前祷告吗？

如果不确定还可以继续询问：

- Who's saying grace? 谁做饭前祷告？

也可以自告奋勇：

- I'll say grace. 我来做饭前祷告。

针对你的询问作答：

- Could you please do it? 你做行吗？

或者你的家人会安排其他人做：

- It's okay. Your brother can say grace tonight. He hasn't in a while. 没事，今晚上你兄弟做饭前祷告。他好一阵子没做了。

❖ say grace 饭前祷告

7 Can you pass the salt, please? 你能把盐递给我吗？

或者还可以说：

- Hey, can I have the salt? 嘿，把盐给我吧？

回答可以说：

- There you go. 给你。
- Here. 给。

8 I'm stuffed. Thanks for making dinner, mom. 我吃饱了，谢谢你做的晚餐，妈妈。

吃饱了，还可以说：

- I'm full. That was really good. 我吃饱了。真的很不错。

对于你的赞美，对方也会高兴的：

- Thanks hon (short for "honey"). I'm glad you liked it. 谢谢你，宝贝。我很高兴你喜欢。

如果你还需要:

- There's plenty left in case you want seconds! 如果你还要的话这还有很多剩下的。
- ❖ stuffed [stʌft] *adj.* 吃饱了的

Eating Conversation

Mom: Kevin, could you please say grace?	妈妈:凯文,你能做饭前祷告吗?
Kevin: Alright…I haven't in a while so I might mess up.	凯文:好的……我有好一阵子没做了,我可能会搞糟的。
Mom: Don't try to weasel your way out of it. Your brother did it last night.	妈妈:别想着逃避,你弟弟昨天晚上做了。
Kevin: Okay, okay. Thank you God, for giving us this food and keeping us healthy.	凯文:好的,好的。感谢上帝,赐予我们食物,让我们保持健康。
Family: Amen.	家人:阿门。
Dad: Good, I'm just gonna dig in…	爸爸:好了,我要开始吃……
Mom: Don't eat all the steak like last time!	妈妈:别像上次那样把牛排都吃完了!
Kevin: (joking) With the way dad eats, the rest of us will starve.	凯文:(开玩笑地说)在爸爸这种吃法下,我们大家就得挨饿了。
Dad: (laughs) Hey, just be glad your mother is a good cook!	爸爸:(笑)嘿,这是因为你妈妈是个好厨师。
Mom: Thank you, dear. But still, leave some for the rest of us!	妈妈:谢谢你,亲爱的。但还是给我们大家留点儿吧!
Dad: Fine, I won't have too much.	爸爸:好的,我不会吃太多的。

❖mess up 搞糟,陷入困境

❖weasel ['wizl] *vi.* 逃避,推诿

❖dig in 开始做……(非正式用法)

文 化 穿 越

　　美国的饮食文化是大部分留学生最头疼的事情。中国留学生一般都会不同程度地想念中国菜。因为虽然美国大城市可以找到中国菜或者中国餐馆，但你始终找不到中国菜的原本味道，大部分在美国的中国饮食都是经过改良的。比如，一直让人很纠结的是为什么美国人喜欢往宫保鸡丁和炖肉里放糖，后来发现，凡是能放糖的东西他们全都放糖。除此之外，传统的美国饮食离不开几样东西，像汉堡、比萨、意大利面、热狗等。唯一让人有些好感的东西就是美国牛排，因为美国的牛肉很不错，有些是从国外进口，一般口感较好。其次就是奶酪，奶酪是美国人的生活必需品，即使不吃主食，也得吃奶酪和生菜。综合上述，你就能明白为什么美国胖人多了。

Section 5 花销储蓄
Spending and Saving Money

吃完饭，趁着休息的时间，我把自己的积蓄和需要的开销计划一下，以便在回家后和亲戚朋友聚会时花销有所节制。朋友们，从这件小事你可以了解我另外一个特点，我还是善于理财的哦。朋友们，你们平时的储蓄、花销怎么样？有点打探隐私了，呵呵。

1 Hey, I want to pick up some groceries. Can I have a little money? 嘿，我想挑些食品杂货。你能给我点钱吗？

或者需要借钱买：

- Can I borrow some money to get some groceries? 我能借点钱去买些食品杂货吗？

买东西也要按计划行事哦：

- Okay. Here's a list of what we need, too. 好的，这是一张单子，上面列出了我们所需要的东西。
- Sure, but don't get too much. 好的，但是别买太多了。
- Here you go. Just don't buy all the name brands. 给你吧，别都买名牌就行。

❖ grocery ['grosərɪ] n. 食品，杂货（其复数是 groceries）

❖ name brand 名牌

2 I'll only get stuff that's on sale. 我只买特价商品。

除了特价的还可以去折扣店：

- I'll just go to bargain shop. 我只去折扣店。

是的，太贵的东西不实惠：

- Yeah, don't splurge on the expensive food. 是的，别在那么贵的食物上挥霍。

❖ on sale 廉价出售，贱价抛售

❖ splurge [splɜːdʒ] *vi.* 挥霍金钱，舍得花钱

3 Can I take your calculator? 我能用你的计算器吗?

有谁随身携带计算器吗:

• I'll take your calculator to help me out, if that's okay. 如果可以的话，我想用你的计算器帮帮我。

• Where is your calculator? I'll take it with. 你的计算器呢? 我要用一下。

有的话可以借用一下:

• Here's the calculator. Keep it turned off so you don't waste the battery. 给你计算器。不用的时候就关了，那样就不浪费电池了。

❖ calculator ['kælkjəˌleɪtɚ] *n.* 计算器

❖ battery ['bætərɪ] *n.* 电池，蓄电池

4 I forgot how to figure out better deals. Can you show me quick? 我忘了怎么计算出更好的折扣了。你能快速给我演示一下吗?

瞧美国人的精明劲儿:

• Will you show me how to calculate the prices? I forget. 你能给我演示怎么计算价格吗? 我忘了。

临时抱佛脚:

• Can we review over the math I need to do to get the better deal? 咱们能复习一下数学吗? 我需要计算出更好的折扣。

各有绝招:

• Okay, get me a piece of paper. 好的，给我张纸吧。

• It's easy. Give me the calculator and I'll show you. 很容易的。给我计算器我给你演示。

5 Excuse me, sir. Can I get the price of this? The sticker is worn off. 打扰一下，先生。我能以这个价买吗? 商标都已经磨损了。

或者还可以说:

• Hey, the sticker seems to be worn off of this. Can you tell me the price? 嘿，这价格标签好像磨损了。你能告诉我价格吗?

很热情的回答：

- Sure thing. Let me scan that for you. 当然可以，我来给你扫一下。
- ❖ sticker ['stɪkɚ] *n.* 标签
- ❖ be worn off 磨损，磨破

6 Could you please tell me if both of these are on sale? 你能告诉我这两个都打折销售吗？

或者还可以说：

- Are both of these items on sale? 这两样东西都打折吗？
- Excuse me. I see one of these things are on sale, but are both? 打扰一下，我看见这些东西当中有些打折，但两种都打折吗？

可根据实际情况回答：

- Yes, both of them are on sale. 是的，都打折销售。
- No, sorry. Only the one kind is on sale. 不，抱歉，只有一种打折。

7 I can't find the store-brand of this. Can you show me where it is? 我找不到这个品牌。你能告诉我在哪里吗？

或者还可以说：

- Can you please help me find where the store-brand is? 你能帮我找到这个品牌的东西在哪里吗？

如果想找便宜点的东西：

- I don't want to get the expensive brand. Is there a cheaper brand of this item somewhere? 我不想买贵的品牌。这东西在哪里有更便宜的牌子吗？

可根据实际情况回答：

- Sure, I think it's right over here. 当然有，我想就在这儿了。
- Sorry, we only carry that brand. 抱歉，我们只有这牌子的。
- The cheaper brand should be in Aisle 8. We might be out of it. 便宜点的品牌应该在 8 号过道，我们可能没有了。

- ❖ store-brand（为某一商店特制的）商品上印制的商店标志

8 I have some coupons to use, too. 我还有些优惠券用。

以下几种说法也同样适用：

- Here, I have a few coupons for those items. 嘿，我有几张那些商品的优惠券。
- Here are some coupons I have. 我这有些优惠券。

如果优惠券还能用：

- Okay, let me add these. 好的，我来加上这些。

万一过期了：

- Oh, I'm sorry, but these are expired. 哦，不好意思，这些都过期了。

❖ coupon ['kupən] *n.* 赠券，减价优惠券

9 I have a store discount card. 我有张商场打折卡。

更明确的表达：

- Here's my discount card. 这是我的打折卡。

接受之人会表达谢意：

- Alright, thank you. 好的，谢谢。

收银员可能会说：

- Sorry sir. We stopped taking these cards. 抱歉，先生。我们已经停止用这些卡了。

10 I really need to save for school. 我真的需要为上学攒钱了。

需要攒钱的理由各种各样：

- I need to save up for that concert. 我需要为那场音乐会攒钱。
- My loan needs to be paid off. 我的贷款需要还了。
- Can we start saving for a vacation? 我们要开始为度假攒钱了吗？
- I'm saving money for when I have kids. 考虑到要小孩，我现在正在攒钱。

❖ save up 储蓄，贮存

11 I want to go to see that band but I need to save money. 我想去看那个乐队的演出，但我需要存钱。

类似这种句型的表达：

- I want my kids to have the best so I'm saving money. 我想让我的孩子生活得最好，所以我在存钱。
- I would love to go on vacation but I need to save first. 我很想去度假，但我需要先攒钱。

交流面对面

Spending and Saving Money Conversation

Kevin:	Excuse me, I wasn't sure if it was on sale or not.	凯 文：	打扰一下，我不确定它是否特价销售。
Cashier:	Was there a sign or sticker on it?	收银员：	上面有标志或标签吗？
Kevin:	There was a sign for the one kind, but this one is a bit different and I didn't know if it was included.	凯 文：	一种有标志，但这种有点儿不同，我不知道是不是包括在内。
Cashier:	Hold on. Let me check.	收银员：	等等，我看看。
Kevin:	Alright.	凯 文：	好的。
Cashier:	Yup, this is on sale. Sorry about the confusion.	收银员：	是的，这个是特价销售的。不好意思弄混了。
Kevin:	Okay, thank you, I'll still take it then.	凯 文：	没事，谢谢你。那我还是买了吧。
Cashier:	Your total is $36.74.	收银员：	总共是 36.74 美元。
Kevin:	Thank you. Have a nice day.	凯 文：	谢谢你，祝你愉快。
Cashier:	Thanks. You too.	收银员：	谢谢，你也一样。

❖confusion [kən'fjuʒən] *n.* 混乱，混淆

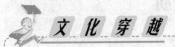

文化穿越

　　对于大部分美国家庭来说，花钱和存钱其实没有什么定律。孩子长大成人后，很多家长就让孩子自己打工养活自己，上大学的学费等更是由孩子自己想办法，不过美国政府有很大一笔教育经费是专门提供给美国上学的孩子的。对于美国学生来说，可以向政府申请到大部分学费，但住宿和吃饭只能靠自己打工了。对于家长的这种做法，其实美国人自己的解释很简单：我们也想给自己孩子钱，但问题是，我们自己都没有钱。由此看出，其实美国家庭是基本不攒钱的。不过这也与美国人的消费观念有关。在美国，很少有用到大笔现金的地方，一般都是信用卡消费。因此在美国，一个人的信誉记录十分重要，它决定了住房、汽车等贷款，甚至手机签约等问题。

Section 6

看望亲朋
Visiting Friends

休息一两天把时差倒过来后，我就着手去探望亲戚朋友了。好久不见他们，确实挺想念的。和他们一起逛逛街、看看电影、吃个大排档……感觉也是非常不错的。来，朋友们，跟着我一起去认识一下他们吧。

① Hey man, do you want to hang out tonight? 嘿，伙计，你今晚想出去逛逛吗？

以下两种表达也可以：

- Wanna (want to) hang out tonight? 今晚想出去逛吗？
- Let's hang out tonight. I don't have anything else to do. 咱们今晚出去逛逛吧，我没什么其他的事要做。

如果对方同意：

- Yeah, let's go out with some other friends too. 好的，咱们也和其他一些朋友出去玩玩。
- Sure, sounds good. Let me get ready and you can come over. 好啊，听起来不错。我准备一下，你就可以过来了。

如果对方另有安排：

- Sorry man. I got a date with my girlfriend. 不好意思，哥们儿。我和我女朋友有约会了。

② You can bring your girlfriend if you want. 如果你愿意的话可以带你女朋友来。

或者可以说：

- Your girlfriend's cool. You can bring her if you want. 你女朋友很不错，如果你愿意的话可以带她来。
- I don't mind if you want to bring your girlfriend, man. 哥们儿，如果你想带你女朋友过来，我不会介意的。

对方得到你的允许肯定会很高兴的：

- Yeah, that'd be awesome. 好的，那太好了。

不过得先问问当事人哦：

- I'll ask her first, but sure. 我要先问问她，但我可以肯定。
- I'm not sure if she'd want to, but I'll check it out. 我不确定她是否愿意来，但我会确认一下的。

3 Let's all celebrate my return with a movie. 为了庆祝我的归来咱们都去看电影吧。

看电影还可以说：

- Let's all go to the movie theatre tonight. 今晚咱们都去电影院吧。
- Let's bring everybody to the movies tonight. 今晚咱们把大家带去看电影吧。

对于这样的提议，一般不会有人拒绝的：

- Awesome, let's meet up and check out the movie times. 太好了，咱们见面再确认电影的放映时间吧。
- Sure, I'll pick everybody up and we'll meet you there. 好的，我去接大家，我们在那儿和你见面。

4 Hey man! What's up? 嘿，哥们儿！怎么了？

老朋友见面，多问候一声又何妨：

- Hey! It's good to see you again, dude. What's up? 嘿！很高兴再见到你，兄弟。最近怎么样？
- What's up? Tell me how you've been while I was gone. 最近怎么样啊？告诉我，我不在的时候你怎么样啊？

生活有好有差，对亲戚朋友就不要隐瞒了：

- Life's been pretty good. 生活还挺不错。
- Nothing much, dude. I just got a new car. 没什么，兄弟。我就买了辆新车。
- My girlfriend and I broke up, but it's not too bad. 我女朋友和我分手了，不过还不是太糟糕。
- There is so much shit going on. Life is crazy right now! 糟糕的事情太多了，现在的生活简直是疯了。

❖ dude [djud] *n.* 哥们儿，伙计

5 How's your family doing? 你的家人怎么样?

> 以下的表达意思都一样:
> - Is your family alright too? 你的家人也都好吗?
> - Has your family been doing well too? 你的家人也都还好吧?
>
> 一般的客套回答:
> - We've been family, you know. Same old, same old. 我们还是一家人, 你知道的。老样子, 老样子。
>
> 还可以回问对方的家人:
> - Yeah, they're alright. I hope your family is cool too. 是的, 他们都挺好, 我希望你的家人也都挺好。
>
> 说明实际情况:
> - They've not been better, but they're okay. 他们前阵子不太好, 不过现在没事了。

6 Alright, it was good seeing you again. I'll catch you later. 好的, 再见到你真好。我稍后联系你。

> 其他的客套招呼:
> - Hey, it was fun seeing you, but I have to go. See you! 嘿, 见到你很高兴, 但我得走了。再见!
> - See you later, man. Good seeing you. 一会儿见, 哥们儿。见到你真好。
>
> 回答可以比较简单:
> - Yeah, bye. 好的, 再见。
> - Good to see you too, later. 见到你也很不错, 一会儿见。

Visiting Friends Conversation

Kevin: Hey, how have you been?

Mabel: Pretty good, pretty good. Wanna go see that new movie?

凯　文: 嘿, 最近怎么样?

梅布尔: 挺不错, 挺不错。想要去看那部新电影吗?

Kevin:	That'd be fun. Let's pick up everyone else and we can go see it.	凯　文：	那肯定很好玩。我去接其他人，我们大家一起去看。
Mabel:	Awesome, they're all really excited to see you again. They wanna hear all of your crazy stories!	梅布尔：	太好了，他们再见到你肯定很兴奋。他们都想听你那些稀奇古怪的故事呢！
Kevin:	Well, I don't have too many crazy stories, but I have a few. Do you want me to drive?	凯　文：	哦，我没太多稀奇古怪的故事，不过也还有几个。你想让我开车吗？
Mabel:	Nah, don't worry about it. I can drive.	梅布尔：	不用，别担心，我会开车。
Kevin:	Alright, let's pick up Dan first. He lives closest.	凯　文：	好吧，咱们先去接丹，他住得最近。
Mabel:	Okay, you get shotgun.	梅布尔：	好吧，你坐到前排座位去吧。
Kevin:	Awesome, I never get shotgun!	凯　文：	太好了，我还从来没有坐过前排！
Mabel:	You're funny. Alright, let's go!	梅布尔：	你可真逗，好了，咱们走吧！

❖ get shotgun 坐到前排座位（俚语）

文化穿越

　　其实，美国人也有同中国人一样走亲访友的习惯。一般情况下，美国人会在感恩节、圣诞节等大的节日出远门，自己开着车到其他州去走访亲戚朋友。去的时候，一般会准备一些礼物，感恩节的话一般会是食物，如火鸡什么的。圣诞节当然都是包装好的礼物。不过，美国人聚会都离不开酒，他们每个人的家里都多少备有几瓶不错的威士忌或者红酒供客人选择。如果是走访别人家，带酒也是不错的选择。衣着方面，如果是跟着朋友一起参加比较正式的宴会或者酒会，需要穿晚礼服等正装出席，但如果是老朋友的个人聚会，衣着随便都是可以的。

Chapter 4

唐人街美食
Eating Out

商定餐馆
Where to Eat

今天打算请朋友们出去吃顿饭，去哪家餐馆呢？去澳拜客吃牛排还是去苹果蜂吃烧烤？天天吃西餐都吃厌烦了，咱们换种口味吧，去中餐馆撮一顿怎么样？

1 Want to go get a bite to eat? 想随便去吃点东西吗？

朋友和熟悉的人之间：

- Hey, want to go get some food? 嘿，想去吃点东西吗？
- I'm hungry. Want to go get something to eat with me? 我饿了，想和我去弄点吃的东西吗？

好的，一起去吃吧：

- Yeah, let me just get ready. 好的，我准备一下啊。

不好意思，已经吃过了：

- Oh man, I just ate. Sorry. 哦，老兄，我刚吃过。抱歉啊。
- ❖ get a bite 随便吃点东西

2 Do you want to in, or out tonight? 今晚你是想在家吃还是去外面吃？

还可以稍微复杂些：

- Hey, do you want to make food or just go out tonight? 嘿，今晚你是想做饭还是去外面吃啊？

在家吃：

- Let's stay in and save some money. 咱们在家吃吧，节省点儿钱。

去外面吃：

- I don't feel like cooking. We should go out. 我不想做饭，我们出去吃吧。

3 I don't want to go anywhere, That's fast food. 我哪里都不想去了，那都是快餐。

厌烦吃快餐：

- I don't feel like eating fast food tonight. 今晚我不想吃快餐。
- Let's go somewhere nice. I'm tired of fast food. 咱们去个好的地方吧，我讨厌吃快餐。

快餐吃多了确实让人腻味：

- Alright, sounds good to me. 好的，听起来不错。
- ❖ fast food 速食，快餐

4 Hey, I don't have a lot of money so let's go somewhere cheap. 嘿，我没有多少钱，咱们去个便宜的地方吧。

节省点儿吧，找便宜的地方吃：

- I don't feel like spending too much money tonight, we should go somewhere cheaper. 今晚我不想花太多的钱，我们去个便宜点的地方吧。
- Let's try not to spend too much money going out tonight. 咱们今晚出去吃，尽量别花太多的钱啊。

嗯，还是节省点儿：

- Alright, that's probably a good idea. 好的，那也许是个好主意。

5 I really like Outback, but I'm not in the mood. How about Chinese food? 我挺喜欢澳拜客的，但我没心情，中餐怎么样？

或者提别的建议：

- Pizza sounds good but I've been eating it a lot lately. How about a burger? 比萨听起来不错，但我最近吃得太多了，来个汉堡怎么样？

好吧，那主意也不错：

- OK, that sounds good to me too. 好的，那对我来说也不错。
- ❖ Outback 澳拜客，美式牛排餐厅
- ❖ not in the mood 心情不舒畅，没有兴致

6 I just saw a commercial for Applebee's. Let's go there! 我刚看到苹果蜂的一个广告，咱们去那儿吧！

类似的说法：

- Oh man, I just saw this commercial for Olive Garden. We should go!
  哦，伙计，我刚看到橄榄园餐厅的这个广告，我们该去那儿！

广告的效应：

- Oh yeah? I saw that too. Let's go! 哦，是吗？我也见过那个。咱们去吧！

❖ commercial [kə'mɜːʃəl] *n.* 商业广告

❖ Applebee's 苹果蜂，美国一家酒吧烧烤连锁餐厅

❖ Olive Garden 橄榄园餐厅，美国的一家著名意大利菜连锁店

交流面对面

Where to Eat Conversation

Debra: Hey, still up to go eat?	黛布拉：嘿，还出去吃吗？
Kevin: Sure, where do you wanna eat?	凯　文：是啊，你想去哪儿吃？
Debra: I don't care, just not fast food.	黛布拉：无所谓，只要不是快餐就行。
Kevin: Alright, how about Applebee's?	凯　文：好的，苹果蜂怎么样？
Debra: Sure, sounds good to me. I love their steak!	黛布拉：好啊，听起来不错。我很喜欢他们的牛排！
Kevin: Oh man, I'm so hungry. Don't even remind me!	凯　文：哦，天哪，我好饿啊，不要再提醒我了！
Debra: Get your shoes on and let's go!	黛布拉：把你的鞋穿上咱们走吧！
(Kevin and Debra arrive at Applebee's)	（凯文和黛布拉来到苹果蜂）
Waitress: Just the two of you?	服务员：就你们两个人吗？
Kevin: Yep, a table please.	凯　文：是的，请安排一张桌子。
(They sit down at a table)	（他们在一张桌子旁坐下）
Kevin: Alright, let's see what's on the menu.	凯　文：好了，咱们来看看菜单上有什么。

❖ I don't care 我无所谓，我不介意

文化穿越

　　美国比较昂贵的餐馆大部分都是法国餐厅和意大利餐厅。光是最后的小费都够在一般餐厅吃一顿了。其实，对于美国本土的饮食文化而言，简单地说是好看不好吃，有的甚至看起来也不怎么样。每天都离不开汉堡、比萨和意大利面。不过美国的牛排很不错，牛排的肉质比较好，也比较适合烧烤，尤其是做一些五成熟或者更生一些的牛排，味道十分不错。

Section 2 ▶ 点餐
Ordering Food

走进餐馆，服务员把菜单呈递上来，看着菜单上这些花花绿绿的菜样，大家都忍不住吞咽口水了。可一时也想不出该点哪个菜才好，矛盾啊，朋友们，还是你们来点吧！

1 Hello, table for two, please. 你好，请来张两人桌。

刚进餐馆：
- Hi there, we need a table for six. 你好，我们要一张六人桌。

服务员领座：
- Sure, right this way. 好的，这边请。

餐馆人多需要等一会儿：
- No problem. There might be a small wait though. 没问题，不过可能要等一小会儿。

2 What do you have to drink here? 你们有什么喝的?

询问饮品：
- What drinks are on the menu? 菜单上有什么饮料?

服务员会给你指明：
- Well, we serve Coke products here. 嗯，我们这里供应可口可乐。
- We serve Pepsi products. 我们供应百事可乐。

3 Do you have any specials? 你们有什么特价食物吗?

询问特价食物或特色食物：
- Are there any specials going on? 有什么特价食物吗?

- I was curious what your specials were for today. 我想知道你们今天的特价食物是什么。

服务员会详细说明：

- Sure, we have a garden salad and sandwich special today. 当然有了，我们今天的特价食物是田园沙拉和三明治。
- ❖ special ['speʃəl] *n.* 特色菜，特价菜
- ❖ garden salad 田园沙拉

4 Do you have a nutrition chart? 你们有营养图表吗?

这一点和中国有点儿不一样：

- Hi there, I was curious if you had a nutrition fact sheet. 你好，我想知道你们是否有营养说明书。

美国餐馆一般会备用：

- We do, let me go get that for you. 有，我去给你拿来。
- ❖ nutrition [nju'trɪʃən] chart 营养图表
- ❖ nutrition fact sheet 营养说明书

5 Do you serve alcohol? 你们提供酒水吗?

美国卖酒水有特定的地方，需问清楚了：

- I was curious if you guys sell alcoholic drinks here. 我想知道你们这里卖酒精饮料吗？

有的餐馆并不一定有酒水服务：

- We do not, I'm sorry. 对不起，我们不提供。

有的餐馆可能有：

- We do, here's our menu of drinks. 提供，这是我们的酒单。
- ❖ alcohol ['ælkə,hɔl] *n.* 酒，酒精饮料
- ❖ alcoholic [,ælkə'hɔlɪk] drinks 含酒精饮料

6 I'd like to get the cheese sticks as an appetizer. 我想点起司条作开胃食品。

一般先点开胃菜：

- Could we get the chicken fingers appetizer, please? 请给我们来鸡柳开胃菜好吗？

服务员应答：

- Sure thing. 好的。
- ❖ cheese stick 起司条，干酪条
- ❖ appetizer ['æpə,taɪzə] *n.* 开胃菜，开胃的食物
- ❖ chicken finger 鸡柳

7 I'd like to order the salmon. 我想点三文鱼。

点自己想吃的食物：

- Hi, I'd like the steak. 嗨，我要牛排。
- I'd like the pasta. 我要意大利面。
- Could I get the double cheeseburger? 给我来个双层芝士汉堡好吗？

回答：

- Alright. 好的。
- ❖ salmon ['sæmən] *n.* 三文鱼，鲑鱼，大马哈鱼
- ❖ pasta ['pɑstə] *n.* 意大利面，意大利通心粉
- ❖ double cheeseburger 双层芝士汉堡

8 Could I get that without meat? 给我来那个，不加肉好吗？

有特殊说明：

- I'm a vegetarian. Could I get this dish without meat? 我是素食者，这个菜不加肉好吗？

饭店一般都会满足你的要求：

- No problem. We serve tofu as a substitute. 没问题，我们用豆腐代替。
- ❖ vegetarian [,vedʒə'terɪən] *n.* 素食者
- ❖ tofu ['tofu] *n.* 豆腐
- ❖ substitute ['sʌbstə,tjut] *n.* 代替物，代用品

9 Could I get this cooked medium rare? 这个给我来三分熟的好吗？

牛排的吃法：

- I'd like a steak, but could I get that well done? 我想要牛排，但是我想要全熟的，行吗？

就这900句 玩转口语

服务员会根据你的要求做：
- Sure. 好的。
- ❖ medium rare 三分熟的，适中偏生的
- ❖ well done 全熟

【补充】餐馆的牛排一般有如下几种：rare 一分熟，medium rare 三分熟，medium 五分熟，medium well 七分熟，well done 全熟。

10 For dessert, could I have a piece of pie? **餐后甜点，能给我来张馅饼吗？**

根据自己的喜好点甜点：
- Could I get a chocolate cookie for dessert? 给我来份巧克力曲奇作为甜点，好吗？
- Could I get some ice cream after my meal? 饭后请给我来些冰激凌，好吗？

回答：
- No problem. Coming right up. 没问题，马上就上来。
- ❖ dessert [dɪˈzɜːt] n. 甜点心，餐后甜点
- ❖ chocolate cookie 巧克力曲奇
- ❖ right up 马上，立刻

Ordering Food Conversation

Kevin:	What looks good to you?	凯 文：	你看点什么好啊？
Debra:	Well, the ribs sound good, but they're pretty expensive.	黛布拉：	哦，听说排骨不错，但就是太贵了。
Kevin:	Hmm, what about the grilled chicken?	凯 文：	嗯，这烧鸡怎么样？
Debra:	Still a bit out of my price range.	黛布拉：	还是有点儿超出了我的价格范围。
Kevin:	You're such a bum!	凯 文：	你真是个小气鬼！
Debra:	I think I'll just get a burger.	黛布拉：	我想我就来个汉堡吧。

Kevin: Alright. I think I want the fried fish and chips.	凯　文：好吧。我想要炸鱼和薯条。
Debra: Ugh, that's gross, dude!	黛布拉：啊，总共就那么多，老兄！
Kevin: Well, it's better than a burger!	凯　文：嗯，总比汉堡要好！
(They both laugh)	（两人都笑了）
Waitress: What can I get for you?	服务员：你们要点什么？
Kevin: Could I have the fish and chips, please?	凯　文：请给我来炸鱼和薯条。
Waitress: And for you?	服务员：你呢？
Debra: Could I get a burger?	黛布拉：我要个汉堡。
Waitress: Alright. Thank you very much!	服务员：好的。多谢你们！

❖ rib [rɪb] *n.* 排骨，肋条
❖ grilled chicken 烧鸡
❖ range [rendʒ] *n.* 范围
❖ bum [bʌm] *n.* 流浪乞丐，小气鬼（美国俚语）
❖ gross [gros] *n.* 总额，总量

文 化 穿 越

　　点餐是中国人到美国后需要熟悉的场景之一。对于刚到美国的中国人可以采取观察战略，看看身边的美国人都点了什么，自己也学着点同样的东西。美国人点餐一般刚开始点饮料和开胃菜，上完开胃菜之后，服务员开始询问主食，一般很多品种的主食都会有沙拉一类的附带食物，你可以选择你喜欢的附带食物。最后是甜点，一般就是蛋糕一类的甜品。不过，有的人没那么讲究，一上来只点主食也是可以的。

Section 3  上菜用餐
Eating

哇，菜上来了，好丰盛啊。先来一口尝尝，味道很不错哦。朋友们，你们也一起来尝尝吧。今天我请客，大家放开肚子吃，不要客气，减肥的朋友也不要太节制，吃一顿饭没什么关系的。

1 Wow. That was good. I'm so full. 哇，太棒了，我吃得好饱。

好吃就多吃点：
- I feel so much better, but so full! 我感觉好多了，但是吃得好饱！
- That was an amazing meal. 这真是一顿美餐啊。

这饭菜确实不错：
- Me too! That was so good though. 我也是，不过还真不错。

2 You eat like a bird. 你吃这么一点啊。

你减肥啊，吃这么少：
- You eat very little. 你吃得这么少啊。

你可真能吃：
- Wow, you eat like a horse. 哇，你真能吃。
- You are a big eater. 你食量真大。

我食量小：
- Yeah, but I feel stuffed. 是啊，但是我感觉饱了。

太饿了：
- I'm very hungry. I can eat anything. 我饿极了，我什么都能吃。
- ❖ eat like a bird 吃得极少
- ❖ eat like a horse 吃得很多
- ❖ a big eater 食量极大的人

3　Don't be picky about food. 别那么挑食。

挑食不好哦：

- Don't be so fussy about your food. 你别那么挑食。
- Don't be such a picky eater. 别那么挑食。

我不喜欢吃怎么办：

- I know it's good for my health, but I just don't like to eat the food. 我知道这对我的健康好，但我就是不喜欢吃这东西。
- ❖　picky ['pɪkɪ] *adj.* 吹毛求疵的，挑剔的
- ❖　fussy ['fʌsɪ] *adj.* 难以取悦的，挑剔的

4　I'm hungry. 我饿了。

怎么这么饿：

- I am as hungry as a hawk/hunter. 我饿极了。
- I have a wolf in the stomach. 我饿极了。
- I can eat an ox. 我饿极了。
- I'm starving! Aren't you? 我好饿！你不饿吗？
- ❖　as hungry as a hawk[hɔːk]/hunter 饿极了，非常饥饿
- ❖　have a wolf in the stomach 饿到极点
- ❖　eat an ox 饿极了

5　I really enjoy fish. 我喜欢吃鱼。

喜欢吃鱼的人注意了：

- Fish is a great dish! 鱼是道很美味的菜！
- I'm really in the mood for some fish. 我真想吃鱼。

那就尝尝吧：

- You know what? That sounds great! 你知道吗？那听起来不错哎。

6　So, what all did you order? 那，你都点了什么？

你点的什么啊：

- That looks great! What was it? 真好看啊！是什么？

你连这道菜都不知道：

- I went with your suggestion and ordered fish! 我听从你的建议点了鱼！
- ❖ go with 跟随，与……持同一看法

7 I could go for a second course. 我想再来一个菜。

加个菜吗：

- Hey man, want to get another course? 嘿，伙计，想再来个菜吗？

不要了，够啦：

- No way! I'm stuffed! 不要了！我吃饱了！

8 The portions at this restaurant are so small. 这个饭店给的分量太少了。

这饭店老板好小气哦：

- I like eating here, but they don't give you enough food. 我喜欢来这里吃，但他们给的食物太少了。

每次都没吃饱：

- That is so true. 没错。
- I agree. I always leave hungry. 没错，我走的时候总是饿的。
- ❖ portion ['pɔrʃən] n. （食物等的）一份

9 Be quiet and eat your food. 别说话，吃你的饭。

小心喷饭哦：

- Don't talk when you eat your food. 吃饭的时候不要说话。
- Keep quiet while your mouth is full. 满嘴食物的时候不要讲话。

对不起，我会注意的：

- Sorry, I won't again next time. 对不起，我下次不会了。

10 This is great, but it could use some more salt. 这很不错，但可能要再加点盐。

好辣啊：

- I really like this, but it is exactly spicy enough for me. 我很喜欢这个，但对我来说确实太辣了。

要不要点别的东西缓和一下：

- Maybe you should ask the waiter for something. 也许你该问服务员要点什么。

Eating Conversation

(Kevin and Debra are waiting their orders)	(凯文和黛布拉在等他们点的菜)
Kevin: So how have you been?	凯　文：你最近怎么样啊？
Debra: I've been alright. How about you?	黛布拉：还好吧。你呢？
Kevin: Oh, not too bad. Just living day by day!	凯　文：哦，还不是太糟糕。就一天天过呗！
Debra: (laughs) Aren't we all?	黛布拉：（笑）我们不都是这样吗？
(The food arrives)	(食物端上来了)
Kevin: Wow, this is great!	凯　文：哇，这很不错！
Debra: I know! Such huge portions.	黛布拉：没错！份量好大。
Kevin: This is my favorite place to eat at night.	凯　文：我晚上最喜欢来这里吃了。
Debra: I know what you mean. I love it here.	黛布拉：我知道你什么意思。我喜欢这里的东西。
Kevin: Waiter, could I get some ketchup, please?	凯　文：服务员，能给我来些番茄酱吗？
Waiter: Sure, one sec.	服务员：好的，稍等。
Kevin: I always need ketchup to eat my fries with.	凯　文：我总是就着番茄酱吃薯条。
Debra: Me too. I can't stand eating them without it.	黛布拉：我也是。没有番茄酱我简直没法吃下去。

文化穿越

　　吃饭的时候需要注意一些细节，比如，刀叉的使用。一般情况下，我们用右手拿刀，左手拿叉子。一般餐桌上会有自助的小包白糖，白糖也分很多种类，包括普通白糖或者低糖白糖。除此之外，胡椒和盐是桌子上必备的。这是因为美国的烹饪方式和中国不太一样，有时候美国的蔬菜和主食是完全不放油和盐的，甚至有时候用糖代替盐，因为美国人比较喜欢吃甜的。因此，点餐的时候，自己别忘了挑选口味，不然，就只能依靠桌子上的盐和胡椒了。

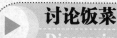
Section 4　▶ 讨论饭菜
Discussing Your Food

就餐的时候，我们经常会对面前的食物品头论足，因为总有些食物是自己最爱吃的或是自己比较挑剔的。如果你想吃什么就提前告知一声哦，万一都是你不喜欢的食物，可就要挨饿了。

1 Wow, this looks great! 哇，这看上去真好吃！

可口的饭菜总让人赏心悦目：
- This looks amazing! 这看上去真棒！
- This looks delicious! 这看上去真好吃！
- It smells good. 闻起来真香。
- It smells nice. 闻起来真香。

2 It's not good. 不好吃。

万一不好吃不合你的胃口：
- It doesn't taste good. 不好吃。

味道很怪哦：
- This tastes strange. 这味道好奇怪。
- This tastes funny. 这味道好怪的。
- This tastes weird. 这味道真奇怪。
- ❖ weird [wɪrd] *adj.* 奇特的，不可思议的

3 It's spicy. 真辣。

各种味道：
- It's too hot. 太辣了。
- It's salty. 好咸啊。

- It's sweet. 好甜。
- It's sour. 好酸啊。
- It's a bit bitter. 有点儿苦。
- ❖ spicy ['spaɪsɪ] *adj.* 辛辣的，辣味的
- ❖ bitter ['bɪtə] *adj.* 苦的，有苦味的

4 Excuse me, could I get a side of ranch dressing? 打扰一下，能给我来份沙拉酱吗？

请求服务员给额外的东西：

- I'd like to dip my fries in some ketchup, could I get some? 我喜欢用薯条蘸番茄酱吃，能给我些吗？

服务员会马上答应：

- Sure, I'll bring that right out. 好的，我马上拿过来。
- ❖ ranch [ræntʃ] dressing 沙拉酱

5 Oh, it looks like you forgot to give me my salad. 哦，你好像忘了给我沙拉了。

如果服务员忘了你点的东西，可以提醒一下：

- Excuse me, it looks like you forgot to give me my fries. 打扰一下，你好像忘了给我薯条了。

服务员会道歉并马上补给你：

- Oh, I'm sorry. Let me get that fixed for you. 哦，对不起，我去给你拿来。

6 Excuse me, could I get this cooked a little longer? 打扰一下，能给我把这个煮得时间长点儿吗？

想吃得熟一点儿：

- This looks a little red inside. Could I get it cooked a bit more? 这里面看起来有点儿红，能给我再煮一会儿吗？

一般会满足你的要求：

- No problem. I'll send it back. 没问题，我会给你送回去的。

7 I'm sorry, but this isn't what I ordered. 不好意思，可这不是我点的。

发现上来的食物不是自己点的:

- Oh no, this isn't the food that I ordered. 哦,不,这不是我点的食物。
- I didn't order this. 我没有点这个。
- This is not what I ordered. 这和我点的不一样。

服务员会道歉并给你换回来:

- I'm sorry. Let me try and get this fixed for you. 抱歉,我去给你换一下。

Discussing Your Food Conversation

(The food comes out of the kitchen)	(食物刚从厨房端出来)
Waitress: Here you go!	服务员:这是你点的东西!
Kevin: Thank you!	凯　文:谢谢你!
Waitress: Let me know if you need anything else.	服务员:如果你们需要其他的东西就告诉我。
Kevin: Oh wow, this looks great!	凯　文:哦,哇,这看上去真好吃!
Debra: Yeah, it does. Give me a fry!	黛布拉:是啊,确实如此。给我根薯条!
Kevin: Get away. You have your own food!	凯　文:走开。你自己有!
Debra: Fine, fine. This burger does look pretty tasty.	黛布拉:好吧,好吧。这汉堡看上去太好吃了。
Kevin: Excuse me, waitress…	凯　文:打扰一下,服务员……
Waitress: Yes? Can I help you?	服务员:哦?需要些什么?
Kevin: Could I get some ketchup?	凯　文:能给我来些番茄酱吗?
Waitress: Sure, I'll bring that right out.	服务员:好的,我马上给你拿过来。
(The waitress brings out ketchup)	(服务员把番茄酱拿来了)
Kevin: Thank you so much.	凯　文:多谢你啊。

❖ Get away. 走开,滚开。

文化穿越

在这里，要提醒大家注意番茄酱的说法。一般美国人管番茄酱叫 ketchup。另外，很多中国人比较喜欢把番茄酱放到比萨一类的食物上面。在美国和欧洲，人们一般不这么吃，而且如果看到你这么做，人家会认为很怪异，不过这是餐饮文化的差异。当然，依照个人口味，如果喜欢番茄酱和比萨一块吃的话，在家自己吃就好，饭店里还是需要注意一下。

Section 5

买单
Paying

　　说好了是我请客的，就我来买单吧，碰到这样的好事大家就不要推脱了，下次你们请我就行啦。不过在这里要提醒大家一句，买单的时候可要稍微多准备几块钱，作为给服务员的小费。

---

1 Could we get the check please? 请给我们看一下账单好吗?

请服务员拿账单:
- Excuse me, could I get the bill? 打扰一下，把账单给我好吗?

回答:
- Sure, just one minute. 好的，稍等啊。
- ❖ get the check / get the bill 看一下账单

---

2 It's on me. 我请客。

请客的各种说法:
- This is my treat. 这次我请客。
- I'll treat you. 我请你。
- I'll take care of it. 我来付钱。
- I'll pay for dinner. 我来付晚餐的钱。
- I'll pay for drinks. 我来付饮料的钱。

别人请客好开心哦:
- Oh! How nice! Thank you. 哦! 那太好了! 谢谢。
- ❖ on me / my treat 我请客

3 Do we pay for the check here, or up front? 我们是在这儿结账，还是去前台？

在哪里结账：

- Do you want us to pay for the bill here, or go to the front desk? 你是想让我们在这里结账，还是去前台？
- Can we pay up front or do we need to pay you? 我们是在前台付款还是付给你就行？
- Where should I pay? 我该在哪儿结账？

去柜台结账：

- Yep, just bring your check to the counter. 是的，把你们的账单放到柜台就行。

给我就行：

- I can take your check. 我可以给你们结账。

❖ the front desk 前台

4 How much should we tip our waiter? 我该给服务员多少小费？

记得给小费哦：

- How big of a tip are you leaving? 你们留了多少小费啊？
- Hey, how much should we tip? 嘿，我们该给多少小费？

小费也有一定数额啊：

- A couple bucks at least. 至少两美元吧。
- Probably two or three bucks. 可能两到三美元吧。

❖ buck [bʌk] *n.* 美元（俚语）

5 Keep the change. 不用找零了。

零钱也可以作为小费给服务员：

- Here's the check, and keep the change. 这是账单，不用找零了。

服务员会很感激你的：

- Thank you! 谢谢你！

6 Can I pay with a credit card? 我能用信用卡结账吗？

刷信用卡还是付现金：

- Do you accept credit cards or just cash? 你们接受信用卡还是只能用现金？

两者都可以：

- We accept both cash and credit. 现金和信用卡都可以。

❖ credit card 信用卡

7 What is this for? 这是什么的钱？

如果对账单有异议：

- What is this charge for? 这项费用是什么？
- What is this amount for? 这是什么的钱？

服务员会向你解释清楚：

- Oh, it's the drinks'. 哦，这是饮料的钱。

8 Could I also get a cookie to go? 给我再来块饼干带走好吗？

需要外带食物：

- Could I get the check, and could I get a brownie to go? 请给我结账，再要个巧克力蛋糕带走好吗？

这可增加费用了哦：

- Sure no problem. Let me update the check for you. 好的，没问题。我来给你改一下账单。

❖ brownie ['braunɪ] n. 巧克力小方饼，果仁巧克力小方块蛋糕
❖ update [ʌp'det] vt. 更新，修改

Paying Conversation

Kevin: Hey, let me handle the check.	凯　文：嘿，我来结账吧。
Debra: No way. You paid last time. I got it.	黛布拉：不用了。你上次付了，我来吧。
Kevin: You drove us out here. I'll pay.	凯　文：你开车载我们来这里的，我来付吧。

Debra: Fine, fine, you can pay. Let's hit the bars later though, I'll buy you a drink.	黛布拉：好吧，好吧，你付吧。不过咱们一会儿去泡吧，我请你喝一杯。
Kevin: Alright. It's a deal.	凯　文：好的。说定了。
Waitress: I can take your bill whenever you're ready.	服务员：你们什么时候准备好了，我给你们拿账单。
Kevin: Sure, I'm gonna pay with my card. Here you go.	凯　文：好的，我刷卡结账，给你。
Waitress: Thanks! I'll be right back with your receipt.	服务员：谢谢！我马上把收据给你拿过来。
(The waitress returns)	（服务员回来了）
Waitress: OK. Just sign the top copy and you're all set.	服务员：好了，你只要在收据的原件上签名就可以了。
Kevin: OK. Have a good night.	凯　文：好的。祝你晚上愉快。

❖handle the check 结账
❖no way 不用，不行
❖hit the bars 泡吧
❖It's a deal. 一言为定，成交。

文化穿越

　　美国结账有几点需要注意。一般情况下，用现金结账的话，服务员会将零钱找给你，之后你需要按照账单的 15% ～ 20% 的小费将零钱直接放到桌上；如果是信用卡支付的话，服务员会直接给你两张单子，需要在一张上面填需付金额和小费金额，另一张自己保存就行。之后消费的金额就会自动在信用卡上扣除。你不用担心服务员多扣小费，一般情况下不会发生这种事情，况且你手里面有一份单据证明，回去后也可以查询网络银行以确认无误。

Section 6　

喝咖啡
Getting Coffee

　　吃完饭后时间还早，不想这么早就回家去，朋友们可以考虑和我一起再去喝杯咖啡，在外面逛逛，消磨一下时间。在这一节里，我给大家介绍一些咖啡种类的常见说法，请大家不要错过，学习完这一节后就是不喝咖啡的人也会对咖啡有个大致的了解。

1 Would you like to go get coffee later? 你过一会儿想去喝咖啡吗?

邀请别人喝咖啡:
- Hey, want to grab a cup of coffee later? 嘿，一会儿想去喝杯咖啡吗?
- Want to go with me to get some coffee later? 一会儿想和我去喝点咖啡吗?

接受邀请:
- Sure. 好的。

拒绝邀请:
- I wish I could, but I'll be busy later. 我想去，可是我一会儿会很忙。
- ❖ grab a cup of coffee 喝杯咖啡

2 Hey, after the movie, do you want to get a cup of coffee? 嘿，看完电影后你想去喝杯咖啡吗?

建议去喝咖啡:
- I was thinking after the show we could go get some coffee. 我在想看完电影后我们可以去喝杯咖啡。

极力赞成:
- Yeah, that would be great. 好啊，那再好不过了。
- Sure! I would like that. 好的! 我喜欢那样。

找借口回绝：

- Sorry, I'll be busy later. 抱歉，我一会儿会很忙。

3 I'll have a small black coffee please. 请给我来一小杯黑咖啡。

有具体的要求：

- Could I have a small coffee with cream, please? 请给我来一小杯加奶油的咖啡，好吗？
- Hi there, could I get a coffee with cream and sugar? 你好，给我来一杯加奶油和糖的咖啡，好吗？

报价：

- Sure, that'll be two dollars. 好的，总共是两美元。
- ❖ black coffee 黑咖啡，不加牛奶的纯咖啡

4 Could I get non-fat milk in my latte? 请在我的拿铁咖啡里放脱脂牛奶好吗？

来杯拿铁：

- I'd like a latte, but could I get that with 1% milk? 我要杯拿铁，不过请在那里面加含 1% 脂肪的牛奶，好吗？
- Hello, I'd like a latte but could I get that with skim milk? 你好，我要杯拿铁，但往那里面加点脱脂牛奶，好吗？

回答：

- No problem. 没问题。
- ❖ non-fat milk 脱脂牛奶
- ❖ latte ['lɑːtei] *n.* 拿铁，拿铁咖啡
- ❖ skim milk 脱脂牛奶

5 Do you want some cream for your coffee? 你想在咖啡里加些奶油吗？

询问往咖啡里面加什么调料：

- I'm getting some sugar for my coffee. Do you want anything? 我要往我的咖啡里加些糖，你想加什么吗？

主动提供服务哦:

- Hey, I'm getting up. Do you want me to grab you some coffee? 嘿, 我要起床了。你想让我给你弄些咖啡吗?

如果需要:

- Yes please. Thank you! 好的, 谢谢你!

如果不需要:

- Oh, no. Thank you! 哦, 不用。谢谢你!

6 Could you tell me what you put in mocha? 告诉我你的摩卡咖啡要加什么?

服务员问顾客:

- Hi, I was curious what you guys put in your chai lattes. 嗨, 我想知道你们想往印地安拿铁里加什么?
- How would you like your coffee, with sugar or cream? 你要什么咖啡, 加糖的还是奶油的?
- Do you take cream and sugar in your coffee? 你要在咖啡中加奶油和糖吗?

顾客问服务员:

- I'd like to get a latte, but can you tell me how it's made first? 我想要杯拿铁, 不过你能先告诉我这是怎么做的吗?

先看看调料单:

- Sure, let me check the list of ingredients. 好的, 让我看看调料单。

服务员会告诉你:

- Oh, no problem. It's a mixture of coffee, milk, and these ingredients. 哦, 没问题。这是用咖啡、牛奶和这些配料混合而成的。

❖ mocha ['mokə] *n.* 摩卡咖啡
❖ chai latte 印地安拿铁

7 Wow, this coffee is strong! 哇, 这咖啡好浓啊!

咖啡太浓了:

- I should add some sugar to this. It's pretty strong! 我该在这里面加些糖。太浓了!
- This coffee is great, but how is it strong! 这咖啡很棒, 就是太浓了。

8 Could I get a latte, but have it iced? 我要杯拿铁，但要冰的，好吗?

往咖啡里面加冰:

- I would like an iced latte. 我想要杯加冰的拿铁。

对方会满足你的要求:

- Sure, no problem! 好的，没问题!

Getting Coffee Conversation

(Kevin and Steve arrive at the coffee shop)	(凯文和史蒂夫到了咖啡店)
Kevin: This place is great!	凯　文: 这地方真棒!
Steve: Yeah, I love it.	史蒂夫: 是啊，我喜欢这儿。
Kevin: Could I get a black coffee please?	凯　文: 我要杯黑咖啡吧?
Steve: Black coffee? Disgusting! Could I have a mocha please?	史蒂夫: 黑咖啡? 难喝死了! 我要杯摩卡吧?
Kevin: Mocha? That's basically just sugar and chocolate!	凯　文: 摩卡? 那基本上就只是糖和巧克力。
Steve: Yeah yeah, I don't want to hear it.	史蒂夫: 是啊，是啊。我不想听啦。
Kevin: Real men drink their coffee black, you know.	凯　文: 你知道，真正的男人都喝黑咖啡。
Steve: Whatever you say (laughs).	史蒂夫: 随便你怎么说（笑）。
Kevin: Really though, I do like some sugar in my coffee some times.	凯　文: 不过说真的，我有时候喜欢往咖啡里放点糖。
Steve: So get some!	史蒂夫: 那就放点吧!
Kevin: I'm not in the mood. I want a nice cup of strong black coffee!	凯　文: 我没心情。我想要一杯上好的浓黑咖啡。
Steve: Whatever works for you, man (laughs).	史蒂夫: 你怎么着都行，伙计（笑）。

❖disgusting [dɪsˈɡʌstɪŋ] *adj.* 令人作呕的

142

文化穿越

咖啡是美国人的每日必需品，尤其是每天早晨，他们不吃早饭也不会忘记喝咖啡。我们经常看见美国人在午后拿一杯咖啡，就着半个百吉饼、一份奶油芝士消遣，具有这个喜好的美国人大约有四成；而百分之十八的美国人贪图方便，一般喝杯咖啡，吃个夹肉的三明治或夹香肠的热狗就算早餐。所以无论是在办公室，还是在餐馆和公共场所都能找到咖啡壶的身影。

Section 7 **去酒吧**
Going to the Bar

酒吧也是我们饭后经常去消磨时间的场所，有时间和朋友们上酒吧喝一杯也是一件乐事。不过我提醒大家一句，在美国去酒吧喝酒，一定要有身份证明，并且达到喝酒的年龄，否则人家是不会把酒卖给你的哦。

口语大放送

1 Could I see you ID? 我能看看你的身份证明吗?

在美国不到一定年龄是不准喝酒的：
• Excuse me, could I check your ID? 劳驾，我能看看你的身份证明吗?

拿出证明：
• Sure, here it is. 好的，给你。

2 What drink specials do you have? 你们有什么特价饮品吗?

询问特价酒：
• Hey, what are your drink specials for tonight? 嘿，你们今晚的特价饮品是什么?

特价酒都列举出来了：
• We have them all listed here. 都列在这里呢。
❖ drink specials 特价饮品，特价酒

3 Can I get a beer please? 请给我来杯啤酒好吗?

来杯生啤：
• Could I get a draft? 给我来杯生啤好吗?

这是有区别的：
• Sure, bottled or draft? 好的，要瓶装的还是生啤?

服务员马上会给你上酒：

- Sure, coming right up. 好的，马上上来。
- ❖ draft [dræft] *n.* 生啤
- ❖ bottled or draft 瓶装的还是生啤，啤酒有所谓 draught/draft beer 或 bottled beer 之分。draught/draft beer 用大桶盛着，一杯杯零售，叫做"生啤酒"；bottled beer 当然是瓶装啤酒了。

4 Could I get a mixed drink? 给我来杯混合鸡尾酒好吗？

想喝什么就点什么：

- Could I get a jack and coke please? 请给我来杯杰克丹尼加可乐好吗？

服务员马上给你送上来：

- Sure, coming right up. 好的，马上上来。
- ❖ mixed drink 混合鸡尾酒
- ❖ jack and coke 杰克丹尼加可乐，一种传统的美国鸡尾酒，是用杰克丹尼威士忌加可口可乐混合而成的。

5 I'll have a draft. 我要一杯生啤。

随便点：

- Draft, please. 请给我生啤酒。
- I'd like a pitcher / jug of beer. 我要一罐啤酒。
- I'd like a light / dark beer. 我要一杯度数低 / 度数高的啤酒。
- ❖ pitcher ['pɪtʃə] *n.* 一罐的量，一壶的量
- ❖ jug [dʒʌg] *n.* 一罐的容量，一壶的容量
- ❖ light / dark beer 淡啤酒，低度啤酒 / 黑啤酒，高度啤酒

6 Put it on my tab. 记在我的账上。

第一杯开始记账，最后一起付账：

- Could I open a tab with this on it? 我可以把这个记在账上吗？

可以记账：

- Sure. 好的。

不能记账：
- We don't have tabs here. Sorry. 我们这里没有记账，抱歉。
- ❖ tab [tæb] *n*. 账款，费用

Going to the Bar Conversation

(At the bar)	(在酒吧)
Kevin: Wow, this place is packed!	凯文：哇，这地方人好多啊！
Steve: You can say that again!	史蒂夫：一点儿都没错！
Kevin: See any good looking girls?	凯文：看到什么好看的女孩子了吗？
Steve: Yeah man! None that would be interested in you though! (laughs)	史蒂夫：当然了，伙计！不过可没有人对你感兴趣哦！（笑）
Kevin: (laughs) Alright, buy me that beer.	凯文：（笑）好吧，给我买那个啤酒。
Steve: Yeah, yeah. I guess I owe you.	史蒂夫：行，行。我想我该欠你的。
(Kevin and Steve drink a couple beers)	（凯文和史蒂夫喝了两杯啤酒）
Kevin: Hey, I think I see a girl I know, I'll be right back.	凯文：嘿，我想我看到一个认识的女孩，我马上回来。
(Kevin approaches Emily)	（凯文走近艾米丽）
Kevin: Hey! I didn't see you there.	凯文：嘿！没想到在这儿见到你。
Emily: Oh hey, Kevin. What's up?	艾米丽：哦，嘿，凯文。最近怎么样？
Kevin: Not much, just hanging out. Hey, I was wondering if you wanted to go see a movie Friday.	凯文：不怎么样，只是闲逛。嘿，我想知道周五你是否想去看场电影。
Emily: Sure, I'd like that a lot.	艾米丽：好啊，我挺想去看的。
Kevin: Alright, I'll call you. Have a good one!	凯文：好的，我会给你电话。玩得高兴点啊！
Emily: You too, Kevin!	艾米丽：你也是，凯文！
(Kevin walks back to Steve)	（凯文回到史蒂夫那里）

| Kevin: | That went amazingly! | 凯　文：喝得太爽了！ |
| Steve: | (laughs) Slow down there, man. | 史蒂夫：（笑）慢点儿喝，老兄。 |

❖ packed [pækt] *adj.* 塞得满满的，拥挤的
❖ You can say that again! 一点儿都没错！
❖ amazingly [ə'meziŋli] *adv.* 令人吃惊地，惊人地
❖ slow down there 慢点儿，慢点儿喝

文化穿越

　　酒吧是美国人生活中必不可少的一部分，尤其是周五晚上。还有周末。说到酒吧，必须提及下美国的法律。在美国，21 岁以下的青少年是不允许沾酒的，商店和酒吧都会检查 ID，当然也会有个别学生弄张假 ID，但大部分的学生都十分遵守规则，无论谁给予 21 岁以下青少年酒喝都会进监狱，警察对此的检查如同中国检查酒后驾车一样严厉和频繁。除此之外，美国的大部分酒吧和夜店只营业到凌晨 2 点。因此，提醒大家尽量不要在凌晨 2 点出门，这时候大街上会有很多酒后闹事的人，当然也有个别的酒吧和夜店会营业到凌晨 4 点。

Chapter 5

购物在 99 美分店

Shopping

Section 1 ▶ 百货商店
Department Stores

周末的时候，去逛逛商场，看看有什么特价商品，也不失为一件乐事，不过我大多数时候只是光看不买，是地地道道的 mall rats 中的一员。哈哈，可别把我当老鼠哦，mall rats 就是指我这样的一类人像老鼠那样在 mall 里钻来钻去。

1 Hey, want to go to the mall today? 嘿，今天想去商场吗？

逛商场去了：
- Hey, I was going to the mall today, want to come? 嘿，我今天要去商场，想去吗？
- Want to come with me to the mall today? 今天想和我一起去商场吗？

等等我呀：
- Sure, let me get my coat! 好的，等我穿上衣服啊！
- Yeah man, what time are you leaving? 好的，你什么时候走啊？
- ❖ mall [mɔl] n. 商场，购物中心

2 I need some groceries. 我需要买些食品了。

要买吃的东西了：
- We're out of groceries. We need to go buy some. 我们没有食品了，我们需要去买些了。
- Looks like we need groceries again. 看起来我们又需要买食品了。
- Bummer. We better go to Wal-Mart today. 懒汉，我们今天该去沃尔玛了。

没钱啦：
- Oh man, I'm out of money! 哦，天哪，我没钱了。
- ❖ be out of 没有，用完

3 I need to get some new shoes. 我需要买新鞋了。

要买新鞋了：

- My shoes are really starting to wear out. I need some new ones. 我的鞋子真的快磨破了，我需要买新鞋了。
- These shoes are getting old. Let's go get you some new ones. 这些鞋子都旧了，咱们去给你买些新的吧。
- Wow, those shoes are gross! You need to go get a new pair. 哇，这些鞋子好大！你得去买双新的。

我也要买：

- I'll come with you. I could use a new pair too. 我和你一起去，我也要买双新鞋。

❖ wear out 磨损，穿破，用坏
❖ gross [ɡros] *adj.* 臃肿的，粗大的

4 Want to come with me to get some clothes? 想和我去买些衣服吗？

想去买衣服吗：

- Hey, I'm leaving to go get some clothes, want to come? 嘿，我要去买些衣服，想一起去吗？
- I'm going to the mall to shop for some clothes, want to come with? 我要去商场买些衣服，想一起去吗？

好啊，我也要买呢：

- Yeah, I need to get some new ones for school. 好的，我需要买些新衣服上学穿。
- Sure man, I need a new pair of pants. 好的，我要买条新裤子。

5 These shirts are pretty nice, but I'm looking for something warmer. 这些衬衫都挺好的，不过我要找些更暖和点的。

挑来挑去都不太合适：

- I need something warmer than that. 我要比那件更暖和些的。
- I like that sweater, but it's just too hot for it right now. 我喜欢那件毛衣，但现在穿太热了。

6 I'd like to see some coats. 我想看看上衣。

> 买上衣：
>
> • I want to buy some coats. 我想买上衣。
> • Have you got any coats here? 你们这里有上衣卖吗？
>
> 导购指路：
>
> • Yes, this way please. 有，这边请。

7 Can we go to the electronics department after this? 买完这个后我们去电器区看看吧？

> 再去买些别的吧：
>
> • I need to get some food. Can we go to the grocery section after we're done here? 我要买些食品，在这里买完后我们去食品区吧？
> • My nephew's birthday is coming up. Want to get him something from the toy department? 我侄子的生日快到了，要在玩具店给他买些什么吗？
> • I need to get a card. Can we go to that aisle after we're done here? 我要买张卡。在这里买完后我们去那个过道吧？
>
> 好的，我也要买：
>
> • Sure, I need something from there, too. 好的，我也要从那里买些东西。
> ❖ electronics [ɪlɛk'trɑnɪks] department 电器区，电器部
> ❖ aisle [aɪl] *n.* 过道，通道

8 Are you having a sale now? 你们现在有打折吗？

> 打折吗：
>
> • Is all the goods on sale? 这些商品都打折吗？
> • Is everything in the store on sale? 商店里的所有东西都打折吗？
>
> 最后一天了，要买就赶紧啊：
>
> • Yes, but today is the last day. 有，不过今天是最后一天了。
>
> 没打折了：
>
> • Sorry, we haven't. 抱歉，没有了。
> ❖ have a sale 降价销售，打折

9 Could I have a look at that ring in the showcase? 我能看看陈列柜里那个戒指吗？

还可以这样说：

- Am I allowed to look at that ring in the showcase? 我能看看陈列柜里那个戒指吗？
- I'd like to look at that ring in the showcase. 我想看看陈列柜里那个戒指。

售货员拿出来给你看：

- Of course. Please wait a minute. 好的，请稍等。
- ❖ showcase ['ʃo‚kes] n. 陈列柜

Department Stores Conversation

Debra: Hey, want to go to the mall today?	黛布拉：嘿，今天想去商场吗？
Kevin: Sure, when do you want to go?	凯　文：好的，你什么时候去？
Debra: Right now.	黛布拉：现在。
(Debra and Kevin head to the mall)	（黛布拉和凯文前往商场）
Debra: Oh, I really need to get some new shoes.	黛布拉：哦，我确实需要买双新鞋了。
Kevin: Alright. We can go to the shoe store after we look for some new shirts.	凯　文：好吧。我们看完衬衫后就去鞋店。
Debra: OK. What kind of shirt are you looking for?	黛布拉：好的，你想看什么样的衬衫？
Kevin: Something kind of dark and neutral looking. Nothing flashy.	凯　文：带黑色的、比较中性的。不要太花哨了。
Debra: Hmm, I don't know, man. It looks like flashy stuff is in right now.	黛布拉：嗯，我不知道，伙计。好像现在都是花哨的东西。
Kevin: Yeah, I think you're right. Well, let's go look at some shoes anyway.	凯　文：是啊，你说得没错。好了，咱们去看鞋吧。

| Debra: Alright, I hope they have something I actually want this time. | 黛布拉: 好的，这次我希望他们有些我确实想买的东西。 |

❖ neutral ['njutrəl] *adj.* 中性的，非彩色的
❖ flashy ['flæʃɪ] *adj.* 艳俗的，花哨的

文化穿越

    沃尔玛（Wal-Mart）在美国超级市场领域处于领军地位。它的物品种类相当齐全，几乎所有能想到的日常用品都可以买到。另外，沃尔玛的价格在同类超市中属于比较低廉的，但如果想买服装或香水类的物品，还是要去梅西百货或者 TJ-MAX，这些地方品种更齐全，价格有时比沃尔玛还低。当然，沃尔玛定期会有一些家电或者生活用品促销，价格比平时便宜很多。

    另外，喜欢收集 Zippo（芝宝）打火机、烟斗或雪茄的朋友可以去雪茄专卖店，不过要出示 ID，你的年龄需要超过 18 周岁。对于喜欢威士忌的朋友，可以去酒水专卖，不过店主需要确认你的年龄超过 21 周岁。其实，大部分的物品都可以在免税店购买，那里会更便宜，一般国际机场都会有一些免税店。

Section 2 ▶ 商品式样品牌
Different Styles and Brands

在商场里，那些琳琅满目的商品有时候让人眼花缭乱，不过试想一下，在那么多的名牌商品中穿行也确实挺养眼的。而我一贯的消费原则是宁可买一件名牌的贵的，也不肯买十件杂牌的便宜的，所以这就需要朋友们来一起帮我挑选一下了。

1 I'm willing to pay a bit for getting a name brand item. 我愿意花点钱买个名牌产品。

一分钱一分货：

- Name brand items are costly, but it's worth it. 名牌产品虽然贵，但是很值。
- I don't mind paying a little extra for name brand quality. 我不介意多花点儿钱买个名牌质量的。

没错：

- Yeah, me too. 是啊，我也是。

和普通牌子没什么区别：

- You're crazy. It's the same thing as a generic brand! 你疯了吧。这和普通牌子的东西一样。
- ❖ generic [dʒɪ'nɛrɪk] *adj.* 一般的，普通的

2 Generic food is just as good as name brand food. 普通的食物和有牌子的食物一样好。

普通牌子也实惠：

- I buy generic food to save money. It's just as good as regular brands. 我买普通的食物省钱，再说也和正规品牌的一样好。
- Generic brands are just a good way to save money. 买普通牌子的东西是省钱的好途径。

要省钱就只能这样喽：

- I hear you. Money is tight and everything helps! 我听你说过，现在钱很吃紧，这一切都有帮助！

那可不一样，不能和名牌比：

- I don't think so. I prefer the taste of a name brand. 我可不那么觉得，我更喜欢名牌。

❖ tight [taɪt] *adj.* 吃紧的，难得到的

3 What's your favorite brand of clothes? 你喜欢什么品牌的衣服？

询问你的喜好：

- What kind of clothes do you like? 你喜欢什么样的衣服？

根据自己的喜好回答：

- I prefer gucci. 我喜欢古琦。
- Hugo boss is the best! 雨果·波士最好！

❖ gucci ['gusi] *n.* 古琦，意大利时装品牌，其产品包括时装、皮具、皮鞋、手表、领带、丝巾、香水、家居用品及宠物用品等。一向以高档、豪华、性感而闻名于世，以"身份与财富之象征"品牌形象成为富有的上流社会的消费宠儿。

❖ Hugo boss 雨果·波士，世界知名奢侈品牌，源于德国，主营男女服装，香水，手表及其他配件。

4 When it comes to clothing, off brand just isn't as good. 说到衣服，杂牌的不是那么好。

杂牌的东西差劲：

- Off brand clothes just look awkward. 杂牌的衣服看起来好劣质。
- I can't buy an off brand product. It just looks wrong. 我不买杂牌产品，看起来太差劲了。

没错，就是这样的：

- I agree. They're not made nearly as well. 没错，它们的做工几乎都不好。

❖ off brand 杂牌，非名牌
❖ awkward ['ɔkwəd] *adj.* 拙劣的，劣质的

5 I can't believe you bought that. Can you exchange it for a different brand? 我不敢相信你竟然买那个。你不能换个别的牌子吗？

我可不喜欢这个品牌：

- I hate that brand! Can you exchange it, please? 我不喜欢那个牌子！请你换一个好吗？
- I really like these, but that brand makes me sick. I think I'll take this back. 我确实喜欢这些，但那个牌子让我觉得恶心。我想还是不要这个吧。

❖ exchange [ɪks'tʃendʒ] *vt.* 交换，调换

6 Do you have this coat in my size? 这上衣你们有适合我的尺寸吗？

询问尺寸：

- Do you have anything that will fit me? 你们有适合我的东西吗？
- Have you any shoes to fit me? 你们有适合我穿的鞋子吗？

说说你要什么尺寸吧：

- What size do you wear? 你穿什么尺寸的？

7 The fit isn't good. 这个尺寸不合适。

这个尺寸不合适：

- It's the wrong size. 这个尺寸不对。
- The size doesn't fit me. 这个尺寸不适合我。

那这个怎么样：

- How about in pink? It's small size. 粉色的怎么样？是小号的。
- How about this one? It's size ten. 这件怎么样？是 10 号的。

8 Can I have a size larger? 可以给我更大尺寸的吗？

大号或小号：

- Is there a large size? 这有大号的吗？
- Do you have large size? 你们有大号的吗？
- Do you have small size? 你们有小号的吗？

马上给你拿：

- Yes, wait a moment please. 有，请稍等。

9　What color do you like? 你喜欢什么颜色?

询问喜欢的颜色:

- What color do you prefer? 你更喜欢什么颜色?
- Which color do you like? 你喜欢哪种颜色?
- Which color do you like better? 你更喜欢哪种颜色?

自己喜欢什么就说什么:

- Light blue. 淡蓝色。
- I like purple. 我喜欢紫色。
- ❖ purple ['pɝpl] *n.* 紫色

10　It's 100% pure cotton. 这是百分之百纯棉的。

这可都是真货:

- It's pure wool. 这是纯羊毛的。
- It's real leather. 这是真皮革的。
- It's best quality cashmere. 这是质量最好的羊绒。
- ❖ leather ['lɛðɚ] *n.* 皮革
- ❖ cashmere ['kæʃmɪr] *n.* 羊绒，开士米羊毛

11　This is the latest model. 这是最新的款式。

这都是最新款式:

- This is the latest fashion. 这是最新的款式。
- This is the latest style. 这是最新的款式。

交流面对面

Different Styles and Brands Conversation

Kevin: Ugh, these chips are gross!	凯　文: 啊，这些薯片好差劲!
Debra: Sorry, I bought the generic kind!	黛布拉: 不好意思，我买的是普通的那种!
Kevin: Why would you do that?	凯　文: 你干吗买那个?
Debra: Sorry! They were cheaper.	黛布拉: 不好意思! 它们更便宜啊。

Kevin: Let's go to the store and get some better ones. These are horrible.	凯 文：咱们去商店买些好点儿的吧，这些太糟了。
Debra: Fine, let's go.	黛布拉：好的，咱们走吧。
(Kevin and Debra go to the local department store)	（凯文和黛布拉去当地的百货商店）
Kevin: Oh, these look good, WISE brand.	凯 文：哦，这些看上去不错，威士牌的。
Debra: Those are OK, but they aren't really a "name" brand, you know?	黛布拉：这些是挺好的，但可不是真正的"名"牌啊，你知道吧？
Kevin: Yeah, I guess not. How about Lays?	凯 文：知道；我想也不是。乐事怎么样？
Debra: Sure, that sounds good to me.	黛布拉：好啊，听起来不错。

文化穿越

很多朋友们出国后会发现，我们一般所追求的品牌，如 NIKE 一类的运动品牌，或者如 CK、LV 一类的时尚品牌在美国都要便宜很多，尤其是香水、化妆品一类的东西。价格上，一般香水和化妆品会比国内便宜三分之二，品牌类服装会便宜一半左右。所以像 LV、GUCCI 一类的时尚品牌在美国用的人比较多。比如一个美国人一个月挣 3000 美元，一个名牌包在打折的时候 500 美元左右，而一个中国人一个月挣 3000 元人民币，一个同样的包却要 7000 元或者 8000 元左右。这样的悬殊差价除了品牌产品外，在各个领域都会有所体现。

Section 3 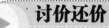 讨价还价
Bargaining at the Market

其实，在讨价还价这一技巧上我是需要多请教大家的，因为我确实不善于砍价。不过在此我要提醒大家，在美国一般的商场是不讲价的，标价是多少就卖多少，只有在农贸市场才有讲价的商品。

1 I'm selling these for ten bucks a kilo. 这些卖 10 美元一公斤。

报价：
- These are on sale for ten dollars a pound. 这些卖 10 美元一磅。

还价：
- How about eight bucks and we call it even? 8 美元怎么样，咱们扯平了？
- ❖ call it even 扯平了

2 I'll give you half that, those look stale. 那个我给你半价，那些看起来都不新鲜了。

想方设法砍价：
- That food looks a little ripe, I'll give you half. 那食物看起来有点儿熟过头了，我给你半价吧。
- That price is good but the food isn't. I'll give you half. 价钱是合适但食物不太好了，我给你半价。

商家不让步：
- Are you kidding? No! 你开玩笑吧？不行！
- No deal, these are worth full price. 不行，那些要全价的。

3 How much are you selling these for? 这些你卖多少钱？

询问价钱：

- What's the price on these? 这些是什么价钱？
- What are these going for? 这些怎么卖啊？

报价：

- Ten Dollars. 10 美元。
- Twelve bucks. 12 美元。

4 That's the final price, take it or leave it. 这是最低的价格了，买不买随你。

这是最低价了：

- I'm not budging here, that's the final price. 我这里不让价了，那是最低价了。
- Our prices are rock bottom. 我们的价格是最低的了。

觉得不合适就不买：

- Fine. I'm leaving. 好吧，那我走吧。

觉得还可以的话就买了：

- Alright, alright, I'll pay it. 好吧，好吧，我买了。
- ❖ the final price 最低的价格，最后的价格
- ❖ take it or leave it 买不买随你，不买就算了
- ❖ budge [bʌdʒ] *vi.* 让步，改变意见
- ❖ rock bottom 最低点

5 I can go down a little, but not that much. 我可以再降点儿，但也不会便宜很多。

做个小让步：

- I can lower the price by a couple dollars, but not that much. 我可以便宜一两美元，但也不会便宜很多。
- No way. Maybe a couple bucks cheaper but that's way too much! 不行了。也许可以再便宜一两美元，但那已经便宜很多了。

双方都让步，成交：

- Alright, we'll go with a couple bucks off then. 好吧，那就便宜一两美元吧。

6 How about I buy two and get one free? 买二赠一怎么样？

买二赠一的优惠：

- Sure, I'll pay that, but if I buy two can I have a third free? 好吧，我买那个，但如果我买两个，第三个免费吗？

合适就卖了：

- OK, just take it. 好吧，你拿走吧。

确实卖不了：

- Sorry, we can't. 抱歉，卖不了。

7 Lower the price and I'll consider it. 价钱再低一些我才会考虑。

再便宜点儿：

- I'll consider it if you cut down the price. 如果你把价钱降低点的话我会考虑。
- If you reduce the price, maybe I'll take it. 如果你降低一下价格，也许我会买。

不能便宜了：

- Sorry, this is the final price. 抱歉，这是最低价了。

交流面对面

Bargaining at the Market Conversation

Kevin:	Excuse me, how much is it for a basket of these apples?	凯 文：劳驾，这些苹果一筐多少钱？
Clerk:	I'm selling them for four dollars per basket.	店 员：4 美元一筐。
Kevin:	How about for these green ones?	凯 文：这些青苹果呢？
Clerk:	Those are also four.	店 员：也是 4 美元。
Kevin:	Four dollars? That's a bit high.	凯 文：4 美元？ 那有点儿高了。
Clerk:	I'm sorry but it hasn't been a good season. I can't budge.	店 员：不好意思，但这水果现在还不到季节，我没法让价。
Kevin:	How about three fifty for a basket?	凯 文：3.5 美元一筐怎么样？

Clerk: Like I said, I really can't budge. I'm sorry. Give me four dollars or nothing.	店　员：就像我说的，我确实没法让价，抱歉。4美元或者你可以不买。
(Kevin begins to walk away)	（凯文走开了）
Clerk: OK, OK, wait. Three fifty it is.	店　员：好吧，好吧，等一下。就3.5美元吧。
(They shake hands)	（他们握了握手）
Kevin: Here you go. Thank you very much!	凯　文：给你。多谢了！
Clerk: Thank you. Have a good day, now.	店　员：谢谢你，祝你愉快。

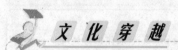

文化穿越

　　谈到讲价，情况与中国有些不同。美国大部分的正规商店都是没法讲价的。不过，在一些特殊地区或场合还是可以的。一般讲价发生在农场，直接与农民买卖是可以讲价的。另外，有时候商品如果只剩最后一件，而且这件商品没有包装或者是样品，有时候商店老板会给你很低的折扣。此外，在买二手商品的时候是可以讲价的。例如，一个崭新的便携式小冰箱可能会超过100美元，但二手的一般可以砍到30～50美元左右。需要注意的是千万不能乱砍价，美国和中国的批发市场不太一样，如果你砍价太离谱，人家不会卖给你。而且，如果你在美国买到十分便宜的东西，往往需要特别注意，有时候特别便宜的东西往往真的会有问题。

Section 4 ▶ 寻找减价商品
Searching for Sales

　　我不知道大家是不是也和我一样，非常关注报纸上的促销打折广告、喜欢特价商品。虽然说不一定买，但我还是其乐无穷地关注这方面的信息，毕竟这也是一个商机。所以，朋友们如果有这方面的消息，不妨告诉我哦。

 口语大放送

1 Have you checked the sales in the paper? 你看了报纸上的销售信息吗？

看报纸上的销售广告：

- The paper came today. Did you see the sales? 今天的报纸来了，你看销售信息了吗？

看过了：

- Yep, here they are. 看了，在这儿呢。

2 Do you guys have a section of things on sale? 你们有什么东西减价销售吗？

礼貌询问能否退货：

- Does your store have a clearance aisle? 你们店有清仓甩卖的东西吗？
- I'm curious if you have any deals or promotions going on. 我想知道你们是否有什么处理品或促销活动吗？

有，天天都物美价廉：

- Yes, we do. It's right over there. 有，我们有。就在那里。
- We sure do. Here's a list of all of our items on sale. 我们当然有了。这单子上有我们所有减价销售的商品。
- ❖ clearance aisle 清仓甩卖

3 These items are on BOGO. 这些东西买一送一。

快来买啊，买一送一：

- These items are buy one get one free. 这些东西买一送一。
- Everything here is buy one, get one free! 这里的所有东西都买一送一。

这可是个好机会：

- Awesome, that's a great deal! 太好了，那可是笔好买卖！
- ❖ BOGO 买一送一，是 Buy One Get One 的首字母缩写

4 This camera is on sale, but it isn't very good. 这款相机特价销售，但质量不是很好。

价钱低质量差：

- It's pretty obvious why these speakers are on sale. 很明显为什么这些音箱会特价销售。
- This would be a good deal if it wasn't in such bad shape. 如果样子不是那么难看的话，这可能会是笔不错的买卖。

一分钱一分货：

- Yeah, it looks like it. 是啊，看上去就是这样。
- Seems like they're just trying to rip off the customer. 看起来他们只是想敲诈顾客。
- ❖ obvious ['ɑbvɪəs] *adj.* 明显的，显著的
- ❖ rip off 敲诈，敲竹杠

5 I can't wait until the sales on Black Friday! 我都等不及"黑色星期五"的清仓甩卖了！

盼着清仓大甩卖啊：

- When Black Friday comes around, the sales are incredible. 当"黑色星期五"快来的时候，清仓甩卖简直让人不敢相信。
- ❖ Black Friday 黑色星期五，每年感恩节的第二天，老美们称之为"Black Friday sale"。据说每年的这一天各个商家都会推出非常优厚的大减价。很多优惠到难以置信的地步。所以每逢这个时候，各大商场门口早早的就会排满了等着进场的人群。
- ❖ incredible [ɪn'krɛdəbl] *adj.* 难以置信的

6 It's always nice to buy holiday stuff after the holiday is over. 节日过后再买节日的东西总是很划算的。

要这样精打细算：

- Buying holiday items late is always very, very, cheap. 节日过后再买节日的东西总是非常非常便宜。

确实是这样：

- Yeah, I heard that. 是啊，我听说了。

7 Oh look, they're having a sale on all women's shirts! 哦，看，所有的女式衬衫都清仓甩卖！

好不容易遇到这样的机会：

- Oh nice, a sale on all men's ties. 哦，太好了，所有的男式领带都打折。
- I was looking for some shoes, looks like they're all on sale. 我看了些鞋，好像都减价销售。

交流面对面

Searching for Sales Conversation

Kevin:	Hey, did you see the paper this morning?	凯　文：	嘿，你看今天早上的报纸了吗？
Debra:	Yeah, why?	黛布拉：	看了，怎么了？
Kevin:	Were there any sales in it?	凯　文：	上面有什么打折的信息吗？
Debra:	Yeah, Best Buy has some stuff going on, and Wal-Mart does too.	黛布拉：	有啊，百思买有些商品打折销售，沃尔玛也有。
Kevin:	Oh, I wonder if they have any cameras on sale. I wanted one of those.	凯　文：	哦，我想知道他们的相机有没有打折的，我想买一个。
Debra:	Yeah, it looks like you get a mail-in refund for fifty bucks when you buy a camera.	黛布拉：	有啊，如果你买个相机，好像可以得到 50 美元的邮寄退款。
Kevin:	Oh wow, that's not bad at all. Let's go check it out.	凯　文：	哦，哇，那太划算了。咱们去看看吧。
Debra:	Alright, let me get ready.	黛布拉：	好的，我准备一下。

(The guys head to Best Buy)	（两人前往百思买）
Debra: Excuse me. I saw an ad where you can get a mail in refund on a camera.	**黛布拉：** 打扰一下，我看到你们的广告，买一个相机有50美元的邮寄退款。
Salesman: Oh, yeah. That sale applies to all of the cameras on the left wall over here.	**销售员：** 哦，是的。这边左面墙上的所有相机都这样销售。
Kevin: Oh, these aren't bad. What do we need to do in order to get the refund?	**凯 文：** 哦，那还挺划算的。我们怎样才能得到退款呢？
Salesman: Just fill out the form online and mail in a copy of your receipt!	**销售员：** 只要在网上填写张表格，把收据复印件寄过来就行。
Kevin: Alright, I'll take it. Thank you!	**凯 文：** 好的，我买一个。谢谢你！

❖Best Buy 百思买，全球最大的家用电器和电子产品的零售和分销及服务集团。
❖apply to 适用
❖fill out 填写

文 化 穿 越

　　对于销售的一些把戏美国人玩得十分周全。每周日的报纸都会像一本书一样厚，原因是里面夹杂着很多商场的打折信息和优惠券（coupon）。带着报纸上的打折信息往往可以买到十分便宜的东西。比如说如果一双 NIKE 鞋的原价是 50 美元，折扣上经常会出现20美元的抵金券，你只要花30美元就可以买到了。另外，沃尔玛的打折信息也有很多，包括各类调料、生活用品等。因此，每次看报纸的时候，一定多留意报纸上的打折优惠券，可以剪下来保存好，等有机会的时候使用。

Section 5

▶ 售后服务
Customer Service

我买东西有一个习惯，就是非常关注商家或厂家的售后服务。因为售后服务好的商品，如果买回来以后确实有问题，对于我们消费者会省去很多麻烦事。这也算是在购物的时候我给大家分享的最后一个小窍门吧。

口 语 大 放 送

1 This camera has broken. I need to return it. 这个相机坏了，我要退货。

东西坏了要退货：
- I bought this camera, and it broke. 我买了这个相机，坏了。
- This camera broke today, but I just bought it. 这架相机今天坏了，这可是我刚买的。

请出示收据：
- Alright, do you have the receipt? 好的，你有收据吗?

2 Hi, I'd like to make an exchange on this shirt. It doesn't fit. 嗨，我想把这件衬衫换一下，它不合身。

礼貌询问能否退货：
- These clothes don't fit. Can I exchange them? 这些衣服不合身，我能换一下吗?

服务周到的商店：
- Sure, just go find something you like and bring it back. 好的，去找一下你喜欢的衣服拿回来换就行。

❖ make an exchange 交换

3 Can I get my money back for this? 这个能退款吗?

拿着东西去退款：
- Hello, I'd just like to get cash back for this. 你好，这个我想退款。
- I'd like my money back, please. 请把钱退给我吧。

要出示收据的：
- OK, but I'll need a receipt to give you cash. 好的，不过我需要收据才能给你现金。

4 I just want to get store credit for this. 这个我只想退款。

没有收据能退款吗：
- I have this shirt but no receipt. Could I get store credit? 我买了这件衬衫但没有收据。我能退款吗？
- I forgot my receipt. Is there any way I can just get store credit? 我忘了带收据了。我有什么办法能得到退款吗？

很想遇到这样的商店：
- Sure, let me scan the item in. 好的，我来把它扫一下。
- ❖ store credit 退货，退款

5 Hi, I had some trouble with an employee. 嗨，我和你们一个员工有点麻烦。

向商店经理投诉：
- One of your employees was very rude to me. 你们一个员工对我很粗暴。
- One of your employees ignored me when I tried to speak to him! 我要和他说话的时候，你们这个员工不搭理我。

经理会妥善处理的：
- I'm so sorry. Did you happen to get their name? 非常对不起，你知道他们的名字吗？
- ❖ ignore [ɪg'nɔr] vt. 忽视，不理会

6 Hi there, I was wondering if you had ties in stock. 你好，我想知道你们这领带还有货吗？

询问是否有货：

- Hello, do you have ties in stock? 你好，你们的领带还有货吗？
- Where could I find the ties? 领带在哪里？

店员会给你指路：

- We do, they're in aisle 8. 有货，在 8 号通道。
- Ties are right over there, past the sign. 领带就在那边，走过这个标志牌就到了。
- ❖ in stock 有存货，现有

7 Hi there, could I place an order? 你好，我能下单吗？

是否能送货呢：

- Do you ship in special items? 特价商品你们送货吗？
- I'd like something but you don't have in stock. Could you ship it to me? 我想要些东西，可是你们现在没货。能给我送过来吗？

可以，留下地址就行：

- Sure, could I get your address? 好的，能告诉我你的地址吗？
- ❖ place an order 订购，下单

交 流 面 对 面

Customer Service Conversation

Kevin: Hey man, this camera is acting funny.	**凯　文：**嘿，这相机有点怪怪的。	
Steve: What's wrong with it?	**史蒂夫：**有什么问题吗？	
Kevin: It won't turn on, even when it's charged.	**凯　文：**打不开了，即使有电也开不了。	
Steve: Oh, it might be a problem with that brand of camera. You should take it back.	**史蒂夫：**哦，可能那个牌子的照相机都有问题。你该把它退回去。	
Kevin: Alright, I'll just get my money back.	**凯　文：**好的，我要把钱要回来。	
(Kevin drives to the store)	（凯文开车去商店）	

Kevin:	Hi there. I bought this camera from you guys yesterday, and it doesn't work.	凯 文:	你好，我昨天从你这里买的这个照相机坏了。
Clerk:	Alright, let's see.	店 员:	好的，让我看看。
Kevin:	Sure, here. There aren't any other issues with it.	凯 文:	好的，给你。这没有什么别的问题。
Clerk:	Do you have your receipt?	店 员:	你有收据吗？
Kevin:	I do, let me get it out of my wallet.	凯 文:	有，我从包里拿出来给你。
Clerk:	Also, did you want to exchange this or get a refund?	店 员:	还有，你是想换一个呢还是想退款？
Kevin:	I'd like a refund, but I already mailed in a coupon for it.	凯 文:	我想退款，不过我已经寄了张优惠券了。
Clerk:	No problem. I can call and get that cancelled for you.	店 员:	没关系。我可以打电话给你取消。
Kevin:	Thank you. I appreciate it.	凯 文:	谢谢你，非常感谢。

❖charged [tʃɑrdʒd] *adj.* 带电荷的，荷电的

文 化 穿 越

　　美国的服务业很发达，甚至超乎你的想象。在美国，几乎所有的东西都可以无缘由的退还，但前提是你需要保留发票，东西不能损坏得太厉害。比如，你在美国买了一辆山地车，骑了一年车依然很新，你可以拿着当初的发票跟商店服务人员说，我不喜欢这车的颜色，想退货。他们会二话不说地退掉，之后向你道歉。除此之外，美国的售后维修也是很到位的。比如，你买了一台笔记本电脑，使用期间无论出现任何问题，公司都会给你退货。如果有任何硬件或者软件方面的问题，公司会马上寄过来你所需要的所有零件或光盘。其他的售后也是如此。

Chapter 6

Kevin 的态度观点

Attitude and Mind

eshaping
our Life
y the
ower of
Positive
Mental
ttitude

Section 1 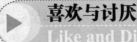 喜欢与讨厌
Like and Dislike

在这里我和大家分享一下态度观点的英语表达。因为我们每个人都有七情六欲，都有自己的想法和观点。比如说我们喜欢什么，我们讨厌什么，都要恰如其分地表达出来，以下这些话，肯定会让你爱憎分明！

1 I like that. 我喜欢那个。

换一种表达也不错：
- I enjoy that. 我很喜欢那个。

还可以用这个很流行的词：
- I'm a fan of that. 我是它的粉丝。

兴趣相同：
- Me too. 我也是。

万一有偏差：
- I don't like it that much. 我没那么喜欢。

2 I really like that. 我真的喜欢那个。

喜欢的方式也可以多种多样的：
- I like that a lot. 我很喜欢那个。
- I really enjoy that. 我真的很喜欢那个。
- That is really great. 那真的很棒。
- I love that. 我喜爱那个。

说到心坎上了：
- Yeah, isn't it cool? 是啊，难道不酷吗？
- I do too. 我也喜欢。

3 I don't like that. 我不喜欢那个。

不喜欢也可以很直接：

- I dislike that. 我不喜欢那个。
- I don't like that very much. 我不是那么喜欢。

萝卜白菜各有所爱：

- Really? I love it. 是吗？我很喜欢。
- I wasn't a fan either. 我也不是粉丝。

4 I really don't like that. 我真的不喜欢那个。

还可以更强烈一点：

- I hate that. 我讨厌那个。
- I despise that. 我鄙视它。
- I don't like that at all. 我一点儿也不喜欢那个。

感觉相同：

- I hate it too. 我也很讨厌。

还有点儿回旋的余地啦：

- It's not too bad. 还不是太糟糕啦。

❖ despise [dɪ'spaɪz] *vt.* 鄙视，看不起

5 That's awesome. 那太棒了。

以下这些简短的表达也非常不错：

- That's cool. 那很酷。
- That's neat. 那很整洁。
- That's fantastic. 那太不可思议了。

好的东西大家的感觉都是一样的：

- Isn't it? It's great. 不是吗？是挺好的。
- Yeah, I know, right? 是啊，我知道，是吗？

❖ neat [nɪt] *adj.* 整洁的，整齐的
❖ fantastic [fæn'tæstɪk] *adj.* 极好的，了不起的

6 That sucks. 那太差劲了。

让你的语言更丰富些吧：

- That's terrible. 那太糟糕了。
- That's awful. 那太可怕了。
- That's horrible. 那很恐怖。

确实如此：

- Yeah, I agree. 是的，我同意你的说法。

有点儿疑问哦：

- You really hate it that much? 你真那么讨厌它吗？
- I didn't think you would dislike it so much. 我觉得你不是那么讨厌它啊。

❖ suck [sʌk] *vi.* 烂，令人讨厌（俚语）

Like and Dislike Conversation

Kevin: Did you listen to that new band I told you about?	凯　文：你听过我跟你说过的那个新乐队的演唱吗？
Mabel: Yeah. They're okay.	梅布尔：听过，挺好的。
Kevin: Just okay? You don't like them?	凯　文：只是好？你不喜欢他们？
Mabel: Not really.	梅布尔：事实上不喜欢。
Kevin: Why not?	凯　文：为什么？
Mabel: I'm not a fan of their singer.	梅布尔：我不是他们歌手的粉丝。
Kevin: Well, what kind of singers do you like?	凯　文：哦，那你喜欢什么类型的歌手？
Mabel: I'm more of a classic rock kind of guy.	梅布尔：我更喜欢古典摇滚歌手。
Kevin: I thought everyone was a classic rock kind of guy.	凯　文：我觉得大家都喜欢古典摇滚歌手。
Mabel: Everyone should be, at least.	梅布尔：至少大家都应该是这样。
Kevin: Well, to each his own I guess.	凯　文：好吧，我想各有所好嘛。

❖classic rock 经典摇滚，古典摇滚
❖to each one's own 各有所好

文化穿越

　　相比中国人与人之间较为复杂的人际，美国人的性格更直接。对于喜欢的人或物，他们会很热情，相反，对待不喜欢的人或物，他们不会有任何兴趣。拿工作和生活态度举例来说，美国人对待工作与中国人不同，美国人不喜欢攒钱，喜欢享受生活。结束一天的工作后，他们会做些自己喜欢的事情，比如去健身房锻炼或是来次野外烧烤。大部分美国人很少加班，而且周末是绝对不工作的。对于不喜欢的事物，有个常用的口语表达是"That sucks."翻译成"太烂了，太糟了，太差劲了。"

Section 2

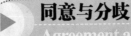 同意与分歧
Agreement and Disagreement

生活中总有一些和我们不谋而合或意见相左的事情，碰到这种情况该怎么办呢？Kevin 跟大家说说自己的想法，自己同意与否，态度一定要分明，千万不要含蓄，否则引起误会可就不太好了。

 口语大放送

1 I agree with you. 我同意你的说法。

英雄所见略同：
- I agree. 我同意。
- I feel the same way. 我有同感。

努力没有白费：
- Cool. 太好了。
- I thought you would. 我觉得你会的。

2 I don't feel the same way about it. 对此，我并不那么认为。

还可以更简洁明了：
- I disagree. 我不同意。
- I don't agree with you. 我不同意你的说法。
- I don't think I agree with that. 我想我不同意那种说法。

你不同意，对方可能不高兴了：
- Oh, that sucks. 哦，那太糟糕了。
- Sorry. I thought you would. 抱歉，我以为你会同意的。

3 I can't believe you feel that way. 我不敢相信你是那么想的。

你的想法和别人不一样：

- I'm surprised you feel that way about it. 我很奇怪你对此会那么想。
- I'm kind of shocked that you felt that way. 你那么想我有点儿震惊。
- I'm surprised you think that. 我很惊讶你那么想。

奇怪也是事实啊：

- Really? I thought it was obvious. 是吗？我以为这很明显。
- I hope that isn't a bad thing. 我希望那不是什么坏事情。

❖ shocked [ʃɑkt] *adj.* 震动的，震惊的

---

4 I'm surprised we feel the same about it. 我很吃惊我们对此想法一致。

太好的事情也会让人不相信啊：

- I'm amazed that we agree on that. 在那件事情上我们能达成一致意见令我很惊奇。
- I thought we would disagree, and I'm surprised that we don't. 我原以为我们会有分歧，没想到竟然没有。
- It's great that we agree on it. 我们对此意见一致真是太好了。

确实如此啊：

- Yeah, it's cool. 是啊，太好了。
- Me too, actually. 事实上，我也是。
- Nah, I thought we would agree. 没有啦，我认为我们会意见一致的。

---

5 I'm glad you think that way. 我很高兴你会那么认为。

咱们想法一致真让人高兴：

- I'm happy you feel that way. 你那么想我很高兴。
- I'm relieved that you feel that way. 你那么想我就放心了。
- That's really cool that you think that way. 你那么想真是太好了。

大家一起高兴吧：

- Thanks. I'm glad you're happy about it. 谢谢。我很高兴你能满意。
- Really? That's cool. 真的吗？那太好了。

❖ relieved [rɪ'livd] *adj.* 放心的，宽慰的

Agreement and Disagreement Conversation

Kevin: I got in an argument with my mom the other day.

凯　文：我几天前和我妈妈吵架了。

Debra: Oh yeah? What was it about?

黛布拉：哦，是吗？为什么？

Kevin: I want to get a new car, and she wants me to get a Chevy.

凯　文：我想买辆新车，而她想让我买辆雪佛兰。

Debra: A Chevy? Ugh, my mom likes Chevy's too. What do you want?

黛布拉：雪佛兰？啊，我妈妈也喜欢雪佛兰的车。你想要买什么样的？

Kevin: I'd rather have something like a Nissan. I've been saving up for a while now.

凯　文：我想买辆像尼桑那样的车。我已经攒了一段时间的钱了。

Debra: Nissans are really nice. If you have the money for it you should buy it anyway.

黛布拉：尼桑确实不错。如果你有钱买的话，无论如何你应该买一辆。

Kevin: I'm glad you agree with me. She'll probably be really mad if I get it anyway.

凯　文：我很高兴你认同我的看法。如果我买辆尼桑的话她可能会疯的。

Debra: It's your money; you can do what you want with it, man.

黛布拉：这是你的钱，你可以拿它做你想做的任何事，哥们儿。

Kevin: I know, right? That's what I tried telling her.

凯　文：我知道，那正是我想要跟她说的。

Debra: I say you should buy it anyway. If she has a problem with it then oh well.

黛布拉：我说不管怎样你都应该买。如果她对此有意见的话过后也就没事了。

Kevin: Good idea. I'm sure she'll disagree with me about it, but she'll get over it.

凯　文：好主意。我肯定她不同意我买辆尼桑，但她总会让这事过去的。

❖argument ['ɑrgjəmənt] *n.* 争执，争吵

❖Chevy ['tʃevi] *n.* 雪佛兰，美国汽车品牌
❖Nissan [ni'sɑ:n] *n.* 尼桑，也叫日产，日本汽车品牌

文 化 穿 越

　　一般在对美国人表达自己观点的时候，要避免中国人一贯的含蓄和兜圈子。同意就说同意，不同意也可以直接说"不"。很多时候，美国人是不理解中国的人情的。中国人认为谦让和容忍是美德，甚至可以换来别人的理解。但在美国有时候事与愿违。举个例子，在钱的问题上，美国人一般不讲面子上的事儿，中国人有时候很慷慨，认为都是好朋友，于是抢着结账，一般这种情况发生时，美国人是不会客气的。时间一长，中国人就会很疑惑为什么每次都是自己抢着结账，而美国哥们儿怎么从来不主动。其实是因为，一般情况下，美国朋友之间都是各花各的，即使彼此是情侣关系。当然，也会有特殊情况，比如人家确实喜欢你，或者说，情侣之间有时候也不分你我。因此，跟美国人切勿含蓄，想表达什么直接说就行。

Section 3 ▶ 信任与怀疑
Trust and Doubt

相信一个人是很重要的，就像 Kevin 一直非常相信大家能说出一口流利地道的英语一样，大家有没有信心？但有时候对一些事情也要有怀疑的态度，要去核实。在这里，Kevin 是要提醒大家要相信自己，要有自己的观点，不要随波逐流。

1 I know I can trust you. 我知道我可以信任你。

信任的程度可以逐渐加深：
- I can trust you. 我可以相信你。
- I definitely trust you. 我肯定相信你。
- I trust you a lot. 我非常相信你。

你信任别人，别人也会信任你：
- I'm glad. 我很高兴。
- I have confidence in you too. 我也相信你。
- That's sweet. I trust you too. 那太好了，我也相信你。

❖ definitely [ˈdefənɪtlɪ] *adv.* 肯定地，确定地
❖ have confidence in sb. 信任某人，相信某人

2 I want to tell you something, but I'm not sure if I should. 我想告诉你一些事情，但我不确定该不该告诉你。

犹豫着该不该相信：
- I'm not sure I can trust you, even though I wish I could. 我不确定我是否能相信你，虽然我希望我能。
- I don't think I can trust you, even though I want to talk to you about something. 我觉得我不能相信你，虽然我想告诉你一些事情。
- I want to have faith in you, but I don't think I should. 我想相信你，但我认为我不应该那样。

对于你的迟疑，对方会反问：

- Why not? 为什么不呢？
- That's not cool. Why wouldn't you trust me? 那不好吧，你为什么不相信我呢？

或许你的迟疑也有一定道理吧：

- I guess that makes sense. We haven't known each other very long. 我想那有道理，我们认识也不是很长时间。
- ❖ have faith in sb. 信任某人，相信某人

3 I don't really want to talk to you about it. 我真的不想跟你说这件事。

类似的表达还可以这样说：

- I don't think I should talk to you about it. 我想我不应该跟你说这件事。
- I'm not sure I should talk to you about it. 我不确定我该不该跟你说这件事。

对方会问你原因：

- Really? Don't you have faith in me? 是吗？你不相信我吗？

对方也可能会泰然处之：

- Okay, that's fine. 好吧，没关系。

4 I feel like I can't trust you. 我觉得我不能相信你。

以下四种表达也很地道：

- I don't think I can trust you. 我觉得我不能相信你。
- I don't really trust you. 我真的不相信你。
- I'm not sure that I trust you. 我不确定我是否相信你。
- I don't think I should rely on you. 我觉得我不应该相信你。

你得说说原因吧：

- Why not? What have I done? 为什么？我做什么了？
- Did I do something wrong? 我做错什么了吗？

相不相信随便你啦：

- Okay. Well, I can't force you to trust me. 好吧，我也不能强迫你相信我。
- ❖ rely on 信任，依赖

5 I think I can trust you. 我想我能相信你。

语气可以逐步加强：

- I believe I can trust you. 我认为我能相信你。
- I'm pretty sure I can trust you. 我非常肯定我能相信你。

对方也非常肯定：

- You can definitely trust me. 你当然可以相信我。
- Yeah, you can trust me. Don't worry. 是的，你可以相信我，别担心。

6 I doubt it. 我怀疑。

不可信：

- It's doubtful! 这很可疑！
- It's chancy. 这不是真的。
- I wouldn't bet on it. 我不相信这个。
- It sounds fishy to me. 听起来可疑。

你不信我信：

- I don't think so. 我不这样认为。

❖ doubtful ['dautfəl] *adj.* 怀疑的，疑惑的
❖ chancy ['tʃænsɪ] *adj.* 不确实的，偶然发生的
❖ bet on 相信，就……打赌
❖ fishy ['fɪʃɪ] *adj.* 可疑的，靠不住的（口语）

7 I won't buy your story. 我不相信你说的话。

我不信：

- I won't believe your story. 我不相信你说的话。
- I don't buy it. 我不相信。

这是真的：

- But, it's true. 可那是真的呀。

Trust and Doubt Conversation

Kevin: Hey mom, can I talk to you about something?	凯文：嗨,妈妈,我能和你说些事吗?
Mom: Sure, what is it, honey?	妈妈：当然可以,是什么事,宝贝?
Kevin: My friend came to me the other day and was telling me about his girlfriend.	凯文：我朋友前几天跟我说了些他女朋友的事。
Mom: Okay. Is something wrong?	妈妈：好啊,有什么不对吗?
Kevin: Well, he said he thinks she's cheating.	凯文：嗯,他觉得他女朋友在欺骗他。
Mom: Have there been a lot of signs?	妈妈：有很多迹象吗?
Kevin: Yeah, quite a few. Their relationship has been going downhill for a while, I guess.	凯文：是的,有很多。我想他们的关系走下坡路已经有一段时间了。
Mom: Either way it doesn't seem like your friend trusts her anymore.	妈妈：不管怎样,你朋友看起来不再相信他女朋友了。
Kevin: That's true.	凯文：没错。
Mom: Trust is needed in a healthy relationship. They need to be honest with each other. If he's not willing to trust her, then the relationship is doomed to fail.	妈妈：良好的关系需要信任。他们需要互相坦诚,如果他不愿意相信她的话,那他们的关系也注定要失败的。
Kevin: Yeah, I agree. I wanted a second opinion, though. Thanks mom!	凯文：是啊,我同意。但我想再听听其他人的意见,谢谢你,妈妈!
Mom: No problem, dear.	妈妈：没关系,亲爱的。

❖ go downhill 衰退,变坏,走下坡路
❖ doomed [dumd] *adj.* 命中注定的,注定失败的
❖ a second opinion 其他的意见

就这 900 句 玩转口语

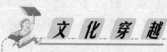

文 化 穿 越

　　美国社会文化在诚信这一点上与中国社会文化略有不同。中国人从小到大，遵循父母和老师的教导，要与人为善但要对别人有所防备。美国这个社会表现出的那种人与人之间的信任是很令人震惊的。无论是在最微小的生活细节还是在企业文化上都体现得淋漓尽致。有时候中国留学生会有很多疑问，是否可以放心地使用信用卡结账？在生活中处理人际关系时，是否可以信任彼此？当然，出门在外，还是万事小心为宜，只是应该给予别人更多的信任。

Section 4 接受与拒绝
Accept and Refuse

> 　　你接受过别人的礼物、建议或别的东西吗？或者你拒绝了？或者是你被别人接受抑或是被拒绝？Kevin 告诉你一个秘密，Kevin 就被拒绝过，这是很糗也是比较伤心的事，就不再提了。不过 Kevin 还是要提醒大家，接受当然是双方都高兴的事，但如果要拒绝别人，光说 No 是不够的，还得有充分的理由才行，特别是那些盛情难却的邀请、动用一大堆关系的请求。这可是一门学问哦，朋友们应该好好学习一下。

1 I wanted you to have this. 我希望你接受这个。

希望别人接受还可以说：

- Here, I want you to take this. 给你，我希望你把这个带走。
- I really want you to have this. 我真的希望你接受这个。
- Will you accept this? I want you to have it. 你会接受这个吗？我希望你接受它。
- I thought you'd enjoy receiving this. 我觉得你会喜欢收到这个的。

2 Thanks, I'd love to take this. 谢谢，我非常愿意接受。

接受别人的东西还可以这样表达谢意：

- Thank you so much. I'll gladly accept this. 非常感谢，我会很高兴接受的。
- I would love to accept this. Thank you. 我很乐意接受，谢谢你。

对方对谢意的回复：

- You're welcome. 不客气。
- Don't worry about it. I'm glad you like it. 别为此担心，我很高兴你喜欢。

3 I don't really want this. 我真的不想要这个。

拒绝还可以委婉点：

- I don't think I want it. 我觉得我不想要。
- I'm not sure I want this. You should have it. 我不确定我想要这个，你应该拥有它。
- I don't think you should have given this to me. 我觉得你不该把这个送给我。

你的拒绝可能会让对方失望哦：

- Really? I thought you would. 是吗？我还以为你喜欢呢。
- Come on, you should take it. 别这样，你应该接受它。

4 I don't think I should take this. 我不觉得我该接受这个。

含蓄的拒绝还可以这样表达：

- I don't think I deserve this. 我不觉得这是我应得的。
- I'm not sure I should get this. 我不确定我该接受这个。
- I'm going to have to refuse. 我得拒绝了。

对方可能会坚持让你接受：

- Why not? Just take it. 为什么不呢？只要接受就行了。
- I think you deserve it. 我觉得这是你应得的。

❖ deserve [dɪ'zɜːv] *vt.* 应受，该得

5 I've actually wanted this for a long time. 事实上，我想要这个已经好长一段时间了。

欣喜地接受：

- I've been thinking about getting this for a while now. 我想要这个已经有一段时间了。
- I've wanted this for a long time now, thank you. 我想要这个已经好长一段时间了，谢谢你。

对方也会高兴送对了：

- That's cool. No problem, man. 太好了，没关系的，伙计。
- You're welcome, I'm glad you like it. 不客气，我很高兴你喜欢。

6 I am sorry to turn you down. 我很抱歉拒绝你。

拒绝你是无可奈何的事：

- I am sorry but I have to turn you down. 我很抱歉，但我必须拒绝你。

没事的：

- Well, it's okay. 哦，没关系的。

❖ turn sb. down 拒绝某人

 7 I am sorry. I am really not in the mood. 对不起，我真的没心情。

不感兴趣：

- Sorry, I am not interested. 对不起，我没有兴趣。

那好吧，下次吧：

- It's okay. Maybe next time. 没关系的，那下次吧。

Accept and Refuse Conversation

Kevin: Hey, Sophie.	凯文：嘿，索菲。
Sophie: Hey, what's up?	索菲：嘿，怎么了？
Kevin: I got some tickets to that concert you were talking about.	凯文：我有你说过的那场音乐会的一些票。
Sophie: Yeah?	索菲：是吗？
Kevin: My other friend changed his mind and doesn't want to go anymore. Can you take a day off work to go?	凯文：我一个朋友改变主意了，他不想再去了。你能请一天假去吗？
Sophie: I can talk to my boss about it.	索菲：我可以跟我老板说说。
Kevin: Cool. Tell me what your boss says as soon as you talk to him.	凯文：太好了，你跟他说了后马上告诉我结果啊。
Sophie: Will do. Thanks for the ticket, man.	索菲：会的。谢谢你的票，哥们儿。
Kevin: You're welcome. Talk to you later.	凯文：不客气，一会儿聊。
Sophie: Yeah, see you.	索菲：好的，再见。

❖ concert ['kɑnsət] *n.* 音乐会，演唱会
❖ take a day off work 歇一天班

文化穿越

　　面对美国人的盛情邀请，中国人经常会有种盛情难却的尴尬。因此，很多时候，在你其实不想参与的情况下，也没有拒绝对方，甚至委屈自己。这就是美国与中国的文化差异。事实上，是中国人自己考虑的太多了，有时候事情本没有想象的那么复杂。接到美国人的邀请后，根据自己的日程安排或者心情，直接回应就好。美国人不会因为你的拒绝而有什么想法，也不会因为你的委曲求全而心怀感激。拒绝别人送的东西的时候，直接说"I don't think I should take this"就好了。

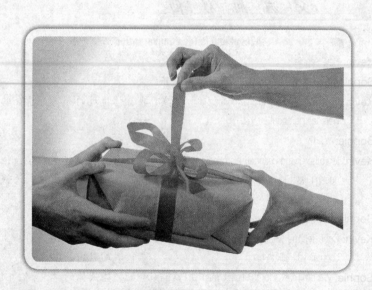

Section 5 ▶ 犹豫与后悔
Hesitate and Regret

　　Kevin 问大家两个问题: 有过犹豫不决、徘徊四顾的时候吗? 对什么事情后悔过吗? 如果你回答说没有, Kevin 可以非常肯定地说, 你真的很牛! 但大多数人肯定会说有吧。没关系, Kevin 告诉大家一些遇到这种情况的时候会用到的英语口语, 你可以淋漓尽致地把自己犹豫和后悔的心情说出来。

1 I'm not sure what I want to do. 我不确定我想做什么。

不确定还可以这样表达:

- I don't think I know what I want. 我觉得我不知道我想要什么。
- I'm really unsure about what I want to do. 我真的不确定我想做什么。
- I'm feeling really indecisive. 我真觉得没法决定。

对方会鼓励你:

- Do you need some encouragement? 你需要些鼓励吗?
- Why not? Just think about it. 为什么不呢? 好好想想吧。
- Don't hesitate too much. You might miss your chance! 别犹豫太多, 你会错过机会的!
- ❖ encouragement [ɪnˈkʌrɪdʒmənt] *n.* 鼓励, 鼓舞
- ❖ indecisive [ˌɪndɪˈsaɪsɪv] *adj.* 无决断力的, 优柔寡断的
- ❖ hesitate [ˈhezəteɪt] *vi.* 踌躇, 犹豫

2 What should I do? 我该怎么办呢?

该怎么办啊:

- Please tell me what to do. 请告诉我该怎么做吧。

你自己都不知道我怎么知道呢:

- I don't know either. 我也不知道。

3 I'm nervous. I don't want to. 我好紧张, 我不想啊。

紧张之下的犹豫:

- I don't want to. I'm too nervous. 我不想啊, 我太紧张了。
- I'm too worried, so I don't want to. 我太担心了, 所以我不想啊。
- I don't want to. I'm worried about the outcome. 我不想, 我担心结果。
- I'm anxious about it. 我很担心。
- I'm having second thoughts. 我再想想啊。

对方会安慰鼓励你:

- Don't be nervous. 别紧张。
- You should, though! Don't let your nerves get in the way. 可是你应该啊! 不要让紧张来妨碍你。
- Don't stress so much, you'll be fine. 别太紧张了, 你会没事的。

❖ nervous ['nɜˑvəs] *adj.* 易激动的, 紧张不安的

❖ outcome ['aut,kʌm] *n.* 结果, 结局

❖ anxious ['æŋkʃəs] *adj.* 焦虑的, 挂念的

❖ have second thoughts 经过重新考虑而改变主意

❖ get in the way 妨碍, 阻碍

 4 I really want to talk to them, but I don't think I should. 我真想和他们谈谈, 但我觉得不应该这样。

在犹豫的边缘徘徊:

- I don't think I should talk to them, even though I want to. 我觉得我不应该跟他们谈, 即便我想。
- I'm not sure if I should talk to them. I'd love to, but I don't know how it will go. 我不确定是否要跟他们谈谈。我想跟他们谈, 但我不知道结果会怎样。
- I would love to talk to them, but I'm getting uneasy thinking about it. 我想跟他们谈, 但我觉得心神不安的。

对方会给你建议:

- Why do you feel that way? 你为什么会有那种感觉呢?
- Maybe you should listen to your heart. 也许你应该听从你内心的感觉。
- Talking to them can't hurt anything. 跟他们谈谈吧, 又不会有什么伤害。

- You're worrying too much. Just chill! 你就是担心太多了,冷静点吧!
- ❖ uneasy [ʌnˈiːzɪ] *adj.* 心神不安的, 担心的
- ❖ listen to one's heart 听从心声, 听从内心的感觉
- ❖ chill [tʃɪl] *vi.* 变冷, 冷静

5 I should have spoken to them. 我应该跟他们说说的。

对没做的事情感觉后悔:

- I should have talked to them. 我本应该跟他们谈谈的。
- It would be better if I had talked to them. 如果我跟他们谈了可能会更好。
- I knew I should have talked to them. I regret not doing it. 我知道我该跟他们谈谈, 我后悔没有去做。
- I knew I should have listened to my gut instead. I thought about it too much. 我知道我应该听从内心的感觉, 是我想的太多了。

早知如此何必当初呢:

- Why didn't you? 那你为什么不做呢?
- You can't undo the past now. 你现在无法修复过去的事情。
- I told you not to get so stressed about it. 我跟你说过不要对此有那么大的压力。
- ❖ gut [gʌt] *n.* 内心
- ❖ undo [ʌnˈduː] *vt.* 取消, 消除, 使复旧
- ❖ stressed [strɛst] *adj.* 紧张的, 感到有压力的

6 I wish I didn't hesitate. 我希望我没有犹豫。

可没有回头路哦:

- I wish I went for it. 我希望我努力去做了。
- I shouldn't have hesitated. 我不应该犹豫。
- I wish I wouldn't have hesitated. 我真希望我没有犹豫。
- I shouldn't have been so indecisive. 我不该那么犹豫不决的。
- I really should have made a decision sooner. 我真应该尽早作决定。

也只能这样安慰了：

- Everyone makes mistakes. 每个人都会犯错误。
- I told you so. 我跟你说过的。
- Try not to regret it too much. You should move on. 别那么后悔了，你应该向前看。

❖ move on 往前走，向前看

 It's up in the air. 还没确定。

还在犹豫中：

- I can't say for sure. 我也说不准。
- I haven't decided yet. 我还没决定。
- I haven't made up my mind. 我还没有拿定主意呢。
- I can't make a decision. 我不能决定。

❖ up in the air 悬而未决的，没有确定的
❖ make up one's mind 拿定主意

Hesitate and Regret Conversation

Kevin:	I am dying to talk to that girl I met the other day.	**凯　文:**	我渴望和我前几天遇到的那个女孩谈谈。
Debra:	Then give her a call.	**黛布拉:**	那给她打个电话吧。
Kevin:	I want to, but I don't want to seem needy.	**凯　文:**	我想打，可我不想让人家看起来觉得我很急切。
Debra:	It's not like you two are dating. And it's been a few days since you saw her. Now would be the perfect time to call.	**黛布拉:**	这又不像是你们两人约会。再说自从你们见面后已经好几天了。现在打电话可是最好的时间。
Kevin:	I don't know; I'm so nervous. She's really cute, and I don't want to mess things up.	**凯　文:**	我不知道，我好紧张。她真的很可爱，我不想把事情搞砸了。
Debra:	You won't mess things up.	**黛布拉:**	你不会把事情搞砸的。

Kevin: You don't know that.	凯　文：你不知道的。
Debra: But if you never try, then you'll regret it later.	黛布拉：但如果你不从来都不试试，那你以后会后悔的。
Kevin: Maybe…	凯　文：也许吧……
Debra: Just call her later tonight.	黛布拉：就今晚给她打电话吧。
Kevin: Okay. I'll try to build up the courage.	凯　文：好吧，我会尽力鼓起勇气的。
Debra: You'll do fine, man.	黛布拉：你会做得挺好的，哥们儿。
Kevin: Thanks.	凯　文：谢谢。

文化穿越

　　在美国这个自由的国度里，应该放开思路，为了自己的理想竭尽全力。美国人的字典里没有后悔两个字，他们对于自己的理想都会竭尽全力的，并且他们认为每个人生来都是有价值的。这也就解释了为什么很多学生为了做自己喜欢的事情而辍学。在这一点上，父母和老师也都是持支持意见的。他们希望自己的孩子能够依照自己的兴趣做一些自己喜欢的事情，快乐地过一生。从某种意义来说，中国学生应该借鉴这种自由至上的思路，放开自我，在这片土地上开始自己新的篇章。

Section 6 · 建议与忠告
Suggestion and Persuasion

和大家一起聊了这么多，在这里 Kevin 给大家分享一些建议，希望对提高大家的英语口语有帮助，也许 Kevin 说的不一定全对，有需要改进的地方也请大家给 Kevin 提出来，Kevin 一定会努力的。好了，建议就在下面的这些表达里面，大家千万不要错过。

1 I want to suggest something to you. 我想建议你一些事情。

给你些建议：

- Can I suggest something? 我能提些建议吗？
- Could I suggest something to you? 我能建议你一些事情吗？
- Can I offer you some advice? 我能向你提些建议吗？
- Let me give you a piece of advice. 我给你条建议。
- I want to suggest something. 我想建议一些事情。

你说吧：

- What is it? 是什么？
- What kind of suggestion? 什么建议？
- Okay. What's up? 好的，怎么了？

2 You should go with me. It will be a lot of fun. 你应该和我一起去，会很好玩的。

我建议你去：

- It will be a lot of fun if you go with me. 如果你和我一起去会很好玩的。
- Go with me! It will be more fun if you do. 和我去吧！如果你去了会更有趣的。
- Please go with me. I promise it will be fun. 和我去吧，我保证会很好玩的。

- I promise it will be a lot of fun if you go. 如果你去的话我保证会很有趣的。

不确定：

- I don't know. 我不知道。

应该行吧：

- Are you sure? I guess I can go. 你确定？我想我能去。

好吧，被你说服了：

- Sure, I'll go. 好的，我去。

3 You should buy it. What harm could it do? 你应该买。这样做有什么坏处呢？

建议某人买东西：

- Go ahead and buy it. It's not like it will do any harm. 去买吧，这又不会有什么坏处。
- There's no harm in buying it. Go for it. 买了它又不会有坏处，去吧。
- Just buy it. It's no big deal. 买吧，没什么大不了的。

接受建议：

- I guess you're right. 我想你是对的。

直接拒绝：

- No, I don't want to. 不，我不想。

犹豫不决：

- I should think about it more first. 我得先好好想想。

❖ go for it 努力争取，加油

4 If you don't do it, you might regret it later. 你如果不做，过后你可能会后悔的。

建议某人做某事：

- You might regret it later if you don't do it. 你如果不做，过后你可能会后悔的。
- Do you want to regret it later if you don't? You should do it. 如果不做，你想后悔吗？你应该去做。
- You could regret it if you don't. Just do it. 你如果不做会后悔的。做吧。

犹豫中：
- Maybe. I'm still not sure. 也许吧，我还是不确定。

对，做吧，过了这个村就没有这个店了：
- That's true. I don't want to regret it. 没错，我不想后悔。

5 It couldn't hurt. You should at least try. 不会有什么事儿的，至少你应该试试看。

你至少该试一下吧：
- Trying won't hurt anything. 试一下又不会有什么事。
- Just try. It couldn't hurt. 只是试一下，不会有伤害的。
- Why not try again? 为什么不再试一下呢？
- You should at least try. It's not like it would hurt anything. 至少你应该试一下，又不会有什么伤害。

接受提议：
- I hope you're right. 我希望你是对的。

还是担心：
- But I'm afraid that it will. 但是我害怕会有。

拒绝提议：
- I don't want to try. 我不想试。

6 Why not go for it? 为什么不努力去做呢？

给予建议的另外一种方式：
- Why not? 为什么不呢？
- Why wouldn't you go for it? 你为什么不努力去做呢？

还没确定：
- Because I don't know if I want to. 因为我不知道我是否想做。

终于醒悟了：
- You're right. I should. 你说得对，我应该去做。

Suggestion and Persuasion Conversation

Kevin: Mom, I really want to buy that Nissan I was looking at.	凯文：妈妈，我真的想买我看的那辆尼桑。
Mom: Kevin, we've already discussed this. I said no.	妈妈：凯文，我们已经讨论过这件事了，我说不行。
Kevin: You shouldn't be so against it. It's my money.	凯文：你不应该那么反对，这是我的钱。
Mom: Those cars are too expensive. You should save your money for something else.	妈妈：那些车太贵了。你应该把钱省下来用在其他的事情上。
Kevin: I earned that money. I worked really hard to save it up. I should have the right to do with it what I want.	凯文：那钱是我挣的，我努力工作节省下来的，我应该有权利做我想做的事。
Mom: You can do what you want with it. I just think it would be a waste.	妈妈：你可以拿它做你想做的事，我只是觉得这是浪费。
Kevin: You get to buy unnecessary things too. You get makeup and clothes all the time.	凯文：你也买不必要的东西啊。你总是买化妆品和衣服。
Mom: Well…I guess you're right.	妈妈：好吧……我想你说得没错。
Kevin: So can I please get the car I want?	凯文：那我能买那辆车吗?
Mom: Okay. You've convinced me. Just be responsible with it.	妈妈：好的，你说服我了。只要你对其负责就行。
Kevin: I promise I will be extremely responsible with my new car. Thanks mom, I'm glad we came to an agreement.	凯文：我保证我会对我的新车非常负责的。谢谢妈妈，我很高兴我们达成一致了。

❖unnecessary [ʌn'nɛsə,sɛrɪ] *adj.* 不需要的，不必要的

❖makeup ['mek,ʌp] *n.* 化妆品

❖convince [kən'vɪns] *vt.* 使信服，说服

❖responsible [rɪ'spɑnsəbl] *adj.* 需负责任的，承担责任的

文化穿越

　　美国人比较看中个人的独立性。受人照顾往往被视为弱者。给对方出主意或提建议时，不能使对方觉得你小看他的能力。不必教人怎么做。中国人则以出主意提建议来表示关心，而且以兄弟姐妹或父母亲人的口吻，或以过来人的口气，这对美国人行不通。举个例子，如果一个美国人生病了，你让他去看医生，这在中国人看来你很关心他，而美国人则不然，他会觉得生病看医生是连三岁小孩都懂的事，根本就不用你说，你这么建议他是不是觉得他很弱智啊？所以对病人表示关心，不必一味地提建议。

Section 7

关心与冷漠
Care and Indifference

在年轻人之间流行这样一句话"我对你如此关心,你却对我如此冷漠。"Kevin 有时候也是一个非常较真的人,对自己喜欢的电影、电视剧或影星等等,如果朋友对此不感兴趣的话,Kevin 是要寻根究底的,哈哈,快闪吧!

1 I'm really interested in it. 我对它真的很感兴趣。

程度可以逐级递进:

- I'm very interested in it. 我对它很感兴趣。
- I'm interested in it a lot. 我对它非常感兴趣。
- I have a lot of interest in it. 我对它非常感兴趣。

两人兴趣一致:

- Really?Me too. 真的吗? 我也是。
- That's cool. 那太好了。

2 I care about it a lot. 我很关心它。

还可以这样表达:

- I really care about it. 我真的很关心它。
- I care about it very much. 我对它非常关心。

这倒令人惊讶了:

- You do? That surprises me. 真的吗? 这倒令我惊讶了。

共同关心:

- Yeah, I do too. 是啊,我也是。

这不关我的事:

- I don't. 我不关心。

3 It's important to me. 这对我很重要。

以下的表达也很不错：

- It's very important to me. 这对我非常重要。
- I find it very important. 我发现这对我很重要。
- It's very important in my life. 这在我的生活中非常重要。

搞不明白了：

- Why is it so important? 为什么它那么重要？

恭喜终于醒悟了：

- That's nice. 那太好了。

4 I don't feel strongly about it. 我对它感觉不怎么强烈。

我可以这样冷漠：

- I don't feel strongly about it at all. 我对它感觉一点儿也不强烈。
- I don't have strong opinions about it. 我对它没有强烈的看法。

强调一下：

- Why not? It's important. 为什么不呢？这很重要的。

不能勉强的事：

- To each his own, I guess. 我想各有所好吧。

5 I don't care either way. 我也不在乎。

还可以这样表达你的不在意：

- I don't care about it. 我对它不在意。
- I don't really care what happens. 我真的不在意发生的事情。

对方的宽容：

- That's understandable. 那是可以理解的。

对方的不理解：

- I think you should. 我觉得你应该在意。

❖ understandable [ˌʌndəˈstændəbl] *adj.* 可理解的，能懂的

6 I don't understand why it matters. 我不明白这为什么重要。

200

怎么也想不明白：

- I don't get why it matters. 我不知道这为什么重要。
- Why does it matter? I don't understand it. 这为什么重要？我不明白。
- I don't see why it matters so much. 我不明白这为什么如此重要。

因为这是事实：

- Because it's really important. 因为这确实重要。

大家都不明白：

- Yeah, me neither. 是啊，我也不明白。

Care and Indifferent Conversation

Kevin: Hey, you know that movie I wanted to see?	凯　文：嘿，你知道我想看的那部电影吗？
Debra: Yeah. What about it?	黛布拉：知道啊，怎么了？
Kevin: I wanted to see it on Saturday. That's when it's premiering.	凯　文：我想周六去看，那可是首映啊。
Debra: Are you asking me to go with you?	黛布拉：你是想问我要不要和你一起去吗？
Kevin: Yeah. Do you want to?	凯　文：是啊，你想去吗？
Debra: I don't know. I wasn't really interested in that movie.	黛布拉：我不知道。我确实对那部电影不感兴趣。
Kevin: Why not? The original was amazing. I've been so excited for the sequel.	凯　文：为什么啊？原剧就非常好，我对续集也非常兴奋。
Debra: Yeah, but the sequels usually suck.	黛布拉：是啊，但是续集通常很差劲的。
Kevin: The trailer looks really good.	凯　文：预告片看起来真的不错。
Debra: I don't know. I guess I'll go if you really want me to.	黛布拉：我不知道，如果你真的想要我去的话，我想我会去的。
Kevin: It's okay. If you really don't want to go I'll find someone else.	凯　文：好的，如果你真的不想去的话，我就只好找其他人了。

Debra: Okay. Sorry, man.

Kevin: Don't worry about it. See you later.

黛布拉：好的。对不起啊，哥们儿。

凯　文：没事儿，一会儿见。

❖premiere [prɪˈmjɛr] *vi.* 首映，初次公演
❖original [əˈrɪdʒənl] *n.* 原著，原剧
❖sequel [ˈsikwəl] *n.* 续集，续篇
❖trailer [ˈtrelə] *n.* 预告片，宣传片

文化穿越

　　在美国，人与人之间经常会将问候挂在嘴边，即使是陌生人与陌生人之间也同样如此。这在中国人看来可能没什么必要，但对别人的问候和关心却是美国文化中很重要的一部分。把你的关心送给大家吧。一般情况下有这么几种口语表达：How are you doing/ how are you/ what's up/ how have you been? 这几种问候意思大体相同，都是比较普遍的说法，what's up 一般回复都是 not much，其他几种自然回答就好，可以说说最近的状况。

Section 8 ▶ 责备与提醒
Scold and Remind

Kevin 为了看电影，竟然把自己份内的家务活给忘了，这不，受到妈妈的责备了。在妈妈面前我总是无力招架的。不过呢，我也确实该受到责备。Kevin 勇于认错，大家是不是该鼓励一下？（是不打自招吧 ^_^）

① Don't do that. 别那么做。

同样的表达还可以说：
- Stop that. 别那么做。
- Stop doing that. 别那么做。

不要操之过急：
- Let's not jump the gun. 别操之过急。

你如果意识到做错了：
- Sorry. 抱歉。

你如果不服气：
- Does it bother you? 这妨碍你了吗？

❖ bother ['bɑðɚ] vt. 烦扰，打搅

② That's not good for you. 那对你没有好处。

类似的提醒：
- It's not good for your health. 这对你的健康不好。

你如果还不明白：
- Why do you say that? 你为什么那么说？

你如果不认同：
- I disagree. It's not so bad. 我不认同，这没那么糟糕。

3 How many times do I have to tell you? Stop it. 我得跟你说多少次？别这么干。

还可以这样不耐烦地责备：

- How often do I have to remind you? Don't do it. 我还要怎么提醒你？别这么干。
- Do I have to remind you so much? Stop that. 我要提醒你多少次？别这么干。
- Do I really have to tell you more than once? Stop. 难道我真的还要跟你再说一次吗？停下。

知错就道歉：

- Sorry, I forgot. 对不起，我忘了。

有点儿不服气的道歉：

- You don't have to be so upset. Sorry. 你不必那么心烦意乱，对不起。
- I didn't mean to. I'm sorry. 我不是故意的，对不起。

4 Don't forget this time. 这次别忘了。

提醒人家别忘了还可以说：

- Try not to forget. 尽量别忘了。
- Try not to forget it this time. 这次尽量别忘了。

对人家提醒的答复：

- Okay. I'll try. 好的，我会尽力的。

你可能经常忘事：

- Sure. I'm sorry. 当然。抱歉。

5 I'll give you one last chance without consequences. 我会不计后果再给你最后一次机会。

还可以更深入点儿：

- I'll let you go one last time. But if you do it again, I'll have to do something about it. 我最后一次让你去，但如果你再做同样的事，我就得对此做些事情了。
- I'll let you go without consequences this time. But next time don't expect the same. 这次我会不计后果让你去，但下次可别期望有同样的事情。

> 对方会明白你的意思：
>
> • Okay. I understand. 好的，我明白。
>
> 你是在开玩笑的吗：
>
> • Seriously? Alright… 认真的吗？好吧……
>
> ❖ consequence ['kɑnsə,kwɛns] n. 结果，后果

Scold and Remind Conversation

Mom:	Kevin, did you do your chores yesterday?	妈妈：凯文，你昨天干家务了吗？
Kevin:	No…Sorry, I thought I told you I went out.	凯文：没有……对不起，我原以为我跟你说过我要出去的。
Mom:	I don't think you did. Why didn't you do your chores earlier if you knew you were going out?	妈妈：我想你没说吧。你知道要出去，为什么不先把家务活干了呢？
Kevin:	I didn't think it would be a big deal. I can do them now if you want.	凯文：我觉得这没什么大不了的。如果你要我做的话我现在就做。
Mom:	Please do. I don't like waking up with dirty dishes in the sink.	妈妈：那就请做吧。我可不喜欢一醒来就是满水池的脏碗碟。
Kevin:	I forgot, sorry.	凯文：我忘了，对不起。
Mom:	It's okay. Just please don't let it happen again.	妈妈：没事，这样的事情别再发生就行了。
Kevin:	I won't. I'll do them right now.	凯文：不会的。我马上就去做。
Mom:	Okay. Thank you.	妈妈：好的，谢谢你。
Kevin:	You're welcome.	凯文：不客气。

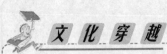

文 化 穿 越

Let's not jump the gun. 别操之过急。这是我们通常用来提醒性情比较急躁的人说的话。那为什么说是 jump the gun 呢？这和"枪"有什么关系？我们想象一下体育赛场的情景：要是一个参加赛跑的运动员在枪还没有响就开始跑，那他就是 jump the gun，要是发生在规模比较大的运动会上，这个运动员还可能会被取消比赛资格。现在，jump the gun 作为俗语已经超越了体育的界限。它可以使用在生活的各个方面，它的意思就是：过早地开始一个行动，或者是过于匆忙地做某事。

Section 9

催促与安抚
Urge and Conciliate

Debra，能不能快一点啊？我妈妈临走之前提醒我需要干的家务活还没干完呢，她马上就要回来了，我可不想再被妈妈说一顿，你快清扫一下吧。大家看看 Kevin 的表面功夫还是做得挺足的。

1　Let's hurry. 快点儿。

各种表示"快点儿"的说法：

- Let's hurry up. 快点儿。
- Let's get a move on. 咱们快点儿吧。
- Let's get going. 咱们走吧。
- Let's get moving. 咱们赶快走吧。
- Step on it. 赶快。
- Come on. 快点。
- ❖　get a move on 赶快

2　Say something. 你说点什么吧。

催促别人继续说：

- Shoot! 说吧!
- I'm listening. 我听着呢。
- Go ahead. 继续说吧。
- Keep talking. 继续说吧。

3　Tell me more. 再跟我说说吧。

想知道更多细节：

- I want to know more about it in detail. 我想知道更多的细节。

比较有礼貌的说法：

- I'd like to know more details. 我想知道得更详细点。
- ❖ in detail 详细地

4 I'd like to hear the story. **我想听听那件事。**

缠着别人说：

- I'd like to know the story. 我想知道那件事。
- I'd like to hear about it. 我想听听那件事。

5 To the point, please. **请抓重点说吧。**

性急的人就这么说：

- Get to the point, please. 请直接说重点吧。
- Stop beating around the bush. 别再绕圈子了。
- ❖ to the point 中肯，扼要，切题
- ❖ beat around the bush 说话绕圈子，拐弯抹角

6 Take it easy. **别着急。**

有的是时间：

- Take your time. 别着急。
- You should take it easy. 你应该放松一下。
- You won't be in a hurry. 你别着急。

7 I know you're angry, but don't get aggressive. **我知道你很生气，但是别咄咄逼人。**

一着急就生气：

- I can see that you're angry. Don't worry so much. 你生气我能理解。别那么担心嘛。
- ❖ aggressive [əˈgresɪv] *adj.* 咄咄逼人的，好斗的

8 Please calm down. **请冷静点。**

别那么急，冷静一下：

- I really need you to calm down right now. 我现在需要你冷静。
- Come on, let's calm down a bit. 拜托，冷静一点儿吧。

嗯，我会听你的：

- You're right. I'll try to. 你说得没错，我会的。

9   I think you need to relax. 我觉得你需要放松。

劝慰性急或紧张的人：

- Can you please relax? 请你放松点好吗？

简单回答：

- Fine. 好的。

10   I feel better now that you talked to me. 你和我说了后我感觉好多了。

你的话很有用哦：

- I really cooled off once you talked to me. 你和我一说我就平静下来了。
- I feel a lot better now that you talked me out of that. 你跟我说了不要那样后我现在感觉好多了。

朋友嘛不用客气：

- That's what friends are for! 这是朋友之间应该做的！
- ❖ cool off 平静下来

Urge and Conciliate Conversation

Kevin:	Please hurry up and clean around here.	凯　文：请快点把这里打扫干净。
Debra:	Why me? I clean as much as you do.	黛布拉：为什么是我？我和你干的一样多。
Kevin:	No! You don't!	凯　文：没有！你没有！

Debra:	Kevin, calm down please. Let's talk about this.	黛布拉:	凯文，请冷静点。咱们谈谈这件事。
Kevin:	No, I can't calm down.	凯 文:	不，我没法冷静。
Debra:	Come on. I'll help clean more.	黛布拉:	别这样。我会帮忙多打扫一些的。
Kevin:	Fine... I'm sorry I got angry.	凯 文:	好吧……对不起，我发火了。
Debra:	That's alright. You have to tell me why you are so quick-tempered.	黛布拉:	没关系。你得跟我说说你为什么这么性急呢？
Kevin:	Because my mom is coming soon and I don't want to look like a mess here.	凯 文:	因为我妈妈马上就要到了，我不想让这里看起来像乱糟糟的一团。
Debra:	Good to hear. That sounds like the Kevin I know.	黛布拉:	很高兴听到你这么说。这听起来才像我认识的凯文。

❖ quick-tempered [ˌkwik'tempəd] *adj.* 性急的，易怒的
❖ mess [mes] *n.* 脏乱的东西，一团糟

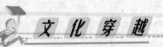

Step on it. 赶快。

在你眼里，很多事真是如火烧眉毛一样紧急，但是你的朋友却是磨磨蹭蹭，你不得不总是催促着他（她），要他（她）快点儿。在英语中，有一个短语非常形象地表达出这个意思，那就是：step on it。这个短语的本来意思是"踩汽车的油门"，表示"加快马力、增加速度"，所以如果别人对你说 step on it，就是催促你快点儿。

Section 10　▶ 支持与鼓励
Support and Encourage

　　其实在很多时候，Kevin 是比较害羞的，更确切地说是缺乏勇气（不要这么直接啦）。你看，在追求女孩子的事情上还是在 Steve 的一再支持和鼓励之下，Kevin 才主动迈出艰难的一步。

口语大放送

1 I'll support you. 我会支持你的。

"支持"的其他说法：
- I'll back you up. 我会支持你的。
- I'm on your side. 我支持你。
- I'm here for you. 我在这里支持你。

对别人的支持表示感谢：
- Thanks. I'm here for you too. 谢谢，我也在这里支持你。
- Thank you very much. 多谢你了。
- Thanks. I'm glad you will. 谢谢，我很高兴你支持我。
- ❖ back sb. up 支持某人
- ❖ be on one's side 支持某人

2 I'll behind you all the way. 我会一直支持你的。

表示一直支持：
- I'm with you all the way. 我会一直支持你的。
- I'm in favor of you all the time. 我一直支持你。

太感谢了：
- Thanks, that's nice of you. 谢谢，你真是太好了。
- I'm really appreciated it. 我非常感谢。
- ❖ all the way 一直，自始至终
- ❖ all the time 始终，一直

3 I'll be available if you need me. 如果你需要我，我随时有空。

给予无私的支持与帮助：

- I'll be there if you need a hand. 如果你需要帮助，我会出现在你面前。
- I'm a phone call away if you need help. 如果你需要帮助，我随叫随到。

表达谢意：

- Thanks, I really need that right now. 谢谢，我现在确实需要你的帮助。
- That's very kind of you. 你真是太好了。

❖ available [ə'veɪləbl] *adj.* 可用的，可得到的
❖ a phone call away 随叫随到

4 You can do it. 你肯定行！

给别人鼓气：

- I trust you can do it. 我相信你能做到的。
- You can make it. 你能做到的。
- I believe in you. 我相信你。

你的鼓励对我很重要：

- Thanks. That means a lot to me. 谢谢，这对我来说意义重大。
- Thank you. 谢谢你。
- Thanks for the support. 谢谢你的支持。

5 You're doing a great job. 你干得很不错。

赞美对方以示鼓励：

- You're doing a really good job. 你干得真不错。
- You're doing fine. 你干得很好。
- You're doing really well. 你干得确实不错。

很感谢你的认可：

- Thanks, man. 谢谢你，哥们儿。
- That's nice of you to say so. 你这样说真是太好了。
- I'm glad you think so. 我很高兴你这么认为。

6 It's going to work out. It always does. 这会解决的，肯定会的。

鼓励安慰遇到挫折的人:

- It will work out. It always does. 这会解决的,肯定会的。
- It always works out. 这总会解决的。

重新打起精神:

- I guess you're right. 我想你是对的。
- Yeah, that's true. 是的,没错。
- ❖ work out 解决,实现

7 Just do your best. 尽你最大努力就行。

只要尽力,没有遗憾就好:

- Try your best. 尽你最大努力吧。
- Do the best you can. 尽你最大的努力。
- Give it your best shot. 尽你最大的努力。

是的,不应该有太多的思想包袱:

- OK, I just think too much. 好的,我就是想太多了。
- ❖ shot [ʃɑt] n. 尝试

8 Keep your chin up. 别灰心。

不要被击倒:

- Don't get discouraged. 不要气馁。
- Don't lose your heart. 不要失去信心。
- Never say die. 永不言败。
- ❖ chin [tʃɪn] n. 下巴
- ❖ discouraged [dɪsˈkɜːrɪdʒd] adj. 灰心的,气馁的,沮丧的
- ❖ lose one's heart 失去信心

交流面对面

Support and Encourage Conversation

Steve: Hey Kevin. You know that girl you wanted to talk to the other day?	史蒂夫：嘿，凯文。你知道前几天你想跟她说话的那个女孩吗？
Kevin: Yeah. Why are you reminding me about it?	凯　文：知道啊。你为什么提起这个？
Steve: I saw her, and she was upset that you never called her back.	史蒂夫：我看见她了，你一直没给她回电话她很伤心。
Kevin: She was?	凯　文：是吗？
Steve: Yeah. I think you should call her.	史蒂夫：是啊，我觉得你应该给她打电话。
Kevin: I don't know. I'll probably just embarrass myself.	凯　文：我不知道。我可能会让自己很难堪的。
Steve: No way, man! You're awesome. I know you'll do fine.	史蒂夫：不会的，伙计。你这么出色，我知道你会表现得很好的。
Kevin: You really think so?	凯　文：你真这么认为吗？
Steve: Of course. And I'm sure she thinks so too. You can do it.	史蒂夫：当然了。我肯定她也是那么想的。你能行的。
Kevin: I'm still nervous.	凯　文：我还是紧张。
Steve: Don't be so worried about it. She thinks you're really cool. I'll be right here to support you, man.	史蒂夫：别那么担心。她觉得你真的很酷，我会一直支持你的，伙计。
Kevin: Thanks for the pep talk. I'm going to call her.	凯　文：谢谢你这番鼓气的话。我会打电话给她。
Steve: You'll do great. I'm here for you!	史蒂夫：你会表现得很棒的。我支持你！

❖ remind [rɪ'maɪnd] *vt.* 提醒，使想起
❖ embarrass [ɪm'bærəs] *vt.* 使难堪，使不好意思
❖ pep talk 鼓励的话

文化穿越

Give it your best shot. 尽你最大的努力。

我们知道，shot 是"发射，射击"的意思。其实"Give it your best shot."这个短语正是起源于射击比赛。当双方选手在射击场上对决的时候，有一方落后了，其教练和队友就会鼓励她"Give it your best shot."也就是说"尽你最大的努力。"实际上这句话还暗含了这样一个意思，也就是说这是最后一次射击了，能不能打中就看你的了，所以要好好把握机会。

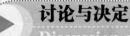

Section 11 ▶ 讨论与决定
Discussion and Decision

现在该是我们最后讨论作出决定的时候了。朋友们，你们还有什么犹豫不决的事情就赶紧决定吧。在这里，Kevin 也和大家分享一些讨论的方法，希望对你们作出决定有所帮助吧。

 口 语 大 放 送

1 I want to talk to you about something. 我想跟你谈些事情。

> 想和对方商讨一些事情：
> - I'd like to talk to you about something. 我想跟你谈些事情。
> - I want to discuss something with you. 我想跟你讨论些事情。
> - Can I talk to you about something? 我能跟你说些事情吗？
> - Could I please talk to you about something? 我能跟你说些事情吗？
>
> 想知道是什么事：
> - Sure. What's up? 当然。什么事？
> - What is it? 是什么？

2 I want your opinion about something. 我想知你对一些事情的看法。

> 你的意见是什么：
> - I'd like your opinion. 我想听听你的意见。
> - Could you give me your opinion about something? 在一些事情上你能给我意见吗？
> - Can you give me your opinion on something? 在一些事情上你能给我意见吗？
>
> 哦，什么意见：
> - Okay. Tell me what's up. 好的，告诉我是什么事。
> - Sure thing. What do you need my opinion on? 没问题。你需要我在什么事上给你意见？

3 I'll tell you all the details. 我会告诉你全部的细节。

我告诉你细节吧：

- I'll tell you all about it. 我会告诉你全部事情的。
- I won't leave out any detail. 我不会遗漏任何细节的。
- I'll explain it thoroughly. 我会把它解释透彻的。
- I'll explain it really well to you. 我会把它给你解释清楚的。

好的，我听着呢：

- Okay. Shoot. 好的，说吧。
- Alright. Start talking. 好的，开始说吧。

❖ thoroughly ['θɜːrəlɪ] *adv.* 彻底地，充分地

4 Give me a definite answer. 给我一个明确的答复。

开门见山：

- I want a definite answer. 我想得到明确的答复。
- I need a definite answer. 我需要一个明确的答复。
- Is it "yes" or "no"? "是"还是"不是"？
- Yes, or no? 是还是不是？

我抱歉：

- Sorry, I can't make up my mind right now. 抱歉，我无法立刻作出决定。

5 It doesn't answer my question. 这可不算是答复。

- That's no answer. 这可不是答复。
- That's not what I want to know. 这不是我想知道的事情。
- You didn't answer my question. 你没有回答我的问题。

6 I'm having trouble deciding. 我很难决定。

作决定比较困难：

- I can't decide. 我决定不了。
- I don't know what I should decide on. 我不知道该作什么决定。
- How should I decide? I don't know. 我该怎么决定呢？我不知道。

需要帮忙吗:

- I can try to help you out. 我会尽力帮你的。
- Just think about it a little longer. 再考虑一下吧。
- What do you need to help deciding on? 你需要帮助做什么决定?

7 Will you help me make a decision? 你能帮我作个决定吗?

帮忙作个决定吧:

- Can you help me decide? 你能帮我决定吗?
- How do you think I should decide? 你觉得我该怎么决定?
- I want to know what you think. How should I decide? 我想知道你的想法。我该怎么决定?

这我可帮不了你:

- It's up to you. 这取决于你。

你再详细说说:

- I'm not sure. Tell me more. 我不确定。再多给我讲讲吧。

我想想啊:

- Okay. Let me think about it a little more. 好的,我再想想。

❖ be up to 由……决定的

8 I've made up my mind. 我已经作出决定了。

已经决定了:

- My heart is set on it. 关于这件事我主意已定。
- The decision is made. 决定已经做出了。
- It's not negotiable. I've decided. 这不容商量。我已经决定了。
- Don't argue. I've already decided. 不要争论了。我已经决定了。
- It's cinched. 事情已确定下来了。
- It's a done deal. 这事情已成定局。

❖ be set on 决心想,一心想
❖ negotiable [nɪ'gəʃɪəbl] *adj.* 可协商的
❖ cinch [sɪntʃ] *vt.* 弄清楚(俚语)
❖ a done deal 已经确定的事,十拿九稳的事

9 You can't say anything to change my mind. 无论你说什么，也不能改变我的决定。

这是最终决定：

- It's written in stone. That's my final decision. 这是不可改变的，是我的最后决定。
- Don't even think about trying to change my mind. 不要想着试图改变我的决定。

不能再商量了吗：

- Is there any room for consultation? 还有商量的余地吗？
- ❖ It's written in stone. 这是不可改变的。
- ❖ final decision 最后决定，最终决定
- ❖ consultation [ˌkɑnsəlˈteʃən] *n.* 商量，商议

Discussion and Decision Conversation

Dad: Son, can I talk to you about something?	爸爸：儿子，我能跟你谈些事情吗？
Kevin: Sure, what is it?	凯文：好的，是什么事？
Dad: Your mother and I have been thinking about moving.	爸爸：我和你妈妈想要搬家。
Kevin: Where to?	凯文：搬哪儿去？
Dad: Not far. But we want to move into a smaller house since you'll be moving out soon.	爸爸：不太远。但我们想搬到一个小一点的屋子里，因为你马上要搬出去了。
Kevin: Well, I think that's a good reason.	凯文：嗯，我觉得这是个好理由。
Dad: Are you okay with moving?	爸爸：那搬家你同意吗？
Kevin: Yeah, of course. Like you said, I'll be getting my own house soon so you guys don't need such a big house.	凯文：同意，当然同意。正如你说的，我马上要搬进我自己的房子，所以你们也不需要一个这么大的房子了。

Dad: Yeah. I'm glad you agree. If you'd like to help us pick out a house you're welcome to.

Kevin: Sure, if you want my help I will.

爸爸：是啊，我很高兴你同意了。如果你想帮我们找一个房子，我们也很欢迎的。

凯文：好的，如果你需要我的帮助，我会的。

文化穿越

"讨论"这个现象在美国挺有意思的。原本很简单的一个事情，往往因为讨论而得不出结果。比如，大学学生有时候会开会讨论决议，大家各持己见，争论得沸沸扬扬，原本10分钟能解决的问题，2个小时都得不出结果。这或许是美国民主的体现。但有些时候，民主也可以使原本简单的事情复杂化。如果中国大学学生会开会，大家一块儿举手表决一个提议，马上就能做出决定。

Chapter 7

今天心情不错

Under a Good Mood

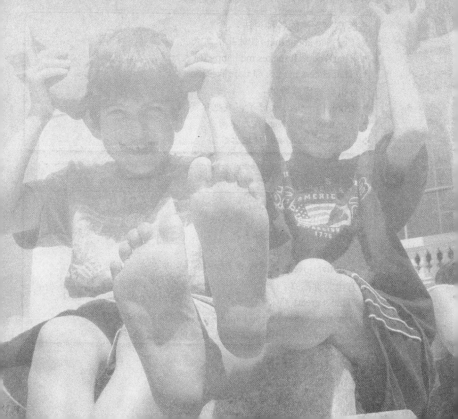

Section 1 高兴与难过
Happy and Sad

人的脸就像是一张纸，把人的心情表露无遗。确实是这样的，高兴的时候觉得一切都是 happy 的；难过的时候一切都好像乌云笼罩了。所以朋友们，哪天你看到 Kevin 满脸阳光灿烂，可以肯定他有什么好事发生了，没准是中奖了呢，但如果看到 Kevin 的脸阴沉沉的，那就最好不要招惹他，说不定会大发脾气哩。

 口语大放送

1 That makes me happy. 那让我很高兴。

表达高兴之情的各种说法：
- I'm glad about that. 我对此很高兴。
- That's cool. It makes me happy. 那太好了，这让我很高兴。
- That cheers me up. 那让我很振奋。

对方也会被你感染的：
- Cool. I'm glad. 太好了，我也很高兴。
- I'm happy for you. 我为你高兴。
- ❖ cheer up 使高兴，使振奋

2 I'm really happy. 我真的很高兴。

丰富一下你的表达方式：
- I'm really glad. 我真的很高兴。
- I'm so happy. 我是那么高兴。
- I'm so glad. 我很高兴。
- I'm overjoyed. 我非常高兴。

对方也为你高兴：
- That's great! 那太好了。
- I'm glad to see you so happy. 看到你这么高兴我也很高兴。
- ❖ overjoyed [,əʊvəˈdʒɔɪd] adj. 狂喜的，极度高兴的

3 | I feel a little better. 我感觉好点儿了。

类似的表达：

- I'm feeling better. 我感觉好些了。
- I'm feeling a bit better. 我感觉好点儿了。
- I have cheered up some. 我高兴点儿了。
- I'm cheering up. 我很高兴啊。

对方对你的关心：

- That's good. I'm glad you feel better. 那挺好，我很高兴你感觉好些了。
- Awesome. If you need anything, just ask. 太好了，如果你需要什么，就说一声。

4 | I've never been this happy. 我从没有这么高兴过。

高兴吧，高兴吧：

- I've never been as happy as I am now. 我从没有像现在这么高兴过。
- This is the happiest moment in my life. 这是我一生中最高兴的时刻。
- This is the best moment of my life. 这是我一生中最好的时刻。

5 | Nothing would please me more. 没有比这更让人高兴的了。

同样意思不同表达：

- Nothing could be more wonderful. 没有比这更让人高兴的了。
- Nothing could be nicer. 没有比这更让人高兴的了。
- I couldn't be happier. 我特别高兴。

6 | That upsets me. 那让我心烦。

伤心的事情太多：

- That makes me upset. 那让我心烦。
- It makes me sad. 这让我很伤心。
- That saddens me. 那让我难过。
- That gets on my nerves. 那让我很生气。

你伤心我也难过：

- I'm sorry. Why does it make you sad? 我很抱歉，这为什么让你伤心呢？

让你伤心难过不是我的本意：

- I don't want you to be sad. 我不想让你伤心难过。

给予安慰：

- Try to cheer up. 尽量高兴点吧。
- ❖ upset [ʌp'set] vt. 使心烦意乱 adj. 心烦的，苦恼的
- ❖ sadden ['sædn] vt. 使悲伤，使难过

7 I'm really down right now. 我现在真的很低落。

难过的时刻总是难熬：

- I'm feeling so down right now. 我此刻感觉那么低落。
- I'm not very happy right now. 我此刻不是很高兴。
- I'm pretty sad right now. 我此刻非常难过。

说出来就会好受点：

- Talk to me about it. 跟我说说吧。
- What's wrong? 怎么了？
- I hope you feel better soon. 我希望你很快就好起来。

8. Why are you so glum? 你怎么闷闷不乐的呀？

给个伤心的理由：

- Why the long face? 你怎么拉着脸啊？
- You're not yourself today. 你今天有点儿不大对劲。
- You seem different today. 你今天有点儿不大对劲。

各种难过的事：

- Yeah, I lost my wallet. 是啊，我把钱包给丢了。
- Yeah, I quarreled with my boyfriend. 是啊，我和我男朋友吵架了。
- ❖ long face 闷闷不乐，不悦的脸色
- ❖ quarrel with 跟……吵架

Happy and Sad Conversation

Mom: Kevin, did you hear about the dog?	妈妈：凯文，你听说过狗的事了吗？
Kevin: No. What happened?	凯文：没有，怎么了？
Mom: It just died. Your little brother was so upset about it.	妈妈：狗死了。你弟弟为此非常难过。
Kevin: When did it die?	凯文：什么时候死的？
Mom: Last night while you were gone. I think we'll be getting another dog, though.	妈妈：昨天晚上你出去的时候。不过我想我们要另外买只狗。
Kevin: Do you think that would cheer him up?	凯文：你觉得那会让他高兴起来吗？
Mom: I hope so. Should I ask him?	妈妈：我希望如此吧。我该跟他说说吗？
Kevin: Yeah. It might make him more upset if you get a new dog without him knowing.	凯文：嗯，如果你没有让他知道就重新弄只狗，会让他更难过的。
Mom: That's true. I'll go tell him.	妈妈：没错，我会跟他说的。
Kevin: Okay. Tell him I hope he cheers up soon.	凯文：好的，告诉他我希望他很快振作起来。
Mom: I will.	妈妈：我会的。

get on one's nerves 惹人生气，让人厌烦

照字面上来看这句话就是碰到某人的神经了，引申为让某人生气的意思。比如说别人一直取笑你，你不高兴就可以说 You get on my nerve。这句话的意思跟 jump on one's back 差不多，jump on my back 就是说某人惹到你，让你生气了。试想如果有一个人在你背上跳啊跳的，那会是什么样的感觉？所以凡是有人惹到你，让你不高兴，就可以警告说 You are jumping on my back!

Section 2 ▶ 惊讶与欣喜
Surprise and Pleasant

今天是一个平常的日子，我像往常一样推门进来。这时，只觉得房间里一团漆黑，还没醒过神来，灯已经亮了，一个人手里捧着燃着蜡烛的蛋糕，妈妈也手捧礼物伸到我的面前，一声 "Surprise" 猛地让我惊醒，今天是我生日，他们给我准备了惊喜派对呢。朋友们，和我一起分享快乐吧。

1 I didn't know that! 我并不知道那件事啊!

惊讶的各种表达:
- I wasn't aware of that. 我不知道那件事啊。
- That surprises me. 那让我很吃惊。
- Wow, that's surprising. 哇，很惊讶哦。

同感:
- Yeah, I was surprised too. 是啊，我也很惊讶。

对方比你更惊讶:
- Really? I thought you knew. 是啊? 我还以为你知道呢。
- ❖ be aware of 知道

2 I'm so surprised. 我很惊讶。

逐级递进:
- I'm really surprised. 我真的很惊讶。
- You surprised me so much! 你太让我惊讶了!

看看对方的反应:
- Awesome. I'm glad I got to surprise you! 太棒了，我很高兴让你惊喜哦!
- Yeah? That's good. 是吗? 那太好了。

3 That's great news. 那消息太好了。

好的消息总是令人欣喜：

- That's wonderful news. 那消息太棒了。
- That news is very nice! 那消息非常好！
- That news is great. 那消息很棒。

对方也有同感：

- I know. I'm really happy about it. 我知道，我对此也真的很高兴。
- I'm glad you think so. 我很高兴你这样认为。
- Yeah, it's alright. 是啊，很好吧。

4 Thanks for the surprise! 谢谢这个惊喜！

对别人给予的惊喜表示感谢：

- Thank you! That surprise was great. 谢谢你！那惊喜太大了。
- That surprise was wonderful. Thank you. 那惊喜真是太棒了，谢谢你。
- I really appreciate the surprise. 我真的很感激这个惊喜。

客套的回答：

- No problem. 不客气。
- I'm just happy that you enjoyed it. 我很高兴你喜欢。
- You're very welcome. 你太客气了。

5 That's very thoughtful of you. 你真是太周到了。

同样对别人的付出表达谢意：

- That's really kind of you. 你真是太好了。
- That's nice of you to think of me. 你想着我真是太好了。

不足言谢：

- It was nothing. 没什么。
- I'm glad you think so. 我很高兴你那么想。

❖ thoughtful ['θɔːtfəl] *adj.* 体贴的，考虑周到的

6 That made my day. 那真让我开心。

人逢喜事精神爽：

- My day is so much better now. 我今天心情比较好。
- That was the best thing that happened all day. 那是一天当中发生的最好的事情了。
- I walk on air today. 今天我很高兴。

我也为你高兴：

- That's great. 那太好了。
- I'm happy I could do that for you. 能为你做那些我很高兴。
- Really? That's awesome. 是吗？那太棒了。

❖ make one's day 使满意……，给……带来幸福

7 Unbelievable! 难以置信！

你就惊讶吧：

- Incredible! 难以置信！
- That's unbelievable! 那真让人难以置信！
- I can't believe it! 我简直不敢相信！
- No way! 怎么会呢！

❖ unbelievable [ˌʌnbɪˈliːvəbl] adj. 令人难以置信的，非常惊人的

Surprise and Pleasant Conversation

Mom:	I know you told me that you didn't want anything for your birthday this year…	妈妈：	我知道你跟我说过今年的生日你不想要任何东西……
Kevin:	Yeah?	凯文：	是吗？
Mom:	But I overheard you talking to Steve about that new game coming out.	妈妈：	不过我无意中听到你跟史蒂夫说起的那款新出来的游戏。
Kevin:	You did?	凯文：	你听到了？
Mom:	Yeah. And you deserve a break lately, with all the hard work you've been doing.	妈妈：	是的，你最近该休息了，你一直在做所有辛苦的工作。
Kevin:	Did you get it for me?	凯文：	你这是给我的吗？

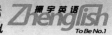
Mom: I did. Happy Birthday, Kevin.	妈妈：是的，生日快乐，凯文。
Kevin: Thank you so much, mom! I wanted this game so bad!	凯文：太感谢你了，妈妈！我很想要这款游戏的！
Mom: I know. I'm glad you like it, sweetie.	妈妈：我知道，宝贝儿，我很高兴你喜欢它。
Kevin: I love it mom. Thank you.	凯文：我很喜欢，妈妈，谢谢你。
Mom: You're welcome. Go enjoy it!	妈妈：不客气，去好好玩吧！
Kevin: I will! Love you!	凯文：我会的！我爱你！

❖ overhear [͵ovəˈhɪr] *vt.* 偶然听到，无意中听到

 文 化 穿 越

walk on air 洋洋得意，飘飘然

在形容一个人很欣喜、很高兴、很得意的时候，中文经常说这个人走路轻飘飘，好像腾云驾雾一样。英文中也有类似的说法，这就是 walk on air。air 就是空气。试想一下，如果一个人走在空气上，是不是有一种像电视镜头中飘飘然、腾云驾雾的感觉呢？所以 walk on air 就是形容一个人非常高兴，走起路来轻飘飘。

Section 3 ▶ 激动与愤怒
Excited and Angry

想看看Kevin兴奋和生气的时候是什么样子吗？先来想象一下：头发根根直竖（成刺猬头了 ^_^），嘴里咿咿呀呀说不出话来（大家证明不是哑巴⊙_⊙），手舞足蹈张牙舞爪（没有发疯 \(^o^)/），Kevin同意上面的部分想象，不过，以下的内容能让你真真切切感受到 Kevin 的兴奋和愤怒。

1 It's very exciting. 太令人激动了。

类似的表达：
- It's really thrilling. 真是太让人兴奋了。

激动的程度：
- I'm too excited to go to sleep. 我激动得睡不着觉了。
- I'm too excited to say a word. 我激动得说不出话来了。

❖ thrilling ['θrɪlɪŋ] adj. 令人兴奋的

2 I can't calm down after that. 那件事后我没法平静下来。

激动或生气后的表现：
- I can't seem to calm down. 我似乎没法平静下来。

对方的建议：
- Just take some deep breaths. 做几下深呼吸就好了。
- Try to calm down. 设法平静下来吧。

3 I'm still mad about it. 我对此仍然很生气。

不能轻易放手：
- I can't forgive that so easily. 我不能那么轻易就原谅了。

生气伤神哦：

- Don't be so angry about it. It's not a big deal. 别那么生气，这没什么大不了的。

④ That's really inconsiderate. 那确实太轻率了。

类似的说法：

- That's so inconsiderate. 那也太轻率了。
- That's really selfish. 那确实很自私。
- That's very selfish. 那非常自私。

当事人道歉：

- I'm sorry. I didn't mean any harm. 对不起，我本不想有什么伤害。

应和回答：

- I know, right? That's terrible. 我知道了，好吧？那很糟糕。

❖ inconsiderate [ˌɪnkənˈsɪdərɪt] *adj.* 轻率的，未慎重考虑的
❖ selfish [ˈsɛlfɪʃ] *adj.* 自私的，只顾自己的

⑤ Why would you do that? 你为什么要做那样的事情？

生气地责问：

- Why would you do something like that? 你为什么要做那样的事情啊？
- What were you thinking? 你在想什么？

事后的推脱：

- I guess I wasn't thinking. 我对这事没想过。

事前没想到影响：

- Sorry, I didn't know it would make you so upset. 对不起，我不知道会让你这么难过。
- I wasn't trying to make you angry. 我没打算要让你生气。

6 That pisses me off. 那太让我生气了。

各种生气的表达：

- That annoys me a lot. 那太让我生气了。
- That makes me pretty angry. 那让我非常生气。
- That's really annoying. 那真让我气愤。

同仇敌忾：

- This annoys me a lot too. 这也让我很生气。

道歉吧：

- Sorry, it won't happen again. 对不起，这不会再发生了。

❖ annoy [ə'nɔɪ] vt. 惹恼，使生气

7 I'm so angry. 我很生气。

赶紧丰富一下你的口语吧：

- I'm really mad. 我真快疯了。
- I'm really angry. 我真生气了。
- I'm extremely pissed off. 这让我非常生气。

关切地询问缘由：

- What's wrong? 怎么了？
- I hope it wasn't because of me. 我希望不是因为我。
- Are you okay? 你没事吧？

8 That's messed up. 一团糟了。

指责：

- That's wrong. 那是错的。
- That's not right. 那是不对的。

附和：

- Yeah, I agree. 是啊，我同意你的说法。

不同意见：

- I don't think it's that bad. 我觉得没那么糟糕。

9 I've heard enough of your excuses. 我已经听够了你的借口了。

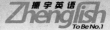
很讨厌听借口：

- I don't want to hear any excuses. 我不想听任何借口了。
- No ifs, ands or buts! 不要找借口了！

很无辜啊：

- But I don't. 可我没有啊。

Excited and Angry Conversation

Kevin: I parked my car over there, man.	凯 文：我把车停到那边儿了，哥们儿。
Steve: Oh yeah, I forgot.	史蒂夫：哦，是的，我忘了。
Kevin: Wait…what the hell is that mark?	凯 文：等等……这到底是什么痕迹？
Steve: Whoa, that mark is huge…What is that?	史蒂夫：哇，这痕迹还很大……那是什么？
Kevin: Did someone key my car?	凯 文：难道有人撬了我的车？
Steve: It kind of looks like it…	史蒂夫：看起来有点儿像那样……
Kevin: Damn it! Why my car? Why would someone do that?	凯 文：该死的！为什么是我的车？为什么有人要做那样的事？
Steve: Because they're a jerk. We can go to a repair shop to see how much it would cost to fix it.	史蒂夫：因为他们是混蛋。我们去修理厂看看修这个要花多少钱？
Kevin: Still, man…that's so messed up that someone did that.	凯 文：可是，天哪……有人做那种事真是太糟糕了。
Steve: Yeah. Hey, if it's expensive I'll help pay for it.	史蒂夫：是啊。嘿，如果比较贵的话我可以帮你付钱。
Kevin: You don't have to do that…	凯 文：你没必要那么做……
Steve: I just don't want you to be too upset over it.	史蒂夫：我只是不想让你那么烦心。
Kevin: I'm okay…I'm just pissed off. Come on, let's go.	凯 文：我没事……我就是太生气了。好了，咱们走吧。

| Steve: Alright, man. | 史蒂夫：好的，哥们儿。 |

❖Damn it! 该死的!
❖jerk [dʒɜˑk] *n.* 混蛋，笨蛋

文化穿越

> piss off 尿尿? 生气?
>
> piss off，看到这个词组千万别认为是"尿尿"的意思，piss off 在字典中是"滚开，滚蛋"的意思，实际上此词是表示"生气，不高兴"的意思，与 angry 同义，在程度上要比 angry 强烈。不过 piss off 可不是什么高雅的词语，piss 其实是"尿尿"的意思 (= pee)，虽然有很多人，包括女生，都使用这个词，但严格地说，如果是在需要 watch your language（小心你说的话）的地方，你还是不用为好。

Section 4 乐观与悲观
Optimistic and Pessimistic

Kevin 一向自认为是一个比较乐观的人，不管是多么糟糕的事情在 Kevin 的眼里都会变好的，虽然遇到挫折，也只是暂时没有成功而已。你看，刚刚面试后，自我感觉良好的 Kevin 就向妈妈报喜了。当然，Kevin 也希望大家做一个乐观的人。

1 Things will go alright. 事情都会好的。

安慰悲观的人或自我安慰：

- Everything will be alright. 一切都会好的。
- It will be okay. 会好的。
- It will work out. 会解决的。

无奈的希望：

- I hope so. 希望如此吧。

积极乐观的态度很好：

- I'm glad you feel that way. 我很高兴你能这么想。

2 I think I will succeed. 我想我会成功的。

对自己充满信心：

- I think I'll do well. 我想我会做得很好的。
- I believe in myself. 我相信我自己。

对方对你的自信很满意：

- I believe in you too. 我也相信你。
- I'm glad that you're self-confident. 你很自信我很高兴。
- That's good to hear so. 很高兴听你这么说。

❖ self-confident [ˌsɛlfˈkɑnfədənt] *adj.* 自信的

3 I'm confident we'll win this game. 我相信我们会赢得这场比赛的。

给自己打气：

- I have faith in winning this game. 我有信心赢得这场比赛。
- I'm sure we can win this game. 我肯定我们能赢得这场比赛。

提醒过于乐观的人：

- First catch your hare then cook him. 先抓到兔子再煮吧。/ 不要过于乐观。

❖ hare [hεr] *n.* 野兔，兔子

4 I hope things will go better. 我希望事情会变得更好。

赶紧学一下这些同类的表达，丰富一下你的口语：

- I really hope things go okay. 我真的希望事情变好。
- I hope things get better soon. 我希望事情很快会变得更好。
- I'm hopeful that things will change. 我希望事情会改变。

对乐观的态度给予肯定：

- I'm sure they will. 我相信会的。
- Yeah, things are bound to get better. 是啊，事情一定会变得更好的。

❖ be bound to 必然，一定

5 I don't think that's going to work. 我觉得那行不通。

还没做自己就先泄气了：

- I really don't think that will work. 我真的不认为那会行得通。
- That's not going to work out. 那行不通的。
- That's not a very good idea. 那可不是个好主意。

反对悲观的想法：

- Why not? I think it will be fine. 为什么？我觉得会好的。

也许事实确实如此吧：

- I agree. It's not going to work. 我同意，是行不通的。

态度很模糊：

- I'm not sure either. 我也不确定。

6 It never works out right. 绝不会起作用的。

悲观的人总是抱有悲观的想法：

- Things never go my way. 事情从没按我的思路发展。
- Nothing ever works out. 没什么事情会解决的。
- Things never work out for me. 对我来说事情绝不会解决的。

也只能安慰一下了：

- Don't say that. Things will be okay. 别那么说，事情会好的。
- That's sad. You shouldn't think like that. 那很让人难过啊，你不应该那么想。
- This will work out right, don't worry. 这会解决的，别担心。

Optimistic and Pessimistic Conversation

Kevin: My interview went really well today.	凯文：我今天的面试进展得很顺利。
Mom: Did it?	妈妈：是吗？
Kevin: Yeah. I think I'm going to get hired.	凯文：是啊，我想我肯定会被录用的。
Mom: That's great, honey. I hope you do.	妈妈：那太好了，宝贝儿。我希望你被录用。
Kevin: Me too. They said I was one of the best people they've interviewed so far.	凯文：我也是。他们说到目前为止我是他们面试过的最好的人选之一。
Mom: I bet you'll get the job!	妈妈：我肯定你会得到那份工作的！
Kevin: I'm going to go call Steve and tell him.	凯文：我给史蒂夫打个电话，告诉他一声。
Mom: Yeah, I bet he'd be happy to hear that it went well.	妈妈：是啊，我肯定他听到面试顺利也会很高兴的。
Kevin: Definitely.	凯文：那肯定的。
Mom: I'll go tell your father too!	妈妈：我也去告诉你爸爸！
Kevin: Okay, mom.	凯文：好的，妈妈。

文化穿越

First catch your hare then cook him. 先抓到兔子再煮吧。/ 不要过于乐观。

这句话的意思非常明显,"先"与"后"的顺序也很清楚明了,表示做事情要一步一步来。这句话是对头脑发热或盲目乐观的人的一种提醒,不要事情还没做就预期结果会多么好,也就是不要过于乐观。但反过来说,First catch your hare then cook him 的这种人也有点过于保守,缺乏激情。

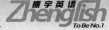
Section 5 ▶ 抑郁与沮丧
Depressed and Desperate

好郁闷啊。不知道怎么回事，最近总是莫名其妙地感觉郁闷和失落。看完以下这些表达，你就能体会到我的这种感觉是何等之深了。当然我的意思是大家在感受我的郁闷时也请给我些建议，让我排遣一下，我也相信大家不会喜欢整天都郁郁寡欢的 Kevin 的，所以我渴望快乐。

① I've been sad for a while now. 我已经难过一段时间了。

感觉抑郁的其他表达：
- I've been feeling blue for a while. 我感觉闷闷不乐已经有一段时间了。
- I've been pretty down for a long time now. 我情绪低落已经很长一段时间了。
- I've been sad a lot lately. 我最近很忧郁。

主动提供帮助：
- Do you need any help? 你需要什么帮助吗？
- I'm here for you if you need me. 如果你需要我，我会在这里陪你。

安慰和祝愿：
- I'm sorry to hear that. I hope you feel better soon. 听到那些我很难过，我希望你很快就好起来。

② I feel really depressed. 我感觉真沮丧。

以下这些表达也非常地道：
- I'm so depressed. 我很沮丧。
- I feel so sad. 我感觉很悲伤。

- I feel blue. 我感觉很郁闷。
- I feel low. 我感觉很低落。
- I feel really down. 我真觉得很失落。

说出来会好一点：

- Talk to me. I want to help. 跟我说说吧，我想帮你。
- Do you want to talk? What's wrong? 你想说说吗？怎么了？
- What's been bothering you lately? 最近有什么事烦扰你吗？

❖ depressed [dɪˈprɛst] *adj.* 沮丧的，消沉的，忧郁的

3 I don't know what to do with myself anymore. 我真不知道我该怎么办了。

不知所措了：

- I feel like I don't know what to do anymore. 我感觉我不知道做什么了。
- I feel so lost now. 我现在感觉好迷茫。

安慰对方：

- Everyone feels like that sometimes. Don't think about it too much. 有时候大家都会有那样的感觉的，别想太多了。

给予建议：

- Do what you used to do. 做你过去常做的事。

4 I don't see the point in anything. 任何事情对我来说都没有意义。

对什么事情都漠不关心了：

- I don't see why anything matters. 我不明白什么事情是重要的。
- Nothing matters to me anymore. 对我来说没有什么事情是重要的了。
- I don't care about anything anymore. 我不在乎任何事情了。

给予建议：

- You should try to do things you used to love. 你应该做些你以前喜欢做的事情。
- Don't talk like that. You have to care about something. 别那么说，你得关心一些事情。

抚慰对方：

- I'm sure you're okay. You're just a little down. 我相信你很好，只不过是有点儿失落罢了。

❖ see the point in 懂得要点，看出好处

5 I feel worthless. 我感觉一文不值。

有点儿自暴自弃了：

- I feel useless. 我感觉好没用。
- I'm pathetic. 我好可怜。
- I'm a waste. 我就是个废物。

给对方打气：

- That's not true at all. You're important to me. 那一点儿都不对，你对我来说很重要。
- You're a great person. Don't say that. 你是个了不起的人。别那么说。
- I feel like that too sometimes. Don't let it get to you. 我自己有时候也那么感觉。别让这事影响你。

❖ worthless ['wɜːθlɪs] *adj.* 无用的，不重要的
❖ pathetic [pə'θɛtɪk] *adj.* 可怜的，可悲的

6 I want to give up. 我想放弃。

有点儿厌世的感觉：

- I'm tired of living. 我厌倦生活了。
- I'm sick of everything. 我对一切都感到厌烦。
- I wish I could just give up. 我希望我可以放弃。

一般的措辞：

- Don't think about that. 别那么想。

建议：

- I want you to seek professional help. 我希望你寻求专业人士的帮助。

表达关心：

- I'm so worried about you. Please don't say those things. 我很担心你，请别说那样的事情。

❖ be sick of 厌恶，厌倦
❖ professional [prə'fɛʃənl] *adj.* 职业的，内行的

Depressed and Desperate Conversation

Kevin: Debra, can I talk to you?	凯　文：黛布拉,我能跟你说说话吗?
Debra: Sure, what's up?	黛布拉：当然可以了，怎么了?
Kevin: I've been really depressed lately…	凯　文：我最近很郁闷……
Debra: I thought something was wrong. Why are you depressed?	黛布拉：我还以为是出什么事了。你干吗郁闷啊?
Kevin: I don't know…I just don't see the point in anything anymore.	凯　文：我不知道……我只是觉得任何事情对我来说都没有意义。
Debra: Hey, don't talk like that, man. I know what you're going through. Don't let the depression get to you.	黛布拉：嘿，别这样说。我知道你正在经历什么，别让这沮丧影响到你啊。
Kevin: But I just don't have any purpose anymore.	凯　文：但我就是没有任何目标了。
Debra: If you did before you can have a purpose again.	黛布拉：如果你做以前的事你又会有目标的。
Kevin: I don't know.	凯　文：我不知道。
Debra: Hey man, I want to come over. We can talk.	黛布拉：嘿，哥们儿，我想去你那儿看看，我们可以谈谈。
Kevin: Okay…I guess you can.	凯　文：好的……我想你可以来。
Debra: Good. I'll see you soon.	黛布拉：好的，一会儿见。

文化穿越

I feel blue. 我感觉很郁闷。

在英语中常会用一些说色彩的词来表示不同的情绪，大家不知有没有注意到。这一节出现了 blue 这个词。blue 是蓝色，属于低沉的冷色调，所以常常用来比喻低落忧郁的情绪。这样看来 feel blue 一定是说心情闷闷不乐了。人的情绪时起时伏，有时甚至连自己也弄不清原委。

就这 900 句 玩转口语

Section 6  耐心与不耐烦
Patient and Impatient

人郁闷的时候，一遇到什么事情就会变得焦躁不安，没有耐性。我和 Debra 在外面散心，原本郁闷的心情已经变得开朗起来了，所以玩得渐渐忘了时间，想打个电话回家告诉妈妈一声，可在这鬼地方手机竟然没有信号，真是急死我了。

口语大放送

1 I'm willing to wait. 我愿意等。

愿意等待还有以下几种说法：
- I'm okay with waiting. 我等一下没关系。
- Waiting isn't so bad. 等一下不是那么糟糕的事。
- Waiting is okay. 等一下没关系。

并不是每个人都愿意等：
- I can't stand waiting. 我可受不了等待。

那就一起等吧：
- Yeah, I'm pretty patient too. 是的，我也很有耐心的。
- ❖ be willing to 乐意，愿意
- ❖ patient ['peʃənt] adj. 有耐心的，能忍受的

2 You just have to be patient. 你得有点儿耐心。

还可以这样劝别人要有耐心：
- You need to learn some patience. 你需要学着耐心点儿。
- All you need is some patience. 你所需要的是耐心。
- Being patient is all you need. 耐心是你所需要的。

接受对方的意见：
- I guess you're right. 我想你是对的。

- I'll try to be more patient. 我会尽量更有耐心的。

有点儿不甘心啊：

- I've been waiting for so long, though. 可是，我已经等了很长时间了。

3 All it needs is a little more time. 所需要的只是多一点时间。

同样的说法：

- It just needs some more time. 所需要的只是多一点时间。
- It needs a little more time. That's all. 需要的只是多一点时间，就这些。

确实不耐烦了：

- But you said that a while ago! 可你刚才就说过了！
- You'd better be telling me the truth. 你最好告诉我真实情况。
- I hope you're right. 我希望你是对的。
- ❖ a while ago 刚才，方才

4 There's a time for everything. 事情要一件一件地来。

做事情不能急：

- One step at a time. 一步一步来。
- Things will work out in the end. 事情最终都会解决的。
- Everything will work itself out. 每件事情都会得到解决的。
- Everything will fall into place. 事情该怎样，就会怎样。
- Everything will come out right in the end, just you wait and see. 你就等着瞧吧，一切最终都会顺利解决。

站着说话不腰疼：

- That's easy to say. 说起来容易。
- ❖ fall into place 落实，有条不紊

5 I don't want to wait anymore. 我不想再等了。

真没有耐心了：

- I don't want to wait any longer. 我不想再等了。
- I'm sick of waiting around. 我讨厌空等。
- I'm tired of waiting. 我讨厌等待。

等等看吧：
- Be a little more patient. 有点儿耐心吧。
- Just hold your horses. 不要着急，耐心一点。

等待是件很烦人的事儿：
- Me too! I'm sick of waiting. 我也是！我讨厌等待。
- ❖ wait around 呆呆地等，空等

6 I want results now. 我现在就想要结果。

以下的表达稍微复杂点儿：
- I want something to happen right now. 我现在就希望一些事情发生。
- I need some results now. 我现在就需要结果。
- I really want results right now. 我现在就想要结果。

无可奈何啊：
- I'm sorry I can't help you. 对不起，我都不了你。

对，不能再拖了：
- I agree. I've tried being patient, but this is taking forever. 我同意，我是想有耐心，但这就永远拖下去了。

交流面对面

Patient and Impatient Conversation

Kevin: Damn, I can't get cellphone service.	凯　文：该死，我手机没信号。
Debra: So? Who do you need to call?	黛布拉：怎么了？你需要给谁打电话吗？
Kevin: I need to call my mom soon to tell her I won't be home until late.	凯　文：我要给我妈打个电话，告诉她我要晚点儿回家。
Debra: Try to point your phone up.	黛布拉：把手机尽量举高点。
Kevin: Still not working. I need to call her as soon as possible!	凯　文：还是不行。我需要尽快给她打电话。
Debra: Here, let's walk forward a little.	黛布拉：咱们再往前走一点儿。
Kevin: Wait, I have a bar! …Gah, it just went away!	凯　文：等等，有一格信号了！……啊，又没了！

Debra:	Do you just wanna use my cellphone? I think I have service here.	黛布拉:	你要用我的手机吗？我想我的手机在这里有信号。
Kevin:	Yes, please.	凯 文:	好的。
Debra:	Okay, here you go. The service isn't too great, but it should work.	黛布拉:	好的，给你。信号不是很好，但应该可以用。
Kevin:	That's fine. I just need to talk to her for a second. Thanks.	凯 文:	好的，我就跟她说一会儿。谢谢。

❖cellphone ['sɛlfon] *n.* 手机，携带式移动电话
❖walk forward 向前走
❖have a bar 有一格信号（特指）
❖go away 消失

文化穿越

Just hold your horses. 不要着急，耐心一点。

hold one's horses 从字面意思来解释就是勒住你的马，停步不走。这个习惯用语起源于十九世纪，是马匹作为重要交通工具时的一个口令，用来要求赶马车的人停下他的那些马匹。但是现在 hold one's horses 被广泛应用在各种场合，意思是"不要着急，耐心一点，不要冲动"。

Section 7 担心与忧虑
Worried and Stressed

说实在的，我最近非常担心 Steve。我成天都不见他的影子，只听说他整天和一帮所谓的哥们儿混在一起，K 歌、泡吧……彻夜不归。Steve 以前可从来不是这样子的，他最近发生什么事了？也不见他打电话，真为他担心。

1 I'm starting to worry. 我开始担心了。

开始担心还可以说：
- I'm beginning to worry. 我开始担心了。
- I'm becoming worried. 我开始担心了。
- I'm starting to get worried. 我开始担心了。

对方的安慰：
- Don't worry too much. 别太担心了。
- I'm sure everything will be okay. 我相信一切都会好的。

2 I've been pretty worried about it. 我对此非常担心。

类似的表达：
- It's been worrying me for a while. 我这段时间很担心。
- I've been worried about it for a while now. 我已经担心一段时间了。
- I'm really worried about it. I have been for a while. 我真的很担心，已经有一段时间了。

忧虑伤身哦：
- How long? That's not good. 多长时间？那可不太好。

还是赶紧采取行动吧：
- Take some action instead of worrying about it. 有所行动吧，别担心了。

❖ take some action 采取行动

3 Is something on your mind? 你有什么心事吗?

还可以关切地询问:

- Do you have something on your mind? 你有什么心事吗?
- What are you worried about? 你担心什么?
- What's on your mind? 你担心什么呢?
- Is anything bothering you? 有什么事让你烦心吗?

是我自己的原因:

- Nothing. I'm just tired. 没什么。我只是累了。

4 I'm so stressed out. 我很紧张。

紧张和压力并存:

- I'm really stressed out. 我真的很有压力。
- I'm very stressed. 我很紧张。
- I feel so stressed. 我感觉很有压力。
- I'm under a lot of stress. 我压力很大。

放松一下就好:

- Try to relax more often. 要尽量经常放松。
- You need to calm down. Live life a little slower. 你需要平静下来, 让生活的节奏慢一点儿。
- ❖ be stressed out 紧张,饱受压力

5 I have way too many things going on. 我有太多的事情要做了。

事情多得喘不过气来:

- I have too much on my plate. 我手头有太多的事情要完成。
- I'm overwhelmed by things. 我都快被事情淹没了。
- I'm having trouble juggling everything right now. 我现在要安排每一件事的话有困难。

建议休息调整:

- You should take a small break from it. 你应该稍微休息一下。
- Don't get overwhelmed. Take on things one at a time. 别被弄得不知所措了,一次做一件事。
- ❖ have too much on one's plate 有很多事情要处理

❖ overwhelm [ˌovəˈhwɛlm] *vt.* 淹没，征服，压倒

❖ juggle [ˈdʒʌgl] *vt.* 耍，弄

❖ take a small break 休息一会儿，小憩

6 I can't handle any more things. 我再也应付不了任何事了。

事情一多压力就大：

- If I get any more stressed I'll freak out. 我如果再有压力的话就要崩溃了。
- I can't be more stressed than this. 这让我太有压力了。
- I can't deal with anything else. 我应付不了其他任何事情了。
- There's so much, I can't deal with it. 这太多了，我应付不了。

尽自己最大的努力：

- Just try to power through it. 尽量努力就行。

给对方鼓鼓气：

- You can do it; don't let it get to you so much. 你能做到的，别太让这难倒你了。

❖ freak out 崩溃

❖ power through 艰苦奋斗，努力

交 流 面 对 面

Worried and Stressed Conversation

Kevin: I'm really worried about Steve.	凯文：我真担心史蒂夫。
Mom: What's wrong with him?	妈妈：他怎么了？
Kevin: He's been going out to parties a lot.	凯文：他出去参加很多的聚会。
Mom: Oh, I see. Have you talked to him about it?	妈妈：哦，我知道。你跟他说了吗？
Kevin: No. I don't want to make him angry at me.	凯文：没有。我不想让他对我生气。
Mom: If you're afraid of that, you could just invite him over before he gets invited to parties.	妈妈：如果你担心他，你就在他被邀请参加聚会之前邀请他来。

Kevin: I suppose I could do that… if you're okay with him coming over all the time.	**凯文:** 我想我可以那样做……但如果他总是过来的话，你没意见吧。
Mom: Of course I am. I don't want Steve to get into trouble.	**妈妈:** 我当然没意见了。我不想让史蒂夫惹上麻烦。
Kevin: Okay … thank you. I've been kind of stressed out about it.	**凯文:** 好的……谢谢你。我对此有点儿紧张。
Mom: That's understandable. I hope he's okay.	**妈妈:** 那是可以理解的。我希望他没事。
Kevin: Me too. Thanks, mom.	**凯文:** 我也是。谢谢你，妈妈。

❖get into trouble 陷入困境，惹上麻烦

文化穿越

I have butterflies in my stomach. 我心里七上八下的。

看了电影《剑蝶》吗? 蝴蝶谷里翩翩飞舞的蝴蝶是不是很美? 大家都知道花丛中自由来去的蝴蝶是大自然的精灵，不过，如果有几只蝴蝶在某人的胃里扑腾乱飞，你猜会是什么感觉呢? 你还会觉得它美吗? have butterflies in one's stomach 很形象地描述了这样的场景，用来形容一个人一种持续不断的恐惧、紧张或忧虑的心情，和中文里说的"心里感到七上八下"很相似。

Section 8 ▶ 期望与失望
Promise and Disappointment

自从上次面试后，我自我感觉一直很良好，就等着人家通知去上班了。今天终于接到面试单位打来的电话。在这里 Kevin 卖一个小关子，朋友们猜猜会是什么结果呢？看来大家都是恭喜我的，先谢谢各位了。可结果是我没有被录用，大家失望了吧，我也非常失望。不过通过这件事情，也让我明白一个道理，凡事要脚踏实地，没有结果的事情不要抱太大的希望，因为期望越高，往往失望也就越大。

 口语大放送

1 I've been really hopeful about it. 我对那件事一直抱有希望。

赶紧学习以下这些表达吧：

- I've been optimistic about it. 我对此很乐观。
- I've been hoping for the best. 我满怀希望。
- I hope the best will happen. 我希望最好的事情会发生。

那就没什么可担心的了：

- That's good. 那挺好。
- I'm sure things will be great if you think so. 如果你那么认为的话我相信事情肯定会很好的。

2 I really think things went well. 我觉得事情进展得很不错。

同类意思不同表达：

- I think things went really well. 我觉得事情进展得很不错。
- I'm pretty sure it went well. 我非常肯定事情进展顺利。
- It went great. 事情进展得很好。
- It went very well. 事情进展得非常好。

听到好消息心里也是一种安慰：

- That's good to hear. 很高兴听到这些。
- Awesome. I hope it works out well for you. 太棒了，我希望这对你有好处。

3 I didn't get what I was expecting. 我没有达成所愿。

事与愿违：

- I wasn't expecting this. 我可没期待是这样的。
- I was hoping for better. 我希望的是更好的。
- This is nothing like what I was expecting. 这和我所期待的一点儿都不一样。
- I didn't want this at all. 我一点儿都不希望是这样。

心存疑虑：

- Is it really that bad? 真有那么糟糕吗？
- Are you disappointed about it? 你对此很失望吗？
- ❖　be disappointed about 对……失望，对……感到失望

4 I'm really disappointed. 我真的很失望。

还可以这样表达失望：

- I'm so disappointed. 我太失望了。
- I'm very disappointed. 我特别失望。
- That's so disappointing. 那太令人失望了。
- That's really disappointing. 那真让人失望。
- He led me on a wild-goose chase. 他让我白费了半天劲。

失望的结果总是令人遗憾：

- I'm sorry to hear that. 听到这我很难过。
- Oh well. What can you do? 哦，是啊。你能做些什么呢？

5 I wish it was better than this. 我多么希望结果比这更好。

希望有时也会让人失望：

- I wish it didn't disappoint me. 我希望这没让我失望。
- I don't want it to be like this. 我可不想像这样。
- I want it to be so much better than this. 我想的比这要好多了。

这都是不值当的事情：

- There's no use in being upset about something you can't change. 为一些你没法改变的事情而烦心是没用的。
- I know. I'm sorry it's not what you were hoping for. 我知道。我很抱歉，这不是你所希望的那样。

6 I think things will go better next time. 我觉得下次事情会更好。

对将来充满希望：

- I hope things will go better in the future. 我希望将来事情会更好。
- Hopefully things will be better in the future. 希望事情在将来能更好。
- I really think things will be better in the future. 我真的觉得事情将来会更好。
- Hopefully things will turn out better next time. 希望事情下次会变得更好。

大家的感觉都是一样的：

- I think so too. 我也那么认为。
- It's good to hear you being optimistic about it. 我很高兴你对此抱乐观态度。
- I hope so. 希望如此。

7 I'm used to being disappointed. 我习惯失望了。

无数次的失望都快变成绝望了：

- Disappointment is common for me. 失望对我来说是很平常的事。
- I'm usually disappointed. 我总是失望。
- Things usually disappoint me. 事情总是让我失望。

要看到光明的一面：

- That's no way to think. 绝不要那么想。
- Don't say that. You have plenty of things to look forward to. 别那么说。你有很多事情可以期待。

❖ look forward to 盼望，期待

交流面对面

Promise and Disappointment Conversation

Kevin: Mom, I have bad news…

凯文：妈妈，我有不好的消息……

Mom: Oh no, what is it?

妈妈：哦，不会吧，是什么？

Kevin: I didn't get the job…

凯文：我没有得到那份工作……

Mom: Really? I thought they told you that you were the best person they had interviewed!

妈妈：是吗？我以为他们跟你说你是他们面试过的最好的人选呢！

Kevin: They did say that…

凯文：他们是那么说的……

Mom: Well I'm sorry, honey. That's really disappointing.

妈妈：哦，真遗憾，宝贝儿。那确实令人失望。

Kevin: I know…I guess I'll just keep applying to places.

凯文：我知道……我想我会继续申请职位的。

Mom: Don't let it get you down too much.

妈妈：别太让这件事来烦扰你了。

Kevin: I'll try.

凯文：我试试看。

Mom: Cheer up, hon. You'll get hired somewhere.

妈妈：振作点，宝贝儿。你总会在某个地方被雇佣的。

Kevin: I hope so.

凯文：希望如此吧。

文化穿越

He led me on a wild-goose chase. 他让我白费了半天劲。

a wild-goose chase 就字面意而言，"追上一群大雁"，这确实是一件很难的事情，实际上是说，忙活了半天，到最后一无所获，等于做了无用功。词源学家认为，"a wild-goose chase"（无益的追求）最早起源于赛马。早在 16 世纪，所谓的"赛马场"是茂密的森林。赛马比赛规定，骑手们须在森林中紧追一匹"头马"，头马性格暴烈，奔跑时毫无路线规律可循。在追"头马"的过程中，很多骑手往往独陷林中，找不到归路。再加上这种赛马的阵形以"一马带路、群马尾随"为特色，与群雁飞翔颇为相似，人们就戏称当时的赛马为"a wild-goose chase"。随着时间的推移，"a wild-goose chase"的比喻意"白费力，徒劳无益的追求"逐渐被人们采用。

Chapter 8

爱上哈佛

Study

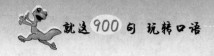

Section 1  熟悉校园和同学
Getting Familiar

过了一段这么长时间的假期，我又要返回学校的生活了，真是让人激动又有些不安。因为我将进入更高一级的学校，要熟悉新的校园环境，结交新的同学，这一切都让人感觉很紧张。但不管怎么说，慢慢就会适应了。

① Hey, what's your name? 嗨，你叫什么名字？

认识新同学：
- I didn't catch your name. 我没有听清你的名字。
- I'm sorry. What was your name? 不好意思，你叫什么名字？

礼貌一点的说法：
- How do I address you? 我怎么称呼你？
- May I have your name? 我能知道你的名字吗？

直接回答：
- Cindy. 辛迪。

自我介绍：
- Oh, I'm sorry. It's Jessica. 噢，抱歉。我叫杰西卡。
- ❖ address [ə'drɛs] vt. 称呼

② Hi there! I'm Kevin. 嗨，你好啊。我叫凯文。

主动介绍：
- Nice to meet you. I'm Kevin. 很高兴认识你，我叫凯文。
- Good to meet you. My name is Kevin. 很高兴认识你，我叫凯文。

客套的回答：
- Nice to meet you, Kevin! 很高兴认识你，凯文。

3 Could you tell me where the science building is? 你能告诉我科教楼在哪儿吗？

问校园里的其他地方：

- I'm looking for the math building. Do you know where it is? 我在找数学教学楼，你知道在哪里吗？
- Do you know how to get to the writing center? 你知道怎么去写作中心吗？
- Where is the campus cafeteria? 校园的食堂在哪里？

指路：

- Yeah, it's just down this walkway and to the left. 是的，就沿着这条路走，然后向左拐。

我也是新来的：

- No, I'm sorry. I'm new here too. 不好意思，我不知道。我也是新来的。

❖ campus ['kæmpəs] n. 校园，校区
❖ cafeteria ['kæfə'tɪrɪə] n. 自助餐馆，自助食堂
❖ walkway ['wɔk,wei] n. 人行通道，走道

4 So where is there to eat on campus? 学校哪里可以吃饭啊？

同样的问法还有：

- What are the places to eat on campus? 学校哪些地方可以吃饭啊？
- Where can I go to get some food on campus? 在学校哪里可以买点吃的呢？

如果你正好知道：

- Well, there's a dining hall, and some coffee shops around. 噢，那边有一个食堂，周围还有一些咖啡店。

❖ dining hall 餐厅，食堂

5 Have you ever had Professor Smith? Is he good? 你和史密斯教授打过交道吗？他怎么样？

还可以这样打听：

- Do you know anything about this professor? Is he any good? 你了解这个教授吗？他怎么样？

根据具体情况回答：

- I've never had him. 我不认识他。
- I hear he's pretty laid back! 我听说他很随和。
- ❖ laid back 随和的，不轻易发脾气的

6 What year are you? 你是几年级的?

根据年级不同来回答：

- I'm a junior. 我是大三的。
- This is my first year, actually. 事实上，我上大一。
- I'm a freshman. 我是大一的学生。
- I'm a sophomore. 我是大二的学生。
- I'm a senior. 我是大四的学生。
- ❖ junior ['dʒunjɚ] n. (四年制大学或中学中) 三年级学生
- ❖ sophomore ['safmor] n. 大学二年级学生
- ❖ senior ['sinjɚ] n. 大学四年级学生

7 Do you know how to check what your advisor is? 你知道怎么查看你的导师吗?

不同的表达：

- How can I check who my advisor is? 我怎么查看我的导师是谁呢?
- Do you know how to check who your advisor is? 你知道怎么查看你的导师吗?

上网查啊：

- Yeah. Just check the information on the university web page. 知道。查一下学校网页上的信息就可以了。

我不知道，你可以问问其他人：

- I'm sorry. I don't know. 不好意思，我不知道。
- ❖ advisor [əd'vaɪzɚ] n. (学生的) 指导老师

8 How do I log in to a computer at school? 我怎么登录学校的计算机系统?

不同的询问方式：

- Do you know how to log in at school? 你知道怎么进入学校的计算机系统吗?

- I need to log in to a computer, how do I do that? 我需要登录计算机，应该怎么做？

操作很简单的：

- You just put in your username and password. 你只需要输入用户名和密码。

❖ log in 登录，注册，进入（计算机系统）

❖ password ['pæs,wɜːd] *n.* 口令，通行密码

Getting Familiar Conversation

Kevin:	It's weird being back in school.	凯　文：	回到学校感觉怪怪的。
Debra:	What do you mean?	黛布拉：	你什么意思？
Kevin:	Like, getting used to everything again.	凯　文：	比如，什么都要重新适应。
Debra:	I don't follow.	黛布拉：	我没明白。
Kevin:	It's rough to get used to studying, meeting new people, and taking notes. All of that stuff.	凯　文：	要习惯学习，又要认识新面孔、记笔记，所有这些事情都让人讨厌。
Debra:	Well, I guess I see your point, but isn't it better than working?	黛布拉：	噢，我想我明白你什么意思了，但是这样难道不比工作好一点？
Kevin:	Yeah, I guess so; it is a lot better than having to work.	凯　文：	是，我也这么认为。这比被逼着工作好多了。
Debra:	So, just think about that when you're doing all of that work.	黛布拉：	所以，当你做那些事情的时候就这么想想吧。
Kevin:	That's a good way of looking at it.	凯　文：	这倒是看待这种事情的一个好方法。
Debra:	I told you. Either way I'm sure you'll get back into the swing of things soon.	黛布拉：	我跟你说过。不论是哪一种方式，我肯定你很快就会熟悉这些事情的。

就这**900**句 玩转口语

| Kevin: You're right. | 凯　文：你说的对。 |

❖take notes 记笔记
❖see one's point 明白某人的意思
❖get back into the swing of sth. 熟悉某种情况，融入某种环境（非正式用法）

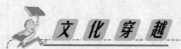
文 化 穿 越

　　对于每个中国留学生来说，刚来到美国校园是件兴奋又胆怯的事情。因为面前的一切都是未知数，不同的国家，不同的语言，不同的文化环境，但这是新生活的开始，也将会是人生中一段重要的旅程。来到校园的时候，一开始要少说多看多思考。其中有这么几点需要注意：一定准备个笔记本随时记录生活中不断出现的新事物的情况，尤其将自己马上需要完成的注册手续等事情记录下来，不然任何遗漏都会对后期的校园生活造成不便；每个学校都有自己的系统，学生拿到学生证后，用学生号登入系统，一切新生需要注册的内容都在里面；另外，住宿、手机、银行账户、保险，甚至 SSN(Social Security Number) 都要陆续办理。具体办理步骤在相关章节都会有详细介绍。

Section 2

学校课程
Curriculum

要开始选课了，面对这一大堆复杂的课程和那些都是生面孔的教授导师，我真不知道该选哪门课好，感觉这些课程都很难，直觉告诉我，比较难的课程我都不会喜欢的。但没办法，我是学生，不管我喜欢与否都是要学的，那就只有多下功夫了。相信大家的感觉也是和我一样的。

 口 语 大 放 送

1 Oh, man, I don't think I'm going to like this class. 噢，天哪，我觉得我不会喜欢这门课的。

我不喜欢这门课：

- This class seems pretty hard. I don't think I'll like it. 这门课好像很难，我觉得我不会喜欢的。
- I don't think I'm ready for this class. It seems hard! 我觉得我还没准备好学这门课程。看起来很难啊！

我也不喜欢，但没办法：

- Me either, but that's life I suppose. 我也是，但我想这就是生活吧。

那你别学好啦：

- Well, you can always drop it. 噢，你随时可以放弃这门课。

❖ drop [drɑp] vt. 停止，中断

2 How do I drop a class? 我该怎么退课呢?

我要退课：

- This class isn't for me. How can I drop it? 这门课不适合我，我该怎么退课呢?

解决方式：

- Just log in online and send a request to drop. 登录网站发个退课申请就行。

3 Is the class info online? 网上有课程信息吗？

还可以说明原因：

- I missed what the class info was. Is it online? 我错过了课程信息，网上有吗？

询问网上的资料：

- Can I find stuff about the class online somewhere? 我能在网上什么地方找到这门课的相关资料吗？

网上一般都有的：

- Yeah, just use the university web page. 有啊，查一下学校的网页就行了。
- ❖ info ['ɪnfo] *n.* 信息，消息

4 When's the test again? 下次考试是什么时候？

有点儿担心考试了：

- When is the test happening? 什么时候考试啊？
- When will we be taking the test? 我们什么时候考试啊？

根据你是否知道作出回答：

- Next Thursday. 下周四。
- I'm not sure. 我也不确定。

5 Did we have homework? 我们有课外作业吗？

具体说明：

- Did we get homework last class? 上节课我们有课外作业吗？

根据事实情况回答：

- No, I don't think so. 没有，我觉得没有。
- Yeah, we did. 有，有课外作业。

6 How long does that paper have to be? 那篇论文得写多长啊？

总是写论文：

- How long should our paper be? 我们的论文要写多长啊？
- How many pages does our paper need to be? 我们的论文需要写几页啊？

差不多就行了：

• Not many. I think six or so. 不是很多，我觉得差不多 6 页吧。

7 Have you got your work done for today? 今天的功课做完了吗？

也可以说：

• Did you finish your homework? 你完成作业了吗？

已经上交了：

• Yeah. I have handed it in to the professor. 是的，我已经交给教授了。

在电脑上做作业要注意：

• I finished my homework but then I deleted it by accident. 虽然我已经完成了作业，但后来不小心把它删除了。

• My computer crashed and I lost it. 电脑死机了，我做的作业（因没有保存）丢失了。

❖ hand in 上交，呈递

❖ crash [kræʃ] *vi.* 电脑死机

8 Why did you choose this course? 你为什么选这门课程？

换个动词表达：

• Why did you take this class? 你为什么选这门课？

讲讲原因：

• Because I will get lots of practice in speaking, and also in writing. 因为我会有很多练习会话和写作的机会。

❖ course [kɔːrs] *n.* 课程

9 I hope he goes over our homework. 我希望他批改了我们的作业。

感情强烈一点：

• I really hope he goes over the homework, I need it. 我真的希望他批改作业，我很需要。

附和一下：

• Me too. 我也是。

Curriculum Conversation

Kevin: This syllabus is pretty in-depth.	凯文：这个教学大纲真的很深奥，很详细。
Classmate: Yeah, it is. I hope this semester isn't too bad.	同学：是啊。我希望这个学期不要太糟糕。
Kevin: Well, it looks like we'll be writing a lot of papers.	凯文：噢，看起来我们要写很多论文。
Classmate: Yeah, but that isn't so bad. You don't have to think to write.	同学：是啊，但这还不是那么糟糕。你不需要去思考该怎么写。
Kevin: I guess you're right.	凯文：我想你是对的。
Classmate: I didn't introduce myself. My name is Julie.	同学：我还没有介绍自己呢，我叫朱莉。
Kevin: Hi, Julie, my name is Kevin.	凯文：你好，朱莉，我是凯文。
Julie: Nice to meet you, Kevin. What's your major?	朱莉：很高兴认识你，凯文。你学什么专业的？
Kevin: Well, I'm a history major, so I have to write almost constantly.	凯文：噢，我是学历史的，所以我几乎经常在写东西。
Julie: Oh, I see! I'm a criminal justice major. It's a lot of memorizing, basically.	朱莉：噢，我明白。我是刑事司法专业的。我主要要记很多东西。
Kevin: Well, that isn't so bad.	凯文：噢，不是那么糟糕啊。
Julie: No, but I think I would rather write.	朱莉：但是，我想我宁愿写东西。
Kevin: (laughs) You're crazy!	凯文：（笑）你疯了。

❖ syllabus [ˈsɪləbəs] *n.* 教学大纲

❖ major [ˈmedʒə] *n.* 专业，主修科目

❖ justice [ˈdʒʌstɪs] *n.* 司法制度，审判

文化穿越

　　美国的课程与中国的不太一样。美国的课程设置是名副其实的学分制。也就是说，每个学期都有学分的底线，每个学生必须修够规定的学分，而且保证成绩在及格以上。无论本科还是研究生都按照这个制度去实施。只不过研究生的课程较少，但课程密度大，论文和阅读没完没了，尤其是美国文科硕士很辛苦。本科课程较多，大概一学期要修 5～6 门课，但课程密度不是很大，一般只要保证期中和期末考试在及格以上就好。另外，美国按季度分为四个阶段，分别是春季学期，夏季学期，秋季学期，冬季学期。但一般夏季学期的课程较贵，一些想提前毕业的学生可以在夏季学期选几门课程，冬季学期情况类似。对于一般学生来说，主要是春季学期和秋季学期，因为很多学校招生也是按照这个制度来进行的，招生日期一过，就不再招收学生了。

Section 3  听讲座
Lecture

> 在学校上课，一些教授的讲座很有意思，所以也就让我有动手做笔记的欲望；可有些教授一讲就几个小时停不下来，让人听得昏昏欲睡的，也不知道该在哪里做笔记了。虽然 Kevin 有这个坏习惯，但还是希望朋友们在这一点上不要学习 Kevin，希望大家在以后的日子里帮 Kevin 改掉这个毛病，学习很重要。

1 I like the way this professor teaches. 我喜欢这个教授的讲课方式。

感情强烈一点：
- I really like how he teaches. 我真的很喜欢他讲课。

根据自己的感觉回答：
- Really? I'm not a fan. 真的吗？我可不是他的粉丝。
- Me too. He's very intellectual. 我也是，他真的很有才。
- ❖ intellectual [ˌɪntɪˈlɛkʃuəl] *adj.* 有才智的

2 These lectures are so boring. 这些讲座真无聊。

不喜欢这样的讲座：
- I'm not a fan of these lectures. 我不喜欢这些讲座。
- I don't like these lectures. They just go on and on! 我不喜欢这些讲座，总是没完没了的！

这些讲座确实没意思：
- I know what you mean. I would much rather actually do things. 我知道你什么意思。事实上，我宁愿去干点什么。

3 Professor Smith, can I ask you a question? 史密斯教授，我能问你一个问题吗？

更礼貌的说法：

- Could I ask you a question, Doctor Stafford? 我能问你一个问题吗，斯塔福德博士？

有什么就问吧：

- Sure, go ahead. 当然可以，问吧。

有点忙：

- No problem, but can it wait a little while? 没问题，但是等一小会儿行吗？

❖ go ahead（经某人允许）开始做

4 Could I get a copy of this lecture? 我可以备份这个讲座吗？

这样也行：

- Is there any way I could get a copy of our lecture? 有什么方法可以拿到我们讲座的备份吗？

很简单的事情：

- Yes, they're available online. 可以，网上就有。

5 How was today's lecture? 今天的讲座怎么样？

也可以说：

- How do you like the lecture? 你认为讲座怎么样？

还行吧：

- I think it was pretty good. 我觉得不错。

催眠曲啊：

- It was so boring that I fell asleep. 太无聊了，我都睡着了。

❖ fall asleep 入睡

6 What was the lecture about? 讲座是关于什么的？

回答讲座的内容：

- How to protect cultural legacies. It was really thought-provoking. 讲的是如何保护文化遗产，很发人深省。

- It was about how to improve your creativity. 讲座是关于如何提高你的创造力的。
- ❖ legacy['lɛgəsɪ] *n.* 遗产
- ❖ thought-provoking['θɔt-prə'vokɪŋ] *adj.* 发人深省的，引人深思的

7 Do you think it's useful to listen to a lecture? 你觉得听讲座管用吗？

不同的观点有不同的回答：

- I think so. 我觉得有用。
- I don't think so. 我不这样认为。

8 What lectures are there to be held this week? 这周有什么讲座啊？

可以具体回答：

- A series of lectures on Jane Austen. 关于简·奥斯汀的系列讲座。

如果你也不知道：

- I don't know. You can ask somebody else. 我不知道，你可以问问其他人。

Lecture Conversation

Kevin: Wow, this lecture has been going on for an hour.	凯文：哇，这讲座都进行了一个小时了。
Amber: Yeah, but I think it's pretty interesting.	安博：是啊，但是我觉得很有意思啊。
Kevin: I guess so. I'm just sick of listening.	凯文：我也这么想，我只是听烦了。
Amber: Me too. But this is what college is all about.	安博：我也是。但这就是大学啊。
Kevin: Yeah, yeah.	凯文：是啊，是啊。
Amber: Are you taking notes?	安博：你在做笔记吗？
Kevin: Yeah, but they're getting worse as time goes on.	凯文：是啊，时间越长我写得越乱。

Amber: That's OK. Just keep it!	安博：没事。继续写！
Kevin: I'm trying. How do you do that?	凯文：我在尽力。 你是怎么做到的呢？
Amber: Perseverance.	安博：坚持不懈。

❖keep at sth. 坚持干，继续做某事
❖perseverance ['pɜːsə'vɪrəns] n. 坚持不懈

文 化 穿 越

　　刚到美国的留学生可以准备一支录音笔，经过老师同意后，可以将讲课内容录下来回家研究。不过一般来说，适应能力快的学生三个月后基本上就可以听懂大部分内容。美国老师讲课的方式与中国老师不太一样，美国老师以提问为主，课堂参与是最后期末成绩评定的一个方面，有时甚至会占到总成绩的20%。因此，性格腼腆的中国留学生需要放开胆量在课上去参与讨论，不过一切讨论内容都基于老师课前留的阅读任务。只有好好思考阅读内容的学生，上课才有的可说。研究生教育更是以自学和讨论为主，老师只是引导和布置任务，课上老师所讲的内容也都是学生提问的内容。

Section 4 ▶ 在图书馆
At the Library

以前在学校，图书馆是我比较喜欢去的地方（我很好学的 ^_^）。我可以在那里看书、借书，还可以在那里学习、上网。可进入新的学校以后，图书馆的规定和设施都不同了，我也晕头转向了。还是问问身边的同学或者图书管理员吧。

口 语 大 放 送

1 Could you help me checking out a book? 你能帮我借本书吗？

询问别人借书：
- Could you help me with checking a book out? 你能帮我借本书吗？
- Do you know how to check out a book? 你知道怎么借书吗？

提供帮助：
- Sure, let me help you. 当然可以，我来帮你。

❖ check out（从图书馆）借书

2 Can you order *1984* for me? 你能帮我预定《1984》吗？

换种说法：
- I'm looking for *Animal Farm*. Could I place an order? 我在找《动物庄园》。我能预定一本吗？

参考回答：
- Sure. Could I see your ID? 好的。我能看一下你的借阅证吗？
- No problem. 没问题。

3 Where can I find the Biographies? 我在哪儿能找到传记类图书？

找其他的书：
- Where is the Fiction section? 小说区在哪儿？
- I'm looking for books on health care. 我在找医疗保健方面的书。

根据实际情况回答：

- Those are on the third floor. 在三楼。
- You can find those on the top floor. 你可以在顶层找到那些书。

❖ biography [baɪˈɑgrəfɪ] *n.* 传记

4 How do I get on the Internet? 我怎么上网？

在图书馆上网：

- Can you get on the Internet in here? 在这儿能上网吗？
- How do I log onto the Internet? 我怎么上网？

热心帮助：

- I'll help you out. 我会帮你解决这个问题。

5 I have a late book. What's the fee? 我有一本到期的书。应该交多少钱？

到期了，不会要罚款吧：

- Is there a late fee on this? 这本书有过期罚款吗？
- I kept this book out for a while. Is there a late fee? 这本书我多借了一段时间。有过期罚款吗？

遗憾地告诉你：

- Yes, you owe 25 cents. 是的，你欠 25 美分。

❖ late fee 滞纳金，过期罚款

6 What time does the library close? 图书馆几点关门？

不太确定的回答：

- I think it's open until 5 o'clock. 我觉得是到 5 点吧。
- I am not sure. Maybe at 6. 我也不确定，或许是 6 点。

7 I can't find that book in the stacks. 我在书库里找不到那本书。

你可以提出建议：

- You could probably get it through inter-library loan. 或许你能通过馆际互借拿到这本书。

- Maybe you have to buy one. 或许你只能买一本了。
- ❖ the stacks（图书馆贮藏使用频率较低的）书库
- ❖ inter-library loan 馆际互借，是图书馆之间根据协议，互相利用对方馆藏来满足本馆读者需求、开展馆际合作的一种形式。

8 Have you checked in the catalog under author and title? 你查过作者和书名目录了吗？

根据实际情况有不同的回答：

- Yeah. I know where to find the book that I want. 是啊。我知道去哪找我要的那本书。
- No. I forgot it. 没有，我忘了。
- ❖ catalog ['kætəlɒg] *n.* 目录

At the Library Conversation

Kevin:	Could you explain to me how to check out a book at the library?	凯　文：	你能跟我解释一下怎么从图书馆借书吗？
Clerk:	Sure, just take the book that you wish to check out to the counter.	管理员：	当然可以，只要把你想借的书拿到柜台来就可以了。
Kevin:	Oh, and they just scan it for you?	凯　文：	噢，他们就给扫描？
Clerk:	Yep, they'll take care of the rest. All you need is an ID.	管理员：	是的，他们会处理剩下的事情。你只需要身份证明。
Kevin:	Will my driver's license work?	凯　文：	驾驶执照可以吗？
Clerk:	Well, what I mean by ID is a library ID.	管理员：	噢，我说的身份证明是图书馆的借阅证。
Kevin:	How do I get one of those?	凯　文：	我怎么办理借阅证呢？
Clerk:	Well, I can sell one to you. They're only ten dollars.	管理员：	噢，我可以卖一张给你，只要 10 美元。
Kevin:	That seems fair, I suppose. Here you go.	凯　文：	我觉得好像很公道。给你钱。

| Clerk: And here you are. Thank you very much! | 管理员：给你，多谢！ |
| Kevin: Thank you! | 凯　文：谢谢你。 |

文 化 穿 越

　　国外正规大学都有很完备的图书馆。在图书馆里进行学术研究是很方便的。另外图书馆也提供很多学习房间，有的甚至是 24 小时开放的。有的学生学累了就在图书馆沙发上睡会儿，醒了后继续学，不过这事儿一般发生在期中和期末前后，那时图书馆爆满，其他时候很少看到美国学生的身影。很多大学图书馆之间都有合作，有的书在本校图书馆里找不到，学生就可以申请向其他图书馆借书，一般只需几天的时间图书馆就会帮学生找来需要的书。

Section 5 考试测验
Tests

怎么又是考试啊？每次考试都这么难，都让人头疼死了。Kevin 不喜欢考试，我相信大部分人的感觉都是一样的。不过作为学生，既然躲不过考试，那就好好学习吧，考好了有一种成就感，考差了也不要太在意，下次努力就好。在这里 Kevin 为自己也为大家祈祷通过人生的每一场考试。

1 Wow, that test was hard! 哇，测试好难啊！

测试好难：

- That test was so hard! 测试那么难！
- I can't believe how hard that test was. 我不敢相信测试怎么那么难啊。

没错，太难了：

- Yeah! It was crazy! 是啊！真是疯了。

2 Did you study for the test? 为了那个测试你学习了吗？

也可以说：

- Did you study at all? 你究竟学习了吗？

学了一晚上：

- Yeah, all night last night. 是啊，昨晚上熬了个通宵。

临时抱佛脚：

- Nope, just winged it. 没有，就是临场发挥的。

❖ nope [nop] *int.* 不，没有

❖ wing it 临时应付，即兴（非正式用法）

3 How do you think you did on the test? 你觉得这次测试你做得怎么样？

考得怎么样：

- What did you think of that test? 你认为那次考试怎么样?
- How do you think you did on the test? 你认为你考得怎么样?

不太好：

- Probably not that great. 可能不是很好。

试题难是学生永远的借口：

- It was so hard! 很难!

4 I hope we aren't tested on this. 我希望我们不要考这个。

考我们擅长的吧：

- I hope we don't get tested on this material! 我希望我们不考这种题材。
- I'm so bad at this. I hope we aren't tested on it. 我这方面很差，我希望我们不要考这个。

学生都不希望考试：

- Me too. I didn't understand it at all! 我也是，我根本就不懂。

5 I'm not ready for the test. 我还没有准备好考试。

考试前的准备很漫长：

- I am not ready for this test. 我还没有准备好这次考试。
- Since I am not fully prepared for the test I don't think I can pass. 我没有准备好考试，我想我过不了了。

感同身受：

- I hear ya. I feel the same way. 我知道，我也有同感。
- ❖ ya [ya:] 在口语中等于 you。

6 I can't find my notes for the open-book test. 我找不到我为开卷考试准备的笔记了。

同情一下：

- I'm sorry to hear that. 听到这个消息我很难过。

安慰并提供帮助：

- Take it easy. You can use mine. 别着急，你可以用我的。
- ❖ open-book test 开卷考试

277

7 I was so nervous about the test that I didn't sleep well last night. 对于这次考试我很紧张，昨晚没有睡好。

考试之前心慌慌：

- I'm pretty terrified to take this test. 我很害怕参加这次考试。
- I am worried about the test, so I scan the whole textbook last night. 我很担心这次考试，所以昨晚我把整本书浏览了一遍。

8 The final exam is just around the corner. 期末考试马上要来了。

考试没完没了：

- The test is coming. 要考试了。
- We are going to have a test. 我们会有一场考试。
- It's time for a test. 要考试了。
- ❖ around the corner 即将来临；在附近

Tests Conversation

Kevin: I don't think I did well on that test.	凯文：我觉得那次考试我考得很不好。
Julie: Me too. It was so hard!	朱莉：我也是。好难啊！
Kevin: I know. I didn't even study the right stuff.	凯文：我知道，我甚至都没有学对东西。
Julie: Well, at least we aren't the only ones.	朱莉：噢，至少我们并不是唯一考得不好的。
Kevin: Why do you say that?	凯文：你为什么那么说？
Julie: I saw people turning it in early because they didn't know what to put down.	朱莉：我看见有人很早交卷，因为他们不知道写什么。
Kevin: Oh, that is good. Maybe he'll curve the test grade then.	凯文：噢，那就好。也许老师会按比例加分。
Julie: Yeah, maybe, but I heard he's pretty strict with the grades.	朱莉：是啊，也许吧，但是我听说他给分很严格的。

Kevin: Oh, yeah? That isn't good. Now I'm really scared.	**凯文：** 噢，是吗？这可不好，现在我真的害怕了。
Julie: Oh, well, don't worry about it. Tests are just like that: you win some, you lose some.	**朱莉：** 噢，这个，不要担心。测试就是这样，有时你考得好，有时你考得不好。

❖turn in 上交，呈交

❖curve the test grade 把考试成绩按比例加分。

文 化 穿 越

　　考试对于美国留学生可以说是家常便饭。级别最低的随堂测试一般叫 Quiz，这种测试一般囊括上节课老师讲座中提及的内容，大部分也来源于笔记。第二级考试叫做 Test，一般指那种比较正式的小型考试，老师会发给学生们一张试卷，试卷上会有各种类型的题，有的老师喜欢出选择题，而有的老师喜欢出主观性问答题，学生在考试的时候跟抽彩券差不多，考什么题得看运气。不过，在挑选一门课程之前，可以先在这个网站上查查学生们对本课程老师的评价：http://ratemyprofessors.com。除此之外，期中和期末考试级别最高，分值相对较多。这也是美国学生一般在这两种考试前拼命看书的原因。

Section 6  奖学金
Scholarship

在学校能够申请到奖学金，那是我一直以来的愿望（Kevin 很有上进心的哦 *^__^*）。因为有奖学金不仅能减轻一下我的经济负担，还能让我偶尔出去旅游一下，放松在学校紧绷的神经。不过新学校的奖学金制度我还没有完全了解透彻，先去向同学打听打听吧。

① Do you qualify for any scholarships? 你有资格申请奖学金吗?

也可以说：

- Did you qualify for any scholarships this year? 今年你有资格申请奖学金吗?

根据情况回答：

- Yeah, a couple. 有啊，可以申请几个。
- Nope. 没有。
- ❖ qualify for sth. 有资格做某事

② Do you have a book of scholarships? 你有关于奖学金的书吗?

询问关于奖学金条款的书：

- I'm looking for scholarships. Do you have any books on them? 我想拿奖学金，你有这方面的书吗?

自己没有：

- I don't, but the library might. 我没有，但是图书馆可能有。
- ❖ look for sth. 期望，盼望

③ What do I need to qualify for this scholarship? 申请奖学金需要什么资格?

换种说法:

- Do you know what I need to do to qualify for this scholarship? 你知道我申请奖学金需要做些什么吗?

不确定:

- I'm not sure. Let me check. 我不确定,我来查一下。

④ I didn't get the scholarship I wanted! 我没有拿到我想要的奖学金!

没有拿到奖学金:

- They didn't pick me for the scholarship I wanted! 我想要的那个奖学金,他们没有给我!

很遗憾:

- That sucks, man. I'm sorry. 真糟糕,哥们。我很遗憾。

⑤ Do you know how much this scholarship pays? 你知道奖学金有多少钱吗?

或者这样问:

- Do you know how much you get with this scholarship? 你知道拿到的奖学金有多少钱吗?

不知道可以这样回答:

- I'm not sure. You'll have to look. 我不确定,你得自己看一下。

⑥ I have won the scholarship. 我得了奖学金。

高兴地祝贺:

- Congratulations! No wonder you are so excited. 恭喜你!难怪你这么兴奋。

表示怀疑:

- You have won the scholarship? I don't buy it. 你得了奖学金?我才不相信你的鬼话呢。
- ❖ no wonder 难怪……
- ❖ buy [baɪ] vt. 相信(尤指不太可能的事情,是非正式的用法)

⑦ What will you do if you can't get a full scholarship? 如果你拿不到全额奖学金你会怎么办?

也可以简单地说：

- What if you can't get a full scholarship? 拿不到全额奖学金怎么办？

信心十足：

- It will never happen. 这种事情不会发生的。

沮丧打消出国念头：

- If so, I won't go abroad and will go on my study here. 如果这样的话，我就不出国了，我将继续在这里的学业。

❖ a full scholarship 全额奖学金

8 I will consider studying abroad on the condition that I get a scholarship. 如果能得到奖学金，我会考虑出国留学。

如果没有奖学金，出国留学将是一笔很大的费用：

- If I obtain a scholarship, I will think of studying abroad. 如果我拿到奖学金，我会考虑出国留学。
- Only if they offer me a scholarship will I go abroad for further education. 只有他们给我提供奖学金，我才能出国进修。

Scholarship Conversation

Julie: Did you apply for any scholarships?	**朱莉：** 你申请奖学金了吗？
Kevin: No, not yet.	**凯文：** 没有，还没有。
Julie: Me either, but I think there are a few I might qualify for.	**朱莉：** 我也没有，但我想有几类奖学金我或许有资格申请。
Kevin: Oh, what ones?	**凯文：** 噢，是哪几类？
Julie: Well, my GPA was pretty high last year, so that's good.	**朱莉：** 噢，我去年的平均成绩很高，所以还不错。
Kevin: I'm jealous. I didn't do so hot last term.	**凯文：** 我真羡慕。我上学期表现没有那么好。
Julie: Yeah, but you might be able to get something from financial aid.	**朱莉：** 是啊，但是你也许能拿到一些助学金。

Kevin: That's true. How can I check?	凯文: 对啊。我怎样才能查到?
Julie: I have a big book of scholarships; I'll show it to you.	朱莉: 我有一本奖学金的大书,我拿给你看。
Kevin: Alright, sounds good. Thanks!	凯文: 好的,听起来不错。谢谢!

❖GPA = Grade Point Average 平均分数
❖financial aid（高等院校的）助学金,助学贷款

文 化 穿 越

　　一般美国的高校都有两种学生奖励机制。一种是奖学金,这一种是颁发给那些学术以及成绩优秀的学生的,分为半奖和全奖。半奖一般是免除学费,但生活费自理。全奖当然就是全部包括,当然机票不算在内。另一种是助学金,这种机制比较复杂,其中美国学生和国际学生的申请机制是不一样的,美国本土学生可以获得更多的钱。助学金一般是对于学生参与学术研究或交流的一种经济上的支持。比如,研究生到别的州去参加会议,就可以申请这种助学金报销旅程的住宿和交通费用。对于其他国家正在申请的学生来说,美国的奖学金是比较难获得的。美国学校会有定量的名额给十分优秀的理科生,除此之外就是美国文科极冷的专业,为了增加更多的生源,会有一定量的奖学金名额。但是,一般情况下,来到美国留学之后,在第二学期或者第二学年申请到奖学金和助学金的几率比较大。因此,没有拿到奖学金的学生别灰心,因为第二学期和第二学年还是有机会的。

Section 7 ▶ 社团协会
School Association

告诉大家一件事情，就是在学校的时候千万不要错过学校社团或俱乐部的活动。看起来你好像要花很多时间在上面，但实际上，你的收获可能更多。你可以在那里认识不同的同学和朋友，更重要的是锻炼自己各方面的能力。所以，朋友们，和我一起去参加学校的社团协会吧！

口 语 大 放 送

1 Do you have a list of clubs? 你有俱乐部的单子吗?

询问学校的俱乐部：
- I am curious about what all of the clubs on campus are. 我想知道学校都有什么俱乐部。

告诉信息的来源：
- Yeah, you can pick it up at the main office. 是啊，你可以在总办公室拿到单子。

2 Do you know when the Club Rush is happening? 你知道俱乐部纳新是什么时候吗?

换种说法：
- I want to join some clubs. Do you know when they're having the rush? 我想参加一些俱乐部，你知道他们什么时候招人吗？

回答具体时间：
- I think it's this Saturday actually. 我想，应当是这周六。
- ❖ rush [rʌʃ] n. 学生联谊会纳新活动（时间）

3 I got promoted to president of my club! 我被提升为俱乐部主席了!

升职的感觉不错:

- I got promoted in my club! Awesome! 我在俱乐部升职了, 太棒了!

表示祝贺:

- Good to hear, man! 听上去不错, 伙计!

4 I got asked to join the Film Club. 我被邀请参加电影俱乐部。

加入别的俱乐部:

- They asked me to join the Soccer Club. 他们让我加入足球俱乐部。

反问对方:

- So did you join? 那你加入了吗?

表达自己的感受:

- I hate that club! 我讨厌那个俱乐部!

5 I'm thinking of leaving the club I'm in. 我正考虑离开现在的俱乐部。

找个离开的理由:

- I want to leave the club I'm in. I'm too busy. 我想离开我现在所在的俱乐部, 我太忙了。

表示理解:

- I don't blame you. School work is more important. 我不怪你, 学习更加重要。
- ❖ I don't blame you. 我不会责怪你。

6 What activities does the Film Club have? 电影协会都有什么活动?

列举一些活动:

- Watching movies, discussing plots, changing DVDs and so on. 看电影, 讨论剧情, 交换 DVD 等等。
- ❖ plot [plɑt] *n.* 情节

7 What should I do if I want to join the Novel Club? 如果我想加入小说协会, 我需要做点什么?

简单而明确的回答：
- Just hand in 5 dollars. 只需要交 5 美元。
- Just go to the office and register. 去办公室注册一下就可以了。
- ❖ register ['redʒɪstə] vi. 登记，注册

8 Would you like to join the Volunteers' League? 你想参加志愿者联盟吗？

根据是否加入作出回答：
- Yes, I'd like to. 是的，我想参加。
- No. I think it will cost much time. 不，我认为加入会花费我太多时间。

School Association Conversation

Kevin: I'm thinking of joining the Student Government Association on campus.	凯文：我正考虑加入学校的学生会。
Julie: Really? That's a lot of work.	朱莉：真的吗？那可是要做很多工作的啊。
Kevin: Yeah, but I think it'll pay off for me.	凯文：是啊，但是我觉得会得到回报的。
Julie: Well, it'll at least look good on a resume someday.	朱莉：嗯，至少将来有一天把它放到简历上看起来不错。
Kevin: Yeah, that's what I'm thinking.	凯文：是啊，我也是这么想的。
Julie: Well, if you look at it that way I think, you should go for it, definitely.	朱莉：噢，如果你的看法和我一致的话，你应该去努力争取，一定要争取。
Kevin: I probably will. I'm just being lazy about it for now.	凯文：我可能会的，只是现在我有点懒散。
Julie: I used to be part of the Video Game Club on campus.	朱莉：我以前是学校电子游戏俱乐部的成员。
Kevin: Somehow I don't think that's quite as prestigious.	凯文：反正我认为这个没有什么值得赞誉的。

Julie: You might be right.　　　　朱莉：或许你是对的。

❖ the Student Government Association　美国大学里的学生会
❖ prestigious [presˈtɪdʒɪəs] *adj.* 有名望的，声誉高的

文 化 穿 越

　　美国学校社团比较红火。一般在新学期会有很多的社团招新，能想象到的主题社团都会涉及，因此，学生可以根据自身兴趣去挑选社团。除此之外，美国学校还有很多学生政治机构，例如学生会，学生政委等，里面的很多职位都是面向全校学生竞选的，有点像美国总统大选，每个人都有机会参选。另外，每个大学都会有各种国际学生社团，中国学生会一般都比较庞大，刚来的中国学生可以加入这个社团寻求一些帮助。

Section 8 ▶ 宿舍花絮
Dorm

在学校住宿舍对于中国的学生来说也许是理所当然的事情，可是在美国，学生宿舍是比较紧俏的，学校需要通过抽签决定谁能够住进去。并且每座宿舍楼可能有不同的规定，以满足学生不同的兴趣。比如说，有的宿舍楼也许会被指定为"24小时安静"的楼，以满足那些比较勤奋的学生的需要；另一些宿舍楼对噪音的规定也许不那么严格，以满足比较爱热闹的学生的生活方式。Kevin 建议大家在搬进一座宿舍楼前，弄清楚这座楼的规定，以免住进去后产生不悦或者误解。

1 Where are the dorm buildings? 宿舍楼在哪里?

宿舍楼在哪里：
- I'm curious about where the dorm buildings are. 我想知道宿舍楼在哪里。

指明方向：
- They're right down the road. 沿着这条路走就行。

2 Do you know what room I was assigned? 你知道我被分到哪个房间了吗?

礼貌询问：
- Could you tell me what room I'm in? 你能告诉我我在哪个房间吗?

热心回答：
- Sure, 253. 当然，你在 253 号。

3 I hope my roommate is nice. 我希望我的室友好相处。

有个好室友是件幸事：

- Hopefully I'll get along with my roommate. 希望我能和室友相处得好。

和室友相处不好很麻烦：

- Yeah, that can be a disaster. 是啊，这可能是个大麻烦。

4 I want to change the room. 我想换寝室。

直接问做法：

- What do I need to do to change the room? 换寝室需要做些什么？

给出建议：

- I think you just need to talk to the RA. 我觉得你只要告诉宿舍管理员就可以了。

❖ RA = Resident Assistant 宿舍管理员

5 Who is our RA? 谁是我们的宿舍管理员？

具体哪个楼层：

- Who's the RA on this floor? 谁是这一层的宿舍管理员？

我也不确定：

- I'm not sure. Let's go check. 我不清楚，咱们去核实一下吧。

❖ go do 在口语中可以这样用，可以不加 to。

6 Which bunk do you want? 你想要哪个铺位？

这时候不要客气，选自己喜欢的：

- I want the one by the door. 我想要挨着门的那个。
- The bottom bunk by the window. 挨着窗户的下铺。

无所谓：

- Anyone is OK. 哪个都行。

❖ bunk [bʌŋk] _n._ 架式床铺，铺位

7 How many people are there in your dorm? 你们宿舍几个人？

具体回答：

- Four including me. 包括我一共四个人。
- Three now. But a new student is going to move in next week. 现在三个，但是下周一位新同学会搬进来。

8 How much do you pay for the accommodation each year? 你每年要交多少钱的住宿费？

可以直接回答：

- Maybe 500 dollars for a dorm like this. 像这样的宿舍大概是 500 美元。

可以概述：

- It all depends. Different kinds of dorms have different charges. 视情况而定。不同的宿舍收费不同。

❖ accommodation [ə,kamə'deʃən] *n.* 住处，膳宿

 交 流 面 对 面

Dorm Conversation

Kevin: So you live in the dorms?	凯文：你住在宿舍？
Julie: Yeah, I just moved in this semester.	朱莉：是啊，我这学期刚搬进去。
Kevin: How is that working out for you?	凯文：你感觉住宿舍怎么样啊？
Julie: It's pretty good; it's hard to adjust to it though.	朱莉：很不错，只是很难适应。
Kevin: I know what you mean. It can't be easy to go from a house to a small room.	凯文：我明白你的意思。从一座房子换到一个小房间不容易。
Julie: It isn't, but it's also nice to be out of your own.	朱莉：是不容易，但是搬出自己的房子也不错。
Kevin: How's your roommate?	凯文：你的室友怎么样？
Julie: She's nice. We're pretty different but I think it keeps things interesting.	朱莉：她很好。我们有很大差异，但是我认为差异让事情变得有趣。
Kevin: Well, at least you're positive.	凯文：噢，至少你很乐观。

Julie: Yeah, I think I have to be or I would never make it here!	朱莉：是啊，我想我必须这样，要不然我也来不了这里。

❖ work out 产生结果
❖ make it 成功

文化穿越

　　美国宿舍文化很有意思。一般情况下，学校的住宿都比校外的租房要贵，因为学校的设施比较齐全，而且不用考虑水电等问题。校内一般有两种宿舍，一种是标准的男生宿舍和女生宿舍，还有一种是男女共同一层的混住公寓，当然公共卫生间是分开的。在学校里住宿学生可以选择单间和合租，合租的话一般是两个人，在一起住之前需要签订一些学校存档文件，包括财产的所有权等等。有一点需要注意，就是室友之间需要有一些底线的原则，例如，在对方不在房间的情况下，切勿将自己的朋友单独留在房间内。

Section 9 ▶ 校园兼职
Part-time Job

边上学边做兼职工作，虽然说能锻炼自己的工作能力，增长见识，还能补充一下自己的花销，但什么事情都有两方面，兼职工作也占用了我很多学习时间，而且快要毕业了，还有很多论文等着要写呢。因此，我现在有些矛盾了，是继续兼职呢，还是一心一意学习？朋友们，帮我出个主意吧。

1 Do you know if anywhere is hiring? 你知道哪里招人吗?

找兼职:
- I'm looking for a job. Do you know anyone who's hiring? 我在找工作，你知道有谁招人吗?

不太清楚:
- I don't know actually, sorry. 事实上，我不知道。不好意思。
- Sorry. I'm not sure. 对不起，我不知道。

2 I hate this job! 我讨厌这份工作。

不喜欢这份工作:
- I don't like this job. 我不喜欢这份工作。
- I can't bear this job. 我不能忍受这份工作了。

3 I need some money. 我需要一些钱。

急需用钱，所以得找份兼职:
- I'm really desperate for money right now. 我目前真的急需用钱。

提供帮助：

- If I hear anything I'll definitely let you know. 如果我听说什么消息，我一定会告诉你的。

❖ desperate ['dεspərɪt] *adj.* 极度渴望的

4 I need to quit my job. 我要辞职。

理由明确：

- I'm doing bad in school because of my job. 由于工作，我在学校表现不好。

给出意见：

- So you should quit it! 那你应该放弃工作。

5 I'd like to move from full time to part time. 我想从全职转为兼职。

指出目的和原因：

- I really need to cut my hours at work so I have time for school. 我真的需要减少工作时间，那样我才有时间来学习。

表示遗憾：

- I'm sorry to hear that. We'll see what we can do. 我很遗憾听你这么说，我们会看一下能做些什么。

6 How's work? 工作怎么样?

感觉良好：

- Great! I am sure I can earn enough to pay for my tuition. 好极了！我肯定能赚够钱交学费。

特别忙：

- So busy I don't even have time to catch my breath. 忙得我连喘口气的工夫都没有。

❖ catch one's breath 休息一下，歇口气（非正式的用法）

7 I enjoy working with my new boss very much. 我很喜欢和我的新老板一起工作。

和老板相处愉快：
- I am getting along with my new boss. 我和我的新老板相处愉快。
- ❖ get along with sb. 与某人和谐相处

8 Do you know how to find a part-time job? 你知道怎么找兼职工作吗？

给出建议：
- There are a lot of ads on the notice boards around campus. 学校的布告栏上有好多这样的广告。
- I hear the bookstore nearby want a salesgirl. You can go there for details. 我听说附近的书店想要一个女售货员。你可以去问问具体情况。

 交流面对面

Part Time Job Conversation

Kevin:	Having a job and going to school at the same time is so hard.	凯　文：	边工作边上学真是太难了。
Steve:	How so?	史蒂夫：	怎么说？
Kevin:	Well, I have so much that I have to do every day.	凯　文：	噢，我每天都有那么多事情要做。
Steve:	Well, sure, but don't you like it more than having a full-time job?	史蒂夫：	噢，当然，但是比起全职工作来说你难道不喜欢吗？
Kevin:	That's true. I do like this much better.	凯　文：	那倒是，我更喜欢这样。
Steve:	Told you, I'm right.	史蒂夫：	我就说吧，我是对的。
Kevin:	But still, I can't focus on my schoolwork with this job.	凯　文：	但是有这份工作，我还是不能把精力集中在学习上。
Steve:	Then quit. School is much more important.	史蒂夫：	那就辞职吧，学习更重要。
Kevin:	Do you think I should? Really?	凯　文：	你认为我该辞职？真的？
Steve:	I do.	史蒂夫：	我是这么认为的。

文化穿越

　　学校兼职需要注意一点。就是 SSN（Social Security Number）的申请。美国法律规定，国际留学生在美国一周可以合法工作 18 小时，但这个小时限制是在有 SSN 合法工作下的。一般所谓的黑工是没有限制的，但一旦被美国相关部门发现，很可能会被遣送回国。办理 SSN，学生需要带着自己的护照和 I-20（I-20 是美国学校发给外国学生用来申请签证好进入美国的通行证。上面载明了持该表学生就读的学校、系所、准予合法在美国居留的期限等重要事项。）以及工作申请表到国际学生处开证明信，之后到相关部门递上申请和证明信。大概等待几周后，SSN 办公室会将 SSN 卡寄给你。拿到这个卡之后，就可以合法工作了。需要注意的是，SSN 和护照以及 I-20 这几样东西是绝对不能丢的，另外 SSN 也不能随便给别人看或者复印。

Section 10 ▶ 毕业舞会
Graduation and Prom

终于等到这一天，等到这一刻了，我们毕业啦！同学之间互相祝贺，家人和远方的亲朋好友也以各种形式送上他们美好的祝福。Kevin 真的很感谢大家在这期间给予的关心和照顾。马上就要各奔前程了，还真有点舍不得。那就借这个机会，咱们出去聚聚，为庆祝咱们毕业，也庆祝咱们的友谊。

1 I love the end of a semester! 我喜欢学期末。

期末真好：
- It's so nice to be at the end of the semester! 期末真好啊！

可以放假喽：
- I know! I love it. 我知道！我喜欢期末。
- ❖ semester [sə'mestə] *n.* 学期

2 I hope I did well this semester! 我希望这学期我学得不错。

总结这学期的表现：
- Hopefully I did alright this semester. 希望这学期我干得还可以。

自己没有好好表现：
- Well, I know I didn't. 噢，我知道我没有好好干。

心里没底：
- Me too. The anxiety is killing me. 我也是，我快担心死了。

3 Congratulations on graduating! 祝贺你毕业了！

随意一点地表扬：
- Great job this semester! 这学期干得不错！

客套回应：
- Thank you! 谢谢！

4 You can check your final grades online. 你可以在网上查最终成绩。

也可以直接说：
- The final grades will be available online. 网上有最终成绩。

5 I hope my GPA is higher now. 我希望我的平均成绩现在高一点了。

担心分数：
- I really tried to get my GPA up. I hope it worked! 我真的努力提高平均成绩了，希望有效。

6 Would you have a dance with me? 你愿意和我跳支舞吗？

欣然同意：
- Alright. 好的。

有约在先：
- Sorry. I'm engaged for the social dance. 对不起，这支交谊舞我已经有约了。
- ❖ engage [ɪn'gedʒ] *vt.* 预定

7 When does the ball begin? 舞会几点开始？

询问舞会时间：
- What time does the dance begin? 舞会几点开始？

直接回答时间：
- At 7 o'clock. 七点。

如果你不知道：
- Sorry. I don't know. 不好意思，我不知道。
- I am not sure. Maybe 6. 我不确定，大概是 6 点。

8 Where can I get my cap and gown? 我到哪里领学士服和帽子呢？

自己想办法：

- You can have them made or rent them. 你可以定做也可以租。

我也不知道：

- I don't know. We'd better turn to the advisor for help. 我也不知道。我们最好找辅导员帮忙。
- ❖ cap [kæp] *n*. (大学师生在特别场合戴的) 方帽
- ❖ gown [gaun] *n*. (大学生在特别仪式上穿的) 长袍

Graduation and Prom Conversation

Kevin: Finally! I'm done with this semester!	凯文：终于完了！我终于过完这个学期了！
Julie: Woohoo! It's been quite a ride.	朱莉：啊！真像一段旅行。
Kevin: Yeah, it has, but it feels so good to be done with.	凯文：是啊，没错，但是结束了感觉真好。
Julie: I know what you mean; I can't wait to finally take a break!	朱莉：我明白你的意思。终于可以休息了，我都等不及了。
Kevin: Well, we can't slack off too much; we have a few more semesters to go.	凯文：噢，我们不能太放松，还有更多的学期没过呢。
Julie: (laughs) That's true! Don't bring me down now, though!	朱莉：（笑）没错！但是现在别泼我冷水！
Kevin: Alright, alright. I won't!	凯文：好吧，好吧。我不会的！
Julie: Hey, do you want to grab some food to celebrate?	朱莉：嗨，你想随便去吃点东西庆祝一下吗？
Kevin: I'd love to. Want to go to the bar after?	凯文：想啊。之后想再去酒吧吗？
Julie: Sounds good to me!	朱莉：正合我意！

❖ slack off 松懈，懈怠
❖ grab [græb] *vt*. (尤指匆忙地) 取，拿，吃

文 化 穿 越

　　毕业对于每个学生来说都是一件令人激动的盛事。美国家庭十分注重毕业典礼，甚至有的家庭会全体出动参加孩子的毕业典礼。对于中国学生来说，这是个让家长顺利拿到 VISA 到美国探亲的不错的借口。美国学校的毕业典礼一般很隆重，参与者大部分着装正式，毕业学生一律都穿学位服到讲台上领取自己的学位。当学生的名字被念到的时候，亲友团们会在底下尖叫欢呼，整个场面激动人心。

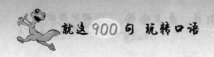

Section 11 ▶ 出国留学
Studying Abroad

虽然毕业了，但我还有另外一个学习计划，我打算出国学习一段时间，也顺便体验一次国外旅游（旅游才是最终目的吧？~(@^_^@)~，这是我心底的秘密，不要这么快就说出来哦）。其实对于这次出国学习，我心里有些激动，也有些担心。朋友们，加油吧，和 Kevin 一起体验留学的生活。

① I can't wait to travel and study! 我等不及去旅行和学习了！

外出留学很激动：
- I'm so excited to study in another country! 要去另一个国家学习，我很激动！

② I wonder what it'll be like in Europe. 我想知道欧洲是什么样的。

换个国家：
- I wonder what China is like. 我想知道中国是什么样子的。

简单概述：
- I'm sure it'll be great! 我相信会很棒！

③ Do you know what studying abroad programs will be available this year? 你知道今年有什么可以申请的出国学习项目吗？

请求帮助：
- I'd like to study abroad. Can you help me? 我想出国学习，你能帮我吗？

提供帮助：
- Sure, here's a pamphlet on it! 当然可以，这里有一个有关这方面的小册子。
- ❖ pamphlet ['pæmflɪt] *n.* 小册子

4 I like studying in another country, but I miss home. 我喜欢在另一个国家学习，但是我想家。

在异国他乡想家了：

- I don't think I'm going through culture shock. I miss my home. 我觉得我克服不了文化冲击，我想家。
- ❖ culture shock 文化冲击

5 I can't wait to get back and tell everyone! 我迫不及待想回去告诉每个人！

要回家喽：

- I'm excited to get home and talk about my trips! 要回家并讲讲我的旅行，我很激动！

6 What do you want to study? 你想学什么？

明确回答：

- I hope to study American literature. 我想学美国文学。

模糊答案：

- I am interested in several majors. I haven't made a final decision yet. 我对几个专业感兴趣，还没有作最后决定呢。

7 Do you have any catalogues from U. S. universities? 你们有没有美国大学的概况手册？

如果有：

- Yeah. Here you are. 有啊，给你。

没有：

- No. But we have catalogues from New Zealand. 没有，但是我们有新西兰大学的概况一览表。
- ❖ catalogue [ˈkætələg] n. 大学概况一览

8 Are you applying to study or work abroad? 你是申请去国外学习还是工作？

或者直接问：
- Why do you want to go abroad? 你为什么想出国？

根据实际情况回答：
- I want to study abroad. 我想出国留学。

 交流面对面

Studying Abroad Conversation

Kevin: Guess what!	凯文：猜猜看！
Julie: What?	朱莉：什么？
Kevin: I'm eligible to study abroad next term!	凯文：下学期我有资格出国学习了！
Julie: Really? Where to?	朱莉：真的吗？去哪里？
Kevin: To Chile, to help build communities and learn about their culture.	凯文：去智利，帮助建立社区，也学习他们的文化。
Julie: That sounds incredible! I'm so jealous.	朱莉：听起来太不可思议了！我好羡慕。
Kevin: It is, but I'm worried I won't be able to get a passport or visa.	凯文：是啊，但是我担心我拿不到护照或者签证。
Julie: Don't worry. The school will help you with those things.	朱莉：别担心，学校会帮你解决这些事情的。
Kevin: I guess you're right. I'm a little nervous though.	凯文：我想你是对的。不过我有一点紧张。
Julie: I would be too, but I'm sure you'll do fine.	朱莉：我也会紧张的，但是我肯定你会做好的。

❖ eligible ['ɛlɪdʒəbl] *adj.* 有资格的
❖ jealous ['dʒɛləs] *adj.* 妒忌的，羡慕的
❖ community [kə'mjunətɪ] *n.* 社区

文化穿越

　　留学在近些年可以说十分流行。家长对自己的孩子都抱有很大期望，希望孩子可以经过国外的历练变得成熟稳重，拥有一个精彩的人生和一份成功的事业。本人认为，留学的意义或许不在于学到的知识，更在于个人对于人生的一种看法的升华。一切眼泪欢笑都会成为人生中挥之不去的回忆与财富。当然，留学也要因人而异，不是所有孩子都适合留学。但最根本的一点在于孩子自身是否愿意去留学，是否愿意承受那份独立与孤独并存的生活。

Section 12 ▶ 签证与护照
Visa and Passport

出国留学首先要办的一件事是申请签证和护照。这可能需要一段比较长的时间，所以提醒各位出国留学的朋友早作准备，免得临时慌乱。同时，也建议大家在申请签证和护照的时候要了解清楚相关规定和条款，以免出现差错耽误时间。

1 Do you know how to apply for a visa? 你知道怎么申请签证吗?

请求帮助：
- I need a visa. Can you help? 我需要签证，你能帮忙吗?

给出指导：
- Sure, start by going to their website. 当然可以，先去他们的网站。
- ❖ visa [ˈviːzə] *n.* 签证

2 Do I need a visa to study abroad? 去国外留学需要签证吗?

换个问法：
- Will I need a visa for this? 这个需要签证吗?

肯定回答：
- Yes, you will. 是的，你需要。

3 How much does it cost to apply for a passport? 申请护照要花多少钱?

不同的表述：
- Do you know how much does this cost? 你知道这个要花多少钱吗?

4 What forms of ID will I need to apply for my passport? 申请护照我需要什么形式的身份证明?

明确答复:

- I believe just 2 forms of photo ID. 我认为只要两种形式的有照片的身份证明就行。

5 Where do I go to apply for a visa? 我去哪儿申请签证?

礼貌询问:

- Do you know where I go to apply for a visa? 你知道去哪里申请签证吗?

乐意帮忙:

- Yeah, I'll take you there if you need. 知道,如果你需要的话我带你去。

6 Do you know where the visa office is? 你知道签证处在哪儿吗?

指路:

- Yeah, just walk along this street and turn left at the first crossing. 知道啊, 沿着这条街走, 第一个路口向左拐。

你问警察吧:

- No. You can ask that policeman there. 不知道。你可以问问那边的那个警察。

❖ visa office 签证处

7 Have you ever been denied a visa before? 你以前签证有被拒绝过吗?

如果有:

- Yes. I was denied my visa when I apply. 有,我申请的时候被拒签过。

没有:

- Never. 从来没有。

❖ deny [dɪˈnaɪ] *vt.* 拒绝

8 I don't need a visa to go to Spain, do I? 我去西班牙不需要签证吧, 需要吗?

> 需要签证：
> - I am afraid you need a visa. 恐怕你需要签证。
>
> 不用签证：
> - Fortunately you don't. 很幸运你不需要。

Visa and Passport Conversation

Kevin: I need to get my passport so I can fly to Chile.

凯文：我需要护照才能飞往智利。

Julia: Where do you get it?

朱莉：你在哪儿拿到护照呢？

Kevin: Actually, I'm not too sure.

凯文：事实上，我也不清楚。

Julia: You should probably find that out.

朱莉：或许你应该把这个搞清楚。

Kevin: Well, I do know it costs a hundred dollars.

凯文：噢，我只知道它得花100美元。

Julia: Wow! That's so expensive.

朱莉：哇！这么贵。

Kevin: It is, but it's worth it.

凯文：是贵，但是值这个钱。

Julia: How about a visa?

朱莉：那签证呢？

Kevin: I have to apply for one, but I'm not too worried about it.

凯文：我得申请一个，但是我并不担心这个。

Julia: Well, I wish you luck, man. I'm gonna miss you.

朱莉：噢，祝你好运，伙计。我会想你的。

Kevin: I'll miss you too.

凯文：我也会想你的。

文化穿越

　　对于想去美国的中国朋友，办理护照一般是在当地的公安出入境管理局。至于美国 VISA 的办理，需要出国人员本人亲自去。一般办理 VISA 前需要到美国使馆网站上下载相关表格，填完后去中信银行缴纳一定的签证费用，还要买使馆的预约电话卡。手续全部办完后，需要打电话给使馆预约签证时间，一定注意要提前预约，甚至提前半个月或者更久，因为有时候预约人数较多，不容易预约到理想的时间。当天去签证需要着装正式，大概要排 3 个小时的队，不过这取决于当天签证的人数是否多。签证官问问题时，切勿多说话，有问有答即可。如 VISA 通过，签证官会发给申请人一张小条，上面是领签证的具体时间和地点等注意事宜。

Chapter 9 Kevin 的爱情
Love

Section 1

约会
Dating

　　我曾经很喜欢一个女孩,总是梦想着和她在一起。每次见到她,我就特别开心,没有她的日子总感觉心里空落落的,好像生活中缺了点什么。终于有一天,我鼓起勇气,邀请她出去约会。

1 I really like you. 我真的喜欢你。

类似的说法还有:

- I like you a lot. 我很喜欢你。
- I think you're cool. I really like you. 我觉得你太酷了,我真的喜欢你。

如果你刚好也喜欢对方, 就可以趁机表白:

- That's sweet. I like you too. 太好了, 我也喜欢你。
- Really? That's really nice of you to say. I like you too. 真的吗? 你这么说真是太好了, 我也喜欢你。

2 Do you want to go on a date? 你想去约会吗?

还可以试探着问:

- I was wondering if you'd like to go on a date. 我想知道你是否想去约会。

或者更直白一点:

- Let's go on a date sometime. 咱们什么时候去约会吧。

如果你也愿意就可以回答:

- Sure, I'd love that. Tell me when you're free. 好啊, 我很想去。告诉我你什么时候有空。

如果你不喜欢这个人, 就可以拒绝:

- I don't think we should go on a date. 我觉得我们不该去约会。
- ❖ go on a date 约会

3 Will you go out with me? 你愿意和我约会吗?

类似的说法还有:

- Do you want to date? 你想约会吗?

你同意的话直接说"yes",如果你不愿意,拒绝就可以了:

- I don't think I want to date you. Sorry. 我觉得我不想和你约会,对不起。

4 Will you be my girlfriend? 你愿意做我的女朋友吗?

愿意的话就赶紧答应啊:

- Of course, I'd love to be your girlfriend. 当然,我很愿意做你的女朋友。
- Yeah, we can be boyfriend and girlfriend. 好啊,我们可以是男女朋友。
- I'd really like that. Yes, I'll be your girlfriend. 我喜欢这样,好的,我愿意做你的女朋友。

但如果你不喜欢这个人,就可以拒绝:

- I just want to be friends. I hope that's okay. 我只是想做普通朋友,我希望那样就好。

5 Let's go to dinner tonight. 咱们今天晚上去吃饭吧。

也可以征询意见:

- We can go to dinner tonight if you want. 如果你愿意的话我们今晚上就去吃饭。

有这样的好事,那就赶紧去吧:

- That sounds good. When do you want to pick me up? 听上去不错,你什么时候来接我?

当然你也可以找理由拒绝:

- I'm sorry, I'm busy tonight. 不好意思啊,我今天晚上很忙。
- ❖ pick sb. up 接某人

6 I'll pick you up at 6. 我六点钟来接你。

相同的说法还有：

- I'll come to get you at 6. 我六点钟来接你。

还可以更殷勤一点：

- I'll come by whenever you're ready. 你什么时候准备好我就过来。

对于对方的热情，你应该表示一下：

- Thanks. See you then! 谢谢，到时候见！

7 I had a great time tonight, thank you. 我今天晚上玩得很高兴，谢谢你。

还可以这样说：

- That was great. Thanks for hanging out with me tonight. 太棒了，谢谢你今天晚上出来陪我一起玩。

如果你觉得确实还不错，就可以说：

- I had fun too. Thanks for everything! 我也玩得很高兴，谢谢你所做的一切。

为下一次约会做铺垫：

- It was fun. We should go out again later this week. 太好玩了，我们应当在本周晚些时候再出来玩一次。

Dating Conversation

Linda: Thanks for dinner, that restaurant was amazing!

琳达：谢谢你的晚餐，那家饭店很棒！

Kevin: I thought you'd like it. I'll take you there again sometime.

凯文：我就知道你会喜欢的。改天我再带你去那儿。

Linda: That'd be awesome. What do you want to do now?

琳达：那太好了。你现在想干什么？

Kevin: We could go to see a movie or go to the arcade.

凯文：我们去看场电影或者去拱廊街道逛逛吧。

Linda: I'm not sure what I want to do...

琳达：我不确定我想干什么……

Kevin: Do you want to get home early?

凯文：你想早点儿回家？

Linda: Definitely not, I'm having way too much fun with you!

琳达：当然不想，和你在一起我玩得特高兴！

Kevin: I'm having fun too! Do you want me to decide on what we should do?

凯文：我也很快乐！你想让我决定我们该做什么吗？

Linda: I'd like to go to the arcade, if that's okay.

琳达：如果可以的话，我想去拱廊街道。

Kevin: Awesome! Arcade it is, then. Let's go.

凯文：太好了！那就拱廊街道了，咱们走吧。

❖arcade [ar'ked] n. 拱廊街道

文化穿越

  与美国人约会要注意细节。首先，在一些正式场合，是比较讲究着装的，参加非正式的 PARTY 穿着可以比较随意，但是正式的宴会或者高档餐厅，穿正装会比较好一些。另外，领带或领结是需要佩戴的。最好不要迟到，如果可能会迟到，需要给对方提前打个电话告知一声，别让对方等。

  约会的地点一般取决于约会的性质，如果是和异性，第一次正式约会要避免去对方家里或者偏僻的地方，不然对方很有可能拒绝你；如果是和同性，就更不能随便往家里请，即使关系再好，两个同性经常在一起腻味，会被误会性取向有问题，因此，需要保持一定距离，这与国内情况不同。

Section 2 ▶ 爱恋
Falling in Love

告诉大家一个好消息，Kevin 恋爱啦！在这里他想借此机会向她表白：多少次我的梦里有你的身影，多少次我在心里一遍遍呼唤你，我只想牵你的手，一起漫步人生路。Linda，我爱你！

1 I really like this girl. I think I love her. 我真的喜欢这个女孩，我想我爱上她了。

爱上"她"的理由：

- She makes me really happy. I think I love her. 她让我觉得很快乐，我想我爱上她了。
- I really think I love her. She's perfect. 我想我真的爱上她了。她太完美了。

跟"她"表白吧：

- You should tell her. 你应该告诉她。
- That's so sweet, you need to tell her. 那太好了，你应该告诉她。

不要莽撞，先和"她"谈谈：

- Do you think she loves you too? You need to talk to her about it. 你觉得她也爱你吗？你得跟她谈谈。

2 My heart beats so fast when I'm around you. 当我在你身边的时候，我的心跳是如此之快。

同样也可以这样说：

- You always make my heart beat faster. 你总是让我的心跳加速。

这时美丽的女孩儿可能会羞涩地说：

- My heart beats faster around you, too. 在你身边，我的心跳也加速。

当然你也可能会听到让你伤心的回答：

- I'm sorry. I'm not sure I feel the same about you. 抱歉，我不确定我的感觉和你的一样。

3 Seeing you always makes me happy. 看到你总让我很快乐。

还可以抒一下情哦：

- You know exactly how to make me happy. 你很清楚怎样使我快乐。

你的他或她可能也会和你有同样的感觉：

- You make me happy too. 你也让我快乐。
- I'm glad I can make you happy. You do the same for me. 我很高兴我能让你快乐，你也同样让我快乐。

4 I'm so lucky to have you in my life. 我的生命中有你是多么幸运。

恋爱中的人话语再甜美一点也不为过：

- I feel blessed to have you in my life. 生命中有你我感觉很幸福。
- Having you in my life is a blessing. 生命中有你是一种恩赐。

对方也会和你有相同的感觉：

- Of course I feel the same. 我当然也会和你有相同的感觉。

- ❖ blessed ['blɛsɪd] *adj.* 幸福的，快乐的，喜悦的
- ❖ blessing ['blɛsɪŋ] *n.* 恩赐，祝福

5 I feel lucky to know you. 认识你我感觉很幸运。

他或她也会这样迎合你：

- I love knowing you too. 认识你我也很高兴。

6 I have something important to talk to you about. 我有些重要的事情要跟你说。

当然也可以这样旁敲侧击：

- I have something important to say. 我有些重要的事情要说。
- I want to tell you something. 我想告诉你一些事情。

对方可能会羞涩地明知故问：

- What is it? 是什么？

7 I love you. 我爱你。

这样的表白也很直接：

- I'm in love with you. 我爱上你了。
- I've fallen in love with you. 我爱上你了。

如果对方也爱你，也可以这么直白地回答：

- I love you too. 我也爱你。

或者含蓄一点儿：

- I feel the same. 我也有同感。

但是如果对方对你根本没感觉，你就自个儿伤心去吧：

- I don't think I love you back. I'm sorry. 对不起，我觉得我并不爱你。
- ❖ be in love with 与……恋爱
- ❖ fall in love with 爱上……

Falling in Love Conversation

Kevin: Hey, I wanted to talk.	凯文：嘿，我想跟你谈谈。
Linda: Sure. What's up?	琳达：好的，怎么了？
Kevin: I have something to tell you.	凯文：我有些事情要告诉你。
Linda: Alright. What is it?	琳达：好啊，是什么？
Kevin: We've become really close and I've always felt a connection between us, from the first time we met.	凯文：我们确实走得很亲近了，从我们第一次见面开始，我就总觉得我们之间有一种联系。
Linda: Me too. I really like you, Kevin.	琳达：我也是。我真的喜欢你，凯文。
Kevin: I like you too. How could I not? You're an amazing girl.	凯文：我也喜欢你。我又何尝不是呢？你是最棒的女孩。
Linda: Aw, that's so sweet of you. Thank you.	琳达：哦，你真是太好了，谢谢你。
Kevin: I'm only speaking the truth. You're my best friend. Actually, you're more than my best friend. I think I've fallen in love with you.	凯文：我只是说实话而已。你是我最好的朋友，事实上，你不仅仅是我最好的朋友，我觉得我已经爱上你了。

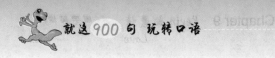

就这900句 玩转口语

Linda: Aw, Kevin. That makes me so happy. I love you too. | 琳达：哦，凯文。这让我很快乐，我也爱你。

❖ connection [kəˈnekʃən] *n.* 关系，联系

文化穿越

　　异国恋情其实没有想象中的那么遥不可及和神秘。美国人也是人，与中国人谈恋爱相比其实差距不是很大。有一点，中国留学在外的男性同胞比较开心的就是如果找了个美国女友，基本上都是 AA 制原则，无论吃饭、看电影，还是合租。不过也有时候是男方付账，这取决于你碰到什么样的女孩儿了。有人会问，与中国女孩儿谈恋爱聊什么都行，毕竟是国语，与美国女友有什么可聊的呢？其实一样，话题都差不多，如果你们能走到一起，说明彼此是有感觉的，有时候爱情好像不需要语言，它可以跨越一切。

Section 3　▶ 求婚
Marriage Proposal

"淡淡的记忆散开，淡淡的回忆袭来，淡淡的思念蔓延，淡淡的爱恋盈满，淡淡的期盼为你。"一路走过这段爱恋的浪漫美好时光，我终于鼓起勇气向 Linda 求婚了。朋友们，请为我祝福吧。

1 I want to ask you something very important. 我想问你一些特别重要的事情。

委婉询问：

- I'd like to ask you something. It's really important. 我想问你一些事情，真的很重要的事情。
- Can I ask you something really important? 我能问你一些特别重要的事情吗？

对方回答：

- Sure. What is it? 当然可以，是什么？
- Of course. You can ask me anything. 当然可以，你可以问我任何事情。

2 You're so important to me. I couldn't live without you in my life. 你对我是那么重要，生活中没有你，我真没法活下去。

这种比较煽情的说法还有：

- I don't know how I could live without you. 没有你，我不知道该怎么活下去。

如果对方也和你一样爱得死去活来：

- I need you too. 我也需要你。

但如果这只是你一厢情愿的爱法：

- I'm sure you could do without me. I'm not that special. 我相信如果没有我你也一样，我并不是你那个特别的人。

3 I love you so much. I feel like that's not going to change. 我是那么爱你，我想那种爱不会改变。

你还可以这样激情地表白：

- I really love you, and I think I will for a long time. 我真的爱你，我想我会永远爱你。
- I love you more than anything. 我爱你胜过任何事情。

他或她和你的感觉一样：

- I love you too. 我也爱你。
- I feel the same way. 我也有同样的感觉。

这样的回答会让你感觉心里空落落的：

- I love you too, but I'm not sure I feel the same way. 我也爱你，但我不确定和你有同样的感觉。

4 Will you marry me? 你愿意嫁给（娶）我吗？

这么直截了当的求婚还有：

- Let's get married. 咱们结婚吧。
- I'd love to marry you. 我想和你结婚。
- Would you be my wife / husband? 你愿意做我的妻子 / 丈夫吗？

接受求婚：

- Yes, I want to marry you! 是的，我想和你结婚。

如果想拒绝，但又不想那么伤害对方，就可以委婉一点儿：

- I don't think I'm ready for that yet. 我想我还没有准备好结婚。

当然也可以回答干脆，毕竟长痛不如短痛：

- No, I can't marry you. I'm sorry. 不，我不能和你结婚，对不起。

5 We should start planning the wedding as soon as possible. 我们应该尽快着手计划婚礼了。

还可以这样表达迫不及待的心情：

- I can't wait. Let's talk about it more. 我都等不及了，咱们再详细谈谈吧。

对方很尊重家长的意见：

- I have to tell my family first. 我得先跟家里说说。
- I want my family to be involved, let's wait a bit to talk about it. 我想让我的家人也参与进来，咱们还是等等再谈吧。

6 I think it's time we took some vows. 我想是我们该许下誓言的时候了。

委婉地求婚：

- I think it's time we settled down... 我想是我们该稳定下来的时候了……
- I want to spend the rest of my life with you. 我要与你共度余生。
- I want to be with you forever. 我要永远与你相守。
- ❖ vow [vau] *n.* 誓言，誓约
- ❖ settle down 定居，安定下来

Marriage Proposal Conversation

(Accepting the proposal)	（接受求婚）
Kevin: I wanted to make tonight extra special.	凯文：我想让今晚变得格外特别。
Linda: Well it was amazing, thank you. Why did you want to make it "extra special"?	琳达：哦，太好了，谢谢你。你为什么想让今晚变得"格外特别"呢？
Kevin: Because I want to ask you something really important.	凯文：因为我想问你一些特别重要的事情。
Linda: You do?	琳达：真的吗？
Kevin: Yeah. I love you so much. You and I are happy together, and I want that to last forever. Will you marry me?	凯文：是啊，我是那么爱你。我们在一起很快乐，我想让这种快乐持续到永远。你愿意嫁给我吗？
Linda: I love you too, Kevin. Yes, I'll marry you!	琳达：我也爱你，凯文。愿意，我愿意嫁给你！
Kevin: I can't wait to start the rest of our lives together.	凯文：我都等不及想与你共度余生了。
Linda: Me too. I'm so happy.	琳达：我也是。我好幸福。

在这里给大家补充一个拒绝求婚的对话

(Refusing the proposal)	(拒绝求婚)
Kevin: Did you have a nice time tonight?	凯文：你今天晚上玩得高兴吗？
Linda: Yes, this is probably the best date I've had in a long time. Thank you.	琳达：是的，这可能是我这么长时间以来有过的最美好的约会了。谢谢你。
Kevin: That's good. I wanted to ask you something.	凯文：那太好了。我想问你些事情。
Linda: Yes? What is it?	琳达：是吗？是什么？
Kevin: I love you more than anything in the world. Will you marry me?	凯文：我爱你胜过这世界上的一切。你愿意嫁给我吗？
Linda: Kevin, I love you too, but I don't think I'm ready for that kind of commitment yet. Please don't take it the wrong way; I just want to wait longer before making that decision.	琳达：凯文，我也爱你，但是我觉得我还没有为那种承诺作好准备。请别误会我的意思，我只是在作出那个决定之前需要更长的时间。
Kevin: It's okay, I understand. I can wait for you.	凯文：没关系，我理解。我会等你的。

❖ take it the wrong way 误会，误解

文 化 穿 越

　　美国人求婚之前的步骤与中国传统上类似，都是彼此到对方家里去征求家长的支持和同意。当然，美国家长也和中国家长类似，也会有不同意的时候，但区别在于，如果是中国婚姻，家长的干预权可能更大一些，甚至拆散一对新人。但美国则不同，美国家长一般就是给予一些意见，无论同意与否，都不会主动干涉新人的决定。当然，如果你娶的是美国黑帮或富人家庭的女儿，有可能会直接被拒甚至勒令不能在一起，除非你们作好罗密欧与朱丽叶式爱情的准备。

Section 4

婚礼
Wedding

　　我和 Linda 终于要走进结婚的殿堂了，我们的亲朋好友也都在为我们的婚礼忙碌。Kevin 在此非常感谢大家，同时我也要对 Linda 说，"在上帝面前，我把我的承诺给你，我将毫无保留地爱你、呵护你，直到永远。"

婚礼计划

1 Let's talk to your family today about wedding plans. 咱们今天去和你的家人谈谈婚礼的计划吧。

还可以这样表达：
- Let's all get together to talk about the wedding. 咱们大家在一起谈谈婚礼的事情吧。

对方可能会回答：
- I'll call them and make sure they're coming. 我会打电话给他们，确保他们会来。

也可以分别说明一下情况：
- I don't think my dad can make it today, but my mom is still coming over. 我想我爸今天来不了，但我妈会过来的。

2 Do you want to get our families together to discuss wedding plans? 你想把咱们家里人都召集在一起讨论一下婚礼的安排吗？

还可以这么询问：
- I want to talk about wedding plans today. Do you think your family is free? 我想今天谈谈婚礼的安排，你觉得你家里人会有空吗？

如果能抽出时间，就说：
- Sure, they can come over in about an hour. 没问题，他们半小时后就能过来。

3 Did you make an appointment with the wedding planner? 你和婚礼策划师约好了吗?

还可以这么说:

- Did you call the wedding planner and make an appointment? 你给婚礼策划师打电话约好了吗?

如果你已经约了可以如实告知:

- I already did it, don't worry. We have an appointment on Thursday. 我已经约好了，别担心。我们周四见面。

如果你没有预约，还想找个借口为自己开脱一下:

- I thought you were going to do it. Oh well, let's call them now. 我以为你预约了。哦，好吧，咱们现在就给他们打电话。

❖ wedding planner 婚礼策划师

4 Where do you want the wedding to be? 你想在哪里举行婚礼?

还可以这样征询意见:

- Do you have any ideas about the wedding location? 你对婚礼的地点有什么想法吗?

结婚可是件大事，有什么想法就说出来哦:

- I've always wanted to have a wedding in my church. It's very classic and beautiful. 我一直想在教堂举行婚礼，既古典又美妙。
- I'd love to have the wedding on a beach. 我想在海滩举行婚礼。
- It doesn't really matter where. Let's just do something simple. 在哪里举行真的无所谓，只要简单一些就好。

5 I want it to be your dream wedding. Tell me what you'd like. 我想给你一个你梦想中的婚礼，告诉我你喜欢什么样的。

女孩儿一定会很高兴的:

- Thank you. I'd love to talk about it more. 谢谢你，我很乐意再详细说说。
- I'm so excited! Let's look up some stuff together. 我太兴奋了！咱们一起来看看要什么东西吧。

结婚请帖

6 Who do you want to send out invitations to? 你想给谁发请帖?

类似的询问：

- Do you have a list of people to invite? 你有需要邀请的客人名单了吗?

如果已经有名单了，还可以再确认一下：

- Let's review over who we want to invite. 咱们来看看该邀请谁吧。

这时对方可以回答：

- I have a list here. Tell me if you want to add or drop anyone. 我这里有份名单，如果你想增加或删掉某人的话就告诉我一声。

也可以说明理由哦：

- I just want a small wedding, so the list is short. 我想一个小型婚礼就行，所以名单比较短。

当然有小的就会有豪华的、大的：

- I want a huge wedding, so I'm still working on the list. Help me add some. 我想要一个盛大的婚礼，所以我还在拟名单。帮我增加一些人吧。

❖ review over 查看，翻阅

结婚礼服

7 Did you buy your dress yet? 你买结婚礼服了吗?

还可以这样说：

- Did you and your girl friend pick out a dress? 你和你女朋友挑选结婚礼服了吗?

如果已有，但还想卖关子，就可以回答：

- I bought the perfect dress. I wish you could see it, but you can't until the wedding day! 我买了套特好的礼服，我希望你能看一下，但你得等到婚礼那天了。

8 Have you found a dress that you like? 你找到你喜欢的礼服了吗?

如果还没有，可就要抓紧时间了：

- I didn't find a dress I liked, so my friends and I are going out again today to look for one. 我还没找到一件我喜欢的礼服，所以我朋友他们和我打算今天出去找一件。

有时候好的东西总有点儿不尽人意：

- I found an amazing dress, but it's expensive so I'm going to shop around more first. 我找到一件特好看的礼服，但就是太贵了，所以我打算先多逛几家商店。

❖ shop around 逛商店，逐店进行搜购

婚礼酒席

 Do you want to pick out a catering service today? 你今天想挑选餐饮服务吗?

你还可以这样建议：

- We should call some caterers today. Do you have any ideas of what you want? 我们今天该给一些承办酒席的人打电话了。你需要什么样的你什么想法吗?

也可以直截了当地说：

- Let's talk about the catering. 咱们来谈谈酒席的事吧。

你可以回答：

- Sure, my mom recommended a few places for us. 好的，我妈妈给我们推荐了一些地方。

❖ catering ['keɪtərɪŋ] n. 承办酒席，提供饮食及服务

 What kind of food do you want for the wedding? 婚礼上你想要什么食物?

还可以这样问：

- Did you figure out what kind of food you want? 婚礼上需要什么食物你想好了吗?

如果你有自己的想法：

- I have an idea of what I want, but let's talk about it together. 需要什么我有点想法，但咱们还是一起商量吧。

如果你还没拿定主意：

- I have no clue who we should hire. Let's look up a few places. 我没有想好要用哪家，我们一起查询几个地方吧。
- ❖ figure out 解决，想出
- ❖ have no clue 不知道

婚礼蛋糕

11 Do you want to pick out a cake? 你想选个蛋糕吗？

还可以这么说：

- What kind of cake do you want? 你喜欢什么样的蛋糕？
- Let's decide on a cake. 咱们讨论一下蛋糕的事吧。

婚礼蛋糕也是婚礼中的一部分，当然要选择自己喜欢的喽：

- Of course! I know I want a white cake, but I'm still not sure of the style. 当然！我想要个白色的蛋糕，但我还不确定要什么样式的。

12 I have a book from the local bakery. Do you want to look at the cakes? 我有一本当地蛋糕坊的书，你想看看蛋糕吗？

如果喜欢：

- This book has a lot of good cakes, but I like this one the most. Do you like it? 这本书上有很多好看的蛋糕，但我最喜欢这个，你觉得呢？

如果不喜欢：

- I don't really like any of these cakes. We should check out another bakery. 这些蛋糕我都不喜欢。我们该上别的蛋糕坊看看。
- ❖ check out 看看，试试（口语）

接待计划

13 I'd like to plan the reception today. 我想今天计划一下接待的事情。

还可以礼貌询问：

- Can we plan the reception today? 我们今天计划一下接的事情好吗？

也可以具体说明：

- Do you want to reserve a place for the reception? 你想预留一个地方用作接待吗？

如果对方也有这种想法：

- Okay. I had an idea of where we could have it and who could perform. 好的，在哪里接待并且由谁来主持，我有个想法。

对方也可以回问：

- Yeah, did you have any plans in mind? 好的，你有什么想法吗？

❖ reception [rɪ'sɛpʃən] *n.* 接待，接见
❖ reserve [rɪ'zɝv] *vt.* 保存，保留

蜜月计划

14 Let's plan out the honeymoon. 咱们来计划一下蜜月吧。

还可以具体询问：

- Where do you want the honeymoon? 你想去哪里度蜜月？

表达迫不急待的心情：

- I can't wait for the honeymoon. Let's plan that next. 我都等不及度蜜月了，咱们接下来计划一下吧。

对方可能的回答：

- Yes! I know exactly where I want the honeymoon to be. 好啊！我非常清楚我想去哪里度蜜月。

很好的回答：

- We can go wherever you want to go. 我们可以去你想去的任何地方。

结婚礼物

15 Thanks for the wedding gifts, everyone! 谢谢你们大家送的结婚礼物！

表达感谢的不同方式：

- I can't thank you guys enough for coming and giving us all these gifts. 你们大家能来，并且还送给我们这些礼物，我真不知道该怎么感谢你们。
- Thank you all for wishing us well. 非常感谢你们大家的祝福。

Wedding Conversation

Linda: Hey Kevin! I want your opinion on something.	琳达：嘿，凯文！我想就一些事情问问你的意见。
Kevin: Sure, what is it?	凯文：好的，什么事？
Linda: I was thinking about the colors for the wedding today and I wanted to ask you about them.	琳达：我今天在想婚礼的色彩，我想问一下你对此有什么意见。
Kevin: Alright, shoot.	凯文：好的，说吧。
Linda: I was thinking we should do a white and baby blue color scheme, but now I think I would like a sea-foam green color better with the white. What do you think?	琳达：我原计划是白色和淡蓝色，但现在我觉得海泡绿和白色搭配更好。你觉得呢？
Kevin: I want it to be whatever you want.	凯文：你想要什么颜色我都喜欢。
Linda: But I can't decide by myself! Which color do you like better?	琳达：但是我自己没法决定！你更喜欢什么颜色？
Kevin: Well, if you're having trouble why don't you pick out your flowers first and base the color around that?	凯文：嗯，如果你难以决定的话为什么不先挑选花，在花的颜色的基础上再决定呢？
Linda: Oh, that's a pretty good idea, sweetie. Thanks! I think I'll go with the green then. Green will go with any flower.	琳达：哦，亲爱的，这是个非常不错的主意。谢谢！我想到时候我会用绿色搭配，绿色和任何花都相配。
Kevin: Sounds good to me, hon.	凯文：听起来不错，亲爱的。

❖**shoot** [ʃut] *vi.* (让某人把话说出来) 说吧，请讲
❖**baby blue** 淡蓝色
❖**scheme** [skɪm] *n.* 计划，方案
❖**sea-foam green** 海泡绿，浅绿色

文化穿越

美国婚礼很有意思。除了电影中那些司空见惯的在教堂里举办的婚礼之外，大部分婚礼的操办方是女方。这貌似与中国相反。因此，如果你觉得在中国结婚开销太大的话，娶个美国女孩吧。其他环节基本与中国类似。不过确切地讲，中国现在的大多数婚礼都西化了，除了不用去教堂，大部分场景和布局都很类似。新人的朋友亲戚也都基本会到场喝彩，当然，无论是新郎还是在场的亲戚朋友，都是正装出席，这是约定俗成的礼节。

Section 5

争吵分手
Break-up

> 爱情婚姻之路没有一帆风顺的，我和 Linda 的婚姻也是如此。争吵已成为我们的家常便饭，相恋时的那种甜蜜已经一扫而光。我们的婚姻已经走到了尽头？还是我们当初结婚的决定太草率？

口语大放送

1 Things have changed. I think we need to talk. 事情已经变化了，我觉得我们需要谈谈。

或者可以开门见山：
- We need to talk. 我们需要谈谈。
- I'd like to talk about us. Things are different. 我想谈谈我们的事，情况有变化了。

谈就谈吧：
- Okay. What's wrong? 好的，怎么了？

2 We've been fighting a lot recently. 我们最近总是吵架。

对这种现状不满：
- We keep fighting and I don't like it. 我们老是吵架，我不喜欢这样。
- Aren't you troubled by how much we've been fighting? 我们总是这样吵架，难道你不觉得烦吗？

这都是面前的事实啊：
- Yeah. I noticed that too. 是啊，我也注意到了。

3 I'm not sure we're working out. 我不确定我们正在解决。

同样还可以说：
- I don't think this is working out. 我不觉得这正在解决。

329

- I don't think we can work together. 我不觉得我们能一起解决。

曾经的那份甜蜜都淡了：

- I agree. We're not happy like we used to be. 是啊，我们不像以前那样快乐了。
- I'm trying, but I know what you mean. 我正在努力，但我明白你的意思。
- Are you just giving up? 你难道就要放弃吗？

4 I really think we should break up. 我真的觉得我们该分手了。

更直接一点儿的说法：

- I'm sorry, but I want to break up. 对不起，但我想分手。

该来的终究是要来的：

- I know… it's okay. I saw this coming. 我知道……好吧。我就知道这会来的。
- I see. Well, I'm sorry it had to come to this. 我明白。哦，对不起，这还是来了。
- ❖ break up 分手

5 I want to break up. It's nothing against you; our relationship just isn't going smoothly anymore. 我想分手，这不关你的事，只是我们的关系不再那么顺畅。

如果还放不下这份感情：

- I don't want to break up yet. 我还不想分手。
- I can't believe we're really breaking up. This is horrible. 我不敢相信我们真的要分手了，这太可怕了。
- ❖ smoothly [ˈsmuðlɪ] adv. 顺利地，平稳地

6 I still like you as a person. Can we remain friends? 我还是挺喜欢你这个人的。我们还能做朋友吗？

同样还可以说：

- Are you okay with still being friends? 咱们仍然是朋友，好吗？
- I don't want there to be any hard feelings. Do you want to stay friends? 我不想有什么芥蒂。你还想做朋友吗？

做不成恋人做朋友也不错：

- Yeah, that's okay. You're still one of my best friends. 好的，那挺好的。你仍然是我最好的朋友之一。
- I guess so. It was fun while it lasted. Thanks for everything. 我想是吧，这份情还能持续我挺开心。谢谢你所做的一切。

既然结束了就不要留恋了：

- I don't think I'm comfortable with that right now. 我觉得现在对此并不是很舒服。
- I need some space after this. 这之后我需要些空间。

 I don't think we should stay friends. 我觉得我们不应该保持朋友关系。

可以说明原因：

- We can't get along. I don't think we should see each other at all anymore. 我们不能和睦相处，我觉得我们彼此还是不要再见了。
- I wish we could stay friends, but all we do is fight. 我希望我们还是朋友，但我们所做的就只有吵架。

分手后不如干脆洒脱一点儿：

- Fine. I guess this is goodbye. 好的，我想这就是再见了。
- I agree. Goodbye, then. 好吧，那再见吧。

如果还想找机会：

- I want to stay friends…can't we at least try? 我还想做朋友……难道我们至少不能试一下吗？

Break-up Conversation

Kevin: We need to talk.

Linda: Okay. What is it?

Kevin: We've been fighting a lot lately. All I seem to do is make you upset, and vice versa.

凯文：我们需要谈谈。

琳达：好吧，什么事？

凯文：我们最近总是吵架。我所做的好像只是让你心烦，反之亦然。

Linda:	Yeah, I know. We used to be happy, but lately we've just been making each other depressed.	琳达:	是啊,我明白。我们曾经是那么快乐,但最近我们只是一直让对方郁闷。
Kevin:	Exactly. That's why I think we should break up.	凯文:	确实如此。那就是我觉得我们该分手的原因。
Linda:	I knew you would say that…and I agree. But I really miss how we used to be.	琳达:	我就知道你会那样说……我同意。但是我真的怀念以前的日子。
Kevin:	Me too. I just don't think we could ever go back to that. We've been through too much.	凯文:	我也是。我只是觉得我们再也回不到以前那样了,我们经历得太多了。
Linda:	I know. So are we going to stay friends?	琳达:	我明白。那我们还是朋友吗?
Kevin:	I'd like that, but if you need a break from me I'll understand. You're still important to me.	凯文:	我很愿意,但如果你要和我断绝关系我也会理解的。你对我仍然很重要。
Linda:	Okay. We can try to stay friends.	琳达:	好吧,我们可以试着做朋友。
Kevin:	Thanks. I'm sorry about all this.	凯文:	谢谢。我对这一切很抱歉。
Linda:	It's alright. I know this is for the best.	琳达:	没关系,我知道这是最好的办法。

❖vice versa 反之亦然

文 化 穿 越

　　确切地讲,美国人分手的方式要比中国人干净利落。中国情侣分手往往会很缠绵,甚至两个人会藕断丝连。但大部分美国情侣分手后,都是各走各的,一般不拖泥带水。因此,如果你与美国女孩分手了,不用顾虑太多,因为她或许忘记你要比你忘记她快得多。当然,这些情况都是美国年轻一代的恋爱观,美国传统一代也会比较保守和讲究。美国离婚率很高,因此,离异的美国人比较惧怕婚姻,有这样的情况:两个人同居多年,但始终不结婚。

Chapter 10

Kevin 侃大山

Free Talk

Section 1 ▶ 买房还是租房
To Buy or to Rent

在 Kevin 看来，现在的状况是：房价涨、地价涨、油价涨，样样都涨，涨了还涨；买房难、租房难、就业难，男女都难，难上加难。其实没错，对我们来说，住房是首要关心的问题。虽然现在楼房盖得越来越高，而房价却节节攀升，买房已成为我们遥不可及的梦想，可租房也不便宜啊。在这里 Kevin 就和大家一起聊聊这个话题。

1 My old house is just too small for me. 对我来说，我的老房子太小了。

想换个新房子：
- I don't like my old house. It's way too small! 我不喜欢我的老房子，它太小了！
- I just don't like being in my old house. 我不喜欢住在我的老房子里。

这房子确实太老了：
- I hear you, sometimes that stuff can be horrible. 我听说了，有时候这房子挺恐怖的。

2 The real estate is always on the rise. 房地产业一直上涨。

房价就没有跌的趋势：
- I heard the price of the house has risen again. 我听说房价又涨了。

房价这么高买不起房啊：
- Yeah, I think buying house is too expensive and I can't afford one. 是啊，我觉得买房太贵了，我买不起。
- ❖ real estate *n.* 房地产，不动产
- ❖ on the rise 在增加，在上涨

3　I need a mortgage loan to buy a house. 我需要按揭贷款来买房。

按揭贷款买房：

- I want to buy a house on mortgage. 我想按揭贷款买房。

付房贷也是一个大问题啊：

- Do you think we can afford the mortgage? 你觉得我们能付得起贷款吗？

❖ mortgage ['mɔːrgɪdʒ] *n.* 抵押借款

4　I'm looking for a new place. 我想重新找个地方。

想换个地方住：

- I'm looking for somewhere new to move in. 我要重新找个地方搬家。
- I need a new place. 我要重新找个地方。

这附近有房：

- I heard of one around here. 我听说附近有一个。

没听说有房：

- Oh yeah? I haven't heard of anywhere but I'll let you know if I found one. 哦，是吗？我没听说什么地方有，如果有的话我会告诉你的。

5　Have you seen any apartments for rent? 你看到哪儿有公寓出租吗？

询问出租房屋信息：

- I'm looking for a house or apartment for rent. Have you seen any? 我正在找出租的房子或公寓，你看到有吗？
- Did you see any ads for apartments in the paper? 你在报纸上看到有出租房屋的广告吗？

没看到有房出租：

- I haven't seen any around, no. 没有，我没有看到附近有。

市中心有房出租，价钱可能比较贵：

- Yeah, I saw one downtown for rent the other day. 有，前几天我看到市中心有一套房出租。

❖ downtown [ˌdaun'taun] *adv.* 在（或往）城市的商业区

6 I'm looking to sign a lease for an apartment. 我想签约租一套公寓。

想租房：
- Hello there, I saw you were renting apartments out. I'd like to sign a lease. 你好，我看到你们有公寓出租，我想签份租约。

有房出租：
- Sure. Can you fill this form out? 好的。你能填下这份表格吗？

❖ lease [lis] *n.* 租约，租契

---

7 How much is the rent? 租金是多少？

询问房屋租金：
- What's the rent for this house? 这间房子的租金是多少？
- I want to know the rent for this apartment. 我想知道这个公寓的租金是多少。
- What does a decent apartment go for around here? 这附近好点儿的房子一个月租金要多少？

附带问一下是否要押金：
- Do you require a security deposit? 你们要求付押金吗？

这个价位有点贵：
- It's 450 dollars per month. 450 美元一月。
- We require a month's rent as a security deposit. 我们要求一个月的租金作为押金。

❖ decent ['disnt] *adj.* 像样的，体面的
❖ security deposit 押金，保证金

---

8 I need to get the household utilities put in my name. 我需要付水电煤气等住房费用。

其他费用：
- I need to put the utilities in my name. 我需要付水电煤气等费用。

租金这么贵包括其他费用吗：
- Are the utilities included in the rent? 租金里面包括水电煤气等费用吗？

❖ household ['haus,hold] *adj.* 家庭的，家用的
❖ utility [ju'tɪlətɪ] *n.* 公用事业

9 Did you pay our water bill yet? 你交水费了吗?

交水电等费用:
* Hey, have you paid the electric bill for this month? 嘿，这个月的电费你交了吗?

正准备去交:
* Not yet, but I'm working on it. 还没有，不过我正准备去交。

已经交了:
* I sent it in last night, actually. 事实上，我昨天晚上已经交了。

To Buy or to Rent Conversation

Kevin: I'm really looking to move into a new place.	凯　文：我真想重新搬个地方。
Debra: Oh yeah? Why is that?	黛布拉：哦，是吗？为什么？
Kevin: Well, my apartment is getting pretty cramped.	凯　文：我的公寓越来越拥挤了。
Debra: You probably just have too much stuff.	黛布拉：你的东西可能太多了吧。
Kevin: Yeah, but I feel like a change of pace too.	凯　文：是啊，但我还是想改变一下。
Debra: Well, I guess I can agree with you. Why don't you check the paper?	黛布拉：哦，我想我能理解你的想法。为什么不在报纸上找找看呢？
(Kevin checks the paper for apartments for rent)	(Kevin 在报纸上找房屋出租的信息)
Kevin: Oh hey, it says there's a bedroom available here.	凯　文：嘿，这里有一间卧室出租。
Debra: Oh yeah? Is it a good price?	黛布拉：哦，是吗？价钱还行吧？
Kevin: Yeah, only a couple hundred a month with utilities included.	凯　文：还行，一个月只需要几百美元，还包括水电费。
Debra: Go for it, man!	黛布拉：去看看，哥们儿！
(Kevin meets with the landlord)	(Kevin 跟房东见面了)

Kevin: Alright, so I just sign here?

Landlord: Yep, here's the lease and you're all set.

Kevin: Thank you very much!

凯 文：好的， 我只需要在这签字吗？

房 东：是的，这是租约，一切都妥当了。

凯 文：非常感谢你！

❖ cramped ['kræmpt] *adj.* 拥挤的，狭窄的
❖ a change of pace 改变步调，换口味
❖ all set 准备就绪，都安排好了

文 化 穿 越

　　在中国的传统观念中，家是一个固定的概念，因此中国人很少没事搬来搬去，除非遇到拆迁。在美国情况就不同，家对于美国人来说是流动的，更确切地说，美国家庭是没有长久固定住所的，因为工作或者生活上的各种原因都会搬来搬去。也因为美国是个车轮上的民族，车的固定性远远超过房子的固定性。另外，美国有搬家的习惯，在一个地方住一段时间后，几个月或者几年，一般情况下很少超过 10 年，他们就会搬到新的住所寻找新鲜感。除此之外，很多美国人都不买房，甚至一直都是租房，这样更方便搬家。

Section 2 ▶ 买车
Buying a Car

　　一直想买一辆属于自己的车，但现在油价一路飙升，而且每个月的汽车保养费用也不便宜，所以 Kevin 一直在买车的天平上摇摆不定。这次终于下定决心，去车市买车去。在这里 Kevin 以自己买车的经历给大家一些建议：首先要考虑汽车的油耗，其次要看汽车的可靠性，此外汽车的价格和安全性能也是大家需要看重的。

1 Why not try this car? 为什么不试试这辆车？

鼓励客户试车：

- Why don't you try this car? 为什么不试试这辆车？
- How about taking this car out for a drive to see if you like it? 为什么不开车出去兜兜风，看看你喜不喜欢？

2 Will you offer any discount right now? 你们现在有什么折扣吗？

很幸运有促销：

- It's still in the holiday sale and I'll give you a real deal at 10 thousand dollars. 现在还是节假日促销，我给你一个最便宜的价一万美元。

3 Is $10,000 a good price for a car? 一万美元买辆车是个好价钱吗？

针对车的价钱征求意见：

- What do you think of $12,000 for a car? 你觉得一万两千美元买辆车怎么样？

还行吧：

- Seems cheap. 看上去不贵。
- Seems about right. 看上去很合适。

4 Where can I find a good deal on a vehicle? 我在哪里买车比较合算?

想买车征求意见:

- I need a new vehicle, any suggestions? 我需要一辆车,有什么建议吗?

给出自己的建议:

- Check the local paper. 查一下本地的报纸。
- ❖ vehicle ['viːɪkl] *n.* 交通工具,车辆

5 What kind of car is safe? 哪种车比较安全?

询问车的安全性能:

- What's the safest car out there? 最安全的车是哪种?

6 Do you know if this car gets good miles per gallon? 你知道这辆车每加仑跑得远吗?

问一下车的耗油量:

- What are the miles per gallon like on this car? 这车每加仑油能跑多少英里?

夸夸这车:

- Pretty great! Around 20-30, not bad for the used. 相当不错! 大概20到30英里,相对于二手车来说已经不错了。
- ❖ gallon ['gælən] *n.* 加仑

7 Could you tell us more about its standard features? 你能告诉我们更多有关这车的标准配置吗?

热心示范以求做成生意:

- Here's a brochure. Get in the car and I will show you. 这里有宣传册。上车来,我给你们展示一下。

Buying a car Conversation

Salesman: May I help you?　　　销售员:我能帮你吗?

Kevin: Yeah. I come here for a sports car.	凯 文：是的。我来这里买辆跑车。
Salesman: Do you like this one? I think it is just the one for you.	销售员：你喜欢这辆吗？我觉得这辆车很适合你。
Kevin: What is the gas mileage?	凯 文：油耗是多少？
Salesman: A quarter will go for a mile.	销售员：跑一英里只需要消耗0.25美元的油。
Kevin: Great! Do you have a black one?	凯 文：好极了！你们有黑色的吗？
Salesman: Yes. This way please.	销售员：有，这边请。
Kevin: OK. How much is it?	凯 文：好的。多少钱？
Salesman: 10 thousand dollars.	销售员：一万美元。
Kevin: How about 9.7 thousand dollars? I'll pay in cash.	凯 文：9700美元怎么样？我付现金。
Salesman: You're a real killer at bargaining. I'll hand that to you. Follow me please.	销售员：你可真是会杀价。卖给你了，请跟我来吧。

❖ sports car 跑车
❖ gas mileage 每英里汽油消耗量，一加仑汽油所行驶的里程

　　前面已经提到，美国是个车轮上的民族。汽车像自行车一样普及，而且价格十分低廉。同样款型的新车中国有可能会比美国贵3倍，美国的工薪阶层买一辆跑车并不是很难，一辆很不错的高档车大概是5万美元到15万美元不等，更确切些，一辆100万元人民币的车在美国也就30.万元人民币左右。这也是为什么很多有钱的中国留学生一到美国就买辆世界级跑车的原因。另外，汽油价格相比中国也要便宜不少。

Section 3

股票基金
Trading Stocks

股市有风险，投资需谨慎。Kevin 一直拿这句话提醒周边买股票基金的朋友，可有时候看着有的朋友买股票一夜之间就赚了，心里也痒痒的，于是也忍不住买一些。可现在股市一直持续走跌，Kevin 也不得不收手了。

1 I want to trade stocks. 我想炒股。

炒股是一种诱惑：
- I've always been curious about trading stocks. 对于炒股，我一直都很好奇。

我可以给你介绍股票：
- Well, I can try and help you understand it if you want. 哦，如果你愿意的话，我可以试着帮你了解股票。

❖ trade stocks 炒股

2 Stock trading seems like such a scam. 炒股看起来像是一个骗局。

炒股赔钱的几率大：
- It seems like I'll lose money if I do this. 好像如果我炒股，我就会赔钱。
- I'm not sure about stocks. They seem like a waste of money. 我对股票不太了解。股票看起来就是浪费钱。

❖ scam ['skæm] n. 骗钱，诈取，骗局

3 Do you know what stocks are low right now? 你知道现在哪支股票的价格低吗？

关注股票:

- Do you know what the popular stocks to buy are today? 你知道今天什么股票最受欢迎吗?

建议上网查一下:

- I'm not sure. You should check the e-trade website. 我不知道,你应该在电子商务网站上查一下。
- I don't know today specifically. Why don't you check online? 我不知道今天具体是哪支股票。你为什么不上网查一下呢?
- ❖ e-trade 电子商务

4 I need to buy 50 shares of DOW stock, please. 请给我买 50 股道琼斯股票。

要经纪人买股票:

- I need 50 shares of Dow Jones, please. 请给我买 50 股道琼斯股票。

买了:

- Sure. 好的。
- Got it! 买了!
- ❖ Dow 道琼斯平均指数 (是 Dow Jones Indexes 的缩写)

5 I lost all of my money buying stocks! 我买股票把钱都赔光了!

炒股赔钱了:

- I wasted so much money buying stocks. 我在股票上浪费了那么多钱。
- I hate the stock market. I wasted so much of my money. 我讨厌股票市场。浪费了我那么多的钱。

股市有风险,投资需谨慎:

- I hear ya. I was never good at it myself. 我明白,我也从来不擅长炒股。
- Bummer man. I'm sorry to hear that. 真倒霉,哥们儿。听到这个消息我很难过。
- ❖ I hear ya. 我明白,我理解。
- ❖ bummer ['bʌmə] n. 令人不愉快、不满意的事物,倒霉

6 This stock has soared almost to the surged limit. 这支股票几乎要涨停了。

股票上涨：

- Great. Stock market prices continue to advance. 太好了，股票市场价格继续上涨。

股票跌停的时候就惨了：

- Oh, man. The stock will be the decline limit. 哦，天哪。这支股票要跌停了。

❖ soar [sor] *vi.* 猛增，暴涨
❖ surged limit 波动极限，涨停
❖ advance [əd'væns] *vi.* 上涨
❖ decline limit 递减界限，跌停

Trading Stock Conversation

Sophie:	I never understood how trading stocks worked.	索菲：	我从来不知道股票交易是怎么回事。
Kevin:	Well it's easy. You just buy while they're low and sell while they're high.	凯文：	哦，这很简单，你只要在低价的时候买进，在高价的时候卖出就行。
Sophie:	Well sure, I understand that much. But what if they just get lower and lower?	索菲：	那是肯定的，这个我明白。但是如果股票一直跌着呢？
Kevin:	Well, I think that means you've failed.	凯文：	哦，我想那就意味着你赔了。
Sophie:	This is too confusing for me. I would never survive the stock market.	索菲：	这对于我来说太复杂了。我从来就没在股市中幸存下来。
Kevin:	I don't mind it.	凯文：	我又不介意。
Sophie:	Do you even buy stocks?	索菲：	你还买股票吗？
Kevin:	Well…no.	凯文：	呃……不买了。

Sophie: See!	索菲：看到了！
Kevin: But if I did, I would make a pretty huge net profit.	凯文：但如果我还买了的话，我就净赚很多钱了。
Sophie: Like hell you would.	索菲：到时候你就会苦不堪言了。
Kevin: I would! I use a simulator online sometimes.	凯文：我当然会赚钱！我有时候在线模拟炒股。
Sophie: Man, you really are a nerd.	索菲：伙计，你真是个呆子。

❖ confusing [kən'fjuzɪŋ] *adj.* 令人困惑的

❖ net profit 净利润

❖ simulator ['sɪmjuˌletə] *n.* 模拟器，模拟程序

❖ nerd [nɜːd] *n.* 讨厌的人，笨蛋，呆子

文化穿越

　　股票涨跌停板制度源于国外早期证券市场，是证券市场中为了防止交易价格的暴涨暴跌，抑制过度投机现象，对每只证券当天价格的涨跌幅度予以适当限制的一种交易制度，即规定交易价格在一个交易日中的最大波动幅度为前一交易日收盘价上下百分之几，超过后停止交易。中国证券市场现行的涨跌停板制度是1996 年 12 月 26 日开始实施的。中国的涨跌停板制度与国外制度的主要区别在于股价达到涨跌停板后，不是完全停止交易，在涨跌停价位或之内价格的交易仍可继续进行，直到当日收市为止。在国外发达股票市场，当股票市场发生巨大波动时，个别股票的涨跌停板限制才启动。

Section 4

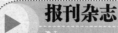

报刊杂志
Newspapers and Magazines

看报纸杂志也是 Kevin 的爱好之一。他关注报纸杂志的新闻信息，也喜欢看里面的花边八卦。不过 Kevin 最喜欢的还是《体育画报》，相信很多男性同胞也是如此，咱们可以抽个时间一起聊聊哦。

1 I got a subscription to *TIME* magazine. 我订了一份《时代》杂志。

买杂志：
- I bought a monthly subscription for *TIME* magazine. 我买了一份《时代》杂志的月刊。

订阅杂志：
- I get the new issues of *TIME* magazine every month. 我每个月都能得到一期新的《时代》杂志。
- I will get all the new issues of *TIME* magazine, because I subscribed. 我订了《时代》杂志，所以我能得到最新一期的。

赞同：
- That's pretty cool. 那很不错。
- That's a good magazine. 那个杂志很好。

不知道是什么类型的杂志：
- What kind of articles do they write? 上面的文章是什么类型的？

❖ subscription [səb'skrɪpʃən] *n.* 预订，订阅

2 They write a lot of articles about politics and current events. 他们写了许多关于时事政治方面的文章。

时政新闻类杂志：
- Most of the articles deal with current events and politics. 大部分文章都是关于时事政治的。

346

- The majority of the magazine focuses around politics and current events. 这一杂志的大部分内容都是关注时事政治的。
- They mostly just write about politics and current events. 他们主要是写有关时事政治的文章。

我爸妈喜欢看：

- Maybe I should buy a subscription for my parents, then. 那也许我应该给我父母订一份。

我对这类杂志不感兴趣：

- That doesn't sound like my type of magazine. 听起来不是我喜欢的杂志类型。
- I don't really like that kind of magazine. 我不喜欢那种杂志。

买一期试试看：

- That's awesome. I'll buy an issue and see how I like it. 很不错。我买一期看看喜不喜欢。
- ❖ current ['kɜːrənt] *adj.* 现时的，当前的

3 I got the newest issue in the mail today. 今天我信箱里收到了最新一期的报纸。

收到最新的报纸：

- My new issue came in the mail today. 今天我的信箱里收到了新一期的报纸。
- I got the latest issue in the mail. 我从信箱里取到了最新的报纸。
- The new issue came in the mail. It was just released today. 我的信箱里有新一期的报纸，是今天才发行的。

效率挺高的：

- You get them right away? Wow, that's impressive. 你这么快就收到了？哇，太不可思议了。

这报纸怎么样：

- How is it? Is there anything interesting in it? 怎么样？有什么有意思的东西吗？
- ❖ issue ['ɪʃjuː] *n.* 发行（物），一次发行量
- ❖ impressive [ɪm'presɪv] *adj.* 给人深刻印象的，令人钦佩的

4 Serious magazines bore me. I prefer magazines that focus around hobbies, like video games. 我不喜欢严肃的杂志。我更喜欢那种关注个人爱好的杂志，比如电子游戏类的。

以下几种说法有点像绕口令：

- I like a few video game magazines more than the boring, serious ones. 比起这些枯燥严肃的杂志我更喜欢那些电子游戏类杂志。
- I'd rather read magazines about video games than the ones about politics. 比起政治类的杂志我更喜欢看电子游戏类的。
- Video game magazines are more interesting to me. The ones about more serious topics tend to bore me. 对于我来说，电子游戏类的杂志更有意思。那些关于严肃话题的杂志让我讨厌。
- I don't like serious magazines. I like lighter ones, like video game magazines or ones that deal with hobbies. 我不喜欢严肃的杂志。我喜欢更轻松一些的，像电子游戏类的或者是关于兴趣爱好的。

喜欢休闲点的杂志：

- I agree, man. Serious magazines can be depressing. 我同意你的说法，哥们儿。严肃的杂志让人感觉压抑。

严肃的杂志有时候也挺有趣的：

- I don't know. Some serious magazines are pretty interesting sometimes. 我不知道。有时候一些严肃的杂志也挺有趣的。

❖ video game 视频游戏，电子游戏
❖ depressing [dɪ'presɪŋ] adj. 压抑的，使人沮丧的

5 My favorite band had an interview in last month's issue of *Rolling Stone*, so I bought it. 上个月那期《滚石乐队》杂志有我最喜欢的乐队的专访，所以我就买了。

因为一个专访就买一本杂志：

- I bought a *Rolling Stone* magazine last month, because it had an interview with my favorite band. 我买了上个月的一份《滚石乐队》杂志，因为上面有我最喜欢的乐队的专访。
- There was an interview with my favorite band in last month's issue of *Rolling Stone*, and I bought it just for that reason. 上个月那期《滚石乐队》杂志有我最喜欢的乐队的专访，所以我买了一份。

那怎么样啊：

- That's cool. Was it a good interview? 真好。那个专访精彩吗？

好像有点不理智：

- That's the only reason you bought it, man? 那就是你买这份杂志的原因吗，伙计？

哦，借我看看吧：

- That sounds awesome. I want to borrow it sometime. 听起来很不错啊。什么时候借给我看看。
- Can I borrow it? I want to read the interview. 能借给我看看吗？我想看那个专访。

6　When is the next issue out? 下一期什么时候出？

询问杂志的出版日期：

- How often does this magazine come out? 这种杂志多长时间出一期？
- When was the newspaper first issued? 这报纸是什么时候开始发行的？
- ❖　come out 出版

Newspapers and Magazines Conversation

Kevin: Hey, do you have the newest issue of *Sports Illustrated*?

凯　文：嘿，你有最新一期的《体育画报》吗？

Store clerk: We might have more behind the counter.

商店职员：柜台后面可能有很多。

Kevin: Oh, could I please get one if you do?

凯　文：哦，你能帮我取一份吗？

Store clerk: Sure, let me check.

商店职员：好的，我看一下。

Kevin: Thank you.

凯　文：谢谢你。

Store clerk: I found a few copies. Let me put some on the rack and then I'll bring you out.

商店职员：我看到好多份。我拿出来一些放到架子上，然后给你取出来。

Kevin: Alright, thanks. Do you read it?

凯　文：好的，谢谢。你看它吗？

Store clerk:	Sometimes, but I don't read it all the time. It's has some pretty cool stuff in it, though.	商店职员：	有时看，但是没一直看。不过里面有很多精彩的内容。
Kevin:	Yeah, I've been buying it for a few months now and I love it.	凯　文：	是啊，我连着几个月都买了，现在特别喜欢。
Store clerk:	I have a few friends that have a subscription to it, so I borrow it when there's an article I want to read.	商店职员：	我有好多朋友都订了这份杂志，所以如果我想读里面的哪篇文章了就找他们借。
Kevin:	That's awesome! I guess I'm that friend for everyone else (laughs). Thank you. Have a nice day.	凯　文：	那太好了！我想我就是其他人的那个朋友（笑）。谢谢，祝你愉快。
Store clerk:	You too.	商店职员：	你也是。

❖ rack [ræk] *n.* 架子

文化穿越

　　美国有很多有名的杂志。例如 *TIME*《时代周刊》www. time. com, *Life*《生活》www. life. com, *People*《人物》www. people. com, *Fortune*《财富》www. fortune. com, *Reader's Digest*《读者文摘》www. rd. com, *Newsweek*《新闻周刊》www. Newsweek. com 等等。相比之下，美国的杂志价格比中国要贵很多，当然按照美国人的收入来看，价格还算可以，而且一般如果订阅时间长的话还会有折扣。

Section 5　　闪婚
Flash Marriage

火车提速，网络提速，现在男男女女的约会和恋爱也跟着大提速。Kevin 从网上看到一幅描写约会恋爱大提速的漫画，其文字注释是这样的：

We met, fell madly in love, got engaged, and had a lovely wedding and honeymoon. Then things turned sour, we grew bitter, separated and divorced. It was quite a busy weekend! 我们相遇，坠入爱河，结婚，举行婚礼，度蜜月。然后慢慢变味，越来越厌倦这种生活，分居，离婚。这是一个多么忙碌的周末啊！

朋友们，你如果有勇气的话也可以感受一下（O(∩_∩)O 哈哈~）。

口 语 大 放 送

1 My girlfriend and I are doing great. 我和我女朋友处得挺好的。

变换一种说法：
- My relationship is going so well. 我和我女朋友相处得很好。
- I have a really good relationship right now. 我现在跟她的关系很不错。

为你祝福：
- That's good, man. 那很好啊，伙计。
- Awesome, I'm happy for you. 太好了，我为你们感到高兴。

2 We haven't been dating too long, but I really like her. 我们约会还没多长时间，但我真的喜欢她。

爱不需要时间：
- I really love her, even though we haven't been together for too long. 我真的爱她，尽管我们还没相处多长时间。

- I know we haven't been dating for long, but I'm so in love with her. 我知道我们还没约会多长时间，但是我已经爱上她了。

有点儿惊讶：

- You think you love her already? 你觉得你已经爱上她了？

清醒一下吧：

- Don't you think it's kind of early for saying that kind of stuff? 你不觉得这么说有点过早了吗？

这么快？祝福你们啊：

- Wow, the relationship is really moving forward fast. I'm glad you two are so happy. 哇，你们进展得真快。你们这么幸福，我感到很开心。

3 I want us to get married. 我想我们该结婚了。

我们结婚吧：

- We should get married. 我们该结婚了。
- Do you think we should get married? 你觉得我们该结婚了吗？
- I think we're going to get married. 我想我们要结婚了。

来得太突然了：

- Marriage already? Well, whatever you want. 现在就结婚？好吧，随便你想怎么样。
- I don't know if you should get married yet. 我不知道你是不是应该结婚。

是有点早，但这是你自己的决定：

- It's pretty early, but if you think it's true love then I don't see why not. 太早了，但如果你觉得是真正的爱情，那我还有什么不可以的呢。

4 Let's have our wedding in Vegas. They have last minute ceremonies there. 咱们在拉斯维加斯举行婚礼吧。他们有快速婚礼。

举行快速婚礼：

- We should go to Vegas for our wedding, since we want to get married soon and everything. 我们应该去拉斯维加斯举行婚礼，因为我们想马上结婚而且一切都妥当。
- Do you want to have our wedding in Vegas? They have speedy ceremonies, don't they? 你想在拉斯维加斯举行婚礼吗？那里有快速婚礼，不是吗？

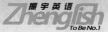
- Let's go to Vegas to get married! It's easy to have a last minute wedding there. 咱们去拉斯维加斯结婚吧！那里的快速婚礼很简单的。

好啊，马上行动：

- That sounds great! Let's plan the trip right now. 听起来不错！咱们现在来计划旅程吧。
- That's a good idea. Let's go as soon as we can! 很不错的主意。咱们赶快去吧！
- ❖ last minute ceremony 快速婚礼，指那些不要求计划的婚礼，基本上只要走到那里就可以结婚了，和下文的 speedy ceremony 和 last minute wedding 是同一个意思。

⑤ Our wedding in Vegas was so awesome! 我们在拉斯维加斯的婚礼棒极了！

这个婚礼很不错：

- We had a fun time in Vegas, and the wedding was great. 我们在拉斯维加斯玩得很开心，婚礼也很棒。
- Vegas is amazing, and our wedding went so well for a last minute thing. 拉斯维加斯太棒了，我们的整个婚礼进行得都很顺利。

为你们祝福：

- That's great. I hope you two are happy together. 很好，希望你们俩在一起很幸福。
- That's good to hear. I want to see the pictures! 听起来很好。我想看照片。

Flash Marriage Conversation

Steve: Hey, Kevin! Do you remember that Donna girl I told you about?

史蒂夫：嘿，凯文！你还记得上次我跟你说的那个叫唐娜的女孩吗？

Kevin: Yeah. You two have been dating, right?

凯 文：记得。你们俩一直在约会，是吗？

Steve: Yeah, but we decided we want to take it to the next level.	史蒂夫：是啊，但是我们决定再向前进一步。
Kevin: What do you mean, bro?	凯　文：兄弟，你什么意思？
Steve: Donna and I are getting married!	史蒂夫：唐娜和我要准备结婚了！
Kevin: Married? Didn't you just meet her a few months ago?	凯　文：结婚？你不是才认识她几个月吗？
Steve: Yeah, but we've become really close. I think we're going to Vegas to get married in one of those drive thru weddings.	史蒂夫：是啊，但是我们已经很亲密了。我们打算在拉斯维加斯举行快速婚礼。
Kevin: Well man, I can't say I agree with your decision, but just do what makes you happy.	凯　文：哦，哥们儿，虽然我不认同你的决定，但是只要你开心就好。
Steve: Thanks for the support, Kevin. Donna makes me happy, and I can't wait until we get married.	史蒂夫：谢谢你的支持，凯文。唐娜让我很开心，我都迫不及待想要跟她结婚了。
Kevin: Yeah, I can see that. I really hope you two are great together.	凯　文：是啊，我能看出来。我希望你们俩在一起幸福。
Steve: Thanks, man! I'll send you pictures of the ceremony!	史蒂夫：谢谢，哥们儿！我会给你送婚礼照片的！
Kevin: Catch you later. Have fun.	凯　文：一会见。玩得开心点。

❖ take it to the next level 向前进一步，向前发展

❖ bro 兄弟（brother 的缩写）

❖ drive thru weddings 汽车通道婚礼，这样的婚礼好比快餐店的汽车通道，你不用下车就可以买到食物，只不过这里不是买食物，而是结婚。在拉斯维加斯，为了方便那些赌高了喝大了的人快速结婚，有的教堂竟开设汽车通道，办理结婚手续。

文化穿越

　　美国人的婚姻观和中国人不同。在美国，两个人即使结婚了也会有各自的隐私自由。另外，很多有钱人在结婚前都要签署一些婚前协定，大部分都是关于离婚后财产划分问题的。也正因为美国人不愿意受婚姻的束缚，因此很多人都一直和自己的情侣保持男女朋友关系而不结婚。很多人认为结婚只是个形式而已，真正的意义是在于两个人是否适合在一起生活。闪婚这种情况在美国也是比比皆是，有的人是出于某种目的，或者纯粹是一见钟情。当然，来得太快的婚姻，离得也相对要快。

Section 6  享受单身
Enjoying Single

看着身边的人一个一个都成双入对了，只剩下自己还形单影只，这样的情形你会怎么面对呢？是觉得孤单自怜、伤春悲秋还是觉得无拘无束、精彩充实？其实 Kevin 就很喜欢单身的生活，因为这样的生活有我想要的自由和乐趣。

口 语 大 放 送

1 Being single is great. I'm not tied down to a relationship. 单身真好。我是不会谈恋爱的。

我喜欢自由，我喜欢单身：

- I love being single. I have so much freedom. 我喜欢单身，我有很多自由。
- Being single is awesome; it's relieving after a bad relationship. 单身真好，结束一段不开心的恋情后，轻松多了。
- It's a huge relief to be single again. 重回单身真是一种很大的解脱。

恭喜你获得自由了：

- I'm glad you're taking the break-up well, man. 哥们儿，你分手处理得很好，我感到很高兴。

是啊，确实还是单身好些：

- I agree, being single is amazing. 我同意，单身的感觉太棒了。

单身会孤单么：

- Don't you get lonely at all, though? 但单身你不觉得孤独吗？
- ❖ be tied down to... 被……束缚住，拴住

2 I used to enjoy being single, but I've been lonely lately. 我以前挺喜欢单身的，但最近感觉挺孤单的。

不要孤单，要恋爱：

- Being single is cool for a while, but I miss being in a relationship. 单身一段时间感觉挺好，但我挺想念恋爱的时候。
- I've been getting pretty lonely lately. I kind of wish I had a girlfriend. 我最近感到特别孤单。有点希望我有个女朋友。

那就试着约会吧：

- You could try dating someone again. 你可以再试着约会。

找谁呢？有合适的对象么：

- Is there someone that you're interested in? 你现在有中意的对象吗？
- Aren't you interested in anybody? 你对谁感兴趣呢？

---

3 I think I'll go out to the bar tonight. Maybe I'll meet some new people. 我想我晚上要去酒吧。在那可能会遇到新朋友。

恢复单身的自由：

- I want to meet some new people. I'll go to the bar. 我想认识些新朋友。我要去酒吧。
- The bar is a good place to meet some new people. I'll go there tonight. 酒吧是认识新朋友的一个好去处。我今天晚上要去那里。

今晚就行动：

- Maybe I could go out tonight, to meet new people. 或许我今天晚上能出去见一些新朋友。

表示支持提议：

- Sounds good to me. 听起来不错。

美好的祝愿：

- Have fun! 玩得开心点！
- Good luck, man. I hope you meet someone! 祝你好运，伙计。希望你能遇到新朋友！

我也要去：

- I'll come with you. 我跟你一起去。

---

4 Being single gives me all the freedom I need. I can hang out with my boys anytime I like. 单身给了我所想要的自由。我可以随时和我的兄弟们一起玩。

重回单身，终于不用被人管了：

- Now that I do not need to report to my girlfriend, I feel all better. 现在我不用向女朋友报告了，我感觉太好了。
- Being single feels like I'm on the top of the world. 单身感觉简直太好了。

❖ be on the top of the world 非常兴奋

Enjoying Single Conversation

Kevin: Man, I'm tired of being single.	凯 文：哥们儿，我厌倦单身了。
Steve: Why don't you go out more often?	史蒂夫：你为什么不经常出去走走？
Kevin: I don't know. I'm just not feeling motivated lately, I guess.	凯 文：我不知道，我只是最近感觉没什么激情。
Steve: Maybe you should try out one of those online dating sites.	史蒂夫：也许你可以试试网上约会的网站。
Kevin: I thought only creepy people joined those.	凯 文：我觉得只有那些古怪的家伙才参加那些。
Steve: Nah, I don't think so. A lot of average guys sign up for that stuff. I think there are a few free ones, too.	史蒂夫：不，我不这么认为。一般很多人注册这种网站。我想那里面也会有一些单身人士。
Kevin: Do you think I could find a girl through that?	凯 文：你觉得我通过那个能找到女朋友吗？
Steve: Maybe, but you could at least get some practice talking to girls.	史蒂夫：有可能，但是至少你能练习一下如何与女孩们交流。
Kevin: Sure, I guess. And after I'm on the site for a while, I could do a speed dating program.	凯 文：嗯，我想是的。而且等我熟悉了网站之后，也许我就能火速约会了。
Steve: No. Only creepy people go to those.	史蒂夫：别啊。只有古怪的家伙才这么做。
Kevin: (laughs) Whatever, man.	凯 文：（笑）无所谓啦，伙计。

❖motivated ['motɪveɪtɪd] *adj.* 有动机的，有目的的；有积极性的
❖creepy ['kriːpɪ] *adj.* 毛骨悚然的，古怪的
❖sign up for 登记注册

　　相比婚姻和束缚，美国人更喜欢自由。因此，美国大学里的男女朋友只是暂时的陪伴关系而已，如果觉得在一起不开心了，也就分开了。男孩追求女孩也很直接和简单，没有太多浪漫的场面和冗杂的环节，喜欢就表达出来，不喜欢就直接拒绝，省时，省力。两个人分手后，有的还依然是不错的朋友。因此，单身这个状态对于美国人来说无所谓，他们随时准备好进入下一场恋情。

Section 7

中性美女
Tomboy

有一天你走在大街上，迎面走来一个人，且看这人的穿着打扮：短发、T恤、牛仔裤、帆布鞋、没有化妆，说话的声音也有些沙哑，你的第一感觉判断这个人的性别，是男还是女呢？告诉你吧，她是女孩，是有男人气质的女孩。没错，她就是一个 tomboy！

① She's such a tomboy! 她真是个假小子！

看，行为举止太男孩化了：
- What a tomboy! 好一个假小子！

我也看出来了：
- I know. 我知道。

其实我自己也是一样的：
- I have been a tomboy since I was born. 我从生下来就很像假小子。

确实是啊：
- You tomboy! 你这个假小子！
- ❖ tomboy ['tɑm'bɔɪ] *n.* 假小子，男孩似的顽皮姑娘

② It's okay to be boyish. 男孩子气也是可以的。

假小子也不是什么奇怪的事：
- Don't worry about it. It's alright to be a tomboy. 别担心，做一个假小子也没什么的。
- ❖ boyish ['bɔɪʃ] *adj.* 男孩似的

③ I like a girl who's tough. 我喜欢坚强的女孩。

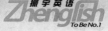
换种说法：

- I like a tough girl. 我喜欢坚强的女孩。

找到知己了：

- Me too, man! 我也是，伙计！
- ❖ tough [tʌf] *adj.* 坚韧的，不屈不挠的

4 Independent girls are so attractive! 独立的女孩很有吸引力！

表示赞同：

- I agree. 我同意。

外加热烈地赞美：

- They're the best kind there is! 她们是最好的。
- ❖ independent [ˌɪndɪ'pɛndənt] *adj.* 独立的，单独的
- ❖ attractive [ə'træktɪv] *adj.* 吸引人的，有魅力的

5 She's kind of a tomboy, but I have a huge crush on her. 她是那种假小子，但我还是狂热地爱上她了。

我喜欢的类型：

- I have such a big crush on that tomboy girl in class. 我狂热地爱上班里的那个假小子。

怎么办，大家都喜欢：

- I think we all do! 我想我们也是！
- ❖ crush [krʌʃ] *n.* 迷恋，迷恋的对象（口语）
- ❖ have a huge/big crush on sb. 狂热地爱上（某人），非常喜欢

6 She works on a farm, but she's still very girly. 她在农场工作，但她还是很有女人味的。

假小子也有很女人的一面啦：

- She maintains her feminine side even though she's so masculine sometimes! 尽管她有时候很男性化，但她仍保持着她女性的一面。
- You? A tomboy? You're kidding, right? You always wear dresses and you act very feminine. 你？假小子？你在开玩笑吧？你经常穿裙子而且行为举止很有女人味啊。

❖ girly ['gɜːlɪ] *adj.* 像少女的，女人气的
❖ feminine ['fɛmənɪn] *adj.* 女性的，柔弱的
❖ masculine ['mæskjəlɪn] *adj.* 男性的，有丈夫气的

Tomboy Conversation

(Steve and Kevin are walking downtown)	（史蒂夫和凯文正在市中心闲逛）
Steve: Did you see that girl?!	史蒂夫：看见那个女孩了吗？！
Kevin: No, which one?	凯　文：没有，哪个？
Steve: How could you miss her?! She was like an 11/10.	史蒂夫：你怎么能没看到呢？！10分她能得11分呢。
Kevin: What kind of scale is that?	凯　文：那是什么级别的？
Steve: The hotness scale, obviously.	史蒂夫：显然是火辣的级别了。
Kevin: Oh, very clever.	凯　文：哦，很聪明呀。
Steve: Thank you. I'd like to think that I'm pretty witty when I want to be.	史蒂夫：谢谢。我觉得当我想变得聪明的时候我就会很聪明。
Kevin: Relax, relax. Don't be in a high key.	凯　文：放松，放松。别高调了。
Steve: Yeah, yeah. Well still that one girl, man. Crazy.	史蒂夫：好吧，好吧。还是那个女孩，伙计。太让人着迷了。
Kevin: You and your girl.	凯　文：你和你女朋友。
Steve: She had such a boyish charm.	史蒂夫：她有一种像男孩一样的魅力。
Kevin: So she was like a tomboy?	凯　文：那她像个假小子？
Steve: Yeah! I love tomboys.	史蒂夫：是啊！我喜欢假小子。
Kevin: Interesting.	凯　文：有趣。

❖11/10 10分能得11分，给女孩打分的标准，表示其性感的程度（俚语）
❖scale [skel] *n.* 等级，级别
❖witty ['wɪtɪ] *adj.* 富于机智的，诙谐的
❖high key 高调的

文化穿越

　　Tomboy 指的是言行举止以及装扮趋于男性的女性。随着时代的前进，这类型的女性越来越多。她们做着男人的工作，甚至比男人还要干练。在美国，有不少这种类型的女孩。她们衣着制服，谈吐专业，在华尔街与男人们一起打拼。尤其是在美国这个自由民主的国度，这类女孩不在乎别人的看法和偏见，她们只做自己喜欢的事情。甚至骑着哈雷摩托在大街上出没于车辆之间。

Section 8 ▶ 月光族
Paycheck to Paycheck

这个月快过完了，我口袋中的钱也光光了，盼着发工资的日子啊！我就是一个典型的月光族，不过我身边有些朋友每个月比我还要"光"呢，且不说一个月工资能有多少，可花钱的习惯就是改不了啊。朋友们，有闲钱的时候也支援支援一下我吧。

1 I really need this next paycheck or I won't be able to make rent. 我盼望下一次的工资，否则我就交不起房租了。

同样的说法：
- I'm going to be unable to pay my rent if I don't get paid soon. 如果再不发工资我就要交不起房租了。

放心吧，一定会好起来的：
- I'm sure you'll be fine. 我肯定你会好起来的。
- ❖ make rent 付房租

2 Could I borrow some money? 能借我些钱吗?

能借点儿钱吗：
- Is it okay if I borrow some money? I really need it. 借我点钱行吗？我确实需要。
- I'm desperate for some money. Could I borrow some? 我急需要钱，能借我一点吗？

可以，不过虽然是朋友也得还啊：
- Sure, but you have to pay me back. 当然可以，但你得还我。

我没钱：
- No, I don't have any to give! 不，我没钱借给你！
- ❖ be desperate for 渴望得到

3 I'm scared I'll have to take out a second mortgage. 我好害怕我又得交第二期的抵押贷款了。

又要还贷款了：

- I might have to file for a second mortgage. 我可能得要申请第二期按揭贷款了。

不要太悲观啊：

- Don't worry. It won't get that bad. 别担心，不会那么糟的。
- ❖ take out 开始
- ❖ file for 申请

4 If I don't find a new job I won't be able to keep up with my money. 如果我找不到新的工作，我的钱可能就不够用了。

换种说法：

- I'm not going to be able to keep up with my spending if I don't get a second job. 如果我找不到第二份工作，我的钱就不够花了。

别担心，我来帮你：

- I'll see if I can find anything for you. 我看看能不能帮你找到。
- ❖ keep up with 跟上

5 I'm afraid I'll have to take a payday loan out to make ends meet. 我恐怕得弄一个发薪日贷款来保持收支平衡了。

收支不相抵：

- I don't think I'm going to be able to make ends meet. 我觉得我没法做到收支平衡。

但也不要太担心啊：

- I'll help you out. Don't worry. 我会帮你的，别担心。
- ❖ payday ['pe,de] *n.* 发薪日，支付日
- ❖ make ends meet 量入为出，收支相抵

6 If this raise doesn't come through, I won't have money for food! 如果这次提薪没有通过，我连吃饭的钱都没有了！

没钱吃饭了：

- I can't even afford to eat this week! 这周我连吃饭的钱都没有了！

过来找我就有饭吃了：

- Why don't you come over? I'll make you dinner. 你为什么不过来？我请你吃饭。

❖ come through 经历，安然度过

Paycheck to Paycheck Conversation

Kevin: Debra, can I talk to you for a second?	凯　文：黛布拉，能跟你谈谈吗？
Debra: Sure, what's up?	黛布拉：当然，什么事？
Kevin: Debra, where do you get all of your money from?	凯　文：黛布拉，你的钱都是怎么来的？
Debra: Well, from my job, obviously.	黛布拉：很显然是我工作挣的。
Kevin: Oh, alright, I was just curious.	凯　文：哦，好吧，我只是好奇。
Debra: Why did you ask me that?	黛布拉：你为什么问我那个？
Kevin: Well, it seems like you've been spending all your money on stuff you don't need.	凯　文：哦，你好像经常把钱花在买一些你不需要的东西上面。
Debra: Well sure, but it's my money.	黛布拉：嗯，好吧，但那是我的钱。
Kevin: I just don't want to see you get into debt. That's all.	凯　文：我只是不想看你欠债。仅此而已。
Debra: I guess you're right. Maybe I should look into budgeting things a little better.	黛布拉：我想你是对的。或许我应该多关注下一些便宜的东西。

❖ get into debt 负债

文化穿越

　　在美国，如果哪个人说自己老是在倒计时等着发工资的日子，那么他听到的回应可能是，"我也跟你一样。"发工资的前几天，往往是最难熬的时候。而且一旦出现问题，工资不能按时发放，他们的生活就会出现很大的问题。有的员工这样的情形更加严重，甚至会要求老板按星期发工资，或是在更短的时间发工资，这样才能勉强维持生活。这可能也和美国人的储蓄消费习惯有很大的关系。

Section 9 ▶ 节假日
Holidays

一年当中，节假日还是蛮多的。在每一个节假日当中，或去旅游、或和家人朋友们聚会、或去参加派对……生活可谓是丰富多彩。这不，圣诞节来了，我也该送妈妈和其他家人朋友们一份礼物。朋友们，我的礼物你收到了吗？

1 Hey! What do you want for your birthday? 嘿！你生日的时候想要什么？

该过生日了，提前安排哦：

- Your birthday is coming up. Do you want anything specific? 你的生日就要到了。你有什么具体的安排吗？
- Do you want anything particular for your birthday? 你生日想要什么特别的东西吗？

呵呵，想送给你生日礼物：

- I'm going to go shopping for your birthday soon. What do you want? 我一会儿去给你买生日礼物。你想要什么？

我是有些想法：

- I have a few ideas. 我有一些想法。

客气一下：

- Nah, you don't have to get me anything. 不，你不用送我什么东西。

随意啦，送什么都喜欢：

- Just get me something you think I'll like! 送一些你觉得我喜欢的就可以了！

❖ come up 开始，发生，出现
❖ specific [spə'sɪfɪk] *adj.* 特殊的，明确的
❖ particular [pə'tɪkjələ] *adj.* 特别的，独有的

2 Have a happy holiday. 假期愉快。

同样的祝福：

- Happy holidays! 假期愉快！

具体的节日：

- Merry Christmas and Happy New Year! 圣诞快乐，新年快乐！
- Happy Hanukkah. 光明节快乐。

回敬祝贺：

- Thanks, you too. 谢谢，你也快乐。

❖ Hanukkah ['haːnəkə] *n.*（犹太教的）光明节

3 I'm hosting a New Year's party. Do you want to come? 我要举办一场新年派对。你想来吗？

直接邀请：

- You're invited to my New Year's party. 你被邀请参加我的新年派对了。
- Do you want to come to my New Year's party? 你想来参加我的新年派对吗？

心动了：

- Sounds awesome, I'll be there. 听起来很不错，我会去的。

抱歉，晚了一步：

- Sorry, I'm already going to another one. 对不起，我已经参加另外一个了。

过年还是想和家人一起：

- I'm staying with my family for New Year's. Maybe next year! 我要和家人一起过年。明年吧！

4 Do you want to come to my family's Easter Sunday dinner? 你想来参加我家的复活节晚餐吗？

我们都欢迎你：

- My family is okay with you coming to my place for Easter Sunday. 我家人想让你来参加我们的复活节聚会。
- Do you celebrate Easter? You're welcome to come over for dinner. 你过复活节吗？欢迎你来我家吃晚饭。

369

- My family is having a big Easter dinner. Do you want to come? 我们家将有一个复活节大聚餐。你想来吗?

哇,太好了:

- Okay, that sounds great. 好的,听上去太好了。

不打算过这个节日:

- No, thanks. I don't really celebrate Easter. 不用了,谢谢。我不过复活节。

可惜,我已经有安排了:

- I have to take my little brother on an Easter egg hunt. Sorry. 我得带我弟弟去参加寻找复活节彩蛋活动。抱歉啊。

❖ Easter ['iːstə] Sunday 复活节
❖ Easter egg hunt 寻找复活节彩蛋活动

5 I'm going to a barbeque for 4th of July. There will be fireworks and everything. 7月4号我要去参加一个烧烤野餐。到时候会有烟花表演以及其他很多活动。

同样的说法:

- I was invited to a 4th of July barbeque. I heard they'll be setting off fireworks. 我被邀请去参加7月4号的一个烧烤野餐。听说到时候会有烟花表演。
- I'm going to see some fireworks on the 4th of July, at my friend's barbeque. 7月4号我要去朋友的烧烤野餐看烟花表演。

我能去吗:

- Sounds fun. Can I come? 听起来很好。我能去吗?

玩得开心点哦:

- That's cool. Have a good time! 好酷。玩得开心点!

碰到同路人了:

- Nice. Me too. 很好。我也是。

❖ barbeque ['bɑːbɪkjuː] n. 烤肉,野餐
❖ fireworks ['faɪrwɜːks] n. 烟火
❖ set off 使爆炸

6 What are you dressing up as for Halloween? 你万圣节穿什么?

万圣节的装扮：

- Are you going to be anyone for Halloween? 万圣节你打算扮成什么？
- What's your Halloween costume going to be? 你的万圣节服装是什么？
- Tell me what you're going to be for Halloween! 告诉我你万圣节准备穿什么吧！

还没买服装呢：

- I haven't picked out a costume yet. 我还没有万圣节服装。

已经买好服装了：

- I just bought a vampire costume. 我刚买了一件吸血鬼服装。

没有确定：

- I have a few ideas for a costume, but I'm not sure yet. 关于装束，我有一些想法，不过还没确定。

❖ costume ['kastum] *n.* 装束，服装
❖ vampire ['væmpaɪr] *n.* 吸血鬼

---

7 Sorry, I can't make it to your Halloween party. I have to take my little sister out trick or treating. 抱歉，我不能去参加你的万圣节派对。我得带我小妹妹出去玩"不给糖就捣蛋"的游戏。

不能参加万圣节派对了：

- I have to take my sister trick or treating, so I can't come to your Halloween party. 我得带我妹妹玩"不给糖就捣蛋"的游戏，所以不能来参加你的万圣节派对了。
- Sorry, but I can't come to your Halloween party. I'm taking my little sister out trick or treating. 不好意思，我不能参加你的万圣节派对了。我要带我小妹妹去玩"不给糖就捣蛋"的游戏。

没关系的：

- It's okay, man. Get her lots of candy. 没关系，哥们儿。要给她弄很多糖果哦。

下次吧：

- Maybe next year, then. 那明年吧。

有些可惜：

- That sucks. Try to have fun with your little sis. 真可惜，跟你妹妹玩得开心点。

❖ trick or treating 不给糖就捣蛋

Holidays Conversation

Kevin: Hey, mom! Merry Christmas!	凯文：嘿，妈妈！圣诞快乐！
Mom: Aw, Kevin. Thank you! You didn't have to get me anything.	妈妈：噢，凯文。谢谢！你没必要给我买什么的。
Kevin: Well, I was hanging out with my friends and I saw this at the mall…I thought you would really like it.	凯文：哦，我和朋友们在逛商场的时候看到这个……我觉得你会很喜欢的。
Mom: Can I open it now?	妈妈：我现在能打开看看吗？
Kevin: Go ahead. It's your gift.	凯文：打开吧，这是给你的礼物。
Mom: (opens present) Oh, I love it! Thank you so much, dear.	妈妈：（打开礼物）哦，我非常喜欢！谢谢你，亲爱的。
Kevin: No problem. I thought I should get you something nice, since I'm going out to a party for New Year's.	凯文：不客气。我觉得应该送你一些好东西，因为我要出去参加一个新年派对。
Mom: That's very considerate of you, honey.	妈妈：你真体贴，宝贝儿。
Kevin: No problem, mom. Happy holidays.	凯文：不客气，妈妈。节日快乐！
Mom: Happy holidays to you too, dear.	妈妈：你也节日快乐，亲爱的。

❖ considerate [kən'sɪdərət] *adj.* 体贴的，周到的

文化穿越

　　美国比较常见的节假日包括万圣节、感恩节、圣诞节等。万圣节大学里一般会有各种化妆晚会，到场的嘉宾必须打扮成电影里一些稀奇古怪的角色，比如：吸血鬼、僵尸、蝙蝠侠、超人等等。有的学校还会有雕刻南瓜灯的比赛。感恩节一般是家人团聚的日子，家长们一般都把孩子接回家去，一般这个日子大家都会吃火鸡。圣诞节在美国是个大节，一般都会放假休息，大部分商店也会关门。亲戚朋友们大家聚在一起说说笑笑，互赠礼物。

Section 10 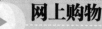 网上购物
Online Shopping

　　我不太喜欢逛街，一是因为逛街比较累，还有一点就是看着那些琳琅满目的商品，头就晕晕乎乎的。不过现在这个问题解决了，在网上购物，简单便捷，点点鼠标，东西就到家了。因此这也激起了我想自己开个网店的热情。朋友们，请多多关注我的网店啊！

1 I just set up an account on eBay. 我刚在易趣上注册了一个账户。

注册账户：
- I made an account on eBay. 我在易趣网上注册了一个账户。
- My account on eBay is brand new. 我在易趣网上的账户是新开的。
- I'm new to eBay. I just made an account. 我是刚来上易趣网的。只是注册了一个账户。

操作很简单的：
- It's a pretty easy site to figure out. 这个网站很容易弄明白的。

不要消费过度哦：
- Cool, just don't shop too much. 好了，不要买太多东西就行。

❖　set up 创立，建立
❖　account [ə'kaunt] *n*. 账户
❖　figure out 想出，理解，明白

2 I'm going to order a few things online. 我要在网上订购一些东西。

网上购物：
- I have to order some stuff online. 我得在网上订购一些东西。
- I'm ordering some things online. 我要在网上订购一些东西。
- I'm making a few orders online. 我在网上下了些订单。

买了什么：

- What did you get? 你买了什么？

我一直都在网上买：

- Yeah? I do that all the time. 是吗？我一直都这样做。

3 I think this site is safe to put my credit card number into. 我觉得在这个网站输入我的信用卡号码是安全的。

不确定是否安全：

- I'm not sure if this is a safe site to be putting in my credit card information. 我不确定在这个网站输入我的信用卡信息是不是安全？

貌似没有想象得那么安全：

- I probably shouldn't shop from this site, it doesn't look too safe. 我或许不应该从这个网站上买东西，看起来很不安全。

没错，你的信息可能会被盗用：

- Yeah, better not do that. You could get your identity stolen. 是啊，你最好不要那样做。你的身份很可能会被盗。

如果有怀疑，就不要用了：

- If you're not sure then don't use the website. 如果你不确定就不要用这个网站了。

我觉得可以试试：

- I doubt there will be any problems. Just go for it. 我觉得没什么问题。大胆试试吧。

❖ identity [aɪ'dentətɪ] *n.* 身份，个性
❖ get sth. stolen 使得某物被偷

4 The shipping cost for this item is ridiculous! 这件商品的运费真是太离谱了。

运费太贵：

- This has a really high shipping fee. 这个运费确实很高。
- The cost for shipping is way too expensive. 运费太贵了。
- I wonder why this product has such a high shipping cost. 我想知道为什么这个产品的运费这么高？

去别的网站看看：

- Try to find it on another website. 试着在别的网站找找。
- Shipping costs might vary depending on the site. 不同网站的运费是不同的。

要不再等等吧：

- Maybe you should wait to get it. 或许你应该等段时间再看。
- ❖ ridiculous [rɪ'dɪkjələs] *adj.* 荒谬的，可笑的

5 I got my package in the mail today! 今天我从邮箱里取到包裹了。

收到货了：

- My order came in the mail. 我买的东西收到了。
- I just got my package from Amazon. 我刚收到了亚马逊的包裹。

这么快啊：

- Cool, open it! 太好了，打开看看！
- That shipped pretty fast. 送得好快。

6 I'm ordering my school books online this year. 我今年要在网上买课本。

网上的东西更便宜：

- I heard it's cheaper to order school books online, so I'm doing that. 我听说在网上买课本更便宜，所以我就在网上买了。
- This year I'll be getting my books online. 今年我要在网上买课本。
- There's a few websites that sell school books, so I'm just getting them from there. 有几个网站卖课本，所以我就从他们那里买了。

我早就从网上买了：

- I did that last year. It can really save you money. 我去年就这么做的。这真的能省钱。

7 I'm going to sell some things online, I heard it's easy. 我要在网上卖东西，我听说这很简单。

网上卖东西：

- I have a few things I want to sell. I think it'll be easier to do it online. 我有些东西想拿去卖。我觉得在网上卖会更容易点儿。

- I hope selling things online is as easy as I've heard. 我希望在网上卖东西能像我听说的那么简单。

没试过：

- I've never done it, but it's probably easy. 我从来没卖过，但是可能会很简单吧。

我帮你卖：

- I can help you out if you need it. 如果你需要的话，我可以帮你。

确实很简单：

- It is easy. There are instructions on the website. 这很简单。在网站上都有说明。

❖ instruction [ɪnˈstrʌkʃən] n. 说明，指示

Online Shopping Conversation

Kevin:	Hey, do you know how to sell things on eBay?	凯　文：	嗨，你知道怎么在易趣网上卖东西吗？
Debra:	I've done it a few times. What do you need to sell?	黛布拉：	我已经卖了很多次了。你要卖什么？
Kevin:	Mostly some old games and movies. Can you help me out?	凯　文：	大多是一些旧的游戏和电影。你能帮我吗？
Debra:	Sure. First you should take a few pictures of what you're trying to sell.	黛布拉：	当然可以。首先，你应该给要卖的那些东西拍些照片。
Kevin:	Okay, you should probably help me out with that.	凯　文：	好的，那你可能要帮我。
Debra:	Sure thing. After that you should come up with a description and a minimum price.	黛布拉：	没问题。之后，你应该作一个描述并设定最低价格。
Kevin:	Do they have instructions on the rest after I make an account?	凯　文：	我注册账号之后剩下的事情他们都有说明吗？

Debra: Yeah, it's pretty straightforward. What do you need to sell stuff for, anyway?	**黛布拉:** 有，很简单的。你卖这些东西到底要干什么？
Kevin: I want some extra cash to buy books off of Amazon.	**凯　文:** 我需要一些额外的现金从亚马逊上买书。
Debra: (laughs) So you're selling on one site and buying on another? That's pretty crazy.	**黛布拉:** （笑）那你是在一个网站上卖东西，在另一个网站上买东西？太疯狂了。
Kevin: You know me, I like to live on the edge. Come on, let's take some good pictures of this stuff.	**凯　文:** 你了解我的，我喜欢有挑战性的刺激的生活。来吧，咱们给这些东西拍些好看的照片。

❖come up with 提出，想出，提供
❖minimum ['mɪnɪməm] *adj.* 最少的，最低程度的
❖straightforward [ˌstreɪt'fɔːwəd] *adj.* 简单的，明确的
❖live on the edge 充满挑战和刺激的生活

文化穿越

　　美国有很多家购物网，其中以 Amazon (http://www. amazon. com), eBay (http://www. ebay. com) 比较出名。网上的价格比较低廉，有时还会有折扣和返款。不过有一点需要注意，在网上购物的时候，一定要挑选大型的知名网站，因为有些小的网站存在欺诈现象，在小网站上购物时信用卡密码有可能被盗。付款前，一定要确认邮寄的费用是多少，以及需要多长时间送达。PayPal 是美国人常用的一种付款方式，相当于中国的支付宝。在 PayPal 上注册一个账号，之后购物就可以省去填个人信息这个步骤，直接点击 PayPal 付款即可。

Section 11 博客
Blog

我的博客我做主！心情不好的时候我在博客上一吐为快，高兴的时候我在博客上把快乐带给大家，偶尔心血来潮的时候，我也在博客上写些小故事或转载一些好玩的东西供大家娱乐。当然了，我也喜欢浏览好友的博客。朋友们，希望有一天你看到我的博客时，好好评论一下，增加一下点击率（拉关系了 O(∩ _ ∩)O~）。

1 My friend has a really interesting blog. 我朋友有一个很有趣的博客。

朋友的博客很不错：

- I have a friend who updates a cool blog. 我有个朋友开通了一个很酷的博客。
- My friends update their blog a lot, and the stuff they write is pretty interesting. 我朋友经常更新他们的博客，他们写的东西都特别有趣。
- I like reading my friend's blog. It's pretty cool. 我喜欢看我朋友的博客，特别酷。

说得我也想看了：

- I might read it too. Send me the link. 或许我也应该看看。发给我链接吧。
- Can I have the link to it? I want to read it. 能把链接发给我吗？我也想看。

❖ update [ʌp'det] vt. 更新

2 I want to start up my own blog. 我想开通自己的博客。

想要一个自己的博客：

- I think I'll start my own blog. 我想要开个博客。
- Starting a blog can't be hard. I'll do it. 开通博客不难。我要开一个。

- I'm pretty sure I'll start up my own blog soon. 我很肯定我马上就能开通博客了。

鼓励对方：

- Go for it. I'll be sure to read it. 去开吧。我肯定会看的。
- That sounds like it could be fun. 听起来很有意思。

3 I need to help with a blog layout. I don't know any HTML. 帮我设计个博客吧。我对 HTML 一点都不懂。

设计博客：

- I need some coding help for my blog layout. 我需要一些编码来帮助我设计博客。
- I want a web designer for my blog. 我想请一个网页设计师来设计我的博客。
- I don't know HTML, so I need to find someone to help me out with my blog. 我不懂 HTML，所以我需要找人帮我设计博客。
- Do you know anyone who can help me out with HTML? I need it for my blog layout. 你知道有谁能帮我解决 HTML 的问题吗？我需要用它来设计博客。

提供帮助：

- I know HTML. 我懂 HTML。
- I have a few friends that could help you. 我有几个朋友可以帮你。

给予建议：

- Maybe you could learn how to do it yourself. 或许你可以自己去学一下。

❖ layout ['leɪ,aut] *n.* 版面编排，设计
❖ HTML = Hypertext Markup Language 超文本链接标示语言
❖ coding ['kodɪŋ] *n.* 编码

4 I had an amazing weekend. I wrote all about it in my blog. 这个周末太有意思了。我把它全部写在博客里了。

疯狂的周末过后更新博客：

- I just updated my blog. I wrote all about my crazy weekend. 我刚更新了我的博客。我把有关于这个疯狂周末的事情都写在上面了。

- My weekend was insane! I wrote an entry in my blog about it. 这个周末太疯狂了！我在博客上记录下来了。

很感兴趣：

- Cool, I'll have to read it. 太好了，我得去看看。

❖ entry ['entri] n. 项目，记录

5 I like to follow celebrity's blogs. 我喜欢看名人的博客。

喜欢看名人博客：

- I read a few blogs that celebrities write. 我读了一些名人写的博客。
- I keep myself updated with my favorite celebrities by reading their blogs. 我通过看我喜欢的名人的博客来了解他们最新的消息。

如果你也喜欢看：

- I do the same thing. 我也这么做。

如果你没有时间看：

- I don't really have the time to do that, but it sounds awesome. 我没时间看那个，但是听起来很不错。

❖ celebrity [sə'lebrəti] n. 名人

6 Are you a blogger? 你是博客写手吗？

我写博客：

- Sure I am. I've been writing a blog for almost three years. 我当然是啦。我都写了将近三年了。

不写博客：

- No, I am not. I don't have time to write blogs. 不，我不是。我没有时间写博客。

7 When did you start blogging? 你什么时候开始写博客的？

具体时间：

- I began blogging when I was a freshman. 我是从上大一的时候开始写博客的。

都快忘了：

- I am not sure. Maybe five years ago. 我不确定。也许是5年前吧。

8 How often do you publish a blog? 你多久发表一篇博客日志？

> 每天都写：
> * Once a day. 一天更新一次。
>
> 写日志的频率不一定：
> * It all depends. Usually every other day. 视情况而定。通常每隔一天。

Blog Conversation

Kevin: Hey Kay, I was reading your blog the other day, and I have a question.

凯文：嗨，凯，我前几天看你的博客了，想问你一个问题。

Kay: Yeah, what's up?

凯 ：嗯，什么问题？

Kevin: Well, first off, I thought it was pretty cool.

凯文：呃，首先我觉得你的博客非常酷。

Kay: Thanks. I don't put much work into it, but it passes the time.

凯 ：谢谢，我没花很多功夫在博客上，但那能打发时间。

Kevin: You're a really good writer. I was wondering if you could help me start up my own blog.

凯文：你的文章写得真好。我在想你能不能帮我开一个博客。

Kay: Sure, I guess so. The site I use is free.

凯 ：当然可以。我用的网站是免费的。

Kevin: Oh, really? How do I make my own page?

凯文：哦，是吗？我怎么做自己的网页？

Kay: I have a friend that helps me out with that stuff, but I can show you some basic HTML if you want a custom page layout.

凯 ：我一个朋友帮我做的，但是如果你想设置一个自定义网页我可以告诉你一些基本的HTML。

Kevin: That sounds great! If you don't mind teaching me, that is.

凯文：太好了。如果你不介意教我的话，那当然好了。

Kay: It's cool. How about we meet up tomorrow in the library and I can teach you some stuff?

凯 ：好的。我们明天在图书馆见面我教你一些东西怎么样？

Kevin: Sounds good. I'll meet you there.

凯文：好的。明天见。

文化穿越

对于中国留学生来说，写博客是一种发泄感情的渠道。在国外留学很少能遇到知心的朋友，大部分时候都是笔记本陪伴左右。虽然人在国外，但一般国内发生的事情都逃不过留学生的洞察力。然而，博客上的信息往往都是留学生生活滋润的一面，主要是让国内的家人和朋友们都放心。其实，一切辛酸自己都会默默忍受着，而出去游玩滋润的一面通常也只是放假的时候。博客上的只言片语，渗透着留学生的生活状态，同时也是他们成长的记录。

Section 12 ▶ 秘密
Secret

> 　　每个人的心中都藏着一个秘密花园。你看，Steve 藏不住了，他把他的秘密告诉我了，说实在的，那根本就不算是秘密了，因为我们都知道 Steve 喜欢 Donna。朋友们，你有什么秘密也可以跟我说哦，My lips are sealed。

口语大放送

1 I've got a secret. 我有一个秘密。

分享秘密：
- I have a secret to tell you. 我有一个秘密要告诉你。

是什么秘密：
- What is it? 是什么？

2 Can I tell you something? 我能跟你说些事吗?

能不能和你分享秘密：
- Can I tell you something secret? 我能跟你说一件秘密的事吗？

当然可以：
- Sure, what is it? 当然可以，是什么？

3 If I tell you this, you have to promise not to tell anyone. 如果我告诉你，你必须保证不告诉任何人。

一定要保密：
- If I tell you this, please don't repeat it. 如果我告诉你，请不要再说出去。

我会的：
- I won't. I promise. 我不会的，我保证。

4 Guess what I heard? You can't tell anyone though. 你猜我听说什么了？不过你不能告诉任何人。

保守秘密：

- I heard the craziest thing today but we have to keep it a secret. 我今天听说了最疯狂的事，但是我们得保守秘密。
- I heard the most insane rumor today, but please keep it to yourself. 我今天听说了最荒唐的谣言，但是请你保守秘密。

询问具体是什么事情：

- What is it!? 是什么？
- ❖ rumor ['rumə] *n.* 流言，谣言

5 No one needs to know about this. 没有人有必要知道这事。

不知道为好：

- It won't hurt anyone if they don't know. 如果他们不知道，就不会受到伤害。

给予承诺：

- Alright…alright. I won't tell anyone. 好的……好的，我不会告诉任何人的。

6 Can this be our little secret? 这能成为我们之间的小秘密吗？

这只限于咱们之间：

- Can you keep this between you and me? 你能保证这件事只有咱们俩知道吗？

保证会保密：

- Sure, I will, I promise. 当然，我会的，我保证。
- ❖ between you and me = between ourselves 只有我们两个知道

7 That was to be kept secret from the others but she let the cat out of the bag. 那件事本来应该对其他人保密的，但她却泄密了。

泄露秘密:

- She divulged the secret to a stranger when she was drunk. 她喝醉的时候把秘密告诉了一个陌生人。
- ❖ let the cat out of the bag 泄露秘密
- ❖ divulge [daɪˈvʌldʒ] *vt.* 泄露

8 My lips are sealed. 我的嘴很紧的。

会保守秘密的:

- Don't worry. Your secret is safe with me. 别担心，我会为你保守秘密的。
- I won't tell anyone about your secret. 我不会把你的秘密告诉任何人的。

Secret Conversation

Steve: Hey man, can I tell you something?	**史蒂夫:** 嘿，哥们儿，我能跟你说一些事吗？
Kevin: Sure, what is it?	**凯　文:** 当然了，什么事？
Steve: You have to promise not to tell anyone.	**史蒂夫:** 你得保证不告诉任何人。
Kevin: Alright, shoot.	**凯　文:** 好的，说吧。
Steve: I want to go out with Donna so bad.	**史蒂夫:** 我特别想和唐娜约会。
Kevin: That's hardly a secret.	**凯　文:** 那已经不算是秘密了。
Steve: Is it really that noticeable?	**史蒂夫:** 那很明显吗？
Kevin: Yes, yes, it is.	**凯　文:** 是的，的确很明显。
Steve: Well, that's awkward.	**史蒂夫:** 噢，好尴尬。
Kevin: Don't worry about it. Everyone wants you two together, anyway.	**凯　文:** 不用担心。反正大家都希望你们俩在一起。
Steve: Well, do you promise you won't tell anyone?	**史蒂夫:** 好吧，你保证不告诉其他人？
Kevin: Relax, man. I promise.	**凯　文:** 放心吧，哥们儿。我保证。

❖shoot [ʃut] *vi.* 快讲（俚语）
❖noticeable ['nɒtɪsəbl] *adj.* 显著的，显而易见的
❖awkward ['ɔkwəd] *adj.* 尴尬的，不合适的

文 化 穿 越

　　秘密这个话题更多的是和隐私有联系。美国人是非常重视个人隐私的，无论是普通朋友还是密友，甚至孩子与父母也是有着绝对隐私的。在中国这种情况或许不是十分突出，死党与死党之间几乎没有什么隐私，父母与孩子之间就更不用谈什么隐私了。中国留学生们在这一方面有可能会有文化上的不适，因为即使有再好的美国朋友，也不可能亲密无间。人与人之间还是会有一定距离的。如果打破这种距离，就会招致美国朋友的反感。

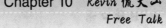

Section 13 友谊
Friendship

　　朋友是一种相知,朋友是一种相伴,朋友是一种相思。人生在世,多么美丽的青春年华都会像流水一样一去不复返,唯有朋友间的真挚友谊不会枯萎,可以天长地久。所以,我要说:"朋友们,珍惜友谊吧!"

1　I'm glad I have you for a friend. 我很高兴能有你这样的朋友。

咱们是朋友:
- I'm happy we're friends. 我很高兴我们是朋友。
- You're a good friend of mine. 你是我的好朋友。

礼貌回应一下:
- Me too! 我也是这么觉得!
- Yeah, you're a good friend of mine too. 是啊,你也是我的好朋友。

2　You're my best friend. 你是我最好的朋友。

最好的朋友:
- We'll always be best friends. 我们一直是最好的朋友。

我们的友谊一直到永远:
- Yeah, our friendship is going to last forever. 是啊,我们的友谊会一直到永远。
- I hope so! You're my best friend too. 希望如此! 你也是我最好的朋友。

3　I'm always here for you. 我会一直在你身边。

好朋友的见证：
- If you ever need anyone, I'm here. 如果你需要有人陪你，我随叫随到。
- I'm here if you need me. 如果你需要我，我会在这里的。

回谢：
- Thanks. Same for you! 谢谢，我也是！
- Thanks, man. I'm here for you too. 谢谢，哥们儿。我也会在你身边的。

4 I want to talk to you about something. 我想跟你说些事。

朋友之间互相倾听：
- I need to talk. Can you listen for me? 我想找人说会话。你能听我说吗？
- I want to talk to someone. Is that okay? 我想找人说会话。行吗？
- Let's talk. I need someone to listen. 咱们说说话吧。我需要有人听我说话。

很愿意倾听：
- Okay, I can listen. 好的，我听你说。
- Sure, I'll try to help you out. 当然，我会尽力帮你的。

5 I can always count on you! 我总是可以依赖你。

朋友之间就是互相依靠的：
- I can always rely on you. 我总是可以依赖你。
- I can always depend on you. 我可以永远信赖你。
- You are a friend who I can always trust. 你是我一直可以信赖的朋友。
- ❖ count on/rely on/depend on 依赖

6 What's true friendship? 什么是真正的友谊？

理解：
- I think friendship is love with understanding. 我认为友谊是基于理解的爱。
- True friendship is in some way a relationship of selfless giving. 真正的友谊在某种程度上是一种无私给予的关系。

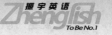
7 Last night I had a big argument with Jane. 昨天晚上我和简大吵了一架。

朋友之间有争执：

- We had a quarrel last night because she stood me up. 我们昨晚上吵架了，因为她放我鸽子。
- I had a row with Jane for she forgot to come to my house and went to see a film with her boyfriend. 我和简吵架了，因为她忘了来我家，和她男朋友去看电影了。

❖ stand someone up 放某人鸽子
❖ have a row with sb. 和某人吵架

Friendship Conversation

Kevin: Is something wrong, Steve?	凯　文：有什么事吗，史蒂夫？
Steve: Eh, I don't know if I want to talk about it.	史蒂夫：呃，我不知道该不该说。
Kevin: Come on, I'm your best friend. You can talk to me about anything.	凯　文：说吧，我是你最好的朋友。你什么事都可以跟我说。
Steve: Well…Donna was talking about breaking up.	史蒂夫：好吧……唐娜说要跟我分手。
Kevin: Aw, that's terrible. Why don't you come over to my place and chill for a bit?	凯　文：喔，那太糟了。你为什么不来我这里放松一下呢？
Steve: Nah, I don't want to burn you out.	史蒂夫：不，我不想连累你。
Kevin: Don't worry about it. You know I'm always here for you, man.	凯　文：别担心。你知道我是随叫随到的，哥们儿。
Steve: Okay…I guess I'll come over.	史蒂夫：好吧……我想我会来的。
Kevin: Cool. I'll make some tea or something.	凯　文：太好了。我会泡些茶水或准备点其他东西。
Steve: Thanks, man. I really appreciate it.	史蒂夫：谢谢，哥们儿。真是太感谢了。
Kevin: Anytime.	凯　文：我随时等着你。

❖chill [tʃɪl] *vi.* 冷静，放松
❖burn sb. out 累垮

文化穿越

　　美国人把友情看得也很重要，但没中国人看得那么重要。举个最简单的例子，在中国，死党与死党之间，可以随时牺牲一些自身利益来帮助对方；在美国，所谓的死党与死党之间，一般涉及个人利益时，美国人很难牺牲自己的利益去为对方做些什么。当求助于美国朋友时，如果他们当时正在处理自己的事情，他们会很直接地告诉你 NO；当然，如果没有什么要紧的事情做，他们也会很热情地过来帮忙。因此，对于美国的人际关系，直来直去就好，不用兜圈子。

Section **14** ▶ 环境
Environment

面对我们的生存环境日益恶化，Kevin 的环保意识也逐渐增强了。保护环境就从我们身边力所能及的小事做起：随手关灯节约能源，参加社区的志愿者活动，捡捡垃圾，净化环境……朋友们，为了我们共同的家园，都行动起来吧！

 口语大放送

1 I'm going to start helping the environment more. 我要开始更多地保护环境。

主张保护环境：

- I'm "going green". 我要走向环保绿化。
- I want to go green. 我想变得有环保意识。
- I want to help out the environment. 我想帮助改善环境。

我也想参与：

- That's cool. Maybe I'll do the same. 那很好，或许我也可以那样做。

行动起来：

- A lot of people are doing that lately. It shouldn't be too hard. 最近好多人都这么做。应该不太难。

2 I'm starting to buy only organic foods. 我开始只买有机食品。

还可以详细地说：

- I'm not buying any food that is grown with chemicals or pesticides.
  我不买那些使用化学物质或杀虫剂的食品。
- All of the food I'm buying is organic. 我所买的食物都是有机的。

有机食物确实有益：

- That's healthier for you and the environment. 这对你的健康和环境都有好处。

❖ organic [ɔr'gænɪk] *adj.* 有机的，有机物的

3 I've been filling up my recycling bin faster than my trash can!
我的回收桶填满的速度比垃圾桶都要快！

换回收桶的速度更快：

- I always have to change my recycling bin before the trash. 我总是先换我的回收桶再换垃圾桶。
- I think I recycle way more than I throw away. 我觉得我循环利用的东西比扔掉的东西要多。

客套回应一下：

- That's good. 很好。

❖ bin [bɪn] *n.* 容器，箱子
❖ trash [træʃ] *n.* 垃圾，废物

4 I'm going to help my friend pick up some litter today. 今天我要帮朋友去捡垃圾。

实际行动，捡垃圾：

- My friend and I are going to pick up litter today. 今天我和我朋友要去捡垃圾。
- I'm volunteering with my friend. We're going to go around and pick up trash. 我和我朋友都志愿去周围转转捡垃圾。
- I'm picking up litter today with a friend. 我今天和一个朋友去捡垃圾。

想加入其中：

- Cool. Can I come? 太好了，我能去吗？
- I'll help you out too, if you want. 如果需要的话，我也去帮你们。

表示祝愿：

- Have fun. 祝你们愉快。

❖ litter ['lɪtə] *n.* 废弃物

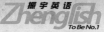
5 I'm trying to conserve energy by turning out the lights when I leave a room. 我离开房间的时候，我都关灯来节省能源。

开源节流：

- I've been turning out the lights when I leave the room, so I can conserve energy. 当我离开房间的时候会把灯关掉，所以我能节省能源。
- I want to conserve more energy. I turn out the lights when I leave a room. 我想节省更多的能源。当我离开房间的时候会把灯关掉。

我也会这样做：

- I do that too. 我也那样做。

这样还可以省钱：

- Yeah, and it lowers your electric bill. 是的，这样还可以减少电费。
- ❖ conserve [kən'sɜːv] vt. 保存，节省

6 I'm going to ride my bike around more often, so I save money on gas and pollute less often. 我经常骑自行车，所以我节省了汽油钱，也减少了污染。

骑自行车减少污染：

- I don't want to pollute so much, so I'll ride my bike around. 我不想有太多污染，所以我去附近的地方就骑自行车。
- If I ride my bike more often I won't pollute as much and I'll save money. 如果我经常骑自行车，就不会造成太多的污染，还能省钱。

主意不错：

- That's a good idea. 是个好主意。

7 Are you doing anything to help the environment? 你做了什么事来帮助保护环境吗？

采取环保措施了吗：

- Are you taking any steps to help out the environment? 你有采取什么措施来改善环境吗？
- What are you doing to save the environment? 你有做什么事情来拯救环境吗？

做了很多事情：

- It's really important to me, so I've been doing a lot. 这对于我来说很重要，所以我做了很多。
- I've been doing some things here and there. 我一直到处在做一些事情。

并不在意环境：

- I'm not too worried about it. 我不是很担心环境。

8 What can we do to protect the environment? 我们可以做些什么来保护环境？

给出建议：

- We can use public transport instead of taking our cars for a start. 我们可以乘坐公共交通设施代替自驾车。
- Don't use disposable things such as disposable wooden chopsticks, disposable paper tissues. 不要使用一次性的东西，比如一次性筷子、一次性餐巾纸。
- ❖ disposable [dɪ'spozəbl] *adj.* 用完即丢弃的，一次性使用的
- ❖ tissues ['tɪʃu] *n.* 纸巾

Environment Conversation

Kevin:	Hey mom. I was thinking of going green.	凯文：嘿，妈妈。我想变得有环保意识。
Mom:	Oh, that's great, honey. Do you need any help?	妈妈：哦，那很好，亲爱的。你需要帮助吗？
Kevin:	Well, I already recycle and buy recycled goods, but I'm not sure what else I could do.	凯文：我已经循环利用东西，也买了可循环利用的东西，但是我不知道还能做些什么。
Mom:	I have a book about it that I can let you borrow.	妈妈：我可以借给你一本关于环保的书看。

Kevin: That'd be great! Are there any programs in the area that I could volunteer in?	凯文： 那太好了！在咱们小区有没有什么项目我可以志愿参加呢？
Mom: I think there's a committee that goes around and picks up litter every weekend.	妈妈： 我想有一个每周末都在附近捡垃圾的委员会吧。
Kevin: Do you think you could look that up for me?	凯文： 你可以帮我找找吗？
Mom: Sure, I'll try to look it up online and I'll get you a phone number.	妈妈： 当然。我试着在网上给你找找，我会给你找到电话号码的。
Kevin: Thanks mom!	凯文： 谢谢妈妈！
Mom: No problem, sweetie.	妈妈： 不客气，宝贝。

❖recycle [ri'saɪkl] *vt.* 使循环，再次使用

文化穿越

美国的乡村绝大部分都是森林，房子和学校周边都是被森林包围着的。在高速路上开车很舒服，两边都是绿色的森林旷野，空气很清新。美国的城市污染比较乡村而言要严重很多，但城市里的绿色植被依然保护得很好，公园随处可见。另外，美国对于垃圾的分类很系统。最重要的是大部分人都会按照垃圾归类来投放垃圾，十分有助于城市垃圾的处理和回收。

Section 15 ▶ 智商与情商
IQ and EQ

通俗地说，IQ（智商）指的是一个人的聪明程度，EQ（情商）指人调控情绪、适应环境的能力。当然，继 EQ 之后，MQ（道德商数）、SQ（成功商数）也纷纷登场，更激发了公众对这些 Q 的好奇。其实我们有时候也在有意无意中通过各种方式参加 IQ 和 EQ 的小测验，希望知道自己的 Q 们是否足以保证成功。然而，IQ、EQ 及其他 Q 真可以决定人的成败吗？我们拭目以待。

1 What's your IQ? 你的 IQ 是多少?

IQ 测试结果：
- What did you score on your IQ test? 你的 IQ 测试分数是多少?

直接回答：
- I scored a 125. How about you? 我得了 125 分。你呢?
- ❖ IQ =intelligence quotient 智商

2 Do you know if you need to take an IQ test for this? 你知道你是否要为这个作一个 IQ 测试吗?

是否需要作 IQ 测试：
- Do you know if an IQ test is required? 你知道是否需要作 IQ 测试吗?

根据情况回答是否需要：
- No, I don't think it is. 不，我觉得不需要。
- Yeah, unfortunately it is. 很不幸，需要做。

3 She's pretty good looking, but man is she dumb! 她长得很漂亮，但人挺笨的!

举个同样的例子：

- He's really good at sports, but not so great at studying! 他体育很好，但学习不好。

自嘲一下：

- Haha. Well, that's alright with me! 哈哈，我也是！
- ❖ dumb [dʌm] *adj.* 愚蠢的

---

4 Did you take the test? What did they say your IQ was? 你作这个测试了吗？你的 IQ 是多少呢？

分数太低不想说：

- A little too low to be proud of! 很低，没有必要炫耀！

还不错：

- Pretty decent, I scored a 120. 相当不错，我得了 120 分。
- ❖ decent ['disnt] *adj.* 相当好的

---

5 I never did well in school, probably for my low IQ. 我在学校一向表现得不好，可能是因为我的 IQ 低。

低智商的结果：

- I probably did so bad in school because my IQ is so low! 我在学校表现得那么糟糕是因为我的 IQ 太低了。

笑着安慰：

- (laughs) Or maybe because you didn't pay attention! （笑）或许是因为你不够专心。

---

6 Which do you think is more important, IQ or EQ? 你认为智商和情商哪个更重要？

根据不同认识回答：

- I think IQ is more important. 我认为智商更重要。
- EQ is of much more importance. 情商更重要。
- I think both are important. I hope I am high in both IQ and EQ. 我认为两个都重要，我希望我的智商和情商都高。
- ❖ EQ =emotional quotient 情商

7 I do think EQ have much influence in promoting. 我真的认为情商对升职有很大作用。

情商很重要：

- I am sure EQ plays a vital role in promoting. 我确定情商对升职起很大作用。
- ❖ have much influence in sth. /doing sth. 对……有很大影响

8 Do you know where can I have a test on EQ? 你知道哪里可以作情商测试吗？

测试情商：

- I wonder if you know where to test EQ. 我想知道你是否知道哪里可以测试情商。

给你些建议：

- I know a famous website. 我知道一个有名的网站。
- I happen to have a book on EQ. Here you are. 我正好有一本关于 EQ 的书，给你。

IQ and EQ Conversation

Kevin: Hey Debra, did you ever take an IQ test?	凯　文：嘿，黛布拉，你作 IQ 测试了吗？
Debra: Yep!	黛布拉：作了！
Kevin: Well, how did you do?	凯　文：哦，作得怎么样？
Debra: Not so great!	黛布拉：不是很好！
Kevin: Me either. I'm pretty ashamed.	凯　文：我也是。我觉得好丢人。
Debra: Don't be. Those things are just a scam.	黛布拉：不要这样，那些东西是骗人的。
Kevin: You think?	凯　文：你这么认为？
Debra: Yeah, there's no way you can measure intelligence that way.	黛布拉：是啊，没有能测量智商的方法。
Kevin: I guess you're right.	凯　文：我觉得你说得很对。

Debra: Of course I am. I'm a genius!

Kevin: (laughs) Whatever you say.

黛布拉：当然了，我是天才!

凯　文：（大笑）随便你怎么说。

❖ scam ['skæm] *n.* 骗局

文 化 穿 越

　　对于美国公司而言，他们选择一个职员的标准绝不仅仅停留在 IQ（智商）上。更确切地说，EQ 更为重要。因为美国公司比较看重一个人的协作能力和专业水平的综合能力。一个成绩很高却无法处理事情的学生对于公司而言是没有意义的，因为他无法为公司创收。相反，一个在学校成绩平平，但却参与过多次相关领域的工作实践或者有过傲人的成果和经历的人，往往受公司赏识。当然，美国公司也看大学期间的在校成绩，但这仅仅是参考之一。

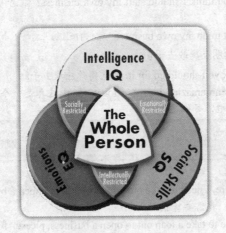

Section 16 ▶ 创业
Starting a Business

　　当从学校出来找工作四处碰壁的时候，当作为上班族钱不够花的时候，我的心中就有一股激情在涌动，自己创业去！自己当老板！在这里，Kevin 要提醒创业的朋友，先从自己擅长的领域去寻找机会，因为做自己熟悉的事情至少在技术或人脉关系上不会比别人差。

1 I think I'm going to start my own business. 我想我要开始创业了。

自己当老板：

* I'm really considering starting my own business. 我正在考虑自己创业。
* Do you think I should start my own business? 你觉得我应该自己创业吗？
* I want to do my own business. 我想自己创业。

可以鼓励朋友勇敢去干：

* I think you should go for it. 我觉得你应该去干。
* That's an amazing idea! Go for it, man! 这真是一个很棒的想法！去做吧，哥们儿！

2 I'd like to take a loan out to open a business. 我想贷款创业。

贷款创业：

* Hi there, I need to take out a loan in order to open a business, please. 你好，我需要贷款创业。
* I'd like to take a loan out to open a business, please. 我想贷款创业。

给出明确答复：

* Sure, just fill this form out. 当然可以，只要填好这张表格就可以了。

❖ take out 获得，领到（正式文件或服务）

3 What financial steps do I need to take to open my own business?
我自己创业需要办理什么财务手续吗？

办理创业手续：

- I really need to open a business, what steps should I take? 我要创业，需要办理什么手续吗？

给出具体的步骤：

- Well, after you've taken out the loan you need to file with the city. 你贷完款之后需要在市里备案。

4 What kind of business do you want to start? 你想开什么样的公司？

想开什么公司：

- What kind of business is it that you need a loan for? 你贷款想开一家什么样的公司？

具体回答：

- I'm looking to open a bakery. 我想开一个面包店。
- I'd really like to start a shoe store. 我喜欢开鞋店。
- ❖ bakery ['bekərɪ] *n.* 面包店

5 What kind of business is your company? 你公司的业务类型是什么？

明确回答：

- I've started an investment banking firm with some of my old colleagues. 我和以前的同事开了一家投资银行公司。

还没有决定，征求意见：

- I haven't decided yet. Maybe you can give me some advice. 我还没有决定，或许你可以给我一些建议。
- ❖ colleague ['kalig] *n.* 同事

6 I need to hire people for my business. 我的公司要招聘一些人。

想要招聘人才：

- I really need to find some people to work for me. 我想招一些人为我工作。

礼貌赞扬：

- Yeah, that's a smart move. 是啊，这是明智之举。

询问有没有现成人选：

- Do you know anyone who would be interesting in working for me? 你知道谁有兴趣来我们公司工作吗？

如果无能为力：

- Sorry, I don't know anyone off the top of my head. 不好意思，我一下子想不出来有谁。

❖ off the top of my head 突然想到

7 What should I name my business? 我该给公司起什么名字呢？

给公司想名字：

- I'm trying to think of a name for my business. 我正给我的公司想名字。

我也帮忙想想：

- Let me think. 让我想想。
- I can help! 我能帮忙。

8 Why do you want to start your own business? 你为什么想自己开公司呢？

明确陈述理由：

- I hate being controlled by others. 我不想受制于人。
- I want to prove I can make use of my ability to earn more money. 我想证明我能凭自己的能力挣更多的钱。

❖ make use of 利用

Starting a Business Conversation

Kevin:	I really want to start a business.	凯　文：	我想开一家公司。
Debra:	What? Why?	黛布拉：	什么？为什么呀？
Kevin:	Well, I've always wanted to have one, and I could be my own boss.	凯　文：	我一直想有个公司，可以自己当老板。

402

Debra: Well sure, but that's a lot of hard work.	黛布拉：确实，但那是一项很艰难的工作。
Kevin: I know, but I'm willing to do it.	凯　文：我知道，但是我很愿意去做。
Debra: Even take the loans and everything?	黛布拉：甚至要贷款还有其他很多事呢？
Kevin: Yep.	凯　文：是的。
Debra: Well, then, I think you should go for it. I believe in you.	黛布拉：哦，那么，我觉得你应该去做。我相信你。
Kevin: Thanks. That means a lot. I think I will.	凯　文：谢谢，这对于我来说很重要。我会努力的。
Debra: I'll help you out however I can.	黛布拉：我会尽我所能帮你的。

文 化 穿 越

　　美国拥有很健全的商业法。政府积极鼓励学生创业，学校大力宣传创业。在这其中，一部分创业者来自比较富裕的家庭。不过美国的情况与中国不同，中国的富人们一般都会将自己的财产继承权给子女，但美国的富人们会将一部分财产捐赠，只借一部分给子女创业。因为在他们的理念中，一切财富都是他们辛勤工作的结晶，与子女无直接关系。他们认为自己的子女必须通过自己的努力来获得财富。另一方面，美国遗产税对于富人来说是个噩梦，与其被政府征税，不如将大笔遗产捐赠给社会，做些善事。他们将大笔遗产捐赠给社会，就可免征其遗产税。

Section 17 ▶ 激情 NBA
National Sports

不记得是什么时候喜欢 NBA 的了！只记得那时候我们一群哥们儿总喜欢围坐在电视机旁或者露天的大屏幕前，看那些球员在球场上奔跑、抢篮板、投球、进球、得分……为他们欢呼，也为他们着迷。NBA 真的太精彩了！下次赛季开始的时候，朋友们别忘了叫上我一起看球赛啊！

1 The NBA is on this Sunday! 这周日有 NBA 联赛！

周末就有比赛：
- NBA starts this Sunday. Are you excited? 这周末美国职业篮球联赛开始了，你激动吗？

心情很激动：
- I can't wait! 我都等不及了！
- ❖ NBA 美国职业篮球联赛 (National Basketball Association 的首字母缩写)

2 Did you catch the game last night? 你昨晚上赶上看比赛了吗？

看比赛了吗：
- Hey, did you see the game last night? 嘿，你昨晚上看比赛了吗？
- Did you catch the game last night? It was a real nail biter. 你昨晚上看比赛了吗？真是一场紧张激烈的比赛。

根据实际情况回答：
- Yeah! It was wild! 是的！太疯狂了！
- No, I missed it! I'm pissed. 没有，我错过了！气死我了。
- ❖ nail biter 激烈紧张的比赛
- ❖ pissed [pɪst] adj. 愤怒的

3 My favorite NBA player is Bryant. 我最喜欢的 NBA 球员是布赖恩特。

最喜欢的篮球明星：

- I think my favorite NBA player will always be Jordon. 我觉得我最喜欢的 NBA 球员会一直是乔丹。
- I'm a huge fan of Oneil. 我是奥尼尔的忠实粉丝。

表达自己的想法：

- Really? I hate that guy! 真的吗？我讨厌那个人！
- Nice! Jordon for life! 太好了！乔丹是我的一生的偶像。

4 My favorite team is the Heat. 我最喜欢热火队了。

球队粉丝：

- I'm a huge Magic fan. 我是魔术队的忠实粉丝。

不喜欢对方说的球队：

- I hate the Heat! Go Bulls! 我讨厌热火队！公牛队好样的！

5 I got tickets to the game, wanna come? 我有这场比赛的门票，你想一起去吗？

邀请去看比赛：

- I've got two tickets to the game this Friday. You should come. 我有两张这周五比赛的门票，你应该一起来。
- Hey, want to see the Lakers game? I got tickets! 嘿，想去看湖人的比赛吗？我有门票！

如果感兴趣，很想去：

- Aw, dude, I would love to! 噢，老兄，我想去！
- Yeah, man, that's intense! 好的，哥们儿，真刺激！

想去，但是没有时间：

- I wish! I gotta work that day, dude. 我想去！但那天我得上班，老兄。

❖ intense [ɪn'tɛns] *adj.* 紧张的，热情的，激烈的
❖ gotta ['gatə] *adv.* 必须去（相当于 have got to）

6 I'm betting on the Mavericks tonight. 我今晚赌达拉斯小牛队赢。

就这 **900** 句 玩转口语

赌比赛：

- I put all my money on the Hornets. I hope they win. 我把钱都押在大黄蜂队了，希望他们能赢。
- If the Lakers don't win, I'll go broke! 如果湖人队赢不了，我会破产的！

赌比赛可不是件好事：

- You shouldn't have bet your money! 你不应该赌钱的！
- Well, that was a pretty stupid thing to do. 噢，那样做很愚蠢。

7 Have you been following NBA for this season? 你最近关注 NBA 本赛季的赛事了吗？

NBA 球迷：

- Of course, tomorrow evening there will be a most exciting game. 当然，明天晚上就有一场激动人心的比赛。

不喜欢这类比赛：

- No. I hate it. 没有，我讨厌比赛。

8 Which team won last game? 哪个球队赢了上次的比赛？

看了比赛的人：

- The Lakers. They have home court advantage. 湖人队赢了。他们有主场优势。

没看比赛的人：

- I missed the game because my boss gave me some work. 我错过比赛了，因为老板给了我一些工作。
- ❖ home court advantage 主场优势

National Sports Conversation

Andy: Hey, did you catch the game last night? 安迪：嘿，昨晚上你看比赛了吗？

Kevin: Which one? 凯文：哪个比赛？

Andy: NFL, man. What else?	安迪：NFL，伙计。还能有什么？
Kevin: I'm more of an NBA guy myself.	凯文：我更喜欢看 NBA。
Andy: What!? How could you not like football?	安迪：什么！？你怎么能不喜欢足球呢？
Kevin: How could you not like basketball?	凯文：你怎么能不喜欢篮球呢？
Andy: Well, don't get me wrong. I like basketball, just not as much as football.	安迪：好吧，你千万别误会。我喜欢篮球，只是不像喜欢足球那么喜欢。
Kevin: You're crazy. The Lakers shot an insane 3-pointer, It was crazy!	凯文：你太疯狂了。湖人队疯狂地投了个三分球，太不可思议了。
Andy: You should have seen the Steelers score a touchdown. I went ballistic!	安迪：你应该看到钢铁人队触地得分了，我都快疯了。
Steve: Will you two shut up already?	史蒂夫：你们两个都闭嘴行吗？

❖ NFL 美国全国橄榄球联盟（National Football League 的首字母缩写）

❖ don't get me wrong 别误会，别把我的意思弄错了

❖ insane [ɪn'sen] *adj.* 疯狂的

❖ 3-pointers 三分球

❖ touchdown ['tʌtʃ'daun] *n.* 触地得分

❖ ballistic [bə'lɪstɪk] *adj.* 失去理智的，狂怒的

❖ shut up 闭嘴，安静

文化穿越

　　美国是个崇尚自由和民主的国家。但在篮球、橄榄球、棒球运动上美国十分有团队合作精神。NBA 是美国的民族运动之一，热爱篮球的民众很多，大街小巷经常可以看到孩子们一块儿打篮球，大学与大学之间会有阶段性的比赛。美国很多家庭在周末或者休息时会带着孩子一块儿去看篮球比赛。在美国知名度比较高的中国篮球运动员是姚明和易建联。

Section 18 运动健身
Exercise and Fitness

Kevin 一直坚信生命在于运动。闲暇的时候和家人朋友们一起运动健身，比如慢跑、徒步行走、骑自行车等，既锻炼了身体又可以和家人一起共度休闲时光，还可以跟大自然亲密接触，呼吸新鲜空气，欣赏美景，是繁忙紧张的生活工作之余减压的好方法。

1 I need to go to the gym more. 我需要多去几次健身房。

需要运动健身：

- I really need to start going to the gym. 我确实需要去健身房了。
- I need to get some more exercise. 我需要做更多的运动。

我和你一起去：

- I'll go with you next time. 下次我陪你去。

2 I want to sign up for a gym membership. 我想报名成为健身房的会员。

想要成为会员：

- I want to get a gym membership. 我想成为健身房的会员。
- I'd like to get a gym membership. 我想成为健身房的会员。
- ❖ sign up for sth. 报名（参加课程）
- ❖ membership ['mɛmʒ,ʃɪp] n. 会员资格

3 How much does a gym membership cost? 成为健身房会员需要多少钱？

询问健身房会员的价钱：

- How much is it for a membership to your gym? 成为你们健身房的会员需要多少钱？

- I really need a membership to your gym. Could you quote me a price? 我真的想成为你们健身房的会员，你能给我说下价钱吗？

明确回答：

- Sure, it's about fifty dollars a month. 当然可以，一个月差不多50美元。

❖ quote [kwot] *vt.* 报价

---

4 Do you have to pay a membership fee? 你要付会员费吗？

需要付会员费：

- Yeah. Not as expensive as you may imagine, 500 dollars each year. 是啊，不像你想的那么贵，每年五百美元。

因为是新开的，不用付钱：

- No, the fitness center is newly-built and it's attracting members. 不用，这个健身中心是新开的，正吸收会员呢。

❖ fitness center 健身中心

---

5 I went to the health club to work out. All my muscles are sore. 我去健身俱乐部锻炼去了，全身肌肉酸痛。

你锻炼过度了吧：

- Did you overdo it with your exercises? 你运动过量了吧？
- What kinds of activities have you done? 你今天都做什么运动了？

❖ muscle ['mʌsl] *n.* 肌肉

---

6 I'm starting to lose weight since I started going to the gym! 自从我开始去健身房后，我的体重减轻了。

去健身房有效果：

- The gym is really working. I feel better already. 去健身房真有用，我已经感觉好多了。
- I've been going to the gym a lot lately, and I'm starting to see results. 最近我经常去健身房，而且我开始看到效果了。

效果这么好，我也想去：

- That's great to hear. Now only if I could do the same. 听到你这番话真高兴。要是我也一样就好了。

❖ lose weight 减肥

7 Do you know where the locker room is? 你知道更衣室在哪儿吗?

健身房的设施:
- Could you show me how to get to the locker room from here? 能告诉我从这儿怎么去更衣室吗?

帮忙指路:
- Yeah, it's right down the hall. 是的，顺着大厅走就能看到了。

询问是否可以用更衣室:
- Are there showers in the locker room I could use? 更衣室里的淋浴我可以用吗?

遗憾地回答:
- There are showers, but they're for members only. 有淋浴，但只有会员才能用。
- ❖ Locker room 更衣室，衣帽间

8 I need a personal trainer. 我需要一个私人教练。

配备私人教练:
- Could I get a personal trainer, please? 请问能给我配一名私人教练吗?
- Do you think I could sign up for a personal trainer? 你觉得我可以签约一名私人教练吗?

当然可以了:
- No problem. Just sign these forms here. 没问题，把这些表格填好就可以了。
- ❖ personal trainer 私人教练

9 Wow, that was a great workout! 哇，健身效果真好!

健身效果不错，但很累:
- What a workout, I feel exhausted! 运动真累,我感觉到筋疲力尽了!

非常同意对方的说法:
- Oh, man, I'm gonna feel that one in the morning! 哦，伙计，我早上也感觉到筋疲力尽了!
- Yeah, man. That was crazy! 是啊，伙计。太疯狂了!

410

不同的看法：

- I feel like a million bucks after that. 做完运动我觉得好舒畅。
- ❖ feel like a million bucks 感觉心情极好，感觉很舒畅 (俚语)

交流面对面

Exercise and Fitness Conversation

Kevin: I need to go to the gym more.	凯 文：我需要多去健身房了。
Debra: Why?	黛布拉：为什么？
Kevin: I'm getting out of shape.	凯 文：我的体型都走样了。
Debra: You look fine.	黛布拉：你看起来还好啊。
Kevin: Well, sure I look fine but I feel horrible.	凯 文：嗯，我看起来当然还好，不过我感觉很糟糕。
Debra: Well, let's go this weekend then.	黛布拉：哦，那这周末我们一起去吧。
Kevin: Alright. Are you a member?	凯 文：好的，你是会员吗？
Debra: Yeah, I'm a member at Silver's Gym.	黛布拉：是的，我是 Silver's Gym 的会员。
Kevin: Oh, really? I heard that place was good.	凯 文：哦，是吗？我听说那儿挺好的。
Debra: Yeah, I have a personal trainer and everything.	黛布拉：是啊，我有一个私人教练还有其他的待遇。
Kevin: Well, sign me up. I'm in!	凯 文：哦，我也报名。我加入会员！

❖get out of shape 体型走样

文化穿越

　　日常生活中，美国人很重视健身。无论是学校还是大中型企业，很多都会有自己的健身房。大学里，美国学生会将大部分业余时间都用在健身上。学校里的健身房设施很齐全，也很专业，还有很多舞蹈等课程的辅导。对于上班族，健身也有着很重要的地位。大部分人每天都要抽出一定时间跑步或者去健身房锻炼。美国人喜欢吃甜食，因此胖子很多，减肥也是他们去健身房的原因之一。

Section 19 ▶ 减肥
Lose Weight

减肥是当今流行的话题，特别是对于女性朋友（其实很多男性朋友也很关注自己的体重，Kevin 就是其中之一 *^_^*）。因为一个人如果太胖的话，影响美观且不必说，最主要的是对身体也有影响。不过在这里 Kevin 要提醒减肥的朋友们，不要过于节食，减肥还是要多运动。

1 I think I'm gaining weight. 我觉得我长胖了。

感觉自己长胖了：
- I feel like I've been gaining weight recently. 我感觉我最近一直在长胖。
- I'm pretty sure I'm heavier than I used to be. 我很肯定我比以前重了。

客套安慰：
- It's not too bad. 还不是太糟糕啦。

关心地询问：
- Are you worried about it? 你很担心吗？

给出建议：
- You should do something about it. 你应该做点什么。

❖ gain weight 增加体重

2 I really want to lose some weight. 我真的想减肥。

想要减肥：
- I want to try and lose a few pounds. 我要争取减几磅。
- I want to get a little thinner. 我想变瘦点。

- I don't want to be this heavy anymore. I'll try and lose weight. 我不想再这么胖了。我要试着减肥。

主动提出帮助对方：

- I'll help you out if you need it. 如果你需要，我会帮你的。

你其实还好啦，不需要减肥：

- You don't need to lose weight. You're fine how you are. 你不需要减肥。你现在的体重正好。

3 What do you think about all the different diets people go on? 对于人们进行各种各样的节食你怎么看？

节食减肥也许有点效果：

- I think some may be effective. 我认为有些或许是有效果的。

没必要，节食会影响健康：

- I don't think dieting is good. It's much better to eat a balanced diet. 我不认为节食有什么好处。均衡饮食要好得多。

❖ effective [ɪ'fɛktɪv] *adj.* 有效的
❖ balanced diet 均衡饮食

4 I'm going on a diet. 我正在节食。

正在节食中：

- I started a new diet. 我开始了新一轮节食。
- My diet is starting today. 我从今天开始节食。

祝对方好运：

- Good luck. 祝你好运。

让对方量力而行：

- Try your best. 尽力而为。

❖ go on a diet 节食

5 I think my exercise and diet plan has been working. 我觉得我的运动和节食计划已经起作用了。

减肥有效：

- I think I'm losing weight. Thanks to my new diet and exercise plan. 我觉得我变轻了，多亏了我的新节食计划和运动计划。

- I lost a little bit of weight so far, because of exercise and diet. 因为做运动和节食，到目前为止，我减了一点肥了。

祝贺对方减肥取得成效：

- That's great! Good job! 太好了！干得不错！
- I'm glad to hear that. 很高兴听到这个消息。
- ❖ thanks to 幸亏，由于

6 I'm back down to my ideal weight. 我又回到我的理想体重了。

达到理想效果：

- I lost all the weight I wanted to lose. 我想减掉的体重都减掉了。
- I lost the extra weight! 我减掉多余的体重了！
- My weight is back down to normal. 我的体重恢复正常了。

祝贺对方减肥成功：

- Congrats! Let's celebrate. 恭喜你！咱们庆祝一下。
- Awesome! Good job, man! 真棒！干得好，伙计！
- ❖ congrats [kən'græts] *int.* 恭喜

7 What should the obese do to lose weight? 太胖的人应该怎么减肥呢？

建议改变饮食习惯：

- They need to change their diet habits and eat healthy foods. 他们需要改变饮食习惯，吃健康的食物。

建议增加运动量：

- They have to increase the amount of exercise they do every day. 他们必须增加每天的运动量。
- ❖ obese [o'bis] *adj.* 极为肥胖的

8 All those diet books and special foods are a racket. 所有的那些减肥书和特效食品都是骗人的。

不要相信减肥药：

- I used to try different health foods, but they didn't work. 我以前试了不同的保健食品，但是没有效果。

❖ racket ['rækɪt] n. 骗局
❖ health food 保健食品

交 流 面 对 面

Lose Weight Conversation

Kevin: Sophie, can I ask you something? I want you to be honest.

凯文：索菲，能问你点事吗？你要老实回答我。

Sophie: Yeah, man.

索菲：好的，伙计。

Kevin: Do you think I'm gaining weight? I feel like I'm heavier than I used to be.

凯文：你觉得我变胖了吗？我感觉我比以前重了。

Sophie: Well, maybe a little. But it's no big deal.

索菲：嗯，可能有点。但没什么大不了的。

Kevin: I don't want it to get out of control, though. Maybe I should go on a diet.

凯文：但是我不想让我的体重失控。也许我应该减肥。

Sophie: Why don't we go to the gym too? I hear the gym in town has a pretty cheap membership plan.

索菲：为什么我们不一起去健身房呢？我听说市中心的健身房有一个特别便宜的会员计划。

Kevin: That sounds cool. What days are you free?

凯文：听起来很不错。你哪几天有空呢？

Sophie: I'm usually free Monday, Wednesday, and Friday mornings. Do you want to go then?

索菲：我一般周一、周三和周五上午有空。你想去吗？

Kevin: Yeah, that sounds great. Thanks for doing this with me!

凯文：好啊，听起来很不错。谢谢你和我一起去。

Sophie: No problem, man. Honestly, I kind of want to lose a few pounds too.

索菲：不客气，哥们儿。老实说，我也有点想减掉几磅呢。

Kevin: Then let's make sure we stay on task. Doing this together should make it easier, right?

凯文：那我们就这么定了。两个人一起会更容易点，是吧？

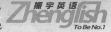

Sophie: Yeah, that's what I'm thinking. Let's meet at the gym at 8 in the morning on Monday.	索菲：是啊，我也是这么想的。我们周一早上8点在健身房见。
Kevin: Alright, I'll see you there.	凯文：好的，健身房见。

❖ out of control 失去控制
❖ It's no big deal. 没什么大不了的。
❖ stay on 留下来继续（学习，工作等）

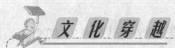 文化穿越

　　减肥是美国人平时经常讨论的话题之一，原因很简单，因为在美国胖子太多了。当然，这与美国的饮食习惯有关。他们喜欢甜食，甚至任何食物都要放糖。他们平时也喜欢吃零食——炸薯片、糖豆儿以及冰激凌一类的甜食。除此之外，美国是个车轮上的民族，美国人结束一天的办公室工作后，就会开车回家。期间很少有机会锻炼。美国有专门针对减肥的节目，谁在规定的期间内减重最多，可以获得奖金。美国有很多特别胖的胖子，他们胖到无法自己系鞋带，无法坐进一般的汽车，甚至上电影院看电影都要占两个以上的座位。

Chapter 11 好莱坞的梦想
Entertainment

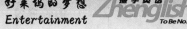

Section 1 ▶ 音乐的狂想
Music

工作累了，心烦了，就娱乐一下吧。听听音乐，在美妙的乐曲声中让沉重的大脑暂时休眠，然后一点一点地逐渐放松，让身心在轻柔的音乐中愉悦开来；再或者随着劲爆的歌曲狂吼几声，把心中的烦恼吼出去。来，一起和Kevin随着音乐动起来！

推荐朋友听歌

1 Hey, man, check out this new band I heard! 嘿，哥们儿，来体验一下我听过的这个新乐队！

还可以这么说哦：

- Hey, dude, listen to this band! 嘿，伙计，听听这个乐队！
- Oh, man, I love this! Listen! 哦，老兄，我喜欢这个！听听！

如果对方被你的激情所吸引：

- Alright, let's hear 'em. 好的，咱们听听吧。
- Sure, dude, let's hear it. 好的，哥们儿，咱们来听吧。

❖ 'em 他们，是 them 在口语中的缩略。

2 This band kicks ass, listen to them! 这个乐队真了不起，听听吧！

也可以这么来表达：

- These guys are really good, check it out! 这些人真的很不错，来体验一下吧！

如果你听了后感觉真的是名不虚传，也可以附和一声：

- Wow, these guys are great! 哇，这些家伙好棒！

❖ kick ass 在此处的意思并不像字面上的那样，而是俚语的用法，表示"了不起，非常厉害"。

评论喜欢的乐队

3 I really like Iron Maiden, but I'm not a big Metallica fan. 我很喜欢铁娘子乐队，不过我可不是金属乐队的铁杆粉丝。

我可不认同你的说法：
- No way. Metallica kicks Iron Maiden's ass any day! 绝不可能，金属乐队任何时候都比铁娘子乐队要棒。

【补充】Iron Maiden 铁娘子乐队。无论在哪个国家，Iron Maiden 这个伟大的名字在重金属乐迷当中都是家喻户晓的。在过去的 20 多年当中，Iron Maiden 始终都是英国最杰出的金属乐队之一，同时，无数的后辈乐队在成长的过程中也都受到了 Iron Maiden 音乐的影响。Metallica 重金属乐队。1981 年在美国洛杉矶组建的重金属乐队，是当今最为成功最有影响力的摇滚乐队之一。

4 This is really good, but it's nothing compared to Slayer. 这确实不错，但和杀手乐队比起来就没什么了。

有什么不同的意见，就表达出来吧：
- Yeah. I can see that, but I still hate Slayer. 是啊，我看到了，不过我还是不喜欢杀手乐队。

❖ compared to 与……相比

【补充】Slayer 杀手乐队。是美国著名速度金属乐队，与金属、大屠杀、"炭疽"乐队并称为激流四巨头；与重金属，铁娘子，潘多拉并称为金属四巨头。

5 They never should have changed singers. They're horrible now! 他们不应该更换歌手的。现在他们多糟糕啊！

如果你肯定这种说法：
- Yeah man, they must be insane. 是啊，他们肯定是疯了。

言辞还可以更激烈一些：
- What the hell were they thinking, getting rid of their singer? This sounds like shit! 他们究竟在想些什么，要丢弃他们的歌手？这听上去就像垃圾！

❖ insane [ɪn'sen] *adj.* 疯狂的，愚蠢的

❖ get rid of 丢弃，抛弃

询问喜欢的音乐

6　What kind of music do you like? 你喜欢什么类型的音乐?

换种说法:

- What kind of music do you listen to? 你听什么音乐?
- What's your favorite music genre? 你最喜欢什么类型的音乐?
- ❖ genre ['ʒɑnrə] *n.* 类型，风格

7　Hey, what are you listening to? 嘿，你在听什么?

很好听，是什么歌:

- This is really good. What is it? 这确实不错。是什么歌?
- This is great! What is it? 这太棒了! 是什么歌?

直接告知:

- Oh, this is The Smiths. They're classic. 哦，这是史密斯乐团的，都是很经典的。
- We're listening to Kiss, duh! 我们在听 Kiss 乐队，废话!

【补充】The Smiths 史密斯乐团。在 20 世纪 80 年代英国的独立音乐背景中，史密斯乐团算是最成功的另类摇滚乐团之一，他们对后来的独立音乐影响很大。

Kiss 吻乐队。1973 年 1 月于纽约组建的美国摇滚乐队，其魅力体现在现场演出上，他们艳丽的化妆、花哨的服饰、令人眼花缭乱的舞台效果，再加上硬摇滚的音乐，创造了广告上说的"天下最棒的摇滚演出"。

演唱会现场

8　This concert is incredible! 这场音乐会简直难以置信!

好听的音乐总是这么吸引人:

- Holy shit, dude! This is great! 天哪，兄弟! 这太棒了!
- This concert is blowing my mind! So good! 这场音乐会让我心醉神迷! 太棒了!

肯定以上的说法:

- I know, right! Incredible! 是啊，没错! 太不可思议了!

- Yeah! This is freaking awesome! 是啊！这太酷了！
- ❖ holy shit 天哪
- ❖ blow one's mind 让某人心醉神迷，神魂颠倒

9 Lift me up, I want to crowd surf! 把我举起来，我想人群冲浪！（演唱会的现场人山人海，你如果想在音乐的魔力中更疯狂一点儿，就可以这么说。）

❖ crowd-surfing 人群冲浪，被人群举到头顶传来传去

10 I'm totally buying their CD. 我会去买他们全部的 CD。

类似的说法还有：
- These guys are amazing. I'm buying their album. 这些人太棒了，我要去买他们的专辑。

对方可以附和说：
- Let's go buy it, dude! 咱们去买吧，伙计！

如果你不认可：
- I want their CD so bad! 我觉得他们的 CD 太差劲了。

❖ album ['ælbəm] *n.* 专辑，一套唱片

11 That band played so loud. I have a headache! 那个乐队的表演太吵了，我都头疼！

认同的请点击同意：
- Me too, man, me too. 我也是，老兄，我也是。

12 Hey, let's try to get backstage after the show! 嘿，演出结束后咱们想办法去后台吧！

类似的表达还有：
- I got a backstage pass. Let's go hang with the band! 我得到了一张后台通行证，咱们去找这乐队玩玩儿吧。
- I really want to meet the band. Let's see if we can get backstage. 我真的想见见这个乐队，咱们看看能不能去后台。

如果你同意这种做法：
- Sure man, it's worth a shot! 好的，哥们儿，这值得一试！

- Awesome dude, I can't wait! 太棒了，哥们儿，我都等不及了！
- ❖ backstage pass 后台通行证
- ❖ worth a shot 值得一试

Music Conversation

(On the way to a concert)	（去演唱会的路上）
Kevin: Have you heard these guys before? They're so good.	凯　文：你以前听说过这些人吗？他们很不错的。
Debra: Nope, but they seem pretty good from what I've heard.	黛布拉：没有，但是他们看起来远比我听说的要好。
Kevin: Let's listen to their CD to get ready for tonight.	凯　文：那咱们听听他们的 CD 吧，也好为今天晚上的演唱会准备一下。
Debra: Alright, I want to learn the words before the show!	黛布拉：好啊，我想在演出之前了解一下歌词！
(They arrive at the concert)	（他们到达音乐会现场）
Debra: Where do we buy tickets at?	黛布拉：我们在哪里买门票呢？
Kevin: I think just the kiosk over there has them for sale.	凯　文：我想那边的小摊棚就卖门票。
Debra: Oh, ok. Well let's go check it out. I don't want to have to wait in line.	黛布拉：哦，好的，那咱们去看看。我可不想排队等。
Kevin: Alright, lead the way.	凯　文：好吧，你带路。
Debra: Ok, get your ID ready.	黛布拉：好的，准备好你的身份证。
Kevin: Oh, damn! I almost forgot about that.	凯　文：哦，该死！我差点儿都忘了那个了。

❖kiosk [kɪ'ask] *n.* 小摊棚，售货亭
❖wait in line 排队等候

文化穿越

朋友们可能会认为在网上下载喜欢的歌曲和电影是件非常正常的事儿。但在美国，几乎没有网站可以提供免费下载，一般都会收取一定费用。盗版光盘在美国是绝对禁止的。美国的版权相关法律很健全，任何剽窃或侵犯版权行为都会被告上法庭。如果留学生携带或者传播大量盗版物品，等待你的可能会是一张法院的传单。

Section 2　▶ 电影的魅力
Movies

> 经典的电影在愉悦我们五官的同时，也给电影本身留下了永久的记忆。Kevin 也很喜欢看电影，每次新片一出来，都会去电影院体会电影的魅力。如果你也是个影迷的话，下次去看电影的时候可以叫上我。

口 语 大 放 送

1 I really want to go see *Inception*. I heard the acting was great! 我真想去看《盗梦空间》，听说演技非常棒！

称赞一部电影，还可以这样表达：

- *Inception* seems really good, especially the acting. 《盗梦空间》看起来确实不错，尤其是演技。
- *Inception* has the best acting I've seen all year. 《盗梦空间》的演技是我一年中所见过的最好的。

2 Wow, that movie kicked ass! 哇，那部电影真棒！

称赞一部电影，还可以这样感叹：

- That was fantastic! 那太不可思议了！
- That movie was awesome! 那部电影太棒了！
- ❖ fantastic [fæn'tæstɪk] *adj.* 极好的，了不起的

3 I'm in the mood to see an action movie. 我想去看部动作片。

如果你对这一提议不感兴趣：

- I'm not really in the mood for that. How about something romantic? 我对那个真没什么心情，爱情片怎么样？
- ❖ action movie 动作片

425

❖ be in the mood 想要做某事，心情舒畅
❖ romantic [rə'mæntɪk] adj. 浪漫的，幻想的

4 Hey, do you want to come over and watch a movie? 嘿，你想过来看部影片吗？

征求意见：

- How about going to a movie? 去看部电影怎么样？
- Want to come over? I have some movies. 想过来吗？我有些影片。

如果你有兴趣，就可以这么回答：

- Sure, I'll be right over! 好啊，我马上过来！

5 Hey, did you see the new Bruce Willis movie? 嘿，你看过布鲁斯·威利斯新拍的那部影片吗？

如果没有看过：

- No, but I saw the trailer for it. 没有，但我看过它的预告片。
- ❖ trailer ['treɪlə] n. 预告片

6 Hey man, it's cheaper if we catch the matinee. 嘿，老兄，如果我们看日场的话会更便宜。

看日场比较便宜：

- The movie will be cheaper if we go before noon. 如果我们中午之前去看这部电影会更便宜。

那就去吧：

- Alright, well we'd better hurry. 好吧，那我们最好快点儿。
- ❖ matinee [,mætən'e] n. 日场，日戏

7 Can I have two adult tickets, please? 请给我来两张成人票，好吗？

想买哪部电影的票：

- May I have two tickets for *Iron Man*, please? 请给我来两张《钢铁侠》的票，好吗？

售票员回答：

- Sure, that will be 15 dollars. 好的，总共是 15 美元。

8 I've heard they're making a new batman movie! 我听说他们新拍了蝙蝠侠电影。

对所说的话表示疑问：

- No way. Really? 不可能吧。真的吗?

表达欣喜之情：

- That's awesome! 那太好了!

9 That movie is a box-office hit. 那部电影是卖座片。

引起轰动的电影：

- That movie is a blockbuster. 那部电影引起了轰动。
- That film created a sensation. 那部影片引起了轰动。
- This movie has been ruling the box office for weeks. 这部电影已经雄踞票房榜首好几个星期了。

❖ a box-office hit 卖座电影，票房爆满
❖ blockbuster ['blɑk,bʌstə] n. 大轰动，最成功的电影
❖ sensation [sɛn'seʃən] n. 轰动

Movies Conversation

Kevin: Hey, want to go see the new batman movie? | 凯　文：嘿，想去看新拍的蝙蝠侠电影吗?

Debra: Yeah! I've been wanting to see that. | 黛布拉：好啊! 我一直想看那部电影。

Kevin: Alright. Let me get dressed and we'll head out. | 凯　文：好的。我穿好衣服咱们就去。

(They arrive at the movie theater) | (他们到达电影院)

Kevin: Could I have one adult ticket for the 5:00 show, please? | 凯　文：请给我来一张5点钟放映的电影的成人票，好吗?

Clerk: Sure, $7. 50 please. | 职　员：好的，7.5 美元。

Kevin: Here you go. | 凯　文：给你钱。

Debra: Same for me.	黛布拉：我也一样。
(They enter the theater)	（他们走进电影院）
Debra: Where do you want to sit?	黛布拉：你想坐哪儿？
Kevin: I don't care, just away from people. I hate that.	凯　文：我随便，只要远离人群就行，我比较讨厌那个。
(After the movie)	（看完电影之后）
Kevin: Holy crap. That was amazing!	凯　文：哇，天哪！简直太妙了！
Debra: I know man. I want to see it again	黛布拉：是啊，我还想再看一遍。
Kevin: I'm definitely renting it when it comes out on DVD.	凯　文：等 DVD 出来后我一定租一张碟。

❖head out 前往
❖holy crap 哇，天哪

文化穿越

　　在美国有个很爽的事儿是可以在第一时间看到全球首映的电影大片，有很多影片会在一个月或者几个月后到达国内，也有的影片甚至不会在国内上映。对于刚上映的电影，电影院价格可达到 10 到 20 美元不等。而美国的 Dollar Show（1 美元影院）经常提供一些过时的电影，也有很多人不会去看首映，而是等待 Dollar Show 的上映。美国的 DVD 很贵，最新出的电影，其票价可以达到 20 多美元一张甚至更多，最便宜的 DVD 也要 5 美元到 15 美元不等。因此，当美国朋友得知在中国可以用不到 1 美元的价格买到最新的大片时，脸都绿了。另外，美国有专门的商店会卖过时的 CD 和 DVD，你甚至可以找到 50 年代的经典老电影，价格在 5 美元左右。当然，全是正版的。

Section 3　▶ 沙发土豆
TV

> 有一段时间我十分沉迷于看电视，整天躺着或坐在沙发上看电视，是一个不折不扣的 couch potato。偶尔看看电视娱乐一下，是可以打发时间的，不过不要像我那样成为 couch potato 哦。

 口 语 大 放 送

1 When is the new episode of *South Park* on? 新的那集《南方公园》什么时候上映？

询问电视剧放映的时间：

- Hey, what time is the new episode of *Family Guy* coming on? 嘿，新的那集《恶搞之家》什么时候上演？

回答：

- I think it starts at 6. 我想 6 点开始吧。
- ❖ 7:30 I think. 我想是 7:30 吧。
- ❖ episode ['epəˌsod] *n.* 一集

2 Oh man, I love this show! 哦，老兄，我喜欢这个节目！

类似的说法还有：

- Dude, this show is hilarious! 老兄，这节目很滑稽！
- ❖ hilarious [hɪ'lɛrɪəs] *adj.* 滑稽的，有趣的

3 God, I can't stand commercials! 天哪，我受不了商业广告了！

广告有时候确实挺烦人，偶尔发泄一下：

- Commercials are so stupid. I don't want any of this stuff. 商业广告太无聊了，我不想看任何这样的玩意儿。

大家都讨厌：
- I hear you. I hate commercial breaks. 是的，我讨厌商业广告。
- ❖ commercial break（广播、电视中插播的）商业广告

4 My favorite show is about to come on! Don't change it! 我最喜欢的节目就要上演了！别换台！

无奈地同意：
- Alright, alright! 好吧，好吧！
- ❖ be about to 即将，刚要

5 The news is so boring. 新闻太无聊了。

肯定地附和：
- Definitely. Who writes these stories, anyway? 确实，到底是谁写的这些故事？
- ❖ boring ['bɔrɪŋ] adj. 无聊的，枯燥的

6 Change the channel! I hate the show. 换台吧！我讨厌死这节目了。

类似的表达还有：
- Dude, change the channel. This show sucks. 老兄，换个台吧。这个节目太差劲了。

我就喜欢这节目：
- No way man, I like this! 不行，老兄，我喜欢看这节目。

7 Is there anything worth watching on this channel? 这个台有什么好看的节目吗？

还有其他什么节目吗：
- Are there any good programs on TV? 电视上有什么好看的节目吗？
- Are there any interesting programs on TV? 电视上有什么有趣的节目吗？

这个片你看过吗：
- Yeah, there is a sitcom *Everybody Loves Raymond*. 有啊，有情景喜剧《人人都爱雷蒙德》。
- ❖ sitcom ['sɪt'kɑm] n. 情景喜剧

TV Conversation

Kevin: Hey man, want to come over and watch TV or something?

凯文：嘿，哥们儿，想过来看看电视或别的什么吗？

Bob: Sure, I'll be right over.

鲍勃：好啊，我马上过来。

(Bob arrives at Kevin's house)

（鲍勃来到凯文家）

Kevin: Hey dude, what's up?

凯文：嘿，哥们儿，怎么啦？

Bob: Nothing. Hey, let's watch that new game show that's coming on at 8.

鲍勃：没什么。嘿，咱们看八点钟上映的那个新的游戏节目吧。

Kevin: Alright, it looked pretty good.

凯文：好的，这节目看起来很不错。

(After the game show)

（游戏节目之后）

Kevin: Shh! The new episodes of *Law and Order* is about to come on!

凯文：嘘！新的那集《法律与秩序》马上就要上映了！

Bob: Dude, that show sucks.

鲍勃：哥们儿，那电视剧太差劲了。

Kevin: Shut up. I like it.

凯文：闭嘴，我喜欢。

Bob: Fine, but we're watching *Family Guy* after this.

鲍勃：好吧，不过这电视剧完了后我们要看《恶搞之家》。

Kevin: Whatever, dude!

凯文：随便你，哥们儿！

就这900句 玩转口语

文化穿越

　　美国的电视媒体很发达。很多优秀的电视节目都是单独加密收费的，因此，电视公司可以保证顾客的利益，电影频道几乎没有广告的骚扰。

　　哥伦比亚广播公司（CBS—Columbia Broadcasting System），美国广播公司（ABC—American Broadcasting Company），全国广播公司（NBC—National Broadcasting Company）为美国三大商业广播电视公司。平时国内朋友们爱看的美剧系列基本被这三家公司所涵盖。美国的传媒业是目前世界上最发达的，当然，相比中国而言，中国的传媒业是刚刚起步而已，发展空间很大，但运作系统是完全不同的。因此，在美国读传媒的朋友回国发展可能需要适应一段时间。

Section 4 散步星光大道
Hollywood Walk of Fame

很多人都被电视电影中那些明星的风采所倾倒，于是不管是其演技还是明星生活的方方面面，都成为我们乐此不彼的谈资。学习一些这方面的英语，八卦一下这些大明星，也会让我们在学习工作之余消遣一下时光。

1 Did you hear the new rumor about Mel Gibson? 你听说过梅尔·吉布森新的传闻吗？

对于这种八卦新闻，如果你感兴趣：

- No, tell me! 没有，跟我说说吧！

如果你不感兴趣：

- No, I didn't, but I don't really care. 没，没听说，不过我也确实不感兴趣。

❖ rumor ['rumɚ] n. 传闻，谣言

2 I heard Mel Gibson was buying a condo around here. 我听说梅尔·吉布森在这附近买了套公寓。

你可以这样回答：

- No way! We have to find out for sure! 不可能吧！我们得查清是否属实！

❖ condo ['kando] n. 公寓

3 Oh god, I love Matt Damon's movies so much. 哦，天哪，我爱死马特·达蒙的电影了。

肯定的回答：

- Me too! 我也是！

否定的回答：

- Really? I think he kind of sucks to be honest. 是吗？说实话我觉得他有点儿差劲。

❖ to be honest 老实说，说实话

4 Quick, turn on the TV! I want to hear my celebrity gossip! 快，打开电视！我想听名人八卦！

如果你对此不屑一顾，可以这么说：

- No! That stuff is stupid! 不会吧！那些东西太无聊了！

❖ celebrity [sɪˈlɛbrətɪ] n. 名人，名流

❖ gossip [ˈgɑsəp] n. 流言，闲话

5 I can't wait to see the new photos of Lindsay Lohan that got leaked! 我都等不及想看林赛·罗韩被泄露的新照片了。

如果你对这些八卦根本就不感兴趣：

- Oh, you and your celebrities. Get a life! 哦，你和你的明星。别那么无聊！

❖ get a life 别那么无聊，做点儿有意义的事

Hollywood Walk of Fame Conversation

Kevin: Did you hear the new rumor about Brad Pitt?

凯文：你听说过布拉德·皮特新的传闻吗？

Kay: No, what happened?

凯 ：没有，怎么了？

Kevin: I heard he overdosed on drugs and got sent to the ER!

凯文：我听说他因服用毒品过量，被送进急诊室了！

Kay: No way. What about his kids?

凯 ：不会吧，那他的孩子怎么样了？

Kevin: I don't know. They're probably on drugs too!

凯文：我不知道，他们可能也有毒瘾吧！

Kay: (Laughs) You're probably right!

凯 ：（笑）也许你说得对！

Kevin: I just don't get celebrities. Could you imagine having that money?	凯文：我只是不理解名人。你能想象一下拥有那么多钱吗？
Kay: I bet if I did, I wouldn't throw it away like they do.	凯　：如果我有那么多钱，我肯定不会像他们那样随便浪费。
Kevin: You got that right! That really pisses me off!	凯文：你说得对！那确实让我很生气！
Kay: Me too. I wish I had the kind of freedom, though!	凯　：我也是。不过我希望有那种自由！

❖piss sb. off 惹某人生气
❖overdose ['ovə,dos] *vi.* 服药过量
❖ER 急诊室，emergency room 的缩写
❖on drugs 有吸毒嗜好的

文 化 穿 越

　　美国好莱坞位于加利福尼亚州洛杉矶市，是美国电影电视工业的中心。好莱坞是一个和巨大的财富和梦幻联系在一起的地方。很多人一夜之间成为世界级明星，也有很多人的梦想始终都未能在这里实现。如果去洛杉矶旅游，有可能会遇到明星连同家人一起出游，也有可能遇到中国明星，但他们在这里一般不太受人瞩目，也不用带墨镜头巾什么的遮盖，他们来此的目的一般也都是购物而已。

　　好莱坞星光大道（Hollywood Walk of Fame）建于 1958 年，是沿着好莱坞大道自东边的高尔街（Gower Street）延伸至西边的拉布雷亚大道（La Brea Avenue），然后顺着丝兰街（Yucca Street）与日落大道（Sunset Boulevard）之间的藤街由北向南推进。除非偶尔因附近施工或其他理由而更换位置外，大道上的星形奖章位置是永久不变的。上面有 2000 多颗镶有好莱坞名人姓名的星形奖章，以纪念他们对娱乐业的贡献。第一颗星于 1960 年 2 月 9 日颁赠予琼安·伍德沃德（Joanne Woodward）。

Chapter 12 打拼在华尔街

The Job Market

Business
Opportunity
Growth

Section 1

求职应聘
Job Hunting

从学校毕业后，Kevin 也一直没有稳定地工作过。仔细想想，也该好好地努力工作挣钱了，否则，也愧对自己这么多年来的所学。先打听一下有关招聘的信息吧，这样也避免自己像无头苍蝇一样四处乱撞。朋友们有什么招聘的信息，也麻烦推荐一下啊。

 口 语 大 放 送

1 I really need to find a job. 我真的需要找份工作。

需要找份工作：

- Man, I need to get a job! 哥们儿，我需要找份工作！
- I need to get myself a job! 我需要找份工作！

确实也该找份工作了：

- Yeah, you do! 是啊，确实是！

2 Do you have today's paper? 你有今天的报纸吗？

从报纸上看招聘信息：

- Do you have the paper? I want to look for a job. 你有报纸吗？我想找份工作。

根据事实来回答：

- Yeah. It's right here. 有，就在这儿。
- No, sorry. I threw it out this morning. 很抱歉，我没有。我今天早上把它扔了。

3 Oh, hey, that store down the road has an opening. 哦，嘿，这条街上的那家商店有一个空缺职位。

有空缺职位：

- I heard there was an opening at the factory. 我听说这家工厂里有个空缺职位。

如果想去应聘：

- Oh, really? I'll go apply. 哦，真的吗？我要去应聘。

如果不感兴趣：

- No way, I don't want to work there! 不行，我不想去那儿工作。
- ❖ opening ['opəniŋ] n. (职位的) 空缺

4 How much does it pay? 工资是多少？

打听工资：

- How much do you make working there? 你在那儿工作能挣多少钱？
- What's the salary for that place? 那地方的工资是多少？

工资不多，但还够用：

- Not much, but it's easier. （工资）不多，但是很轻松。
- Enough to pay the bills, I'm sure. 我确定足够支付账单。

5 Have you seen anywhere that's hiring? 你知道哪儿有招聘的吗？

询问招聘信息：

- Do you know anyone who's hiring? 你知道有谁在招聘吗？

如果不知道：

- No, I don't. I'm sorry. 很抱歉，我不知道。

如果知道：

- I have. The market down the street is hiring! 知道，这条街上的市场正在招聘！

6 Do you think you could get me a job? 你觉得你能给我找份工作吗？

能帮忙找份工作吗：

- Could you put a good word in for me at your job? 你能替我说说好话，让我去你那儿工作吗？
- I really need a job. Do you think you could help me get one where you work? 我很需要一份工作。你能在你们公司帮我找份工作吗？

如果你愿意推荐朋友：

- Sure, I'll put a word in. 当然，我会帮你说好话的。

如果你们公司不缺人：

- I think we're full right now, actually. 实际上，我想我们公司现在不需要人。

❖ put a good word in 说好话，替人美言

---

7 What kind of job are you looking for? 你在找什么样的工作?

想找什么类型的工作：

- What kind of job do you want? 你想要什么样的工作？

回答具体某方面的工作：

- I'm trying to find a job in civil engineering. 我想找土木工程方面的工作。

❖ engineering [ˌɛndʒəˈnɪrɪŋ] n. 工程（学）
❖ civil engineering 土木工程（学）

---

8 Do you have the vacancies for full-time job? 你们有全职的工作空缺吗?

正好有职位空缺：

- Yeah. We need a sales manager. 有，我们需要一个销售经理。
- You're so lucky. We do have a vacancy. 你真幸运，我们的确有一个空缺。

目前不招人：

- I'm sorry. There're no vacancies at present. 对不起，目前还没有空缺。
- I'm sorry. The new appointments have all been filled. 对不起，新的职位都已经招满了。

❖ vacancy [ˈveɪkənsɪ] n. 空缺

Job Hunting Conversation

Kevin: I need to find a job. Did you get the paper today?

凯　文：我要找份工作，你有今天的报纸吗？

Mabel: Yep, here ya go.

Kevin: Alright. Let's see... Looks like there's an opening at the grocery store.

Mabel: That wouldn't be so bad.

Kevin: Yeah, probably not. Do you know where it is?

Mabel: Yep, right down the road.

(Kevin goes to the store)

Kevin: Hello, could I speak to the manager on duty?

Clerk: Sure, one second.

Manager: Hello, what can I do for you?

Kevin: Hi, I saw in the paper you guys were hiring. I'd like to fill out an application.

Manager: No problem. Here you go.

Kevin: Thank you. Have a great day!

梅布尔：有，给你。

凯　文：好的，我看看……这家杂货店好像有个职位空缺。

梅布尔：那应该不会太糟。

凯　文：是啊，可能不错。你知道在哪儿吗？

梅布尔：知道，就在这条街上。

（凯文去这家商店）

凯　文：你好，能跟你们值班经理谈谈吗？

职　员：当然可以，稍等。

经　理：你好，我能帮你做什么？

凯　文：你好，我在报纸上看到你们店里在招人，我想填一张应聘表。

经　理：没问题，给你。

凯　文：谢谢。祝您愉快！

❖ here ya go = here you go 给你
❖ grocery ['grosərɪ] *n.* 杂货店
❖ fill out 填写

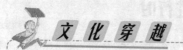
文化穿越

在美国的留学生获得美国学位后一般会有一定期限的 OPT 临时工作许可（注：OPT 是 Optional Practical Training 的缩写，是美国移民局授予外籍学生的校外工作许可）。文科硕士一般是一年，STEM（Science, Tech, Engineering & Mathematics）专业的学生 OPT 可以延长达 29 个月之久。一般情况下，在毕业后便可以申请 OPT，被公司录取后，就可以在美国合法工作了，在这期间，如果美国公司重视你，他们可能会为你申请 H1B 签证（注：H1B 签证是美国为引进国外专业技术人员提供的一种临时工作签证），有了 H1B 签证之后，便可以申请绿卡。但拿到 H1B 是很难的，拿到绿卡就更难了。不过，毕业后能留在美国工作 1-2 年也是很好的，不但可以挣回学费，还可以获得宝贵的工作经验。

Section 2  面试进行时
Interview

接到通知让我去面试，心里挺高兴的，毕竟现在找工作比较困难，有面试机会的话就一定要好好把握。不过临到面试的时候还是有点儿紧张，很担心对方会问一些比较刁钻的问题。在这里 Kevin 提醒大家，面试的时候一定要信心十足，表述自己时一定要条理清楚，多说说自己的优点哦。

（From Perspective of Employer 从老板的角度）

1 What are some of your life goals? 你的人生目标是什么？

要取得什么样的成就：

- What would you like to achieve in life? 在你的人生里，你想要取得怎样的成就？

参考回答：

- I want to be working for an excellent company like yours in a job. My long-range career goal is to be the best technician in this field. 我希望在像贵公司这样优秀的公司里找到一份工作，我的长期职业目标是成为这一领域最好的技师。
- ❖ long-range ['lɔŋ'reindʒ] *adj.* 长期的，远期的
- ❖ technician [tek'nɪʃən] *n.* 技术人员，技师

2 How do you feel about stealing? 对于偷窃你是怎么想的？

这个问题比较刁钻：

- Do you consider stealing to be wrong? 你认为偷窃是错误的吗？
- Would you ever steal from an employer? 你曾从老板那儿偷过东西吗？

避免正面交锋：

- I think I have the excellent moral quality and I won't do such a thing.
  我觉得我有优秀的道德品质，我不会做这样的事情。
- ❖ moral ['mɔrəl] *adj.* 讲道德的，品性端正的

3 Would you consider yourself to have a good work ethic? 你认为自己有优良的职业道德吗？

询问对职业道德的认识：

- As far as work ethic goes, where do you stand? 谈到职业道德，你有什么看法？
- Are you willing to work hard for the money? 你愿意努力工作挣钱吗？
- ❖ ethic ['ɛθɪk] *n.* 道德规范

4 What is your past job experience? 你有什么工作经验？

询问工作经历：

- Could you tell me about some jobs you've had in the past? 能跟我讲讲你过去做过的一些工作吗？
- What is your history as far as jobs are concerned? 你有什么工作史吗？
- Is this your first job? 这是你的第一份工作吗？
- Have you got any experience in advertising? 你有广告方面的经验吗？

据实回答：

- Not really. I'm almost straight out of school. But I tried to stand on my own feet by doing part-time jobs such as tutoring. 基本没有。我才离开学校，但我努力地做过家教之类的兼职工作来自食其力。
- Yes, I've worked in a private company as a sales manager for 3 years. 有，我在一家私企做了3年的销售经理。
- ❖ stand on one's own feet 独立自主，自食其力

5 Do you drive yourself to work? 你开车上班吗？

怎样上下班：

- Do you have reliable transportation? 你有固定的交通工具吗？

6 We would like to start you off at 3,500 Yuan a month, not including bonus and overtime pay. 我们可以付你起薪每月 3500 元，不包括奖金和加班费。

工资的问题可以商量：

- Salary can be negotiated once we officially offer you the job. 正式聘用的话，薪金方面还可以再商量。
- ❖ bonus ['bonəs] *n.* 奖金，额外补贴

7 How do you handle your conflict with your colleagues in your work? 你如何处理与同事在工作中的意见冲突？

表明自己的做法：

- I will try to present my ideas in a more clear manner in order to get my reasons across. 我要以更清楚的方式，提出我的看法，把我的理由讲清楚。
- ❖ conflict ['kɑnflɪkt] *n.* 冲突
- ❖ get sth. across 被传达，把……讲清楚

 交流面对面

Interview Conversation

(Kevin answers the phone)	（凯文在接电话）
Kevin: Hello.	凯文：你好。
Manager: Hello, this is the manager of the marketplace grocery store.	经理：你好，我是市场杂货店的经理。
Kevin: Oh, hello there, how are you?	凯文：哦，你好吗？
Manager: Doing good. I was curious if you would like to come in for an interview tomorrow afternoon?	经理：很好，我想知道你明天下午能过来面试吗？
Kevin: Sure. Thank you so much!	凯文：当然可以，非常感谢！
Manager: No problem. Have a good day.	经理：不客气，祝你愉快。
(Kevin goes to his interview)	（凯文去面试）

Manager: Hello, what's your job experience?	经理：你好，你有什么工作经验吗？
Kevin: Well, I've had a job almost my whole life, and I'm great with customer service.	凯文：在我目前走过的整个人生中，我只做过一份工作，我比较擅长客服。
Manager: Excellent, excellent. Now could you complete this work ethic quiz for me?	经理：很好，很好。你能完成这份职业道德测试吗？
Kevin: Sure thing.	凯文：当然可以。
(Kevin finishes the quiz)	（凯文做完了测试）
Manager: Alright then, we'll review this and give you a call back.	经理：那好吧，我们会审核这份测试，然后给你电话。
Kevin: Thank you.	凯文：谢谢您。
(Kevin gets a call back from the store)	（凯文接到杂货店的电话）
Manager: Hi Kevin, looks like you've got the job.	经理：你好，凯文，看来你可以来上班了。
Kevin: Great! Thank you so much!	凯文：太好了！非常感谢您！

❖ **marketplace** ['markɪt,ples] *n.* 市场

文化穿越

在美国，面试的过程其实与在中国类似，只不过美国公司的关注点与中国企业不太一样。美国企业更注重个人工作经验和修养。个人工作经验体现在相关领域的成就或工作经历上，这也是很多美国学生在校期间很注重实习和社会实践的原因。因为找工作的时候，除了需要简历外，还要有自己的学术履历 (Curriculum Vitae)，有时还需要个人在校期间的成绩点数 (GPA)，另外就是求职信 (Cover Letter)。专业对于找工作固然很重要，但平时的实习机会也一定要重视。另外，在美国面试主要有两种形式，一种是现场面试，另一种是电话面试，地理位置较远时，一般会采取后一种。面试问题取决于你应聘的岗位和领域，如果你应聘的是某专业的教师，那么面试官就会问一些比较学术和专业性的知识。

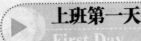

Section 3 ▶ **上班第一天**
First Day

面试后一直在惴惴不安地等待公司的回复，终于等到通知说我可以去上班了，心里那个高兴劲儿啊都没法形容，面试前的一路过关斩将都闯下来了。今天是上班的第一天，来到公司报到后，老板就给我布置了工作任务，并且还规定了工作着装，公司的规定还很严格，希望自己能坚持下来。

1 Hello there, nice to meet you! 你好，见到你很高兴！

上班第一天跟同事打招呼：

- Hi, nice to meet you. I'm new here. 你好，见到你很高兴，我是新来的。
- Nice to meet you. I'm the new guy! 见到你很高兴，我是新来的。

客套地回应：

- Nice to meet you too! 见到你我也很高兴！

2 How do I do this properly? 这个我怎么做比较合适？

询问如何正确做某事：

- What's the correct way that I should be going about doing this? 做这个有什么正确的方法吗？

给出建议：

- Just read this safety manual at first. 先读一下这份安全手册。
- ❖ manual ['mænjuəl] *n.* 手册

3 What would you like me to do? 你想要我做些什么？

询问自己具体的工作：

- What would you have me do today? 今天要我做些什么？
- What will I be doing today? 我今天要做些什么？

给出一项具体的工作：

- Could you stack these boxes behind you? 能把你身后的那些箱子堆放到一起吗？

❖ stack [stæk] vt. 堆放

---

4 Who do I talk to if I have a question? 如果我有问题跟谁讲呢？

有问题找谁解决：

- Who should I let know if I need something? 如果我需要一些东西跟谁要呢？

直接告知对方：

- You can come to me, Carol, or any other employee. 你可以来找我、卡罗尔，或者其他员工。

---

5 When is our first paycheck? 我们什么时候发工资？

询问工资发放日期：

- Do you know when we'll be getting paid? 你知道我们什么时候发工资吗？
- I was curious when payday was? 我想知道什么时候发工资？

直接告知对方：

- You will be paid in 6 weeks. 6 周之后会给你发工资。

我也不知道：

- I'm not sure. You'll have to ask your manager. 我不确定，你得问你们经理。

❖ paycheck ['peɪˌtʃɛk] n. 工资支票

---

6 How long's our lunch break? 我们午餐休息多长时间？

询问午餐时间：

- How long do we have for lunch? 我们有多久时间吃午饭？

447

告知时间：
- An hour. 一个小时。
- We have an hour long lunch break from 12 to 1. 12 点到 1 点我们有一个小时的午休时间。

7 Can I make personal phone calls during office hours? 我可以在上班时间打私人电话吗？

如果公司允许打电话：
- Of course, you can. But don't chat over the phone. 当然可以，但是不要煲电话粥。

如果不允许上班时间打电话：
- I am afraid you can't. 恐怕不行。

8 I am new to the whole working world and would appreciate your guidance. 我没有什么工作经验，请您多指教。

换一种说法：
- This is my first day here. I may bother you a lot if there is something I don't understand. 我今天第一天来上班，有什么不明白的就要多麻烦您了。

First Day Conversation

Kevin: Hey! I'm Kevin.	凯文：嘿！我是凯文。
Boss: Nice to meet you, Kevin. Today we'll just be introducing you to job duties.	老板：很高兴见到你，凯文。今天我们会给你介绍一下你的工作职责。
Kevin: Sure, where do we start?	凯文：好的，我们从哪儿开始呢？
Boss: Well…	老板：嗯……
(Boss explains job duties)	（老板讲解工作职责）
Boss: So, we'll get you a uniform now. What size do you wear?	老板：那么，我们现在发给你一套工作制服。你穿多大号的？
Kevin: I wear a medium.	凯文：我穿中号的。

Boss: Alright, here you go. You can wear any kind of pants, just no jeans.	老板：好的，给你。除了牛仔裤之外，你可以穿任何其他类型的裤子。
Kevin: Alright, is there a policy against facial hair?	凯文：好的，对胡须有什么规定吗？
Boss: No, just try to keep yourself clean cut and looking proper.	老板：没有，只要保持干净得体就可以了。
Kevin: Alright then, I'll see you tomorrow. Have a good day!	凯文：好的，那明天见，祝您愉快！
Boss: You too.	老板：也祝你愉快。

❖ uniform ['junəfɔrm] *n.* 制服
❖ medium ['midɪəm] *adj.* 中等的
❖ jeans[dʒinz] *n.* 牛仔裤
❖ facial hair 面部毛发

文化穿越

　　美国企业文化与中国大相径庭。当然，在美国工作也是很累的，这年头挣钱没有不累的，尤其在资本主义国家。但不同的是，美国人在工作一天之后，绝不加班加点地干活，即使分派的任务没完成也不会加班。只要下班时间一到，就立马走人，因为即使你加班，也没人给你加班费。还有一个原因就是，美国人很注重个人价值，在工作岗位上的每一个人，无论领导还是普通职员都是平等的，大部分的美国领导者都很平易近人而且很尊重职员。但在工作中，一定要实事求是，千万不能模棱两可，因为美国人很重视一个人的诚信，做错事情要敢于承认，做得出色也不用谦虚。在美国，大部分的工作与薪水都是按劳分配的，这一点在非技术性工作上尤为明显。比如，沃尔玛的收银员可以倒班多干活，持续一段时间下来，薪水也是十分可观的。这也是很多中国人宁可在沃尔玛当收银员，也不愿意留在国内工作的原因。

Section 4

職場培訓
Training

公司规定，新进来的员工必须要接受为期一周的培训，这一步骤也是为了让我们这些新员工更详细地了解公司各方面的制度，同时熟悉自己的业务。不过 Kevin 还要告诉大家，其实这个培训的过程也是公司考核你的过程，所以一定要好好表现啊。

口语大放送

（From Perspective of Employer 从老板的角度）

1 For safety precautions, always wear glasses. 为了安全起见，要一直戴着眼镜。

工作的时候要保护眼睛：

- Always wear eye protection while on the job. 在工作的时候要一直戴好眼罩。
- Always wear protective eye wear while working. 在工作的时候要一直戴好眼罩。
- ❖ precaution [prɪˈkɔːʃən] *n.* 预防措施

2 Never mix chemical A with chemical B. 不要把化学物质 A 和 B 混用了。

工作中需要注意的问题：

- If you're cleaning, don't mix these two things together. 在打扫卫生时，不要把这两种东西混在一起。
- Be careful not to breathe in fumes while you're cleaning a tight spot. 在打扫密封场所时，注意不要吸入烟雾。

知道了：

- Understood. 明白。
- ❖ mix A with B 把 A 和 B 混合在一起

❖ fume [fjum] *n.* (有害、浓烈、或难闻的) 烟，气
❖ tight [taɪt] *adj.* 密封的，不漏的

③ To file paperwork, you sort it alphabetically. 把那些文件按照字母顺序归类。

把文件按照顺序排列：

* Just sort those papers from A-Z please. 把那些文件按字母顺序归类。

没有问题：

* Sure. No problem. 好的，没问题。

❖ alphabetically [ˌælfəˈbetɪklɪ] *adv.* 照字母顺序排列地

④ I need you to clean the bathrooms. 我需要你帮忙打扫一下卫生间。

打扫卫生：

* This is where the mop and the bucket are. 拖把和水桶在这儿。
* Could you clean the bathrooms for me, please? 请帮忙打扫一下卫生间，可以吗？

马上回应：

* No problem. 没问题。
* I'll get right on it. 我马上去。

❖ mop [mɑp] *n.* 拖把
❖ bucket [ˈbʌkɪt] *n.* 水桶

⑤ For the first day of training, we need you to watch this video. 今天是第一天培训，我们想让你看一下这段视频。

看录像了解工作职责：

* Please watch this video; it will broadly cover your duties and safety procedures. 请看这段视频，它基本涵盖了你的工作职责和安全程序。

礼貌回应马上就看：

* No problem. 好的。

6 I would like to set up a time with you to go over the training manual. 我想跟你约个时间一起看一下培训手册。

先抽时间了解:

- I want you to spare some time to scan the training manual. When are you free? 我希望你抽出一些时间来看一下培训手册。你什么时候有空?
- ❖ set up 准备,安排
- ❖ go over 反复研究,仔细琢磨

7 The manager is going to give you a training workshop next week. 经理下周会给你们开个培训会。

或者说:

- There will be a training that you must attend on time. 有一个培训,你一定要按时参加。
- ❖ workshop ['wɜːkˌʃɒp] n. 专题讨论会

8 The training period can vary widely. 培训时间大不相同。

培训时间根据职责不同:

- Training time depends solely on your duties. 培训时间只取决于你的职责。

Training Conversation

Carol: Hello, I'm Carol, I'll be training you today.	卡罗尔: 你好,我是卡罗尔,今天由我来给你们培训。
Kevin: Hello, nice to meet you. I'm Kevin.	凯 文: 你好,很高兴见到你,我是凯文。
Carol: Do you have any questions?	卡罗尔: 你有什么问题吗?
Kevin: I do have a couple. What do I do if the customer can't afford their items?	凯 文: 我确实有几个问题。如果顾客支付不起他们的物品我们该怎么做?

Carol: Just politely ask them if they would like to come back, and set their items off to the side.	卡罗尔：只要礼貌地问他们能不能下次再来，然后把这些物品放到一边。
Kevin: And what if they threaten me?	凯　文：如果他们威胁我呢？
Carol: Just call for the manager.	卡罗尔：给经理打电话就行。
Kevin: Alright, that makes sense. So what will we be doing today?	凯　文：好的，这个行得通。那我们今天要做什么？
Carol: Well, let me show you how to scan an item into the cash register.	卡罗尔：嗯，我给你示范一下怎么把物品扫描到收银机里。
(Carol demonstrates how to do this)	（卡罗尔演示如何做）
Kevin: Oh alright, so just have the barcode facing the window.	凯　文：哦，好的，只要把条形码对着这个窗口就可以了。
Carol: Exactly, and if they have any vegetables, just weigh them using this button.	卡罗尔：完全正确，如果他们买的是蔬菜，只要按这个按钮称一下重量就可以了。
Kevin: Alright, that seems pretty easy.	凯　文：好的，看起来挺简单的。
Carol: You'll get used to it. Well that's it for today. Have a great night!	卡罗尔：你会习惯的。那今天就到此为止。祝你度过一个美好的夜晚。
Kevin: You too!	凯　文：你也一样！

❖ set sth. off 把……放在一边
❖ threaten ['θrɛtn] *vt.* 威胁，恐吓
❖ make sense 讲得通，言之有理
❖ cash register 收银机
❖ demonstrate ['dɛmən,stret] *vt.* 演示，示范
❖ barcode [bar'kod] *n.* 条形码

文化穿越

　　美国企业对于刚入职的员工会给予一定的培训，时间长短不一，取决于工作性质。在培训期间，刚入职的员工和正式员工的基本福利是一样的，不会有特别大的差别。另外，培训期间其实也是美国企业观察员工的一种方式，他们很注重培训期间员工的表现以及细节上的问题。例如，一个员工是否准时上班，是否按时完成任务，最重要的是是否有诚信。因此，在美国企业里工作，要时刻注意自己的言行，在细节上尤其要注意。

Section 5 ▶ 出勤与迟到
Arriving at Work Late

天哪，都这个时间了，我上班岂不是要迟到了？我可不想没上几天班就迟到，给人留下不好的印象，再说我现在还在试用期呢。于是赶紧穿衣服起床，忙忙碌碌了一会儿后就出门了。真不凑巧，今天还赶上堵车了，车子像蜗牛一样不紧不慢地往前挪。上班肯定得迟到了，真是急煞我了！

 口 语 大 放 送

1 Crap! I'm going to be late for work. 天哪！我上班要迟到了。

要迟到啦：

- Oh, no, I'm gonna be late! 哦，不要啊，我要迟到了！
- ❖ crap [kræp] *int.* 天哪

2 We need to hurry up. 我们要快点儿。

心急如焚，担心迟到：

- Can we hurry up? It's getting late. 我们能不能快点？要迟到了。
- Hurry up, or we'll be late. 快一点儿，不然我们就迟到了。

3 I can't be late for work. 我上班不能迟到。

上班不能迟到，后果很严重：

- I can't be late for work again. 我不能再迟到了。
- If I'm late again, I'll get fired! 如果我再迟到我就会被开除了。

只能安慰一下同时加快速度：

- Well, let's hurry up! 噢，咱们快点儿吧。

4 What happens if I'm late? 我要是迟到了会怎么样呢？

- What will happen if I'm late for work? 如果我上班迟到了会怎么样呢?

迟到或许会被开除:

- You'll probably get fired. 你可能会被开除。

5 I may be late for work tomorrow. 明天上班我可能会晚到一会儿。

提前告知自己可能迟到:

- I have an appointment tomorrow. I might be late for work. 明天我有个约会,上班可能会晚到一会儿。

表示理解,谢谢告知:

- That's fine. Thanks for letting me know. 好的,谢谢你告诉我。

6 My bus was late so I am late for work. 公共汽车来迟了,所以我迟到了。

可能是个借口:

- I was late because I didn't catch the bus. 我迟到是因为我没有赶上公交车。

7 My car broke down. 我的车抛锚了。

车子出问题导致迟到:

- My car ran out of gas on the way to work. I had to push it to a gas station. 我的车走到半路没油了,我只好把车推到加油站。
- ❖ break down 发生故障
- ❖ run out of sth. 用光,耗尽

8 I was only late by five minutes. 我只迟到了 5 分钟。

还好只迟到了 5 分钟:

- I was only five minutes late. 我只迟到了 5 分钟。

Arriving at Work Late Conversation

Kevin: Oh, no! I'm gonna be late!	凯　文：哦，不！我要迟到了！
Debra: Well, hurry up and get ready!	黛布拉：噢，快点儿准备好！
Kevin: I can't! I need to stop at the post office.	凯　文：不行啊！我要在邮局停一下。
Debra: Well, what will happen if you're late?	黛布拉：哦，你要是迟到了会怎么样？
Kevin: I could get fired!	凯　文：可能会被开除。
Debra: Just forget about the post office, then.	黛布拉：那就别想什么邮局了。
Kevin: I can't! I need to mail out this package. I'm screwed!	凯　文：不行啊，我要寄这个包裹。我都晕头转向了。
Debra: Well, talking about it isn't going to help. Let's go.	黛布拉：噢，说这些没用。咱们走吧。
Kevin: You're right.	凯　文：你说的对。

❖ screwed [skrud] *adj.* 搞糟的，搞砸的

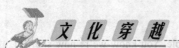

　　迟到在美国企业文化里其实不是什么新鲜的事情。当然，如果你刚到一个公司，在未熟悉自身业务的情况下，还是按章办事比较保险。很多美国职员在对自己的职责和工作任务了如指掌的情况下，有时候会偷懒，但只要不被老板发现，或者你跟老板很熟也没问题。但有一点是必须保证的，就是你最终工作完成的时间和质量必须按照公司进度进行，否则迟到会成为你在老板手中的把柄。

Section 6 请假
Taking a Leave

　　我有点儿事需要请个假，我该怎么跟老板说呢？万一不准假该怎么办呢？这个问题一直在我心里纠结，搞得心神不宁，也没法儿专心工作。几次腹稿演练之后，终于鼓起勇气敲响了老板办公室的门，没想到老板二话不说就批准了，这可真是意料之外的事情。

1 I need to take a leave on the 29th of this month. 这个月 29 号，我要请一天假。

想要请个假：

- Is it alright if I take a leave next Thursday? 下周四我请一天假可以吗？
- Could I take a leave on the 26th? 26 号我能请一天假吗？

批准了：

- No problem. 没问题。

不能准假：

- I'm sorry that may not be possible. You know we're now short of hands. 对不起，那不太可能，你知道我们现在缺少人手。

❖ take a leave 请假

2 I want to ask for a leave to go to the Bahamas with my family. 我想请假和我家人一起去巴哈马群岛。

想请假去旅游：

- I've always wanted to visit Europe. I should ask for a leave to go there. 我一直想去欧洲旅游，应该请个假去那儿。

得到批准：

- Go for it! 去吧！

有紧急任务，不能请假：

- I'm afraid I have to let you down. We're just assigned to an urgent task. 恐怕我得让你失望了，我们刚分配到了一个紧急任务。
- ❖ ask for (a) leave 请假

3 I asked for leave. 我请假了。

因病请假：

- I was absent on sick leave last Tuesday. 我上周二因病请假了。
- I have to ask for sick leave. 我得请个病假。
- ❖ absent ['æbsnt] *adj.* 缺席的，不在场的

4 He is not working today. 他今天请假了。

某人因为生病请假：

- Tom has taken lots of time off lately, has not he? 汤姆最近常请假，是不是？
- As she had a high fever, she asked for leave. 她因为发高烧而请假。
- He's on sick leave today. 他今天请病假了。

5 May I have one day off tomorrow? 我明天能请一天假吗？

明天能不能请假：

- Am I allowed to have one day off tomorrow? 我明天请一天假吗？
- Could I have one day off tomorrow? 明天我能请一天假吗？
- May I ask for leave tomorrow? 我明天能请假吗？

询问请假的理由：

- What happened to you? 你怎么了？

6 I'm asking for a week's leave. 我准备请一星期假。

要请一个星期的假：

- I want to ask for leave, about a week. 我想请大约一周的假。
- I'd like to ask for a week's leave. 我想请一周的假。
- I want to ask for leave for a week. 我想请一周的假。

关心询问有什么事情：

- Why? What happened? 为什么啊？发生什么事了？

7 I'm sorry I can't come to work today. I'm running a temperature. 很抱歉我今天不能来上班，我在发烧。

生病发烧了不能上班：

- I'm sorry. I got sick. I have to tell you I won't be in today. 很抱歉，我生病了。我得跟你说我今天不能上班。
- I'm not feeling well. I'll ask for a day's leave to see the doctor. 我感觉不舒服，我要请一天假去看医生。

准许请假但是不要影响工作：

- No problem. But you'd better ask someone else to take over what you're now in charge of. I hope you'll get better soon. 没问题。但是你最好找个人来接替你现在负责的工作。希望你早日好起来。

❖ temperature ['temprətʃə] n. 高烧，发烧

8 Fill in an absence form, and I will sign it. 填张假条，我帮你签字。

写请假条：

- Submit the absence request, and I'll sign it. 填一下请假申请，我来签名。
- Fill in an absence form, and I will approve it. 填一下请假表，我来批准。

表示谢意：

- Thank you very much.

❖ submit [səb'mɪt] vt. 提交，呈递
❖ approve [ə'pruv] vt. 批准，通过

Taking a Leave Conversation

Kevin: Man, I need to take a leave! 凯　文：哥们儿，我需要请个假！

Steve: I hear ya, dude. But what's up?	史蒂夫：我听说了，伙计。但发生什么事情了？
Kevin: I was thinking of seeing my father. He's ill.	凯 文：我想去探望我父亲。他生病了。
Steve: Well, I'm sorry to hear that.	史蒂夫：听到这个我很难过。
Kevin: It's OK. Nothing serious. I'm gonna talk to my boss about it tomorrow.	凯 文：没关系。不是很严重。我明天就去跟我老板说这件事。
(The next day)	（第二天）
Kevin: Carol, I'd like to take two days off if it's all right with you.	凯 文：卡罗尔，我想请两天假，可以吗？
Carol: Sure, what's up?	卡罗尔：当然可以，怎么了？
Kevin: My father was ill and he is in hospital now. I'm worried about him and I can't concentrate on my work.	凯 文：我父亲生病住院了。我担心他，无法专心工作。
Carol: Oh, sorry to hear that. Well, all you have to do is fill out this form and I'll sign it for you.	卡罗尔：哦，听到这个很难过。好的，你只要填好这张表格，我签字就可以了。
Kevin: Oh alright, that's not so bad! Thanks Carol.	凯 文：哦，没事，还不是很糟糕！谢谢你，卡罗尔。
Carol: No problem, Kevin.	卡罗尔：不客气，凯文。

❖what's up 怎么了
❖concentrate on sth. 专心于某事

461

文化穿越

其实在美国工作有时候会遇到请假这种状况，不过一般中国人都不会轻易请假，除非病得爬不起来。在美国工作，一般请假老板都会批准，但你需要回报的是按时完成任务。有时候美国的老板不在乎你平时是否积极或者出色，他们只看最后的成果。工作任务完成得好，平时的小错误都视而不见，但如果最后你没能完成任务，不好意思，老板会一笔一笔跟你算账，甚至派给你很多任务把你挤兑得主动辞职。

Section 7

调班加班
Shifts and Overwork

上班一段时间后，Kevin 和同事也混得挺熟了，大家相处得都很不错（看来 Kevin 的人缘还是很不错滴 ^_^），所以其他同事有什么困难的话，Kevin 也很乐意帮忙。这不，为了 Bob 的约会，Kevin 自愿代他上班，老板 Carol 对 Kevin 的表现也很满意，都表示要给他加班工资呢，一举两得啊。

1 Oh man, I have to work late tonight! 哦，天哪，我今晚得工作到很晚！

很不幸，今晚要加班：

- I'm working late tonight. Such a bummer. 我今晚要工作到很晚。真倒霉。
- I feel for you. It'll be fine, man. 我很同情你。会好的，伙计。

❖ bummer [ˈbʌmɚ] n. 令人失望或不愉快的局面（非正式用法）
❖ feel for sb. 同情，怜悯（某人）

2 Do you think you could stay late tonight? I need to come home early. 你今晚上能晚点儿回去吗？我今天要早点儿回家。

问对方能否加班：

- Do you think you could work late for me tonight? 你今晚能帮我加会儿班吗？
- Are you busy? Could you work late tonight? 你现在忙吗？今天晚上能加会儿班吗？

如果你没空或者不想加班：

- I'm busy, sorry. 对不起，我很忙。

如果和对方关系不错，也有时间：

- Sure, no problem. 好的，没问题。

3 Will I get paid extra if I stay late? 我加班有加班费吗？

询问有没有加班费：

- Will I be paid more than usual for staying later? 我加班的话，工资会比平时多吗？

根据事实回答：

- Yes, you will be. 是的，有加班费。
- No, sorry. 抱歉，没有。

4 How long should I stay tonight? 我今天晚上要加班多长时间？

询问加班时间长短：

- Do you know how long I have to stay? 你知道我要加班多长时间吗？
- I'm staying late tonight. Do you know how long that will be? 我今天晚上要加班，你知道要加班多长时间吗？

不知道确切时间：

- I'm not sure. 我不知道。

如果知道就告诉对方：

- Probably until around 8, or when someone else comes in. 可能要到 8 点左右，或者到有其他人来了。

5 I can work late on Fridays. 周五我可以加班。

说说什么时间可以加班：

- Typically I can work late on Thursdays and Saturdays. 通常我周四和周六可以加班。
- I can't work late on Mondays, but weekends are fine. 我周一不能加班，但是周末可以。

给予回答：

- Alright. Excellent. 好的，很好。
- Good to know. 知道了。

❖ typically ['tɪpɪklɪ] adv. 代表性地，典型地

6 Could I pick up some extra hours? 我能加班吗？

主动询问是否可以加班：

- I need money. Is there any way I could get extra hours? 我需要钱，有可能让我加班吗？
- I really could use some extra hours this week. 我这周能加班。

如果可以不妨帮忙：

- I'll see what I can do for you. 我看看有什么能帮你的。

如果确实无能为力：

- I'm sorry. I'm not able to give any out. 对不起，我没办法给你分配。

❖ give sth. out 分发

7 Hey Bob, got any shifts I can take? 嘿，鲍勃，我能换班吗？

询问是不是可以帮别人代班：

- I'm looking to pick up some shifts. Do you have anyway? 我正在看谁需要换班，你需要吗？
- I need some extra money. Does anyone want me to cover for them? 我需要多挣些钱，有人需要我替班吗？

根据自己的情况回应：

- Sorry man, I need money too. 抱歉，伙计，我也需要钱。
- Sure, can you work for me Friday? 好的，周五你能替我上班吗？

❖ shift [ʃɪft] n. 轮班，换班
❖ cover for 代替，顶替

8 I have some extra hours this week I don't need. 我这周的工作时间太多了。

抱怨自己工作时间太长：

- I don't need all these hours. 我不想工作那么长时间。
- They gave me too many hours this week! 他们这周给我安排的工作时间太多了！

劝导对方或者安慰一下：

- Bummer, but money is money, man. 真倒霉，但钱就是钱，哥们儿。
- That sucks, but it could be worse. 真糟，不过还好。

9 I have some extra shifts, want one? 我有些多余的班可以换，你需要吗？

自己太忙问问对方能不能替班：

- I'm pretty swamped this week. Could you take a shift from me? 我这周真是忙得应接不暇了，你能帮我替个班吗？

自己很闲，乐意效劳：

- No problem. I could use it. 没问题，我有时间。

❖ swamped [swɑmpt] *adj.* 忙碌的

Shifts and Overwork Conversation

Bob: Hey Kevin, want to cover my shift next Thursday?

鲍勃：嘿，凯文，下周四能替我上班吗？

Kevin: Sure, have something special coming up?

凯文：当然可以，你有什么特别的事吗？

Bob: Yeah, a date with my wife.

鲍勃：是的，跟我妻子约会。

Kevin: Oh I see, no problem, man! I'll get ya covered.

凯文：哦，我明白了，没问题，哥们儿！我会替你去上班的。

Bob: Thanks, man. I really appreciate it.

鲍勃：谢谢，哥们儿。真是太感谢了。

(Later that evening)

(那一天晚上)

Kevin: Hey Carol, just so you know I'll be picking up Bob's shift next Thursday.

凯　文：你好，卡罗尔，那么你知道我下周四要替鲍勃上班了。

Carol: Oh, alright, I'll change the schedule for you.

卡罗尔：哦，好的，我会给你换值班表。

Kevin: Thanks!

凯　文：谢谢！

Carol: It looks like that's going to be overtime, so you'll get bonus pay also.

卡罗尔：看起来是要加班了，那么你也会得到奖金的。

Kevin: Wow hey, that works for me! Thanks, Carol.

凯　文：嗯，正合我意！谢谢你，卡罗尔。

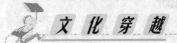

美国人热衷于加班。比如说教师这一职业，拥有 10 年教龄的美国中学教师平均年薪 4 万美元，高于欧洲的 3 万美元，但这正是由于美国教师工作时间比欧洲多了近 1/3 而打拼出来的。不过，问题的另一面是，美国社会竞争之激烈，现在生活是很难想象出来的。美国法律规定加班能够取得基本工资 1.5 倍的加班费，而时时担忧"稍不留神"就有可能被划入"穷人"的普通人（包括那些所谓的中产阶级）绝不会放弃任何赚钱的机会！

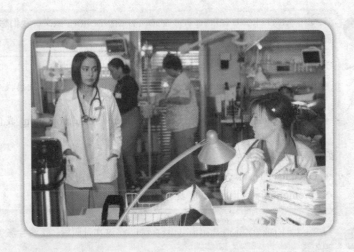

Section 8 ▶ 升职加薪
Promotion and Getting a Raise

由于 Kevin 工作主动积极，且常常自愿承担更多的工作职责，各方面表现优良，老板 Carol 决定给 Kevin 升职加薪。这倒是 Kevin 始料不及的事情，但不管怎么样，这都是努力工作的结果。朋友们，咱们出去喝一杯，庆祝一下吧。

① Kevin, we'd like to talk to you about a promotion. 凯文，我们想跟你谈谈关于升职的事。

升职前的谈话：
- I would like a chance to talk to you about being promoted. 我想找个机会跟你谈谈关于升职的事。
- Could we talk later? You're being considered for a promotion. 我们一会儿能聊一聊吗？我们正在考虑给你升职。

好事啊，赶快答应：
- Of course! Thank you so much! 当然可以！太感谢了！
- ❖ promotion[prə'moʃən] n. 提升，晋级

② Does this promotion come with a raise? 这次升职后，工资会涨吗？

工资问题很关键：
- Will I also be receiving a raise? 我的工资也会涨吗？
- Will I be able to achieve a raise, also? 我的工资也会涨吗？

放心吧，肯定会的：
- Yes. We will discuss that later. 是的，我们稍后讨论此事。

得过一段时间喽：
- Not at the present moment. 现在还不会。

❖　achieve [ə'tʃiv] *vt.* 完成，达到，实现

3　Your new responsibilities will mean more pay. 你的新工作职责将带来更多的薪资。

升职意味着涨工资：

- This promotion will increase your pay by quite a bit. 这次升职也会让你的工资有所提高。
- Your pay will be raised substantially. 你的工资也会大幅度地提高。
- ❖　substantially [səb'stænʃəlɪ] *adv.* 相当多地，大幅度地

4　You're a great worker, and you deserve this. 你是一名优秀的员工，这是你应得的。

被老板赏识：

- You're a fantastic worker, and we believe you will do well. 你是一名优秀的员工，我们相信你会做得很棒。
- We think you're the man for this job! 我们认为你是这份工作的合适人选！

表达信心：

- Thank you. I won't let you down! 谢谢，我不会让你们失望的！
- ❖　fantastic [fæn'tæstɪk] *adj.* 极好的，难以置信的
- ❖　let sb. down 让某人失望

5　With the new promotion, you will be receiving a brand new company car! 鉴于你的升迁，公司将会给你配一辆新车！

业绩提升了，公司自然给出不错的福利：

- Along with the promotion, you will receive a set of keys to the store. 随着你的升迁，公司会给你一套店里的钥匙。
- This promotion also comes with a reserved parking space. 除了升职，还会给你一个预留的停车位。

真是太好了：

- Oh wow, thank you so much! 哇，太感谢你了！
- I'm so grateful! 真是太感谢了！
- ❖　brand new 崭新的，全新的

6 Could you spare any time to talk about my current salary? 你能抽空跟我谈谈现在的工资问题吗?

想谈谈工资问题了:

- May I talk to you about my current salary? 我能和您谈谈我现在的工资问题吗?

一般不会被拒绝:

- Sure. What's wrong? 当然,怎么了?

7 Nowadays I almost can't make ends meet. 我现在几乎入不敷出了。

工资总是不涨:

- I'm always unable to make ends meet. 我总是入不敷出。
- My salary isn't enough to support the family. 我的工资不够我养家。

给你涨薪:

- In consideration of your contribution, I would like to give you a pay raise. 鉴于你的贡献,我决定给你加薪。

考虑给你涨薪:

- Actually, you've made a good impression on me because you always keep your nose to the grindstone. I'll think this over and get back to you as soon as possible, OK? 事实上,你给我的印象很好,因为你总是勤勤恳恳地工作。我考虑一下,尽快给你答复,可以吗?

❖ consideration[kənsɪdəˈreʃən] *n.* 体贴,关心
❖ contribution[ˌkɑntrəˈbjuʃən] *n.* 贡献
❖ grindstone[ˈɡraɪnˌston] *n.* 磨石,砂轮
❖ keep your nose to the grindstone 努力不懈

交流面对面

Promotion and Getting a Raise Conversation

Carol: Kevin, we have good news!	卡罗尔:凯文,有好消息!
Kevin: What's that?	凯 文:什么好消息?
Carol: You're up for a promotion!	卡罗尔:你要升职了!

Kevin: Really? But I just get started!	凯　文：真的？但是我才刚来！
Carol: Well, you showed initiative, and we could use someone like you in a manager position.	卡罗尔：哦，你表现很积极，我们需要像你这样的人做经理。
Kevin: Well, I'm honored, really I am.	凯　文：哦，真是太荣幸了。
Carol: However, with a pay increase comes more responsibility.	卡罗尔：但是，随着工资的上涨，工作职责也会更多。
Kevin: I understand.	凯　文：我明白。
Carol: We'll have to try out some average duties from day to day to see if you can handle it before you get the job.	卡罗尔：在你得到这份工作之前我们会尝试每天给你加一些任务，看看你能不能处理好。
Kevin: Fair enough. Thank you very much!	凯　文：这样很好，非常感谢你！
Carol: No problem. See you tomorrow, Kevin!	卡罗尔：没什么。明天见，凯文！

❖ initiative [ɪ'nɪʃɪɪtɪv] *n.* 主动性，积极性
❖ responsibility [rɪˌspɑnsə'bɪlətɪ] *n.* 责任，职责，责任心

文 化 穿 越

　　美国公司的晋升制度和国内外企类似。简单地说，活干得好，能够给公司创造利益，自然就会被提升。当然，机会是有限的，必然存在竞争。中国的企业文化为什么让员工有种窒息的感觉，因为相比之下，中国企业的机会更少，竞争的人更多。在美国，情况也是类似的，在涉及利益竞争的时候亚洲人在美国其实是不受人欢迎的，因为亚洲人比较聪明又吃苦耐劳，而美国人相对来说比较懒惰，因此他们比较害怕和亚洲人竞争，但这个世界就是弱肉强食，没有谁对谁错，只存在谁能谁上。

Section 9 ▶ 工作压力
Work Pressure

虽然升职加薪了，但承担的责任更大了，需要干的工作更多了，休息的时间越来越少了，压力也越来越大，心情也感觉越来越压抑了。我该怎么办呢？我还能承受多久？朋友们，你们有什么好的点子让我减压一下吗？

1 This job is getting really rough. 工作真的是越来越艰难了。

工作实在是太难了：
- This job is really starting to wear on me. 我开始对这份工作感到恼火了。

不喜欢：
- I'm not liking the direction this job is headed. 我不喜欢这份工作的发展方向。

考虑辞职：
- I think you should quit before it's too late. 我认为你应该趁现在还不太晚就辞职。

坚持才能取得胜利啊：
- Stick in there! You'll be fine. 坚持下去！你会好的。

❖ rough [rʌf] *adj.* 艰难的，艰苦的
❖ wear on 使烦躁不安，使恼火
❖ stick in 放入，陷入，植入，附上

2 Today at work, I wasn't able to do all the stuff I had to do! 今天工作的时候，我无法完成我所有的工作任务！

没完成当天的工作，难过：

- I didn't even have enough time today to finish my work! 我今天甚至没有足够的时间完成工作！
- Today sucked, I wasn't even able to finish all of my work. 今天真糟糕，我甚至没能完成所有的工作。

安慰一下：

- Don't stress over it. There's always tomorrow. 不要压力太大了，总会有明天的。

3 My boss is such an asshole. 我的老板真是个混蛋。

工作真多，老板太过分了：

- God, my boss is really a jerk. 天哪，我老板真垃圾。
- My boss can be such a dick! 我老板真是个讨厌的家伙！

估计大多数老板都是如此：

- I think most bosses are like that! 我想大部分老板都那样！

说不定是好心，先冷静：

- Take it easy. He means well, I'm sure. 冷静点儿，我肯定他是出于好心。
- ❖ asshole ['æshol] *n*. 讨厌的人（粗话）
- ❖ jerk [dʒɜ·k] *n*. 蠢人，古怪的人（俚语）
- ❖ dick [dɪk] *n*. 家伙

4 It is very close to the deadline. 快到截止日期了。

截止日期快到了：

- So we must give an outline about it then. 我们到时必须要给出一个大纲了。

真希望可以推后：

- Is there any way we can push back the deadline by a week? 有什么办法可以将截止日期推后一周吗？

放心吧：

- We're on a pretty tight schedule, but we should be able to finish it just on time. 我们已经安排得很紧凑了，但应该会按时完成工作的。
- ❖ push back 把……向后推

5 How do you handle pressure? 你怎么处理压力？

要保持平衡：
- The appropriate way to deal with stress is to make sure I have the correct balance between good stress and bad stress. 处理压力的恰当方法就是保持正面压力和负面压力之间的适当平衡。

运动减压：
- From a personal perspective, I manage stress by visiting the gym every evening. It's a great stress reducer. 从个人角度来说，我处理压力的方法就是每天晚上去健身房。这是很好的减压方法。

分清轻重缓急：
- Prioritizing my responsibilities so that I have a clear idea of what needs to be done then. It has helped me effectively manage pressure on the job. 将职责的优先顺序排出来可以使我清楚知道应该做什么，这帮助我有效地处理工作上的压力。

❖ appropriate [ə'proprɪ'et] *adj.* 适当的，相称的
❖ perspective [pə'spɛktɪv] *n.* 视角，观点；远景
❖ prioritize [praɪ'ɔrə,taɪz] *vt.* 把……区分优先次序
❖ have a clear idea of 清楚知道

6 I don't know how much longer I can stand this. 我不知道我还能忍受多久。

好累，坚持不下去了：
- I'm not sure how much longer I can hold out. 我不知道我还能坚持多久。

辞职吧：
- I think you should quit now and get it over with. 我觉得你应该现在就辞职，把事情赶快解决了。

❖ hold out 坚持，不屈服
❖ get sth. over with 完成或结束必须要做的讨厌的事情

Work Pressure Conversation

Kevin: Work is becoming impossible.	凯 文：工作越来越难以完成了。
Debra: Why is that?	黛布拉：为什么？
Kevin: I have so many things to do. I'm so stressed out that it isn't even funny.	凯 文：我有太多的工作要做，我太累了，甚至觉得很没意思。
Debra: Well just chill out today, you have the day off.	黛布拉：今天你休假，放松一下吧。
Kevin: Yeah, but all I can think about is the deadlines I need to meet.	凯 文：是的，但是我满脑子想的都是需要面对的截止日期。
Debra: At work?	黛布拉：工作上的？
Kevin: Yeah, I have to have the entire back room re-organized by Friday.	凯 文：是的，截止到周五我得把整个里屋重新整理一下。
Debra: What else?	黛布拉：还有其他的吗？
Kevin: I need to come up with a new marketing scheme for our dairy products also.	凯 文：我还要给我们的奶制品提出新的市场策划。
Debra: It sounds to me like they're just using you, man.	黛布拉：听起来他们好像只是在利用你，哥们儿。
Kevin: You think?	凯 文：你这么想的吗？
Debra: Yeah man, I would quit if I were you.	黛布拉：是啊，如果我是你的话就辞职。

❖ be stressed out 饱受压力，紧张的
❖ chill out 冷静下来，放松
❖ have the day off 休假，不用工作
❖ come up with 提出，想出，提供
❖ scheme[skɪm] n. 计划，方案

文化穿越

　　美国人最大的健康问题是来自精神上的压力，而精神压力的一个主要来源是工作。美国人的工作时间比多数工业化国家都长。美国人每年比日本人几乎多工作一个月，比德国人几乎多工作三个月。工作时间长，心理上的压力也比较大，很多人因此而得了精神忧郁症，甚至引起工作场所发生暴乱。

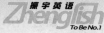
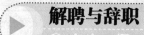

Section 10　▶ 解聘与辞职
Quitting/Resignation

工作的压力整天让我喘不过气来，我感觉我的神经绷得太紧了，说不定哪天就崩溃了。Steve 看到我这个样子后，建议我辞职，可我拿不定主意，毕竟这份工作还不错。经过一晚上的思考之后，我还是决定向老板 Carol 提出辞职。

1 I'm thinking of quitting my job. 我正在考虑辞掉我的工作。

想辞职：
- I've been thinking about pulling the pin. 我一直在想辞职的事。
- I really want to quit my job. 我真的想辞掉工作。

怎么突然想辞职呢：
- How has this idea occurred to you out of the blue? 你怎么突然有了这个念头？

早就该辞职了：
- I think you should. Do it today! 我觉得你应该辞掉。今天就去吧！

记得要提前交辞呈：
- You should at least put in a two weeks' notice. 你至少应该提前两周提交辞呈。
- ❖ pull the pin 离职
- ❖ out of the blue 突然，出乎意料

2 I'm here to put in my two weeks' notice. 我来这儿是提交辞呈的。

递交辞呈：
- I'll be leaving in two weeks. Here's my notice. 我两周后将离开，这是我的告知单。

477

表示遗憾：

- Thank you for the notice. I'm sorry it's come to this. 感谢你的提前告知，我很遗憾走到这一步。

3 This job has become too much for me to handle, I quit. 工作太多了，以至于我无法处理好，我辞职。

实在受不了太多的工作：

- I'm quitting. This job has proven the best of me. 我要辞职。这份工作我已极尽所能。

表示祝福：

- To each his own, we'll miss you around here. 人各有志。这里的同事们会想念你的。

❖ to each one's own 人各有志，萝卜白菜各有所爱

4 Well, I'm bored with my job. 呃，我厌烦了我的工作了。

工作无聊，厌烦了：

- My work is pretty boring. 我的工作太无聊了。
- I'm tired of my present job. 我厌烦了现在的工作。

想接受新的挑战：

- I want to change a more challenging one. 我想换份有挑战性的工作。
- I wish to seek a more challenging job. 我想寻找一份更具挑战性的工作。

进一步发挥能力：

- I'd like to have an opportunity to further develop my abilities. 我想有机会进一步发挥我的能力。

❖ be bored with... 厌烦……

5 I quit! 我辞职！

主动辞职：

- I resign. 我辞职。

抱怨一下：

- I hate this job. I'm outta here! 我讨厌这份工作，我将会离开这里！

提交辞职信：

- This is a letter of my resignation. Have a good day. 这是我的辞职信。祝您愉快。

直接走人：

- I'm not putting in a notice. I quit today! 我不写离职申请，我今天就辞职。

表示惋惜：

- I'm sorry to hear that. Thank you. 很遗憾听到这个消息。但还是谢谢你。

❖ outta [autə] *adv.* 离开，出去（是 out of 口语发音的省略）

6 I quit last week. When will I get my last paycheck? 我上周辞职了，什么时候能拿到最后一次的工资？

会很快发给你的：

- It should arrive by mail soon. 工资很快会寄给你。

7 I quit, so I have to clean out my desk. 我辞职了，所以我得清理下我的办公桌。

走的时候，把随身物品也带走：

- I just quit today. I'm going in to clean out my desk later. 我今天辞职了，稍后我要清理一下我的办公桌。

祝愿：

- Good for you, man! 祝你好运，老兄！

顺带提醒：

- Just be careful. Not having an income is not good. 小心点儿，还没有拿到工资可不是好事。

❖ clean out 把……打扫干净

Quitting/Resignation Conversation

Kay: You look horrible man.　　　　　凯　　：哥们儿，你看起来很糟糕。

Kevin: I feel horrible.	凯　文：我感觉很不好。
Kay: And why is that?	凯　：那是为什么呢？
Kevin: This job is overworking me like crazy!	凯　文：工作太累了，我都要疯了。
Kay: Well, have you considered quitting?	凯　：那你考虑辞职了吗？
Kevin: No, not necessarily. I'm afraid I won't be able to find a new job.	凯　文：没有，没必要。我怕找不到新的工作。
Kay: Dude, that doesn't matter, if you feel like crap you should quit.	凯　：哥们儿，如果你感觉不好就应该辞职，那没关系的。
(The next day)	（第二天）
Kevin: Alright, today I'm quitting my job	凯　文：好吧，今天我要去辞职。
Kay: Good for you, man. Good luck!	凯　：真替你高兴，哥们儿。祝你好运！
Kevin: Thanks. I'll need it!	凯　文：谢谢。我需要好运！
(At Carol's work)	（在卡罗尔的办公室）
Kevin: Hey Carol, can I speak with you?	凯　文：嘿，卡罗尔，能跟你聊会儿吗？
Carol: Sure, what's up, Kevin?	卡罗尔：当然，有什么事吗，凯文？
Kevin: Well, this job is great, but I'm just not fitting in the way I would have hoped. I'm quitting.	凯　文：恩，这份工作很好，但是我不像我期望的那样能适应这份工作。我想辞职。
Carol: Are you sure? You're one of our best.	卡罗尔：你确定？你是我们最优秀的员工之一。

文化穿越

　　最后说说辞职。美国公司很少裁人，除非遇到极大的经济困难，会有裁人指标。一般情况下，都是员工自己辞职，即使公司想让你离开，也会用尽各种方法让你自己递辞呈。不过，美国企业文化有一点很好，一般在你离开公司前会把你该得的福利以及你的工资一次性结清，不会拖欠，这或许和美国相关的法律比较严格有关。公司有任何对员工的不利行为都是违法的。

Chapter 13 Kevin 出游

Travel

Section 1  旅游计划
Travel Planning

> 长时间的工作，确实让人身心疲惫。于是今年的年假，Kevin 打算制定一个旅行计划。不过到底是利用这段时间去做一次家庭旅游呢，还是找几个朋友来一次公路旅游？Kevin 还没有确定。朋友们，你们有什么建议吗？

1 I want to go on a vacation. 我想去度假。

想去度假放松一下：
- I should go on a vacation. 我应该去度假。
- I'd really like to go on a vacation. 我真想去度假。
- Going on a vacation would be nice. 去度假会很不错。

这可是件不错的事：
- Yeah, I agree. 是的，没错。
- It's kind of an odd time of year to go on a vacation. 这个时节去度假可是件美妙的事。
- ❖ go on a vacation 去度假
- ❖ odd [ɑd] *adj.* 奇特的

2 I wonder what kind of places I could travel to. 我想知道我可以去哪些地方旅游。

为旅行作计划：
- I want to do a little bit of traveling. 我想做点儿旅行方面的计划。
- I should travel more. 我应该更多地旅行。

你还是去旅行社打听一下吧：
- You could ask a few travel agencies what's available. 你可以去问问旅行社看看有什么地方可去。
- ❖ travel agency 旅行社

3

Do you want to take a road trip? 你想进行一次公路旅行吗?

公路旅行怎么样:

- Would you like to take a road trip? 你想进行一次公路旅行吗?
- We could always take a road trip, if you want. 如果你想的话，我们可以进行一次公路旅行。
- Taking a road trip might be cool. 公路旅行可能会很不错。

很不错的想法:

- Yeah, man. That sounds awesome. 是啊，听起来很不错。
- Let's do it. 那咱们行动吧。
- ❖ take a road trip 进行一次公路旅行

4

We're thinking of taking a trip to the mountains. 我们想去山上旅行。

旅行计划:

- I'm going on a trip to Europe. 我打算去欧洲旅行。
- We want to arrange a trip to Hawaii. 我们想安排一次去夏威夷的旅行。
- I'll have a week to do sightseeing in that beautiful city. 我将在那个美丽的城市游览一周。
- ❖ sightseeing ['saɪtˌsiɪŋ] n. 观光，游览

5

I'm supposed to go on a vacation with my family later this year. 我打算今年年底和家人去旅游。

全家人一起去旅游:

- My family wanted to take a vacation later this year. 我家人想在今年年底去旅游。
- I have a family vacation to go to later in the year. 今年年底我们一家人要去旅游。

那太没劲了:

- That sucks. Family vacations are the worst. 太没劲了，家庭旅游最差劲了。

玩得高兴点儿吧:

- I hope you have fun. 希望你们玩儿得愉快。

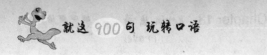
6 I need to look up some hotels. 我要查一下酒店。

旅行前预订酒店：

- I should call a few hotels. 我应该打几个酒店的电话问问。
- I could look up some hotel rates. 我要查一下酒店的价格。
- I need to find out hotel rates. 我要找找酒店的价格。

事不宜迟哦：

- Go for it. 去吧。

我帮你吧：

- I'll help you out. 我会帮你的。
- ❖ look up 查阅

7 I should find some friends to split the cost with. 我应该找些朋友分担一下费用。

找人拼"游"吧：

- I hope some friends will come along, so we can split the cost. 我希望找些朋友一起去，这样我们能一起分担费用。
- I might have a few friends that will split the cost with me. 我可能找几个朋友，和我分担一下费用。
- I'll call some friends to see if they want to come along and split the cost. 我会打电话叫些朋友看看他们是不是想一起去，这样能分摊一下费用。

我看能行：

- That's a good idea. 这主意不错。
- Yeah, I bet you could get at least 4 people to go. 嗯，我敢肯定你至少能叫上四个人。
- ❖ split [splɪt] vt. 分担，分享
- ❖ come along 一起来，随同

Travel Planning Conversation

Kevin: I've been wanting to take a vacation lately.　　凯　文：最近我一直想去旅游。

Mabel: Oh yeah? To where?	**梅布尔：** 哦，是吗？去哪儿？
Kevin: I don't know, maybe Florida. I was going to ask my family about it.	**凯　文：** 我不知道，也许去佛罗里达吧。我要问一下我的家人。
Mabel: You wanted a family vacation? No way.	**梅布尔：** 你想家庭旅游？不会吧。
Kevin: What's wrong with it?	**凯　文：** 怎么了？
Mabel: Those are never any fun. We could have a road trip down there with a few other friends.	**梅布尔：** 家庭旅游一点儿意思都没有。我们可以和几个朋友去那里做一次公路旅行。
Kevin: Sure, I guess that sounds cool.	**凯　文：** 嗯，我觉得这听起来不错。
Mabel: It'll be awesome. We just need to call a few hotels, get some rates, and split the cost.	**梅布尔：** 会很棒的。我们只要找几家酒店，带些钱，一起分担费用就行。
Kevin: Yeah, that's actually a really good idea. I'll call some of my friends and ask them about it.	**凯　文：** 是啊，那确实是个不错的主意。我给几个朋友打下电话问问他们。
Mabel: I'll call some travel agencies.	**梅布尔：** 我会联系一些旅行社的。

❖No way. 不会吧，不可能。
❖get some rates 带些钱

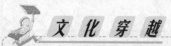 文 化 穿 越

　　对美国人来说，只要有放假的机会就绝不在原地待着。美国的公共管理很到位，无论是公共交通还是公共设施都很人性化。比如，在正规的公共场所，都有饮水机；公厕都有足够的手纸；公路标识基本准确。因此，外出游一般只有两点需要注意，一是怎么去，二是在哪里住。其他的都不是什么问题。一般情况下，寒假往南走，暑假往北走，春假就随便了。

Section **2**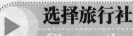

选择旅行社
Choose the Travel Agency

确定要去旅游后，我就着手联系旅行社了。因为有时候找旅行社组团旅游比自己一个人出去旅游要省事很多。例如，旅行的住宿和交通等问题就不用我去担心了。运气好的话，遇到打折的旅行社，还会给自己省一笔哦，但愿我有那样的好运。

1 I need to shop around for travel agencies. 我要到周围的旅行社看看。

打听旅行社：

- I have to look for a travel agency. 我得找家旅行社。
- I should look at different travel agencies. 我应该看看不同的旅行社。

所谓货比三家嘛：

- Yeah, there's a bunch of them out there. 嗯，那边有好多旅行社。
- I bet you could find a good deal. 我肯定你能找到一家合适的。

❖ shop around 四处看看
❖ a bunch of 一大堆

2 I looked up some travel agencies online. 我在网上找了几家旅行社。

从网上找找看：

- I went online to look up some travel agencies. 我在网上找了几家旅行社。
- I was doing research on travel agencies. 我在做旅行社的调查。

哦，那找到合适的旅行社了吗：

- Did you find anything good? 你发现有什么好的旅行社了？
- I hope your search was successful. 我希望你能成功找到。

❖ do research on... 对……进行研究，对……进行调查

3 I talked to the travel agent, and they gave me some rates. 我和这家旅行社谈过了，他们给了我一些优惠。

打听旅行社的优惠条件：

- I spoke with a travel agent. They gave me some rates. 我和一家旅行社谈过了，他们给了我一些优惠。
- I got some rates from a travel agent. 我从一家旅行社享受到了优惠。
- The travel agent I spoke with gave me some rates. 我谈的那家旅行社给了我一些优惠。

哦，是什么：

- Tell me what they offered. 告诉我他们提供了什么。
- Did they offer a good deal? 他们提供优惠价格了吗？

❖ travel agent 旅行社，旅行代理人

4 I picked a really good travel deal from the travel agency. 我从旅行社选了一个很好的旅行套餐。

从旅行社选优惠套餐：

- I got a really nice travel deal from the travel agency. 我从旅行社选了一个很好的旅行套餐。
- The travel deal I got is amazing. 我选的这个旅行套餐太棒了。
- I picked a great travel deal. 我选了一个非常不错的旅行套餐。

是吗，你都选了什么套餐：

- That's good. 太好了。
- Tell me what you picked. 告诉我你选了什么。

5 I think I've decided on a travel agency. 我想我已经选定了一家旅行社。

确定旅行社：

- I've picked out a travel agency. 我已经挑了一家旅行社。
- I decided on a travel agency. 我选定了一家旅行社。
- I know what travel agency I want to use. 我知道我需要什么样的旅行社。

快告诉我是哪家：

- Cool. Which one? 太好了。是哪家？
- Are you sure you picked a good one? 你确定你挑了一家不错的？

❖ pick out 挑选出

6 What kind of tours do you have? 你们都有哪些旅行路线呢？

询问旅行线路：

- What kind of tours are available? 你们都有哪些旅行路线呢？
- What kind of tours do you offer? 你们都提供哪些旅行路线呢？
- What kind of tours are there? 这都有哪些旅行线路？

你先看看旅行小册子吧：

- Well, we have many tours. Here is our travel brochure and you can have a look. 嗯，我们有好多旅行线路。这是我们的旅行小册子，你可以看一下。
- Let me give you some brochures. We have a "Grand Tour" and "The Wonderful All-day Tour". 您看看这些小册子。我们有"大旅游"和"精彩一日游"。
- We have some fun week-long getaways. 我们有一些有趣的周旅游线路。

❖ brochure [broʃur] n. 小册子，宣传册
❖ getaway ['ɡɛtəˌwe] n. 旅行，假期旅游

Choose the Travel Agency Conversation

Kevin: Hello.	凯 文：你好。
Travel Agent: Hi there, sir. How can I help you today?	旅行社：你好，先生。我能帮你什么吗？
Kevin: I was wondering what kind of rates you offer for hotels in Florida.	凯 文：我想知道入住佛罗里达的酒店你们提供什么优惠。
Travel Agent: At this time of year? I could find some really cheap ones.	旅行社：每年的这个时候吗？我确实能找到一些便宜的。
Kevin: That's great. Could you give me some examples?	凯 文：太好了。你能给我些实例吗？
Travel Agent: Well, here's a list of the hotels we work with.	旅行社：好的，这是和我们有合作的酒店名单。

Kevin: Wow, there are some pretty big names here.	凯　文：哇，这上面有好多知名酒店啊。
Travel Agent: Yup. The rates vary, but if you give me a few on the list that you like I can call them up for you.	旅行社：是的。优惠也有好多种，但如果这名单上有你喜欢的酒店的话，我可以给他们打电话问一问。
Kevin: That would be awesome. This seems like the best deal I've found.	凯　文：那就太好了。这看起来是我找到的最好的旅行待遇了。
Travel Agent: I'm glad you came to us, sir.	旅行社：我很高兴你来我们这里，先生。
Kevin: Here, I'd like to know the rates on these hotels.	凯　文：嘿，我想知道这些酒店的优惠条件。
Travel Agent: Alright. If you give me a few minutes I can get the information for you right now.	旅行社：好的。你稍等几分钟，我马上给你找这些信息。
Kevin: Thank you very much.	凯　文：多谢你了。
Travel Agent: You're very welcome.	旅行社：您太客气了。

❖work with 与……共事
❖yup [jʌp] int. 是的（俚语，相当于 yes）

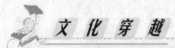 文 化 穿 越

　　美国的旅行社太多了，但基本上都是私人的。一般情况下，如果身处美国的大城市，短程旅行可以选择中国人自己的旅行社，而且价格方面也相对便宜。如果不选择旅行社，选择他们的旅行巴士也不错，价格很便宜。例如，从华盛顿到纽约，往返也就 50 美元左右；从波士顿到纽约，便宜的时候，往返也就 20 美元左右。但很多美国年轻人都属于背包客，经常和朋友一块儿自驾车之后徒步旅行。走累了，找个汽车旅馆住一宿，之后继续前行。

Section 3

参观游览
Sightseeing Tour

很遗憾，在找旅行社方面没有那么好的运气。于是我决定找几个朋友一起自行出游。其实这样也挺好的，很自由，还能一起分摊旅行费用。我们决定进行一次环球影城的旅行。朋友们，和Kevin一起去旅游吧。

口 语 大 放 送

1 When was this museum built? 这座博物馆是什么时候建成的?

参观博物馆或其他建筑物：

- Do you know the time period this was built in? 你知道这是在什么年代建造的吗?

告知建筑物的建造时间：

- It was build over 100 years ago. 大约一百多年前建的吧。
- The exact date is unknown, but it's at least 100 years old. 确切的日期不知道，但至少有100年了。
- It was recently built. 是最近建的。

❖ exact [ɪg'zækt] *adj.* 确切的，精确的

2 Is this a historical area? 这是历史古迹区吗?

想参观历史名胜：

- Is this area historical? 这个地区是历史古迹区吗?
- Is there anything historical about this area? 这一地区有什么历史古迹吗?
- Are there historical landmarks nearby? 这附近有历史古迹吗?

有啊，有很多：

- Yes, there are many historical landmarks here. 有，这里有很多历史古迹。
- Yes, and we'll see most of the historical landmarks on the tour. 有，旅行途中我们会看到很多历史古迹。

有，但不是很多：

- There are a few historical places in the area, but not many. 这一地区有一些名胜古迹，但不是很多。

❖ historical [hɪs'tɔrɪkl] *adj.* 历史的，历史上的
❖ landmark ['lænd,mɑrk] *n.* 标志性建筑

---

3 I want to enjoy some natural scenery. 我想欣赏自然风光。

我还是喜欢大自然的风光：

- I'd like to go some scenic sites. 我想去一些风景名胜地区。
- I want to enjoy things that are different from cities. 我想领略一些与城市不同的东西。

❖ scenery ['sinərɪ] *n.* 风景，景色
❖ scenic sites 风景名胜

---

4 The scenery is beautiful. What's more, the air is fresh here. 这景色真美。而且，这里的空气也很新鲜。

多么美丽的景色啊：

- What a beautiful pacific place this is! 多么美丽宁静的地方啊！
- I've never dreamed it would be so beautiful. 我从没想到会这么漂亮。
- I've never seen a water fall like that before. 我从未见过那样的瀑布。

❖ what's more 而且，再说
❖ pacific [pə'sɪfɪk] *adj.* 平静的，宁静的
❖ water fall 瀑布

---

5 How long is this tour? 这趟旅行要多长时间？

询问旅行要花费的时间：

- Is this a long or a short tour? 这是长途旅行还是短途旅行呢？
- Does this tour take long? 这趟旅行要花很长时间吗？
- Is this tour short? 这是短途旅行吗？

这时间不太长吧：

- It's a full hour tour. 足足一个小时的旅程。
- The tour isn't very long. It's about a half hour. 这趟旅行不会花很长时间，差不多半个小时吧。

6 Where does this tour lead through? 这趟旅程要去哪里啊？

有点晕哦，都不知道要去哪里旅行：

- Where do we go during this tour? 我们这趟旅游要去哪里啊？
- What do we see through this tour? 我们这趟旅游要看什么景观啊？
- What kind of places do we go to during this tour? 我们这趟旅游要去什么地方啊？

城市观光吧：

- We'll go through many well-known streets and a few buildings. 我们会去参观很多著名的街道和一些建筑物。
- ❖ lead through 引领，带领

Sightseeing Tour Conversation

Kevin: Are you guys enjoying yourselves?	凯文：你们玩得还高兴吗？
Kay: The Universal Studios tour was a good pick, Kevin.	凯 ：这次环球影城的旅行是个不错的选择，凯文。
Kevin: Thanks. I'm glad you guys are enjoying this.	凯文：谢谢。我很高兴你们都喜欢这次旅行。
Kay: Of course, this stuff is pretty cool.	凯 ：当然，这趟旅行非常好。
Kevin: Yeah, I thought the Disney World tour would have too many kids.	凯文：是啊，我觉得迪斯尼世界的旅行会有很多孩子。
Kay: Good thinking.	凯 ：没错。
Kevin: Do you guys want to go back to the hotel after this?	凯文：这趟旅行后你们想回旅馆吗？

Kay: If we're tired, yeah. But if we still have some energy we could just walk around the city.

凯 ：如果我们累了就回去。如果我们还有精力的话就在这城里走走。

Kevin: That's true. We'll decide when this is over.

凯文：没错。那结束后我们再决定吧。

Kay: Sure thing.

凯 ：好的。

❖the Universal Studios 环球影城

❖pick [pɪk] *n.* 挑选，选择

❖the Disney World 迪斯尼世界

❖energy ['ɛnɚdʒɪ] *n.* 精力，能量

文化穿越

　　在美国旅游的时候，如果选择旅行社，基本上都是走马观花，旅行社开车带你到一个地方，之后给你 10 分钟的自由活动时间，然后再开到下一个景点。因此，在这期间游客能做的事情就只有拍几张照片而已。但如果选择自助游，感觉就完全不同了，观光的时间可以自行支配，所以总能观赏到很别致的景色，当然也会有些累。不过只要计划好路线，将目的地的几个景点串起来，之后寻找一条最佳路线，就可以拥有一个愉快充实的旅行了。

Section 4 ▶ 旅途遇到麻烦
Trouble

前面我已经说过，自助旅游一路上可能会遇到一些我们意想不到的麻烦。真不幸，被我说中了（他们都说我是乌鸦嘴）。 Mabel 走丢了，Steve 的车半路熄火了，而我把脚扭伤了……看来这次旅行的麻烦事还真不少。

① **I have some bad news. 我有些不好的消息。**

旅途遇到麻烦的事：

- I got some bad news. 我有些不好的消息。
- I have something bad to tell you. 我有些不好的事情要告诉你。

怎么了：

- What is it? 是什么？
- Oh crap. What happened? 哦，天哪。发生什么事了？

② **I think we lost track of someone. 我觉得我们有人走丢了。（我觉得有人和我们走散了。）**

旅途中有人走丢了：

- I think we lost someone. 我想我们丢了一个人。
- I'm pretty sure someone got lost. 我非常肯定有人走丢了。
- We should call them. I think they're lost. 我们应该给他们打个电话，我想他们是迷路了。

那还愣着干什么，赶紧找啊：

- Let's try calling them. 咱们给他们打电话吧。
- Let's go to find them. 咱们去找他们吧。
- ❖ track [træk] *n.* 行踪，足迹

3 My car ran out of gas. 我的车没油了。

旅行途中车没油熄火也是让人头疼的事：

- I just ran out of gas. 汽油刚用完了。
- My car just stopped. It's out of gas. 我的车刚停了，没油了。
- My car is out of gas and won't start. 我的车没油了，发动不起来了。

那只能请求别人帮助了：

- Crap. We should set up flares. 天哪，我们应该打开闪光灯。
- Let's flag someone for help. 咱们打旗号叫人来帮我们吧。

❖ flare [flɛr] *n.* 闪光信号，照明灯
❖ flag [flæg] *vt.* 打旗号表示，打旗号使（车子等）停下

4 I don't remember where we parked the car. 我不记得我们把车停哪儿了。

自驾游的麻烦比较多：

- I don't know where we parked my car. 我不知道我们把车停哪儿了。
- Do you remember where we parked? This parking garage is so big and I forget. 你还记得我们把车停哪儿了吗？这停车场太大了，我忘了。
- I forget where we parked the car, and this parking garage is huge. 我忘了我们把车停哪儿了，这停车场太大了。

那可真麻烦了：

- Crap. I don't remember either. 天哪，我也不记得了。

有我呢，别担心：

- I remember, don't worry. 我记得，别担心。

❖ parking garage 停车场

5 I just fell. I think my ankle is sprained. 我刚摔倒了，我想我把脚踝给扭伤了。

旅行途中摔倒：

- I just injured myself by falling. 我刚摔倒了，把自己弄伤了。
- I just fell. I think I'm injured. 我刚摔倒了，我想我受伤了。
- I'm injured. My ankle feels sprained. 我受伤了，我感觉我的脚踝受伤了。

自备急救：

- I have a first aid kit. 我有急救药箱。

严重的话就去医院吧：

- Let's get you to the doctor. 我们带你去看医生吧。
- I'll drive you to the hospital. 我开车送你去医院。
- ❖ ankle ['æŋkl] *n.* 脚踝
- ❖ sprain [spren] *vt.* 扭，扭伤
- ❖ first aid kit 急救药箱

6 I lost my wallet. 我钱包丢了。

钱包丢了没钱了：

- I can't find my wallet. 我找不到钱包了。

还有其他的印象吗：

- Where did you last use it? 你最后一次用钱包是在哪里？
- Do you have any idea where it is? 放在哪里了你有印象吗？

7 My cell phone just died and I forgot my charger. 我手机关机了，我忘带充电器了。

旅行途中手机关机可就失去联系了：

- I forgot my phone charger and it just died. 我忘带充电器了，手机关机了。
- I don't think I brought my cell phone charger, and it's dead. 我想我没带充电器，手机关机了。

那就用我的吧：

- You can use my phone for now. 你暂时可以用我的手机。

不是吧，怎么不准备齐全呢：

- That sucks, man. 那太糟糕了，伙计。
- ❖ charger ['tʃɑrdʒɚ] *n.* 充电器

8 I'm sorry. I'll try to fix things. I don't want to ruin our vacation. 对不起，我会尽力搞定一切的，我不想破坏我们的假期。

不要因为我而破坏了假期的气氛：

- I hope I didn't ruin our vacation. I'll try and fix things. 我希望我没有破坏咱们的假期，我会尽力搞定一切的。

不要因为我而破坏了假期的气氛：

- I hope I didn't ruin our vacation. I'll try and fix things. 我希望我没有破坏咱们的假期，我会尽力搞定一切的。
- I'm going to try and fix things, so I don't ruin our vacation. 我会尽力搞定一切的，所以我不会破坏咱们的假期的。

别担心，这样的事多了去了：

- Don't worry about it, man. It happens. 不要为此担心，伙计。这种事太多了。
- You didn't ruin our vacation. It's okay. 你没有破坏咱们的假期，没事的。

❖ It happens. 这种事太多了，有时候就是这样的。

Trouble Conversation

Steve: I have some bad news, man.	史蒂夫：我有些坏消息，伙计。
Kevin: What happened?	凯　文：发生什么事了？
Steve: My car just broke down.	史蒂夫：我的车坏了。
Kevin: What happened to it?	凯　文：怎么了？
Steve: It overheated and stopped running. I need to get the radiator fixed.	史蒂夫：太热了，熄火了。我要把这散热器拿去修一下。
Kevin: That's terrible. How much is this going to cost?	凯　文：那太糟糕了。那要花多少钱啊？
Steve: Either several hundred dollars, or I'll have to buy a new car altogether.	史蒂夫：或者花几百美元，或者我得买整个一辆新车。
Kevin: Why would you have to buy a new car? Can't they fix it?	凯　文：你为什么得买辆新车呢？他们不能修理吗？
Steve: They're not sure. Either way we don't have a way to get home for a few days.	史蒂夫：不一定。总之我们得花几天的时间才能到家了。
Kevin: I'll call around some cheap motels and see if we can get a room there…	凯　文：我打电话问问一些便宜的汽车旅馆，看能不能在那里订到一个房间……

Steve: Yeah. Sorry, man.	史蒂夫：好的。对不起啊，伙计。
Kevin: It happens.	凯 文：这种事太多了。

❖overheat ['ovəˈhit] *vi.* 过热
❖radiator ['redɪˌetə] *n.* (汽车等的) 散热器，冷却
❖motel [moˈtɛl] *n.* 汽车旅馆

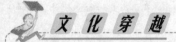 文 化 穿 越

　　旅行途中会出现很多问题。例如，如果是自驾游，出行前一定要确保汽车的状况良好，没有硬伤，不然如果出现问题，就可能会是事故，即使不是事故，车坏在旷野等地方，就只能打电话求助了。另外，预定酒店也是需要注意的，每个地方的税会不同，因此酒店税后的价格才是真正的价格。到酒店后，需要注意的是尽量不要使用房间内的非免费物品，因为每个酒店都会提前扣掉房间的押金，如果使用了房间内的非免费物品，有时候你的押金就拿不回来了。除此之外，就是安全问题，很多大城市都有自己的穷人区，旅游时需要尽量避开穷人区，尤其是晚上可能会有危险。

Section 5 拍照留恋
Photo Taking

这次旅行虽然有不少麻烦事，但乐趣还是很多的。朋友们从我们拍的这些旅行照片中也能感受出来。我很想多拍些照片，把我们旅行中的点点滴滴都记录下来，可惜我的相机没有电了……

1 I just got a new camera for the vacation. 我为这次度假刚买了个新相机。

拍照准备相机：
- I purchased a new camera for the vacation. 我为这次度假买了个新相机。
- I recently bought a new camera for the vacation. 我最近买了个新相机去度假。
- I needed a new camera for the vacation, so I bought one. 我去度假需要个新相机，所以我就买了一个。

拿出来看看吧：
- Can I see it? 我能看看吗?
- Cool. What model is it? 太好了。是什么型号的?

2 I need more film. 我需要更多的胶卷。

胶卷都用完了：
- I ran out of film. 我的胶卷用完了。
- I'm out of film. 我把胶卷用完了。

我这儿有：
- Here, I have some. 给你，我有些。

去买些吧：
- We should go buy more. 我们应该再去买些。

❖ film [fɪlm] *n.* 胶片，胶卷

3 My batteries died! 我的电池没电了。

相机的电池没电了：

- My batteries are dead! 我的电池没电了。
- I ran out of batteries! 我的电池用完了。

去买些吧：

- Let's go get some more. 咱们去买些电池吧。

❖ battery['bætərɪ] *n.* 电池，蓄电池

4 Do you have extra batteries? I need them. 你还有多余的电池吗？我要一些。

问问同行的人有没有：

- I need extra batteries. Do you have some? 我还需要电池。你有吗？
- I need any extra batteries. You might have. 我还需要电池，你可能有吧。
- I need to get some extra batteries. I ran out. 我再要些电池，我的用完了。
- Do you have any more batteries? 你还有电池吗？

有的话就掏出来：

- I do. Here you go. 我有，给你。

实在是没有了：

- No, sorry. 没有了，抱歉。
- No, I don't. Let's buy some more. 我没有了，咱们去买些吧。

5 Are we allowed to take pictures here? 这里允许拍照吗？

询问是否允许拍照：

- Can we take pictures here? 我们能在这里拍照吗？
- Are pictures not allowed during this part of the tour? 旅行的这段期间不允许拍照吗？
- Is it okay to take pictures here? 在这里拍照行吗？

禁止拍照：

- No, cameras are not allowed right now. 不行，现在不允许拍照。

允许拍照：

- Yes, pictures are allowed here. 可以，这里允许拍照。

❖ take picture 拍照

6　Would you take a picture of us? 您能给我们照张相吗？

请求别人拍照：

- Will you take a picture of us? 您能给我们照张相吗？

看来摄影技术还不错：

- OK. Stand back a little… Move right. That's right. Ready? One, two, three! This one is great. 好的，往后站一点点……往右移一下。好的，准备好了吗？一、二、三！这张很不错。

7　Take a picture of that. 给那个拍张照吧。

选景点拍照：

- Take a photo of that. 给那个拍张照吧。
- Take a snapshot of that. 给那个按个快门。

挺好看的，拍一张：

- Okay. 好的。
- I already did. 我已经拍了。
- ❖　take a photo 拍照
- ❖　snapshot ['snæpˌʃɑt] n. 快照，快相

8　I took a lot of pictures. 我拍了很多照片。

这次旅游拍了很多照片：

- I have a lot of pictures. 我拍了很多照片。
- I got a lot of photos. 我拍了很多照片。

上传到网上看看：

- You should upload them later. 你应该一会儿把照片传到网上来。
- I want to see them! 我想看看！
- ❖　upload [ˌʌp'lod] vt. 上传，上载

交流面对面

Photo Taking Conversation

Kevin: Do you have any extra batteries?　　凯　文：你还有多余的电池吗？

Mabel:	Nah, not with me. Why?	梅布尔:	没有，我没带。干什么？
Kevin:	My camera is running low on battery…	凯　文:	我的相机电池电量不足了……
Mabel:	That sucks. I still have my camera on me. Do you want me to take some pictures?	梅布尔:	那太糟糕了。我的相机还有电池，你想让我拍照吗？
Kevin:	Sure. I got the camera on my phone, too. I'll use that if you don't want to take pictures.	凯　文:	好的。我的手机也带摄像头。如果你不想拍的话就借给我拍吧。
Mabel:	Alright. Hey, take a picture of that!	梅布尔:	好的。嘿，拍张那个的照片！
Kevin:	Yeah, that's awesome. I'm glad I remembered this.	凯　文:	好的，太美了。我很高兴我还记得这个。
Mabel:	Yeah. Upload those pictures as soon as we get back!	梅布尔:	是啊。我们一回去就把这些照片上传到网上去吧。
Kevin:	I definitely will. My parents are going to be jealous they didn't come along.	凯　文:	我肯定会的。我爸妈没有一起来一定会很嫉妒的。
Mabel:	(laughs) Yeah, probably! This is the coolest vacation I've ever had.	梅布尔:	（笑）是啊，很可能哦！这是我所度过的最美好的假期。

❖ run low on battery 电池电量不足
❖ jealous ['dʒɛləs] *adj.* 妒忌的
❖ come along 一起来

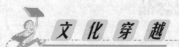

文化穿越

　　一段旅行能给你留下的只有两样东西，一段美好的回忆和一些旅行照片。拿着相机随时记录旅程，写旅行博客，一是记录自己走过的地方，二是与他人分享自己的快乐时光。如果使用的是单反相机，注意至少要备用两块电池，还要有足够大容量的记忆棒。另外，如果条件允许，再带上一部像素较高的手机或者一般相机，因为有些景色是来不及用单反相机抓拍的或者有时很难确保随时将单反相机带在身边，这时手机就派上用场了，但一定确保像素够高。除此之外，手机的视频文件较小，所占的存储容量也相对较小。

Section 6 ▶ 购买纪念品
Buying Souvenirs

Kevin 有一个习惯，每到一个地方旅游，都会买一些当地有特色的纪念品。一是作为礼物回去送给亲朋好友，另外一点就是为了纪念自己到此一游，因为 Kevin 觉得实物比印象要留得久远。朋友们，我也给你们每人准备了一份呢。

1 I'm looking for a souvenir. 我在找纪念品。

需要给朋友买纪念品：
- I need a souvenir for my friend. 我需要给朋友买个纪念品。

生意上门，好好招呼：
- Sure, let me show you what I have. 好的，我给你看看我这有些什么。
- ❖ souvenir [ˈsuvəˌnɪr] n. 纪念品

2 Where is the nearby gift shop? 附近的礼品店在哪儿？

询问礼品店：
- Could you tell me where the gift shop is? 你能告诉我礼品店在哪儿吗？
- Is there a gift shop nearby? 这儿附近有礼品店吗？
- Can you point me to the nearest gift shop? 你能告诉我最近的礼品店在哪儿吗？

指路：
- It's in that building over there. 那边那栋楼里面就有。

3 Are these souvenirs authentic? 这些纪念品是真的吗？

为了保险还是问问真假吧:

- Are these authentic? 这些是真的吗?

店家不会跟你说是假的:

- Yes, they are. 是啊, 是真的。
- ❖ authentic [ɔ'θɛntɪk] *adj.* 真的

4 I want a souvenir, but not from a store. 我想买纪念品, 但不想从商店买。

不想从商店买纪念品:

- I don't want a store-bought souvenir. 我不想从商店买纪念品。
- ❖ store-bought ['stɔ:bat] *adj.* 现成的, 店里买的

5 What do you think my mom would like? 你觉得我妈妈想要什么?

征询意见:

- What kind of souvenir would my dad like? 你觉得我爸爸想要什么
  礼物?

直接给对方一些选择:

- I can show you what I have. 我给你看看我有什么。

6 Do you want a souvenir from my trip? 我这次旅行你要什么纪念
品吗?

要不要给你带礼物回来:

- Should I bring you back a souvenir? 我要不要给你带纪念品回来?

有礼物当然要了:

- Yes, please! 要啊, 当然要!

帮你省省钱吧:

- Nah, I don't need one. 不用了, 我不需要。
- ❖ bring back 带回来

7 Here's a small souvenir from Washington. 这是在华盛顿买的小
纪念品。

送人礼物：

- This is for you. 这是给你的。
- Here's something for you. 这儿有些东西给你。

表达谢意：

- That's very nice of you. 你真是太好了。

8 I thought I'd buy some more souvenirs. 我想我要再多买一些纪念品。

要买纪念品：

- She spent the whole morning buying souvenirs. 她花了一整个上午的时间买纪念品。
- Every time I arrive at a new place, I will buy some souvenirs. 每到一个新地方，我都会买一些纪念品。

 交流面对面

Buying Souvenirs Conversation

Kevin: Hey, good to see you!	凯　文：嗨，见到你真好！
Debra: Welcome back!	黛布拉：欢迎回来！
Kevin: Hey, I got you something!	凯　文：嗨，我给你带了点儿东西！
Debra: Really? What is it?	黛布拉：真的吗？是什么？
Kevin: I got you a hand carved elephant from India!	凯　文：我给你从印度带了一个手工雕刻的大象。
Debra: Oh, snap!	黛布拉：哦，天哪！
Kevin: Yeah! It's totally authentic.	凯　文：是啊。完全是真的。
Debra: Awesome! I love it!	黛布拉：真棒！我喜欢！
Kevin: Glad you like it!	凯　文：很高兴你喜欢。
Debra: Definitely! I'll keep it forever!	黛布拉：那肯定的！我会一直保存的。

❖carve [kɑrv] vt. 雕刻

❖Oh, snap! 哦，天哪！（感叹词）

文化穿越

　　在参团出游的游客中，以购物为主要目的的旅游者只是少数，但在旅游者中需要或愿意购买物品，特别是纪念品的人却有很多。某些游客尽管在出游前并没有购物的愿望和打算，但在参观游览中，偶然发现了颇引人注目的纪念物品和土特产时，也往往会情不自禁地购买。一般说来，在旅游中购物，大体有以下四种类型：一是馈赠型：这种类型的购物主要是为了作为礼品赠送亲朋好友，以表达感情和礼貌。这种类型的购物在旅游者中占有很大比重。二是纪念型：这种类型的购物是为了留作自己曾到该地旅游过的纪念或凭证。因此，具有民族特色、地方特色的旅游商品大受欢迎。三是实用型：有些旅游者对某地生产的实用工艺品、衣着用品、文化用具等慕名已久，借旅游之便前往购买。因此，质量好、款式新，特别是具有地方特色的名牌产品最受旅游者的欢迎。四是业务型：有些旅游者从专业兴趣出发，为了业务方面的需要，到处寻找能为事业带来益处的物品，正是为了业务的原因，他们要买些样品带回去。这种类型的购物在旅游者中只占少数一部分。

Section 7  入住宾馆
Hotel

　　自助旅行需要自己提前联系好旅游目的地的酒店或宾馆，这样就不至于在旅行的时候忙乱了。在这里，Kevin 提醒大家，在入住酒店或宾馆的时候，一定要了解清楚酒店或宾馆的服务，以及退房的时间。否则，我们可能会无意中增加开销。

① I'm looking for a hotel room online. 我在网上找个酒店房间。

网上预定房间：
- I'm looking online for a hotel room. 我在网上找个酒店房间。
- I'm trying to find a hotel room online. 我尽量在网上找个酒店房间。

找到了吗：
- Have you found anything yet? 你已经找到了吗？
- How's the search going? 找得怎么样啊？

② I found a decent hotel room. It's a nice price. 我找了一间相当好的旅馆房间，价格也很合适。

这样的房间很实惠：
- I found a pretty cheap hotel room that looks nice. 我找了一间很便宜的旅馆房间，看起来还不错。
- The hotel room I found was nice and pretty cheap. 我找的这间旅馆房间挺不错，价格也非常便宜。
- I found a fairly nice hotel room for a good price. 我以一个合适的价格找了一间非常不错的旅馆房间。

那去看看吧：
- Cool. Let's go with that one. 太好了，咱们就去那家吧。
- Let me see the room. 我去看看房间。

再看看其他的吧：

- Shop around a little more. Just in case. 再四处看看吧，以防万一嘛。
- ❖ decent ['disnt] *adj.* 体面的，还不错的
- ❖ fairly ['fɛrlɪ] *adv.* 颇为，相当地
- ❖ shop around 四处看看
- ❖ in case 以防万一

3 I reserved the room. 我订了个房间。

已经预定房间了：

- I got the room reserved for us. 我给咱们订了个房间。

真是太好了：

- Awesome, thanks. 太好了，谢谢啊。
- That's good. 太好了。

4 How long will you be staying? 您要住多长时间？

询问停留的时间：

- How long will you be with us? 您要住多长时间？
- How many nights will you be staying? 您要住几个晚上？

直接回答：

- Three nights. 三个晚上。

5 Hi, I'm here to check in to my room. 你好，我来这里对我预定的房间进行入住登记。

登记入住：

- Hi there. I'd like to check in to the room I reserved. 你好，我想对我预定的房间进行入住登记。
- Hello. I'm checking into a room. 你好，我是来入住登记客房的。
- Hi, I'd like to check in. 嗨，我想进行入住登记。

请出示身份证明：

- Hello. Can I see some ID? 你好，能让我看看身份证明吗？
- Hi there, sir. Let me see your ID and I can get your key. 你好，先生。让我看看你的身份证明我才能给你钥匙。

- Alright. Give me your ID and I'll see what room you have. 好的。给我看看你的身份证明，我才能知道你预定了哪个房间。

❖ check in 入住登记

6 Is it a key or a card? 是用钥匙还是用门卡？

酒店房间的门该怎么打开：

- Do you guys use a key or a card? 你们是用钥匙还是用门卡？
- Do we use a key or a card to unlock the door? 我们是用钥匙还是用门卡来开门？

刷门卡：

- It's a card that you swipe. 是刷门卡的。
- You get two cards. 你有两张卡。

有钥匙啊：

- It's just a key. 只有一个钥匙。

❖ unlock [ʌn'lak] vt. 开，开启
❖ swipe [swaɪp] vi. 刷……卡

7 Are we paying for room service? 我们要支付客房服务的费用吗？

客房服务费用怎么算：

- Does room service come with the room? 这个房间有客房服务吗？
- Do we have to pay extra for room service? 我们要另外支付客房服务的费用吗？
- How much extra is room service? 客房服务要另收多少费用？

包括在套餐内了：

- Room service is included in the package you bought. 客房服务包括在你预定的套餐里面。

得另外支付：

- No, I'm sorry. You'll have to pay extra for room service. 没有，抱歉。你得另外支付客房服务的费用。

❖ room service 客房服务
❖ package ['pækɪdʒ] n. (有关联的) 一组事物，一揽子交易

8 Do you have pamphlets with the local attractions? 你们有当地旅游景点的小册子吗?

酒店服务要全面:

- Do you have any information on local attractions? 你们有当地旅游景点的信息吗?
- I'd like some information on the attractions in the area. 我想要这一地区旅游景点的一些信息。
- Could I please have a pamphlet with information on attractions around here? 能给我这儿附近旅游景点信息的小册子吗?

有, 这里有:

- Of course. Here you go, sir. 好的。给你, 先生。
- ❖ pamphlet ['pæmflət] *n.* 小册子

9 When do we have to be out of the room by? 我们应该什么时候退房?

结账退房的时间:

- What time is checkout?/ When's checkout? 什么时间结账退房?
- You need to check out by 12 o'clock a.m.. 你需要在中午 12 点以前退房。
- Noon is your checkout time. 结账退房时间是中午。

中午之前:

- Please check out before noon. 请在中午之前退房。
- ❖ checkout ['tʃɛk,aut] *n.* (从旅馆等的) 结账离开时间
- ❖ check out 结账离开

10 I'm checking out of my room. 我在办理退房手续。

结账退房:

- I'd like to check out. 我想办理退房手续。
- I'm checking out today. 我今天办理退房手续。

服务员的礼貌用语:

- I hope you had a nice stay here. Have a good day! 希望你在这里住得愉快。玩得开心!

Hotel Conversation

Kevin: Hello there. We'd like to check into our room, please.

凯文：你好。我们想登记入住预定的房间。

Clerk: Sure. Can I see your ID?

职员：好的。能给我看看你们的身份证明吗？

Kevin: Here you go.

凯文：给你。

Clerk: Alright, let me look you up real quick.

职员：好的，我马上给你查一下。

Kevin: Sure.

凯文：好的。

Clerk: Looks like you boys are in 211.

职员：你们好像是211房间。

Kevin: Okay. Thank you.

凯文：是的。谢谢你。

Clerk: Here's your keycard. Just swipe it to unlock the door.

职员：给你门卡。刷一下就能把门打开了。

Kevin: Do we only get two?

凯文：只给我们两张卡吗？

Clerk: Yes, I'm sorry. Make sure you don't lose it or you will be charged a fee. Also, there is free for housekeeping, but just put the sign on the door if you don't want them to come in.

职员：是的，对不起。请确保不要丢失，否则是要收费的。还有，这里有免费的客房服务，但如果你不想让他们进来的话在门上贴个标贴就可以了。

Kevin: Alright, thank you. Have a nice day.

凯文：好的，谢谢你。祝你愉快。

❖ real quick 立即，很快
❖ keycard [kiːˈkɑːrd] *n.* 门卡，出入证
❖ housekeeping [ˈhaʊsˌkiːpɪŋ] *n.* 客房服务

文 化 穿 越

　　酒店这一块儿是很需要注意的。首先，酒店的预订需要货比三家，同样级别的酒店价格相差是很大的。预订一个酒店之前，需要查看对于酒店的各种评价，尤其是差评，做到心里有数。另外是依据旅行路线，确保酒店的位置比较方便旅行。如果是一个人的旅行，就找一些打折的酒店，如果是两个人或者多个人旅行，大家可以一块儿平摊房费。Check in（入住）的时候，只需要告诉前台你的姓名就可以了，或者提供下你的预订确认码。Check out（结账）的时候确保是在中午12点前，不然酒店会将另一天的钱也算入账内。除此之外，就是之前章节提到的尽量不要使用房间内的收费物品，否则押金就没了。

Section 8  旅行归来
Back From the Trip

由于 Steve 的汽车坏了，我们不得不在旅行途中多呆了两天，这一路上确实有点儿累了。不过总的来说，这次旅行还是很不错的。我要先睡一觉，明天一早就把旅行中拍的照片传到网上，大家就可以欣赏了。

1 That trip was a lot of fun. 那趟旅行真好玩。

一次快乐的旅行：
- I had a lot of fun on our trip. 我在旅行途中玩得很高兴。
- That was so much fun. 那太好玩了。
- I had fun. Did you guys? 我玩得很开心。你们呢？

大家都玩得很开心：
- I agree. I had a lot of fun too. 没错，我也玩得很开心。
- Yeah man, that was an awesome vacation. 是的，哥们，这是一个很不错的假期。
- It was good. 很不错。

2 It's so nice to be home. 回到家真好。

想念家的味道：
- It's great to be back. 回来真好。
- Being back home I feel so nice. 回到家我感觉真好。
- It's good to be back home. 回到家感觉很不错。

没错，同感：
- Yeah, I feel the same way. 是啊，我也有同感。

在家也希望还是假期：
- It kind of sucks that our vacation is over, though. 不过我们的假期结束了还真有点儿不舒服。

3　I'm so tired from the trip. 这次旅行我很累。

旅行好玩但也很累：
- I'm pretty exhausted from the trip. 这次旅行我特别累。
- That trip wore me out. 这次旅行把我累垮了。

确实如此：
- Me too. I'm gonna crash. 我也是，我要去睡觉了。

不过你也可以在我这里休息：
- You're welcome to stay here if you're too tired to go back home. 如果你太累了不想回家的话也欢迎你住这儿。

❖ exhausted [ɪgˈzɔːstɪd] *adj.* 精疲力竭的
❖ wear out 耗尽，使精疲力竭
❖ crash [kræʃ] *vi.* 宿夜，睡觉（俚语）

4　I'm going to upload my pictures right away. 我要马上把我的照片传上去。

赶紧把我们旅行的照片发到网上去：
- I'm uploading my pictures right now. 我马上把照片传上去。
- I'm going to post my pictures up now. 我要马上把我的照片贴上去。
- I have to upload my pictures right away. 我得马上把照片传上去。

你传完后我去看看：
- Cool. Tell me when they're all uploaded. 太好了。你传上去的时候告诉我一声啊。
- Alright. I'm going to in the morning. 好的，我明天早上去看。

5　I'm going to call my parents and tell them how the trip went. 我要打电话给我爸妈，告诉他们这次旅行的情况。

把旅游见闻告诉父母：
- I'm going to give my parents a call to tell them how the trip went. 我要给我爸妈打个电话，告诉他们这次旅行的情况。
- My parents are probably wondering how the trip went, so I'll give them a call. 我爸妈可能想知道这次旅行的情况，所以我要给他们打个电话。
- I'll give my parents a call to tell them all about the trip. 我要给我爸妈打个电话，把这次旅行的所有事情都告诉他们。

他们肯定会很喜欢的：

- Yeah, I bet they'd like that. 是啊，我肯定他们会很喜欢的。
- Okay. 好的。

6 Was it a good trip? 旅行还好吗？

旅行归来问候：

- Did you have a good journey? 你旅途愉快吗？

挺不错的：

- Yeah, I have a lot of fun. 挺好的，我玩得很开心。
- Yeah, but I just felt a little tired. 还行，就是感觉有点儿累。

交 流 面 对 面

Back From the Trip Conversation

Kevin:	I'm so tired, man. I can't believe we had to stay here for 2 extra days.	凯 文：	我好累啊，哥们儿。真不敢相信我们在这里多呆了两天。
Steve:	I'm really sorry about that. I didn't know my car would break down.	史蒂夫：	真的很抱歉。我没想到车会坏。
Kevin:	Nah, it's not your fault. I'm just glad to be home.	凯 文：	不用抱歉，这不是你的错。我只是很高兴终于到家了。
Steve:	Yeah.	史蒂夫：	是啊。
Kevin:	We still had a lot of fun.	凯 文：	我们还是玩得很开心的。
Steve:	That's true. It was a good time.	史蒂夫：	没错。那是一段美好的时光。
Kevin:	Do you want to upload the pictures?	凯 文：	你想把照片传上去吗？
Steve:	Can we do that later, man? I'm so exhausted.	史蒂夫：	我们能一会儿再弄吗，伙计？我都筋疲力尽了。
Kevin:	Yeah, me too. We'll do it in the morning.	凯 文：	好的，我也是。我们明天早上弄吧。

Steve: Do you mind if I crash here?

史蒂夫：我在这儿睡一晚你不会介意吧？

Kevin: Not at all.

凯　文：当然不会。

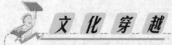

文 化 穿 越

　　旅行中还有一段比较美妙的时光就是坐在回程的车上或飞机上回忆和整理旅程的照片和日记。如果是自助游，一般一周左右的旅程就比较累了。回程之前需要确保汽油已经加满或者航班是否变更，如果回程中没油儿了或者到机场后得知飞机延迟了，就悲剧了。总而言之，建议大家抓住每一个旅行的机会，多出去走走，欣赏一下别处的风景。

Chapter 14 生病怎么办?
Sickness

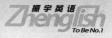

Section 1 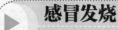 感冒发烧
Suffering From a Fever

由于旅途的劳顿，我的身体内也发生了剧烈的化学反应。这不，一吹风，我就感冒发烧了。头晕晕乎乎的，还一个劲地打喷嚏流鼻涕，一测体温，竟然达到 39.6 度。妈妈着急了，赶紧带我去看医生。

1 I think I'm coming down with something. 我感觉我生病了。

感觉不舒服：

- I don't feel well. 我感觉不舒服。
- I feel sick. 我感觉不舒服。

测下体温：

- Oh geez. Let me get the thermometer. 哦，天哪，我去拿体温计。

要不去看看医生吧：

- That's not good…maybe we should take you to the doctor. 那可不好……也许我们该送你去看医生。
- ❖ come down with something 生病了，不舒服
- ❖ geez [dʒiz] *int.* 哎呀，天哪
- ❖ thermometer [θə'mɑmətə] *n.* 体温表，温度计

2 I feel like I have a fever. 我感觉我发烧了。

不同程度的发烧：

- I feel really warm. Do I have a fever? 我真觉得挺热的。我是不是发烧了？
- I think I have a fever. Can you check? 我好像发烧了。你看看？
- I have a bit of a fever. 我有点儿发烧。
- I have a high temperature. 我在发高烧。

量下体温看看：

- Sit down and take your temperature. 坐下来量一下体温。
- Here is the thermometer. 给你体温计。
- ❖ have a fever 发烧

3 Crap, it says I have a bad cold. 天哪，我严重感冒了。

严重感冒：

- Damn it, I have a cold. 真糟糕，我严重感冒了。

一点儿小感冒：

- I have a slight cold. 我有点儿感冒了。

发高烧：

- God, it says I have a pretty bad fever. 天哪，我发高烧了。
- I have a high fever. The thermometer is reading 39 degrees. 我发高烧了，温度计上显示是 39 度。

躺一会儿吧：

- Don't strain yourself. Go lay down. 别太累了，去躺下吧。

多喝点水：

- Drink some water and have a better rest. 喝点儿水，好好休息。
- ❖ have a cold 感冒，受凉
- ❖ strain [stren] vt. 劳累，操心

4 I have a headache. 我头疼。

头痛的程度逐渐递增：

- My head hurts. 我的头很痛。
- My head is pounding. 我的头痛得实在厉害。
- I have a splitting headache. 我的头像裂了似地疼。
- ❖ pounding ['paʊndɪŋ] n. 猛击，重击
- ❖ splitting ['splɪtɪŋ] adj. 裂开一样的，剧烈的

5 I have a runny nose. 我流鼻涕。

鼻子的症状：

- My nose is running. 我流鼻涕。

- My nose won't stop running. 我一个劲地流鼻涕。
- I have a stuffy nose. 鼻子堵了。
- ❖ runny ['rʌnɪ] *adj.* 流鼻涕的
- ❖ stuffy ['stʌfɪ] *adj.* （鼻子）塞住的

6 I hope I don't have anything too serious. 我希望不要太严重了。

快点儿好起来吧：

- I hope my illness isn't that bad. 我希望我的病不是那么严重。
- This sickness had better go away in a few days. 这病最好几天后就好了吧。
- I really hope I get better soon. 我真希望快点儿好起来。

要去看医生吗：

- If it doesn't go away we can call the doctor. 如果还没好的话我们可以叫医生。
- I'll take you to the doctor if it stays the same. 如果还是和原来一样的话，我带你去看医生。
- ❖ sickness ['sɪknəs] *n.* 疾病
- ❖ go away 离开，走开

7 I'm feeling dizzy, I need to lie down. 我感觉晕晕乎乎的，我要去躺一下。

感冒了要好好休息：

- I need to rest a bit. 我需要休息一会儿。
- I'm gonna go rest some. 我要去休息一下。
- I have to lie down. I need rest. 我要躺下来，我需要休息。

让我来照顾你吧：

- Yes, go lay down. I'll bring you some water. 好的，去躺下吧。我给你端点儿水过来。
- I'll get some medicine for you. Get some rest. 我给你拿点儿药。你休息会儿吧。
- ❖ dizzy ['dɪzɪ] *adj.* 头晕目眩的

8 My fever is getting worse. I need to see a doctor. 我发烧越来越严重了，我需要看医生。

感觉越来越严重了：

- Please take me to the doctor, I feel worse. 请带我去看医生，我感觉更严重了。
- I need to go to the doctor's, I feel terrible. 我需要去看医生，我感觉很不舒服。
- Will you take me to the doctor? I think it's getting worse. 你带我去看医生好吗？我觉得变严重了。

那现在就去看医生：

- Okay, let's get you to the doctor. 好的，我带你去看医生。
- I'll take you. Let's go right now. 我带你去，咱们现在就去。

Suffering From a Fever Conversation

Kevin: Mom, I feel really sick…	凯文：妈妈，我真觉得不舒服……
Mom: You look terrible! Do you have a fever?	妈妈：你看起来很不好！你发烧了？
Kevin: Yeah, and it's pretty bad.	凯文：嗯，很严重。
Mom: Did you take your temperature?	妈妈：你量体温了吗？
Kevin: I did. It said I have a fever of 39.6.	凯文：量了。我发烧到39.6度。
Mom: That's awful. Let's get you to the doctor.	妈妈：那太严重了，我带你去看医生。
Kevin: Will you drive me?	凯文：你开车带我去吗？
Mom: Of course. Let me get my coat and we'll go.	妈妈：当然了。我穿上大衣咱们就走。
Kevin: Could you grab mine too?	凯文：把我的大衣也拿上好吗？
Mom: Sure. And take a bottle of water! You need to stay hydrated.	妈妈：好的。再带一瓶水！你需要补充水分。
Kevin: Okay. I'll go wait in the car.	凯文：好的，我去车里等你。

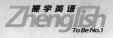
❖grab [græb] *vt.* 抓，拿
❖hydrated ['haɪdretɪd] *adj.* 含水的

文化穿越

　　在美国，你什么都可以有，但是千万别有病。因为在美国看病是公认的比较贵的事情之一（其实这点在中国很多人也有同感）。美国的医疗系统很发达，但只对美国人才有用，其他留学生买的保险在平时根本没什么用处。如果感冒了，除了自己吃点药在家扛着外没什么别的选择。因为第一，医院随便开点药，可能就会要你上百美元。第二，如果你跟你的朋友尤其是美国人说你感冒了，人家会躲你远远的。更别提什么关心或者照顾了。因此，在美国感冒生病是件比较痛苦的事儿。

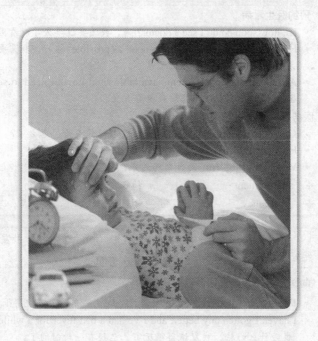

Section 2 ▶ 预约医生
Doctor Appointment

妈妈在车上给医生打了个电话，告知我的病情后，医生就马上答应应诊了。我们到达那里后，医生给我做了一个检查和化验，结果显示是我的肺部严重感染，可能还需要一个小手术。这么严重，幸亏妈妈及时把我送来看医生。

① Excuse me. I need to see a doctor right away. 打扰一下，我需要马上看医生。

预约医生看病：
- Hi, how soon could I see a doctor? 嗨，我还要过多久才能看医生？
- Hello, I need to see a doctor as soon as possible. 你好，我需要尽快看医生。
- Are there any appointments available right now? I need to see the doctor. 现在还有预约吗？我要看医生。

医务接待人员进行询问：
- Let me check for you. What's wrong? 我给你看看。怎么了？
- Is it an emergency? 是急诊吗？
- What's the problem? 是什么问题呢？
- ❖ appointment [ə'pɔɪntmənt] *n.* 约定，预约
- ❖ emergency [ɪ'mɜːdʒənsɪ] *n.* 急诊，紧急情况

② I've had a fever for a few days and it's getting worse. 我发烧已经好几天了，现在越来越严重了。

向医务接待人员讲明自己的病情：
- I've had a terrible fever for the past few days. 我前几天发烧得很严重。
- I haven't gotten any better, and I've had a bad fever for a while now. 我没什么好转，我发烧得很厉害，已经有一段时间了。

- My fever has been getting worse these past few days. 前面这几天我发烧越来越严重了。

接待人员告知预约时间：

- We have an appointment open at 4. 我们四点开始预约。
- A doctor can see you at 4 this afternoon. Is that okay? 你可以今天下午四点来看医生。可以吗?

接待人员给予建议：

- We have an appointment at 4, but if you feel too bad to wait, you should go to the hospital. 我们四点有预约，但如果你感觉很严重的话就别等了，你应该去医院。

---

3 That works. I don't think I need to go to the hospital. 那行，我觉得我没必要去医院。

预约时间确定：

- That time is fine. Thank you. 那个时间可以。谢谢你。
- That will work for me. Thank you very much. 那对我来说没问题，多谢你了。

医务接待人员提醒你：

- Alright. Be sure to have your medical insurance card and an ID. 好的，一定要带上你的医疗保险卡和身份证明。
- Okay, bring your insurance paperwork and an ID. 好的，带上你的保险文档和身份证明。
- ❖ medical insurance card 医疗保险卡
- ❖ paperwork ['pepɚ'wɝk] *n.* 书面材料，文档

---

4 I'm here to see the doctor. I have an appointment for 4 o'clock. 我来这儿看医生，我们约了四点钟。

应预约去看医生：

- I made an appointment earlier for 4 o'clock. My name is Kevin. 我早些时候预约了四点钟的，我的名字叫凯文。
- I'm here for my 4 o'clock appointment. 我预约了四点钟的。

医务人员索要资料：

- Okay Kevin, please give me your medical insurance card and a photo ID. 好的凯文，请把你的医疗保险卡和身份证给我吧。

- Do you have your medical insurance information and a photo ID? 你带医疗保险资料和身份证了吗?

5 Here's my ID and medical insurance. 这是我的身份证和医疗卡。

向医务接待人员提交资料:

- My insurance is the same from the last time I visited. Here you go. 我的医疗保险还是和上次来的时候一样,给你。
- I've switched insurance companies since I was last here. Here's my new information. 自从上次来这里后我已经换了保险公司,这是我的新资料。

医务接待人员给予指引:

- Alright, please sit down. The doctor will be right with you. 好的,请坐吧。医生马上就来。
- Good, the nurse will be right out to take you to see the doctor. 好的,护士会马上出来带你去看医生。

6 Thank you for seeing me, doctor. I've had a terrible fever for a few days now. 谢谢你来看我,医生。我发烧很严重,已经好几天了。

向预约的医生陈述病状:

- Thank you, doctor. I have a really bad fever that won't go away. I was wondering if something worse could be going on. 谢谢你,医生。我发烧很严重,还没有退烧。我想知道会不会有更严重的事情发生啊。
- My fever is getting worse, and I'm afraid something more could be wrong with me. 我发烧越来越严重了,我担心会不会有更严重的情况。

医生给你做检查:

- Okay, I'm going to take some blood work and see how high your fever is now. 好的,我给你验一下血,看看现在烧得多高。
- I'll take your temperature and we can take some blood. 我给你量一下体温,还可以验一下血。
- I want to take some blood to see if anything shows up. I'll check your temperature too. 我要验一下血才能知道有什么情况。我也会给你量一下体温。

Doctor Appointment Conversation

Kevin: Hello, Doctor.

凯文：你好，医生。

Doctor: Hi Kevin. The lab sent back the results to your blood work, and it doesn't look good.

医生：嗨，凯文。化验室把你的验血结果送回来了，看起来不太好啊。

Kevin: What's wrong?

凯文：怎么了？

Doctor: You've developed a serious infection in your lungs, and you need to get better treatment. We're sending you to the hospital.

医生：你的肺部严重感染了，你需要更好的治疗。我们会送你去医院。

Kevin: What kind of treatment do I need?

凯文：我需要什么样的治疗？

Doctor: They'll put you on very strong antibiotics, make sure you stay hydrated and rested, and if it doesn't get better you may have to get surgery.

医生：他们会给你用效果非常强的抗生素，确保你有充足的水分和休息，如果还没有好转的话你可能就需要手术了。

Kevin: Surgery? For an infection?

凯文：手术？就因为一次感染？

Doctor: Yes. There's a build-up of fluid in your lungs and they may have to do minor surgery to remove it.

医生：是的，你肺部积有粘液，他们可能需要一个小手术才能清除掉。

Kevin: Do I need to tell my mom to take me to the hospital?

凯文：我要告诉我妈妈送我去医院吗？

Doctor: No, we called an ambulance for you. It will be here in a few minutes. Do you have any more questions for me, Kevin?

医生：不用，我们给你叫了救护车。几分钟就到了，你还有什么问题要问我吗，凯文？

Kevin: No. Thank you, doctor.

凯文：没有了，谢谢你，医生。

❖infection [ɪnˈfɛkʃən] *n.* 感染，传染
❖antibiotic [ˌæntɪbaɪˈɑtɪk] *n.* 抗生素，抗菌素
❖build-up [ˈbɪldʌp] *n.* 逐渐增加或积累

就这 **900** 句 玩转口语

❖fluid ['fluɪd] *n.* 流体，液体
❖minor ['maɪnə] *adj.* 较小的，不严重的
❖ambulance ['æmbjələns] *n.* 救护车

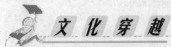

　　在美国看病最麻烦的事儿就是预约。美国与中国情况不同，美国一般看医生需要打电话预约，这也是为什么感冒发烧一类的小病一般大家都不去医院的原因，有等待预约的时间，病早好了。而且即使你顺利见到了医生，也是先需要在医院填一堆表，表上经常都是病和药的名字，估计 GRE 考满分的学生看这些也费劲，况且还发着烧，脑子都不清醒，还怎么可能会正确地填表。总之，如果不是什么必须要去医院的病，自己给自己看就行了。不过直接去急诊的话可以省去预约这个环节，但这只针对于十分紧急的情况。

Section 3 去医院
Going to the Hospital

我预约的那家诊所做不了肺部手术，他们给我叫了救护车送我去别的医院。当我把这一结果告诉妈妈的时候，妈妈也开始担心了，赶紧忙前忙后去医院给我办理相关手续。

1 I'm going to the hospital. 我要去医院。

看来需要去医院了：
- I have to go to the hospital. 我得去医院。
- The doctor said I need to go to the hospital. 医生说我需要去医院。

这么严重啊：
- That's terrible! Will you be alright? 真糟糕！你还好吧？
- How long do you need to stay there? 你要在那里呆多长时间呢？

2 I'm going in an ambulance. 我坐救护车去。

叫救护车去医院：
- They called an ambulance to take me. 他们叫了辆救护车来带我去。
- I'll be arriving at the hospital in an ambulance. 我坐救护车去医院。

要不我开车送你去吧：
- Are you sure I don't have to give you a ride? 你确定不需要我开车送你去吗？

3 I'm scared to go to the hospital. 我害怕去医院。

害怕去医院：
- I'm afraid of the hospital. 我对医院有恐惧感。
- I'm frightened. I don't like going to the hospital. 我很害怕，我不想去医院。

给予安慰：

- It won't be too bad. At least you'll get better. 不会太糟糕的，至少你会康复。
- Me too. But try not to be too stressed. You don't need that right now. 我也是，但不要太紧张，你现在没必要那样。

❖ frightened ['fraɪtnd] *adj.* 受惊的，害怕的

❖ stressed [strest] *adj.* 紧张的，感到有压力的

4 I want to register the department of internal medicine. 我想挂内科。

挂号：

- I need to register the department of orthopedics. 我要挂骨科。
- I'd like to register the department of traditional Chinese medicine. 我要挂中医科。

工作人员一般会说：

- OK. Please fill out the form and the registration fee is $5. 好的，请填写一下这张表格，挂号费是 5 美元。

❖ internal medicine 内科

❖ orthopedics [ˌɔːrθəˈpiːdɪks] *n.* 外科，骨科

❖ traditional Chinese medicine 中医

❖ registration fee 挂号费

5 What floor is the pharmacy on? 药房在几楼？

询问医院的科室：

- Which floor is the emergency room on? 急诊室在几楼？
- Where is the clinic office? 门诊办公室在哪里？

对方会告知你：

- It's on the first floor. 在一楼。

❖ pharmacy ['fɑːrməsɪ] *n.* 药房

❖ emergency room 急诊室

6 I hope I recover quickly. 我希望快点儿康复。

去医院给自己祝福:

- I hope I have a speedy recovery. 我希望很快就康复。
- I want to have a speedy recovery. 我希望很快就康复。

对方也会为你祝福:

- I hope you do too. 我也希望你快点儿康复。
- I'm sure you will. You're a strong person. 我肯定你会的。你是一个坚强的人。
- Don't worry. I'm sure you'll be fine. 别担心，我肯定你会好的。
- You'll be in good hands. 你会好起来的。

❖　recover [rɪ'kʌvə] vi. 恢复健康（其名词是 recovery）

❖　speedy ['spidɪ] adj. 迅速的，快的

❖　be in good hands 情况很好

Going to the Hospital Conversation

Kevin:	The doctor said that I need to go to the hospital.	凯　文:	医生说我得去医院。
Mom:	The hospital? What's wrong?	妈　妈:	医院？怎么了？
Kevin:	I have an infection in my lungs.	凯　文:	我的肺部感染了。
Mom:	That sounds terrible!	妈　妈:	那听起来很严重啊！
Kevin:	I'll probably need surgery as well.	凯　文:	我可能还需要手术。
Mom:	This sounds so serious. Oh, my poor baby. Are you going to be okay?	妈　妈:	这听起来太严重了。哦，我可怜的孩子。你还好吗？
Kevin:	Don't worry. I should be fine.	凯　文:	别担心，我会好的。
Mom:	Oh, thank goodness. I'll start driving over to help you with the paperwork.	妈　妈:	哦，谢天谢地。我马上开车去帮你办理手续。
Kevin:	Okay, thanks mom. I love you.	凯　文:	好的，谢谢妈妈。我爱你。
Mom:	I love you too, sweetie.	妈　妈:	我也爱你，宝贝儿。

文化穿越

　　去医院看病需要注意一些事项。如果需要填表，有个小技巧，凡是病史那一栏全画无就好，不用细看，不过这只针对真的没有病史的人，如果有的话，您还是一条一条看清楚为佳。另外，医生开药的时候会询问你的意见，这时切勿像跟在中国看病一样随医生开，一是药很贵，二是美国医生基本都是西医，他们开的药一般有时候很夸张的。例如，我有个在美国上学的朋友经常失眠，之后他去医院看医生，医生给他开了几瓶药。回来后才发现这几瓶药都是治疗精神的药物，后来一瓶也没吃，慢慢也睡着了。他如果吃了这些药，估计睡眠是好了，但精神很难保证不出问题。

Section 4 ▶ 手术及护理
Operation and Care

　　人在生病的时候是比较脆弱的。马上要进手术室了，虽然医生一再地跟我说只是一个小手术，不要担心。但说实在的，长这么大，我还是头一回进手术室，心里还是挺紧张的。妈妈在旁边一个劲儿地安慰我，鼓励我，渐渐地，我也不那么害怕了。

1 I have to get an operation. 我得接受手术。

接受手术:
- I'm getting surgery. 我要接受外科手术。
- I have to get surgery. 我得接受外科手术。

祝你快点儿好起来:
- That sounds awful. I hope it goes well. 那听起来好恐怖，我希望手术顺利。

2 What kind of operation am I getting? 我要接受什么手术?

请求医务人员告知具体情况:
- Could you explain the operation, please? 请你说一下这手术好吗?
- Can you please tell me what the operation will be like? 你能告诉我一下这手术会怎么样吗?
- I'd like to know more about the kind of operation I'll be getting. 我想更多地了解我将接受的这个手术的情况。

医务人员告知大致情况:
- Of course. It's a simple operation. We just have to remove some fluid from your lungs. 当然可以。这是一个简单的手术，我们只是需要把你肺部的粘液清除掉就可以了。

533

- Yes. It won't be too bad. We're just getting rid of excess fluid from your lungs. 好的，不会很糟糕的，我们只是把你肺部多余的粘液清除掉。
- We're only operating a bit on your lungs, so we can get the extra fluid out. 我们只要在你的肺部做个小手术，那样我们就能把多余的粘液清除出去了。

❖ remove [rɪ'muːv] vt. 移除，去掉

❖ get rid of 除去，去掉

---

3 Am I going to have local or general anesthesia? 我是要进行局部麻醉呢还是全身麻醉？

手术前进行麻醉：

- Am I going to get knocked out or will only one area be numbed? 我是要全身麻醉呢还是只需麻醉一个地方就行？
- What kind of anesthesia will be used? 将用哪种麻醉呢？
- Please tell me about the anesthesia you will be using on me. 请告诉我你们将对我用哪种麻醉。

不用担心，你不会感到痛的：

- We're going to use general anesthesia, so you'll be unconscious the whole time. 我们会用全身麻醉，所以在整个过程中你是没有知觉的。

❖ local anesthesia [ˌænəs'θiːʒə] 局部麻醉

❖ general anesthesia 全身麻醉

❖ get knocked out 昏睡，昏倒

❖ numb [nʌm] vt. 使失去感觉，使麻木

❖ unconscious [ʌn'kɑnʃəs] adj. 不省人事的，失去知觉的

---

4 How long will the operation take? 手术要花多长时间？

手术时间很长吗：

- Will it be a long operation? 手术会很长吗？
- Is this operation going to take long? 这个手术会花很长时间吗？

别担心不会很久的：

- The operation should only take a little more than an hour. 这个手术应该只要花一个多小时的时间。
- It's not going to take very long. 不会花很长时间的。

5 I need to fast before my operation. 手术前我需要禁食。

手术前的注意事项：

- I can't eat or drink for 3 hours before my operation. 手术前三个小时我不能吃喝。
- I have to fast for 3 hours before the surgery, right? 手术前三个小时我得禁食，对吗？

要确保手术成功这是必须注意的：

- Yes, most surgeries require a fasting period beforehand. 是的，大多数手术需要预先禁食一段时间。
- That's correct. You can't eat or drink before the surgery for at least 3 hours. 没错，至少手术前三小时你不能吃喝。

❖ fast [fæst] *vi.* 禁食，斋戒
❖ beforehand [bɪˈforˌhænd] *adv.* 预先，事先

6 I'm going into surgery soon. 我马上就要手术了。

马上要手术了，有点儿紧张：

- I'll be getting my surgery in a bit. 我一会儿就要手术了。
- I'll get my operation soon. 我马上就要手术了。

别担心有我在呢：

- I'll be in the waiting room. 我会在候诊室的。
- Tell me how it goes when it's finished. 结束的时候告诉我手术的进展情况。

7 My surgery went fine. 我的手术进展顺利。

手术进展顺利：

- I'm sore, but the surgery went alright. 我好痛，但手术进展还好。
- My operation was successful. 我的手术很成功。
- I'm in some pain, but at least the surgery went well. 我有些疼，但至少手术进展顺利。

那我放心了：

- I'm glad to hear you're okay. 听到你没事我很高兴。
- That's great! I'll have to plan a visit to see you. 太好了！我正打算去看你呢。

8 How long will it take to recover? 要多长时间才能康复呢?

询问手术后的康复时间:
- Will the surgery take long to recover from? 这手术要花很长时间才能康复吗?
- It won't take long to recover from, will it? 不会花很长时间康复,是吧?

不会花太长时间的:
- If it is successful, it will only take a few days. 如果成功的话,只要花几天的时间。
- It shouldn't take more than a few days to recover from. 康复的话应该不需要花几天的时间。
- The operation won't take too long to recover from. 手术康复不会花太长时间的。
- ❖ recover [rɪ'kʌvə] vi. 恢复,康复

9 Will I need to change my diet temporarily? 我需要暂时改变饮食吗?

手术后饮食注意事项:
- Do I need to change my eating habits for a while? 我需要暂时改变饮食习惯吗?
- Should I change my eating habits at all? 我该完全改变饮食习惯吗?

该吃什么还吃什么:
- No, that won't be necessary. 不用,那没必要。
- Not at all, you can eat what you want. 一点儿都不用,你可以吃任何你想吃的东西。

饮食上需要注意几天:
- Yes, but only for a few days. 是的,不过只需几天就行。
- ❖ temporarily ['tempərerɪlɪ] adv. 暂时地,临时地

10 It's time to take your temperature. 现在是给你测体温的时间。

术后护理:
- Your temperature must be taken twice a day. 你的体温应该一天测两次。
- I'll take your pulse. 我要给你测脉搏。

礼貌答谢：

- All right. Thank you very much. 好的，多谢你了。
- ❖ pulse [pʌls] *n*. 脉搏

11 How often am I supposed to take this pill? 这药我一天吃几次？

该怎么服药：

- How can I take the medicine? 这药我该怎么吃？

服药的方法：

- Two capsules three times daily. 一天三次，一次服二粒胶囊。
- One tablet, three times daily. 一天三次，一次一片。
- Take the medicine after eating. 饭后服药。
- ❖ take the medicine 服药
- ❖ capsule ['kæpsl] *n*. 胶囊

Operation and Care Conversation

Kevin: I have to go into surgery soon.	凯文：我马上要进手术室了。
Mom: I know, honey.	妈妈：我知道，宝贝儿。
Kevin: I'm pretty nervous about it.	凯文：我很紧张。
Mom: Don't worry, you'll be okay. The surgeon said it was a simple operation.	妈妈：别担心，你会没事的。医生说了只是一个简单的手术。
Kevin: I hope I heal up fast, though.	凯文：不过我希望很快就好了。
Mom: I'm sure you will. You're a strong person.	妈妈：肯定会的。你是一个坚强的人。
Kevin: Thanks for the reassurance, mom.	凯文：谢谢你的安慰，妈妈。
Mom: No problem, sweetie. I'll be there the second you get out of surgery.	妈妈：不客气，宝贝儿。你从手术室出来的时候我会在这里的。
Kevin: Okay. I love you.	凯文：好的，我爱你。
Mom: Love you too.	妈妈：我也爱你。

❖heal up 痊愈，治愈
❖reassurance ['riə'ʃurəns] n. 安慰，安心

文化穿越

　　在美国且不说去医院做手术的费用非常昂贵，手术前的准备工作也有一大堆，最繁琐的依然是填表，填表的内容主要是个人信息等等。当然如果病情严重到需要做手术了，应该会有朋友跟着一起来，到时候他们会处理填表等相关手续的事情。此外，美国对于医疗这一块儿的审核工作很严格，对于病人的病史和相关药物的使用情况也非常负责，因为医院害怕万一有遗漏，术后造成不利影响会吃官司。

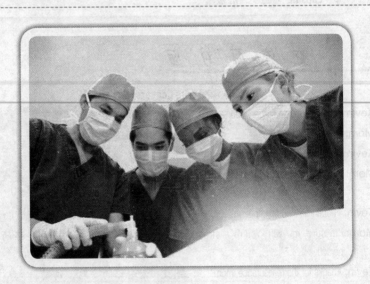

Section 5 住院出院
Living in the Hospital

手术后，一切都感觉良好，不过医生告诉我要在医院观察一段时间后才能出院。没办法只能住院了。朋友们得知这一消息后，都接二连三地来医院看望我，给我送礼物还给我带来好吃的，Steve 的女朋友还托他给我带来了泰迪熊！有你们这些朋友,Kevin 感觉很幸福!

1 I will be in hospital for at least a week. 我至少要住院一个星期。

不想住院啊：
* I'll probably be in hospital for a little over a week. 我可能要住院一个多星期。
* I hope I don't have to stay for more than a week. 我希望我住院不要超过一星期。
* If everything goes okay, I should probably get out in about a week. 如果一切都顺利的话，我应该大约一个星期就能出院了。

希望一切都好：
* I hope everything goes okay. 我希望一切都顺利。
* I guess that's not so bad. 我想那还不是很糟糕。

2 This is your bed. Please let us know if you need any help. 这是你的床位。如果你需要什么帮助，就告诉我们。

病房的其他设施和规定：
* The toilet is over there. 厕所在那边。
* We supply hot water. 我们供应热水。
* Smoking is not allowed here. 这里不准吸烟。

表达谢意：
* OK. Thank you very much. 好的，多谢你了。

3 The hospital isn't so bad. 这医院还不是那么糟糕。

医院的情况还行吧：

- Staying in hospital isn't as bad as I thought. 呆在医院不是我想象的那么糟糕。
- It's not so bad here. 这里还不是那么糟糕。
- Staying here isn't too terrible. 呆在这里还不是那么糟糕。

那我就放心了：

- That's good. 那还不错。
- I'm glad you're not worrying about it as much. 我很高兴你没有那么担心。

4 The food in the hospital is terrible. 医院的食物很差劲。

医院的食物实在是不敢恭维：

- I hate the food they serve. 我讨厌他们提供的食物。
- The food is so bad. 这食物太糟糕了。
- The meals they serve are awful. 他们提供的伙食很糟糕。
- I really don't like the food here. 我确实不喜欢这里的食物。

一般都这样：

- Hospitals usually don't have good food. 医院一般都没有好的食物。
- That's to be expected. 那是预料之中的。
- That doesn't surprise me. 那不让我感到奇怪。

5 I'm glad I'm getting so many visitors. 我很高兴有这么多人来看望我。

朋友来医院探病：

- I've been getting a lot of visitors. It makes my stay here easier. 有很多人来看望我，这让我感觉呆在这里很舒心。
- I really appreciate all my friends coming to see me. 我非常感谢所有来看望我的朋友。
- I'm happy that my friends are visiting me. 我很高兴我的朋友们都来看望我。

这倒是件令人高兴的事：

- That's great. I'm glad they've cheered you up. 那太好了，我很高兴他们让你高兴起来了。

❖ cheer up 使高兴，高兴起来

---

6 I'm tired of being in hospital. I hope I get to leave soon. 我讨厌住在医院。我希望快点儿离开。

我要快点出院：

- I hope I get out soon. 我希望快点儿出去。
- I want to leave soon. 我想快点儿离开。

会很快好起来的：

- I'm sure you'll get out soon. 我肯定你会很快出院的。

---

7 You can discharge from hospital. 你可以出院了。

医生通知可以出院了：

- You can go through the discharge formalities. 你可以办理出院手续了。
- You can go home tomorrow. Congratulations! 你明天可以出院了，祝贺你！

出院后有什么注意事项吗：

- Thank you! What should I do after I go home? Any suggestions? 谢谢！出院后我应该做些什么？有什么建议？

❖ discharge [dɪs'tʃɑrdʒ] vi. 允许……离开
❖ go through 经受，被通过
❖ formality [fɔr'mælətɪ] n. 正式手续

---

8 I'll be leaving soon. I'm excited! 我马上就要出院了。真高兴！

马上就要出院喽：

- I'm excited to leave! 我好高兴要走了。
- I'm so happy I can leave soon! 我好高兴我能马上出院了。
- I'm really happy I'm getting out of here. 我很高兴我就要离开这儿了。

太好了：

- That's great! I'm excited for you! 太好了，我也为你高兴。

9 Good morning! I've come to go through the discharge formalities. 早上好！我来办理出院手续。

办理出院手续：
- I want to come to go through the discharge formalities. 我想来办理出院手续。

交住院费：
- Congratulations! This is your bill from the admission office. 1200 dollars in all. 恭喜你啊！这是住院部开的账单，总共是 1200 美元。
- ❖ admission office 住院处

Living in the Hospital Conversation

Kevin: Hey man, thanks for visiting me.	凯 文：嘿伙计，谢谢你来看我。
Steve: No problem. Here, my girlfriend wanted me to give you this.	史蒂夫：不客气。给，我女朋友要我把这个给你。
Kevin: A teddy bear? (laughs)	凯 文：泰迪熊？（笑）
Steve: She thought it would be cute.	史蒂夫：她觉得这个很可爱。
Kevin: Well, it is. Tell her I say thanks.	凯 文：嗯，是的。跟她说谢谢啊。
Steve: Sure. How have you been doing after the surgery?	史蒂夫：好的。手术后你感觉怎么样？
Kevin: I'm healing up pretty fast, I think.	凯 文：我觉得恢复得很快。
Steve: Are you going to go home soon?	史蒂夫：你很快就要回家了吗？
Kevin: I should be home within the next few days, as long as everything goes alright.	凯 文：只要一切都顺利的话，我应该几天之内就能回家了。
Steve: Okay. Well, I'll take you out to dinner when you get better. You must be getting tired of the terrible hospital food.	史蒂夫：好的。嗯，你好了的时候我带你去外面吃饭。你一定讨厌医院里糟糕的伙食了。

Kevin: I think I'm getting used to it, surprisingly. But thank you! It would be great to go out after this.

凯 文: 很奇怪,我觉得我都快习惯了。不过还是谢谢你!出院后出去吃肯定不错。

❖ cute [kjut] *adj.* 漂亮的,可爱的
❖ surprisingly [sə'praɪzɪŋlɪ] *adv.* 惊人地,出人意外地

文 化 穿 越

　　一般情况下,对于美国人来说住院就算是比较重大的疾病了。美国很多州的乡村环境很好,空气和森林随处可见。这些对于人的呼吸系统很有益,另外加上美国的蔬菜和水果还有肉类等都是经过卫生监管部门严格检查的,因此美国人很少生病,一般的感冒在美国人看来就算是比较严重的病了。对于住院,与中国情况类似,只不过在美国花的是美元就是了。

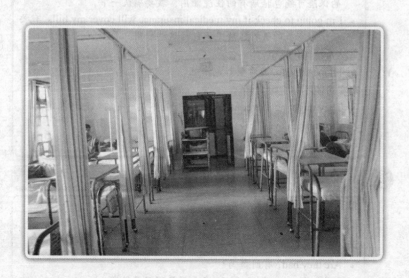

Section 6  医疗保险
Medical Insurance

手术的时候花了一大笔钱，平时交的医疗保险在这时候派上用场了。出院后，我就找医院要求报销医疗费用，可让我大吃一惊的是医院说我的保险不包括这次医疗的费用。难道以前交的保险都打水漂了？是不是搞错了？我得赶紧咨询一下保险公司核实一下。

口语大放送

1 I need to check and see if my insurance covers my hospital bills. 我要确认一下我的保险是否包括住院费用。

确认医疗保险的费用范围：
- My insurance might cover all of my hospital bills. I need to check. 我的保险可能包括所有的住院费用，我要确认一下。
- I'm going to check if my medical insurance will cover my bills. 我要确认一下我的医疗保险是否包括这些费用。

当然希望都包括了：
- I hope they do. 我希望都包括吧。

事实可能不一定哦：
- They might not cover all of them. 可能不是所有的都包括在内吧。

❖ insurance cover 保险范围
❖ medical insurance 医疗保险

2 I got my hospital bills. 我拿到了医院的账单。

拿到医疗费用账单：
- I got my bills today. 我今天拿到了账单。

这么多？没错吧：
- Are they bad? 有问题吗？
- I hope they aren't too high. 我希望费用不是很高。

3 My medical insurance doesn't cover all of my bills. 我的医疗保险并不包括所有的费用。

医疗保险只包括一部分费用:

- My hospital bills aren't completely covered by my medical insurance. 我的住院费用并不全部包括在医疗保险里面。
- My medical insurance won't pay off all of my bills. 我的医疗保险并不能支付我的全部费用。
- I'll have to pay some of the bills myself. 我得自己付一部分费用。

天哪,那你得付多少啊:

- That sucks. How much do you have to pay? 太糟糕了,你得付多少啊?
- ❖ completely [kəm'plɪtlɪ] *adv.* 完整地, 完全地
- ❖ pay off 付清, 支付

4 My health insurance is going to cover all of my bills. 我的健康保险会包括所有的费用。

这样的保险谁都想买:

- My hospital bills are going to be paid by my health insurance. 我的住院费用将由我的健康保险支付。
- I don't have to pay any of my bills. My health insurance covers it. 我不需要支付任何费用,我的医疗保险都包括了。
- ❖ health insurance 健康保险, 医疗保险

5 I just changed my health insurance, so my new information will be different from your records. 我刚更改了健康保险,所以新的信息会和你的记录有所不同。

换保险了:

- I have a different health insurance plan. I'll show you my new information. 我有别的健康保险计划了,我要把新的资料给你看看。

与人方便自己方便:

- Thank you. 谢谢你。
- It will only take a minute for me to get this on your record. 我只要花一分钟的时间就能把这些填到你的记录上。

就这 **900** 句 玩转口语

6 My health insurance is the same. 我的健康保险还是和原来的一样。

我的保险范围没变:

- I have the same health insurance. 我的还是原来的健康保险。
- I've always had the same medical insurance. 我的一直都是一样的医疗保险。

这省去了很多麻烦事:

- That makes things easier then. 那就容易多了。
- That's good. 那太好了。

Medical Insurance Conversation

Kevin: Hi there.	凯 文: 你好。
Clerk: Hello. How may I help you?	职 员: 你好。我能帮你什么吗?
Kevin: I have a few questions about my health insurance.	凯 文: 我有几个关于医疗保险的问题。
Clerk: Yes? What is it?	职 员: 是吗? 是什么?
Kevin: I got a bill for the surgery I had a few weeks ago, and the hospital said my insurance didn't cover it.	凯 文: 我有一张几周前手术的医疗账单,医院说我的保险不包括这些费用。
Clerk: Do you have a copy of the bill?	职 员: 你有这张费用单的复印件吗?
Kevin: Yes, here you go. I knew my insurance wouldn't cover the ambulance bill, but I thought it was supposed to cover any emergency operation.	凯 文: 有,给你。我知道我的保险不包括叫救护车的费用,但我觉得它应该包括所有的急诊手术费用。
Clerk: Ah, yes. Your insurance should take care of this. There must have been a mistake.	职 员: 啊,是的。你的保险应该包括这些。这一定是出错了。
Kevin: Oh! That's good to hear.	凯 文: 哦! 听你这么说真高兴。

546

Clerk: I'll take care of it for you. Just give me your home phone number and I'll let you know what happens.	**职　员：** 我给你看一下，你把你家的电话告诉我，一有消息我就告诉你。
Kevin: Thank you very much. Have a great day.	**凯　文：** 多谢你了。祝你愉快。
Clerk: You too, sir.	**职　员：** 你也一样，先生。

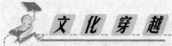

文化穿越

　　美国的医疗费用极其昂贵，看病的费用高得惊人，大部分美国人都未雨绸缪，为自己和家人购买了医疗保险。美国的医疗保险体制分为公私两大块，大部分美国人参加由商业保险公司提供的私人医疗保险，少部分美国人（包括社会特殊群体和社会弱势群体）参加由政府提供的社会医疗保险。一般人可能会认为，美国穷人没有医疗保险，富人才有。穷人看不起病，就只有等死。其实在美国，各大医院都有一部分钱专门用来支付没有保险的人的紧急医疗费用。更好笑的是，他们不会问你是哪里来的人，只要你没有医疗保险，你就能接受免费紧急治疗。此外，美国也有针对留学生的医疗保险，其中有一家叫做 ISO (http: // www.isoa. org) 的保险公司，里面的国际留学生医疗体系很不错，很多国际留学生也都会买这个险种。它是根据年龄段来划分交钱的额度，最便宜的大概是 30 多美元一个月，与同类保险相比性价比较高。

Chapter 15 享受公共服务

Public Service

Section 1

邮局
Post Office

在上一章里，我们说到医疗保险的问题，在这一章，我们展开一下，把一般的公共服务都和大家分享一下，我们就先说邮局吧。在美国，你会发现每家门口都有个小小的邮政信箱，我家当然也有一个了。我们平常寄信不一定非要到邮局去，把信贴好邮票放在自家的信箱里就行。不过如果你要寄一些特殊的信函或包裹等等，还是去一趟邮局吧。

① Hello, I'd like to ship this package. 你好，我想寄这个包裹。

类似的说法还有：
- Could I ship this package? 我能寄这个包裹吗？
- I need to ship this package. 我要寄这个包裹。
- Hi, I have a package and I'd like to ship. 嗨，我有个包裹要寄。

工作人员的回答：
- Sure, can I see it? 好的，我能看看吗？
- Sure, hand it here, please. 好的，请放在这里。

② Hey there, could I buy some stamps? 你好，我能买些邮票吗？

相同的说法有：
- Hey man (if male), could I get some stamps? 你好，我能买些邮票吗？

还可以询问邮票的种类：
- What kind of stamps do you guys have? I need some. 你们有什么类型的邮票？我要一些。

对方把邮票展示给你看：

- These are the stamps that we have in stock right now. 这些是我们现有的邮票。

❖ hey there 你好，相当于 hello。

③ Could you help me open up a P. O. box? 你能帮我打开邮箱吗？

乐意提供帮助：

- Sure, let me help you. 好的，我来帮你吧。

❖ P. O. 邮局，post office 的首字母缩写。

④ How much is postage to Alaska? 到阿拉斯加的邮费是多少？

询问邮资还可以这样说：

- How much is it to ship to California? 把这个寄到加州要多少钱？
- How much do I have to pay to ship a package to Oregon? 寄一个包裹到俄勒冈要多少钱？
- What's the postage rate for a package going to Florida? 往佛罗里达寄一个包裹邮资是多少？

对方会告诉你：

- You need a 25-cent stamp. 你需要一张 25 美分的邮票。
- From here, you'll need a 50-cent stamp. 从这里的话，你需要一张 50 美分的邮票。
- Just a 5-cent stamp. 一张 5 美分的邮票就行。

❖ How much... 是询问价钱多少的句型。

❖ postage ['pəʊstɪdʒ] n. 邮资，邮费

⑤ Where is the drop box for a UPS package? UPS 包裹的投递箱在哪里？

如果你知道投递箱在哪里：

- It's right behind the door. 就在门后边。

❖ UPS: United Parcel Service 的缩略语，联合包裹服务公司。

⑥ Do you sell envelopes here? 你这儿卖信封吗？

你还可以这么询问：

- I need an envelope to mail this, do you sell them here? 我需要一个信封来寄这个，你这儿有卖吗？

如果没有这一项服务：

- Sorry, we don't sell those here. 抱歉，我们这里不卖这些。

❖ envelope ['envə,ləp] *n.* 信封

Post Office Conversation

Kevin:	Hey man, I need to go to the post office, want to come with me?	凯 文：	嘿，哥们儿，我要去邮局，想一起去吗？
Steve:	I can't, dude. I've got to hit up the lundromat and do my clothes. Maybe after that?	史蒂夫：	不行啊，我还得去洗衣店洗衣服，洗完之后再去吧？
Kevin:	Alright, sounds good, dude. Hey, do you have any stamps? I never remember to keep mine.	凯 文：	好吧，听起来不错，哥们儿。嘿，你有邮票吗？我总是忘记拿邮票。
Steve:	No way. No one uses snail mail nowadays anyway! Just email stuff dude, it's the 21st century.	史蒂夫：	没有。现在没有人用蜗牛邮件了！发电子邮件吧，哥们儿，现在是 21 世纪了。
Kevin:	Some of us have bills, smart guy.	凯 文：	我们有些人还是会有账单的，聪明的家伙。
Steve:	Yeah yeah, I guess you have a point.	史蒂夫：	也是，也是，我想你的话也很有道理。
Kevin:	Well hey, do they have an after-hours drop box?	凯 文：	嘿，他们会有非工作时间的投递箱吗？
Steve:	Probably, they usually have some of those in the parking lot.	史蒂夫：	可能有吧，他们通常在停车场有这种投递箱。

Kevin: Well, maybe I'll just drop my mail off there and head out to do laundry with you later.	凯　文：哦，我可能先去那里投信，然后再和你去洗衣服。
Steve: Really? Dude you totally should. I'm going to be so bored.	史蒂夫：真的吗？哥们儿，你确实该这样，我都快无聊死了。
Kevin: (Laughs) Alright, we'll see man.	凯　文：（笑）好吧，一会儿见，哥们儿。

❖hit up 去某地，做某事

❖laundromat ['lɔndrəmæt] n. 自助洗衣店

❖snail mail 蜗牛邮件，形容速度非常慢

❖have a point 正确，中肯，很有道理

❖after-hours drop box 非工作时间的投递箱

文 化 穿 越

　　在美国，平时我经常会给其他州的朋友或者国内的亲戚朋友寄些东西。现在简单给大家说说信封的注意事项。由于不同邮局的要求不同，所以地址等位置的填写也会不同，但大体内容是一样的。收件人以及寄信人的地址、姓名、邮编、电话都需要写上。我邮寄重要信件或物品时，一般用双语，先写一遍英文，之后是中文，但最重要的是完成填写后，一定要把最终目的地用英文和中文写在醒目的地方（例如：To Beijing，北京）。一般情况下平均一周时间可到达。由于不同地方邮费标准不同，查阅相关邮局网站即可，美国邮政局的网址：http://www.usps.com/。

　　一般经常旅游的朋友可以去收集美国不同城市的邮戳，邮局会有专门的地方免费盖戳，另外专门会有收集这些邮戳的册子，邮局都有售。纽约联合国的地下邮局可以制作含有自己大头像的邮票，之后可以寄给家人，很有纪念意义。另外经常旅游的朋友会明白，最珍贵的不是将一张空白的明信片带回国去，而是从美国的当地寄回家里，这样上面会有每个地方的邮局专用邮戳。

在中国出门在外，没钱是万万不能的，可是在美国，"有钱"也是万万不能的。为什么呢？因为在美国很少有人用现金交易，大多数交易都是用支票。为了适应这个现金越来越少的社会（Cash-less society），对于初到美国的人来说，去银行办理相关的支票账户以及储蓄账户手续是必不可少的一个环节。

1 Good morning, I'd like to open a new account. 早上好，我想新开一个账户。

这句话类似的说法还有：

- How are you today? I would like to open a new account. 今天怎么样？我想新开一个账户。
- Could I open a new account, please? 我能新开一个账户吗？

这时对方可能会这样回答：

- Sure, I just need two forms of I. D.. 好的，我需要两张身份证明的表格就行。

2 Hello, could I start a new checking account? 你好，我能新开一个活期账户吗？

如果想开一个别的账户：

- Hi there, I need to start a savings account. 你好，我需要开一个储蓄账户。

对方可能会这样回答：

- Yeah, just let me see your I. D. and Social Security Card, please. 好的，请把你的身份证和社保卡给我看看。

❖ checking account（美）活期账户，相当于 current account（英）

❖ savings account 储蓄账户

❖ Social Security Card 社保卡

3 I need to transfer funds to a different account. 我需要往别的账户上转钱。

类似的说法有：

· Hi there, I need to transfer my funds to a different account please. 你好，我要把我的钱转到别的账户上。

这种业务手续比较简单：

· Just fill out this form. 填写这张表格就行。

4 Hi, I'd like to make a deposit. 嗨，我想存钱。

如果你想表达存钱的确切金额：

· Hey there, could I deposit 100 dollars? 你好，我能存 100 美元吗？

回答：

· Sure, just give me the cash and fill out this form. 好的，把钱给我，填写一下这张表格。

· No problem, just fill this out. 没问题，把这个填写了就行。

❖ deposit [dɪ'pɑzɪt] *n. & vt.* 存款

5 I want to make a withdrawal of 50 dollars from my checking account. 我想从活期账户上取 50 美元。

类似的表达你也要学会哦：

· I need to take some money out, please. 我要取些钱。

· Hey there, could I withdraw some cash? 你好，我能取些现金吗？

对方会回答：

· Yeah sure, just fill this out. 好的，当然可以，只需要填写一下这个。

· withdrawal [wɪθ'drɔəl] *n.* 提款

6 I would like to sign up for a checking card. 我想申办一张借记卡。

申办借记卡：
- Hi, how are you? I'd like to sign up for a checking card. 嗨，你好？我想签约一张借记卡。

提供帮助：
- Sure, let me assist you. 好的，我来帮你。
- ❖ sign up 签约
- ❖ checking card 借记卡，相当于 debit card

7 I need to take out a loan. 我要贷款。

更委婉的说法有：
- Could you help me take out a loan please? 你能帮我贷一笔款吗？

查看信誉度：
- Let me just check your credit. 让我看看你的信用度。

查问信息：
- Sure, let me have your name so I can assist you. 好的，请告诉我你的名字，这样我才能帮你。
- ❖ take out a loan 借款，贷款

8 Hi, could I get some checks? 嗨，我能买些支票吗？

更直截了当的说法有：
- Hey there, I need to get some checks please. 你好，我需要买些支票。

这可能和中国不同，人家会要求：
- Sure, what's your account number? 好的，你的账号是多少？

9 I need to pay a fee for over-drafting my account. 我要给透支账户还款。

你还可以这样表达：
- I over-drafted my account and I need to pay the fee. 我的账户透支了，我需要还款。

这时对方会报出你需要还款的金额：
- Sure, that will be 40 dollars. 好的，一共是 40 美元。
- ❖ pay a fee 缴纳费用
- ❖ over-draft 账户透支

 交流面对面

Bank Conversation

Kevin:	Hi there, I'd like to open a new account and deposit 50 dollars.	凯文:	你好，我想新开一个账户存50美元。
Clerk:	No problem. Just fill this out for me.	职员:	没问题，把这个填了给我就行。
Kevin:	Alright, hey, can I ask you a question?	凯文:	好的，嘿，我能问你个问题吗？
Clerk:	Sure.	职员:	当然可以。
Kevin:	What do I need to take out a loan?	凯文:	我该办什么手续才能贷款？
Clerk:	Well, usually we require multiple forms of I. D. and a credit check.	职员:	嗯，通常我们会要求身份证明和信用调查的各种表单。
Kevin:	Oh OK, that doesn't sound so bad.	凯文:	哦，好的，听上去还可以。
Clerk:	You can come in Monday through Friday, from 6 a.m. until 5 p.m..	职员:	你可以在周一至周五的早上6点到下午5点这个时间段来。
Kevin:	Sound good to me, thanks for the help!	凯文:	对我来说都行，谢谢你的帮助！
Clerk:	Anytime.	职员:	不用客气！有事随时开口。
Kevin:	Here's the form, and the cash.	凯文:	这是表单和钱。
Clerk:	Alright, let me just put in your information. You're all set, have a great day.	职员:	好的，我来把你的信息输进去。都办好了，祝你愉快。
Kevin:	You too.	凯文:	你也是。

❖ multiple ['mʌltɪpl] *adj.* 多样的，复合的
❖ credit check 信用检查
❖ be all set 准备就绪，一切妥当

　　关于美国银行，留学生第一次接触到的便是学校所介绍的附近当地银行或 BOA（Bank of America）。不管是美国当地银行还是美国几大著名银行，第一次申请一般会是借记卡（Debit Card）。信用卡只有等申请到 SSN（Social Security Number 社会保险号）才能办理。

　　美国留学生有几样东西是决不能丢的，护照、I-20、SSN，另外就是借记卡或信用卡。你或许会奇怪，信用卡或借记卡丢了取不出钱，对，没错，但在美国是可以随便刷卡的，收银员会问及你要用的是信用卡还是借记卡（借记卡可以透支当信用卡使用），如果你说借记卡，那么需要输入 4 位密码，但如果你说信用卡，最后签名即可，因此你的卡如果丢失，别人可以签你的名字刷卡。

　　另外，在此建议大家不要轻易申请信用卡，因为很多银行的信用卡年费是很高的，有的甚至还有很多附加条款，留学生如果注意不到，有时候会很麻烦，甚至会吃官司。来美国有几种方法可以携带钱，现金、电汇、旅行支票、信用卡存款等，一般额度大的需要跟学校确认，因为有时学校规定交款方式，甚至会规定 MASTER CARD 或 VISA。除了现金外，本人常用的是电汇，速度快，手续费少，而且安全，但第一次去美国如果需要带大额度的钱，可以将钱存入国内信用卡内，但最好不要在美国用国内信用卡取款，因为手续费会非常高。

Section 3  博物馆
Museum

作为风景和文化结合的产物——博物馆，不仅是一个国家的文化景致，更是一个城市历史文化的汇集地，其发达程度也正在成为一个社会文明程度的重要标志。Kevin 有时间的话会经常去博物馆，且不说博物馆的门票一般比较便宜，更重要的是通过参观不同的博物馆，你能领略到各种不同文化。

1 I need one ticket to the museum, please. 我要一张博物馆的门票。

更直接的表达：
- Admission for one, please. 请给我一张门票。

告知价格：
- Sure, that will be 12 dollars. 好的，12 美元。
- No problem, 10 bucks please. 没问题，10 美元。
- ❖ admission [əd'mɪʃən] *n.* 允许进入

2 Wow, this is a really interesting piece! 哇，这真是个有趣的东西。

看到眼前一亮的东西：
- I really love how this looks. 我真的很喜欢这图案。
- This is amazing! 这太神奇了！

3 Let's go to the gift shop! 咱们去礼品店！

博物馆也会卖一些纪念品：
- Hey, let's go check out the gift shop. 嘿，咱们去礼品店看看。

如果你愿意，可以这样附和：
- Sure, man. Lead the way. 好的，老兄，带路吧。

4 When was this painting created? 这幅油画是什么时候创作的?

相同的表达还有:

- What year is this from? 这是哪年的?

如果你知道确切的年份:

- This was painted in 1963. 这是 1963 年画的。

5 Is this a reproduction? 这是复制品吗?

你还可以这么说:

- Is this piece a reproduction? 这是复制品吗?

如果确定是复制品:

- Yes, this is a reproduction. 是的，这是复制品。
- ❖ reproduction [ˌrɪprə'dʌkʃən] *n.* 复制品

6 Are any of these for sale? 这些出售吗?

询问出售的东西:

- Is this for sale? 这个卖吗?
- Are any of the things on display for sale? 这些展览的东西出售吗?

如果可以卖:

- Yes, the prices are listed here. 是的，价格列在这里了。

如果不行的话，也只能表示遗憾了:

- No, I'm sorry but these are not for sale. 抱歉，但这些都不卖。
- ❖ for sale 出售，待售
- ❖ on display 展览，公开展出

Museum Conversation

Kevin: Wow, this piece is really great, is it for sale?

凯文： 哇，这件东西真的很不错，这卖吗?

Guide: No, this one isn't for sale actually. It's a very special painting for the artist's mother.

导游： 不卖，这件确实不卖，这是为了纪念艺术家的母亲而作的一幅特别的画作。

就这 900 句 玩转口语

Kevin: Oh I see. Well, it's absolutely amazing. I love how the colors accent off each other.

Guide: You have a good eye for art!

Kevin: Thank you! I used to major in art.

Guide: Oh really, well you really must appreciate this section.

Kevin: I do, I'm a big fan of how the artist plays colors off of each other.

Guide: I agree. It's one of his strong points.

Kevin: Beyond some technical issues, these are some of the best paintings I've seen hung around the city.

Guide: Well, thank you for coming in. It isn't often that I get to talk to someone so interested in art.

凯文：哦，我明白了，不过绝对是非常精巧的，我喜欢这颜色与颜色之间互相衬托。

导游：你真有艺术眼光。

凯文：谢谢！我以前是主修艺术的！

导游：哦，是吗，那你肯定真欣赏这幅作品。

凯文：确实，我对艺术家的着色技巧特别着迷。

导游：我同意你的说法，这是他的强项之一。

凯文：除了一些技术问题，这些是我在这个城市见过的一些最好的画作了。

导游：嗯，谢谢你来这里，我和这么对艺术感兴趣的人谈话也不是经常的事。

❖ accent ['æksɛnt] *vt.* 突出，强调
❖ have a good eye for... 对……有眼光，对……有鉴赏力
❖ strong point 强项
❖ beyond [br'jand] *prep.* 越出，越过
❖ hung around 逗留，闲逛

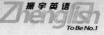

文 化 穿 越

　　美国的博物馆很系统化。一些地方的博物馆很值得一看，尤其是位于纽约和华盛顿的博物馆。纽约的 The Metropolitan Museum of Art (http://www. metmuseum. org) 是比较著名的，内部很大，全部看完至少需要大半天的时间，甚至一整天。The Museum of Modern Art（MOMA. ，http://www. moma. org) 现代艺术博物馆，喜欢现代艺术的朋友们可以来这里看看。Solomon R. Guggenheim Museum (http://www. guggenheim. org) 里面，会有不同著名艺术家的作品，此馆外围设计很醒目。

　　以上提及的博物馆是纽约比较著名的三座，当然也是 city pass 所包括的。(city pass 是类似于包票的东西，包括一些博物馆和著名建筑游览的门票，会比单价便宜很多，美国很多著名大城市都会有。) 至于华盛顿，那里的博物馆如果要认真看的话，要看上至少半个月的时间。有很多世界著名的博物馆，例如：Smithsonian Institution National Museum of Natural History（http://www. mnh. si. edu）; National Museum of the American Indian (http://www. nmai. si. edu）; Smithsonian National Air and Space Museum (http://www. nasm. si. edu) 等。

　　在美国每个著名博物馆和景点都会有一个挤压纪念币的机器，一般是 1 美元可以挤压一个纪念币，纪念币上是景点的 LOGO，可以自己选择式样，自己压制。另外，专门有一个纪念币册子，在很多地方都有售。

Section 4

电话亭
Telephone Booth/Collect Calling

其实随着手机的普及，美国付费公用电话正逐渐淡出历史舞台。但无论怎么普及，人们总会有忘带手机和手机没电的时候。所以公用电话有时候还是会用到的，在这一节，我就给大家简单讲解一下公用电话的口语。

① Hi there, where is the nearest public phone? 你好，最近的公用电话在哪里？

这个表达也是非常不错的哦：

- Excuse me, is there a phone booth around here? 打扰一下，这附近有公用电话吗？

如果对方知道，就会回答：

- Yeah man, right over there. 有，伙计，就在那儿。
- The nearest phone is right around the corner. 最近的公用电话就在拐角处。

❖ phone booth 公用电话亭
❖ around the corner 在拐角处

② Hello there, I'd like to make a collect call. 你好，我想打个对方付费电话。

你还可以更礼貌地说：

- Could I make a collect call, please? 我能打个对方付费的电话吗？

接线员问你的信息：

- Yes, may I have your name? 好的，能告诉我你的名字吗？

[补充] 接线员要把你转接给对方，所以一般要问清楚你的姓名以及对方的姓名和号码等。

❖ collect call 对方付费电话

3 Operator, could I make a collect call to Samantha Heart? 接线员，我能打个对方付费的电话给萨曼莎·哈特吗？

打对方付费的电话一般会有一些特殊的要求：

• Absolutely, could I have your credit card number? 当然可以，能告诉我你的信用卡号吗？

4 Hi, I have a calling card. 嗨，我有张电话卡。

如果你想更明确一点儿：

• Hello operator, I'd like to use my calling card. 你好接线员，我想用我的电话卡。

对方一般会要求：

• Sure, could I have the code on the back? 好的，能告诉我背面的卡号吗？（这一般相当于在中国用 IC 卡打电话一样，要输入卡号和密码。）

❖ calling card 电话卡

5 The phone over there needs to be fixed. 那边那部电话需要修理了。

你还可以说：

• Excuse me, your phone is broken. 抱歉，你的电话坏了。

道歉，并给出解决方法：

• Oh man, I'm sorry, we'll get that fixed. 哦，伙计，对不起，我们会修理的。

6 Sorry to have to keep you waiting. 抱歉，让您久等了。

如果你占用公用电话太长的时间，而恰好后面还有人在等着用电话，你打完后可以这么礼貌地对等待的人说，对方也会很理解地说声：

• That's okay. 没关系。

Telephone Booth Conversation

Kevin: Hello operator, could I make a collect call to Denver. My card number is 789.

凯　文：你好接线员，我能打个对方付费的电话到丹佛吗，我的卡号是789。

Operator: Sure, let me patch you through. Do you accept the fee?

接线员：好的，我来给你接通，你接受这费用吗？

Kevin: Yes.

凯　文：好的。

Operator: One moment please.

接线员：请稍等。

Kevin: Alright.

凯　文：好的。

Operator: We're experiencing some trouble. Would you care to use a different phone?

接线员：我们这儿正有些麻烦。你介意用别的电话吗？

Kevin: Yeah, I guess so. (angry)

凯　文：是的，我想是的。（生气）

(Kevin tries another pay phone)

（凯文试另一部付费电话）

Kevin: Hello operator. Could I make a collect call to Denver?

凯　文：你好，接线员，我能打个对方付费的电话到丹佛吗？

Operator: Sure, what's your card number?

接线员：好的，你的卡号是多少？

Kevin: 789. I just bought it today.

凯　文：789。我今天刚买的。

Operator: Ok, you're all set. Please hold.

接线员：好的，都好了，请别挂电话。

Kevin: Thank god!

凯　文：谢天谢地！

❖patch through 接通（电话）

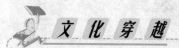

文化穿越

　　美国的电话网络系统与国内不同。对于手机而言，有以下几家主流公司，AT&T, T-MOBILE, SPRINT, VERIZON 等。其中有很多需要注意的地方。中国学生一直认为美国的手机一般比中国的便宜甚至免费，实际上这种便宜是有条件的。例如：如果想购买最新的 IPHONE 手机，有两种途径，一种是直接购买，大概价格平均在 700-800 美元之间；但如果与 AT&T 公司签两年或者一年的绑定合同，便会便宜到 199 或 299 美元一个，但条件是每个月最低月费为大概 70 美元左右，这样算下来，一年将要花在电话上的费用便是 800 多美元，加上手机 200 美元的费用，大概是 1000 美元左右，这样貌似比国内也便宜有限。一般的手机也是同样套路，但会比 IPHONE 便宜很多，另外人多的话，可以跟公司签 FAMILY PLAN，这样大家可以平摊一个套餐，但分钟和短信是大家平分的，一旦超出，费用也会另算。美国手机唯一的优势是每天晚上 9 点后和周末都是免费，另外使用同一家通讯公司业务的人，其手机之间的通讯服务也是免费的。美国本土学生更倾向于使用 VERIZON，但公司里面，只有 AT&T 与 T-MOBILE 是使用 SIM 卡的，因此，想将手机带回国刷机的朋友可以选择这两个公司。

　　以下是几种和中国国内联系的方式。留学生里最常用的是 SKYPE 视频通话，QQ 腾讯或者 MSN。这三种都有视讯功能，可以随时和家人视频，而且是免费的，至于哪种更清晰，每个人都有自己的偏好。

Section 5

社区居委会
Neighborhood Community

在美国，社区居委会的服务比较齐全，社区居民也真正是社区的主人。居民小区管理员经常召集小区居民开会，讨论小区的一些具体问题，比如小区居民不遵守规定而乱扔垃圾、不文明居民制造影响别人的噪音等都是会议讨论的话题。小区要增加建筑或者什么公共设施，也需要小区居民会议的批准。所以，在这些时候，你可以充分行使你作为居民的权利。

口语大放送

1   I would like to raise a question. 我想提个问题。

在居民会议上：

- I want to publicly ask something. 我想公开问些事情。

大家对于你的提问，也会让你充分表述的：

- Sure, what is it? 好的，是什么？
- ❖ raise a question 提出问题

2   We need better security in the neighborhood. 我们社区需要更好的安全措施。

社区安全：

- We need to raise security awareness. 我们需要提高安全意识。
- Our neighborhood needs better security. 我们社区需要更好的安全措施。
- ❖ awareness [ə'wɛrnɪs] n. 意识，觉悟

3   Someone must be leaving their trash out. I've been seeing raccoons in my yard all week. 有些人务必要把他们的垃圾扔出去，我整个星期都看到有浣熊在我院子里。

类似的句子还可以这样说：

- We need to clean our trash up better, raccoons are raising hell all over the neighborhood. 我们需要把垃圾清理得更干净，浣熊把整个社区都搞得乱糟糟的。

【补充】浣熊是北美常见的动物，在一些影视剧中也经常出现在居民区附近，比如电视剧 *Men In Trees* 中经常出现的那只浣熊让人既爱又恨。

❖ trash [træʃ] *n.* 废物，垃圾
❖ raccoon [ræ'kun] *n.* 浣熊

④ My pet went missing, could we put up some posters? 我的宠物走失了，我们能张贴些广告吗？

发动社区里的人帮忙：

- My dog ran away last night and I can't find him, could everyone work together to look around? 我的狗昨晚上跑出去了，我找不到它，大家能帮忙四处找找吗？

通常大家也都乐意帮忙：

- Absolutely, I hope we find her soon! 当然可以，我希望我们能很快找到它。

❖ put up 张贴
❖ poster ['postɚ] *n.* 广告，海报

⑤ We need to mow our lawns more often. 我们需要经常修剪草坪。

如果你同意这一建议：

- I agree, things are slipping. 我同意，情况有点儿糟糕了。

相反，如果有不同的意见：

- Get out of here. My lawn looks great! 别开玩笑了，我的草坪看起来非常好！

❖ mow [məu] *vt.* 割草，刈草
❖ slipping ['slɪpɪŋ] *adj.* 渐渐不好了，渐渐糟糕了（俚语的用法）
❖ get out of here 别开玩笑了，别骗人了

6 We will be holding a fundraiser this Saturday, please bring party favors. 这周六我们将举行一个资金筹集活动,请带派对礼物来。

当然还可以更具体一点:

- We're holding a fundraiser this weekend. It would be nice if everyone could bring some chips or drinks. 这周末我们将举行一个资金筹集活动, 如果大家带些炸薯片和饮料过来肯定会更好。
- ❖ fundraiser ['fʌndˌrezɜ] n. 资金筹集活动
- ❖ party favors 派对小礼物

7 I would like to cast a vote. 我想投票。

也可以更具体一点儿:

- I want to cast a vote about loud music policies. 我想对关于嘈杂音乐的政策投票。

还可以寻求其他人的投票:

- I'm casting a vote. All in favor raise your hand please. 我要投票, 赞成的请举手。
- ❖ cast a vote 投票
- ❖ in favor 赞同, 支持

8 I would like to veto the vote on loud music. 我想对嘈杂音乐投否决票。

你还可以寻求其他人的支持:

- I'm going to veto the last vote. All in favor please raise your hand. 我想投最后否决票, 赞成的请举手。
- ❖ veto ['vito] vt. 否决, 反对

交流面对面

Neighborhood Community Conversation

Kevin: I've been having a real issue with raccoons getting into my garbage. It's annoying to say the least.

凯　文: 我有一个问题是关于浣熊进到我的垃圾桶里的, 太恼人了, 至少可以这么说。

Brenda:	Yeah I've seen them poking around in my yard at night too! Someone needs to put a stop to this!	布伦达：	是啊，晚上的时候我也看到它们在我院子里到处跑！真应该有人来制止这件事！
Paul:	We need to hire a pest control company.	保　罗：	我们需要雇一家害虫防治公司。
Kevin:	Now we're talking! I'll look into it in the morning.	凯　文：	现在咱们讨论吧！早上我会调查这事的。
(After meeting)		（会后）	
Kevin:	Paul, thanks for bringing me that flour yesterday. You're a life saver.	凯　文：	保罗，谢谢你昨天给我把那面粉带回来，你真是个救命的大好人。
Paul:	Oh, no problem, man. We have too much anyway.	保　罗：	哦，没关系的，哥们儿，不管怎么说我们交情都这么好。
Kevin:	Well, I'll pay you back somehow, just ask.	凯　文：	不管怎样我会回报你的，你尽管说就行。
Paul:	Well actually, I could really use a ladle if you happen to have one.	保　罗：	嗯，实际上，我真需要一个长柄勺，如果你有的话。
Kevin:	I do, I never use it either! I'll bring it over tomorrow.	凯　文：	我有，我也从来不用它！我明天给你带过去。
Paul:	That would be perfect. Thank you!	保　罗：	那太好了，谢谢你！

❖annoying [ə'nɔɪɪŋ] *adj.* 讨厌的，恼人的
❖to say the least 退一步说，至少可以这么说
❖poke around 闲逛，到处打探
❖put a stop 停止，制止
❖ladle ['leɪdl] *n.* 勺子，长柄勺

文 化 穿 越

在美国，也有这种类似居委会的机构，不过大部分都是物业来担当。很多社区对于抽烟，宠物，噪音都有特殊的规定。抽烟一般会被划定区域或者规定离建筑物多少米以外的地方才可以抽烟。宠物有的社区是禁止的，因为很多住户反映宠物给社区造成了环境污染。对于噪音限制，一般是汽车的鸣笛和派对的时间，汽车一旦进入社区就不许鸣笛，有些州的法律也明确了这一点。另外，对于邻居的派对过于吵闹可以给予口头警告，如果不管用，还可以报警。

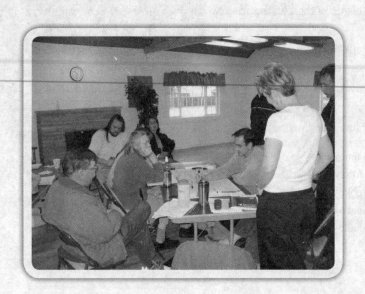

Section 6　 警察局
Police Station

　　我们经常从好莱坞大片中看见 FBI 的身影，可实际上美国的警察局是地方的，是地方执法部门，它并不归美国联邦政府管，因此地方警察局的权限主要是维护地方治安。当然警察局这个地方也没什么可怕的，如果有必要，还可以带小孩子进去参观，以了解更多的安全知识。

① Good morning officer, I need to file a complaint. 早上好，警官，我要投诉。

如果是针对具体的某个人：

- Hello officer, could I file a complaint against John? 你好，警官，我能对约翰提出申诉吗？
- Officer, I need to file a complaint about our neighbors. 警官，我要投诉我的邻居。

那些警察同志经常会回答：

- Sure, just fill out this form for me. 好的，填写这个表格就行。

② Hello officer, could I sign up for a parking pass at my college? 你好，警官，我能登记一张校园停车证吗？

你还可以说明原因：

- Hey there, I go to Edinboro University and I need a parking permit. 你好，我要去艾丁波尔大学，我需要一张停车证。

警察同志一般会要求你：

- Sure, let me see your driver's license and registration please. 好的，请给我看看你的驾驶证和行车证。

❖ parking pass 违规停车罚单

❖ parking permit 停车证

❖ registration [ˌrɛdʒɪˈstreʃən] *n.* 登记，注册（driver's registration 行车证）

3 I need to pay a ticket I got last week. 我要付一张上周的交通罚款单。

交罚款单：

• I got a parking ticket last week and I need to pay it. 我上周有一张违规停车罚单，我来支付它。

• I got a traffic violation the other day and it said to come in here and pay it. 我前天有一张交通违规单，据说是来这里缴费。

警察会很乐意的：

• No problem, just sign here. 没问题，在这里签字吧。

❖ violation [ˌvaɪəˈleʃən] *n.* 违反，违规

4 Hello, I'm here to make a payment on my fine. 你好，我来这里交罚款。

你还可以这么说：

• Good morning, I need to make a payment on my ticket fine. 早上好，我有一张罚款单要支付。

警察一般会让你填一张单子：

• Ok, just fill this out for me. 好的，把这个填了给我就行。

❖ make a payment 付款，支付

❖ fine [faɪn] *n.* 罚款，罚金

5 Hello officer, I need to report someone missing. 你好，警官，我要报案，有人走失了。

向警察报案：

• Officer, I haven't seen or heard from my close friend in a week. I need to make a report. 警官，我已经有一周没看到也没听到我好朋友的消息了，我要报案。

警察询问具体信息：

• I'm sorry to hear that. What was his or her name? 听到这消息我很难过，他或她叫什么名字？

Police Station Conversation

Kevin: Hello officer, I'm here to pay my parking ticket.

凯文：你好，警官，我来这里交违规停车罚单。

Officer: No problem. May I have you license number and 15 dollars please?

警官：没问题，请给我你的驾照号码和 15 美元好吗？

Kevin: Sure, let me go and get the license plate number for you.

凯文：好的，我去把车牌号拿来给你。

(Kevin leaves to record his plate number)

（凯文去记录车牌号）

Kevin: Here you go.

凯文：给你。

Officer: Alright, let me just put in your info.

警官：好的，我来输入你的信息。

Kevin: Do you guys get a lot of parking tickets a day?

凯文：你们一天有很多违规停车罚款单吗？

Officer: Oh, more than you would believe.

警官：哦，比你想象的还多。

Kevin: (Laughs) Yikes, I'm sure you've seen quite a few angry people today.

凯文：（笑）哎呀，我肯定你今天见过不少愤怒的人吧。

Officer: More than a few!

警官：比不少还多！

(Kevin and the officer laugh)

（凯文和警官都笑了）

Officer: Alright, you're all set. Have a great night.

警官：好了，都办好了，祝你有个愉快的夜晚。

Kevin: You too.

凯文：你也一样。

❖info ['ɪnfo] *n.* 资料
❖quite a few 不少，相当多

文化穿越

在美国，警察其实不太受人民喜爱。因为任何事件警察都需要走审查程序，一个程序下来会很久，因此，一般性事件美国人是不报警的。对于留美的学生来说，手机里需要有三个号码，一个是美国最亲近朋友的号码，一个是警察局号码，最后一个是大使馆或领事馆号码（大城市）。出入警察局的人除了罪犯外，其他的多是被贴了罚单的百姓，他们需要按时交罚金。除此之外，一般学校内会有警察局驻点，晚上警车会在学校周边巡逻，如果很晚在学校里溜达，有可能会被警察检查证件，因此学校 ID 要随身携带。

Section 7 理发店 Hair Salon

在美国，去理发店理发也是一笔不菲的开销，因为你除了要付理发的费用外，还要额外给理发师小费。还有一点和咱们国内的一样，就是大多数的理发师在给你剪头发的时候会向你推销各种额外的消费，有时候你一不留神，就会中了他们的"圈套"，从而多消费很多美元。

1 Hey there! I just need my hair cut, please. 你好！我要剪头发。

如果你和理发店的人很熟：

- How are you today? Just a trim today. 今天怎么样？这次稍微修剪一下就行。

理发师一般会回答你：

- Sure, sit down in the chair over there. 好的，坐在那边的椅子上吧。

❖ trim [trɪm] vt. 修剪，修整

2 Oh wow, I really love the shampoo. Is it for sale? 哦，哇，我真的很喜欢这洗发水，这卖吗？

你还可以这样询问：

- This stuff is amazing! Where can I get it? 这东西太神奇了！我在哪里能买到？

如果这洗发水刚好在理发店有卖：

- Ha! Well we have it for sale right over here! 哈！我们这儿刚好有卖的！

❖ shampoo [ʃæmˈpu] n. 洗发剂，洗发水

575

3 Hey, could you cut my hair a little shorter? 嘿，你能把我的头发稍微剪短些吗？

把头发剪短些：

- Could I get this cut a little shorter, please? 请把这稍微剪短些好吗？
- I love it, but could you go a bit shorter? 我挺喜欢的，但是你还能再稍微剪短些吗？

理发师一般会遵照你的要求：

- Sure, no problem! 当然可以，没问题！

4 What should I put in my hair to keep it soft? 我该在头发上抹什么才能让头发保持柔顺呢？

征询建议：

- I want to keep my hair soft, what do you recommend? 我想让头发保持柔顺，你有什么建议？

理发师会向你推销：

- Well, we have a product on sale that would be perfect for you! 嗯，我们有一款热销产品，对你应当非常适用。

❖ recommend [ˌrekəˈmend] vt. 推荐，建议

5 What do I need to do to keep my hair like you've made it? 我要怎么做才能使头发保持得像你打理的这样？

向理发师咨询：

- I love what you've done with my hair! What do I need to do to make it look like this all the time? 我很喜欢你给我做的头发！我要怎么做才能一直保持像这样子呢？
- Wow this looks great! What should I put in my hair to make it stay like this? 哇，看起来非常好！我该在头发上抹什么才能保持像这样子呢？

理发师也会趁机向你推销产品哦：

- Thanks! Just use the product we have at the counter. 谢谢！用我们柜台上的这款产品就行。

6 What do I owe you? 我该付你多少钱？

付款：

- Hey thanks a lot! What do I owe you? 嘿，多谢！我该付你多少钱？
- This was great! How much? 这太棒了！多少钱？

对方会告诉你：

- That will be 12 dollars. 总共 12 美元。
- You're welcome! The haircut comes to 15 dollars! 不客气！总共是 15 美元。

Hair Salon Conversation

Kevin: I don't usually come here to get my hair cut.	凯　文：我不经常来这儿剪头发。
Monica: Oh yeah? Well I won't bite, don't worry.	莫妮卡：哦，是吗？不过我不会吃了你的，别担心。
(Kevin and Monica laugh)	（凯文和莫妮卡都笑了）
Kevin: (Laughs) I'll trust you.	凯　文：我相信你。（笑着说）
Monica: So how would you like your hair cut?	莫妮卡：那你想把头发剪成什么样式的？
Kevin: Just a little trim, an inch off each side, I think.	凯　文：修一下就行，我觉得两边各修一寸就可以了。
Monica: No problem!	莫妮卡：没问题！
(Kevin gets his hair cut)	（凯文在剪头发）
Kevin: Thanks for the haircut!	凯　文：谢谢你给我理发！
Monica: My pleasure! I'll ring you out up front.	莫妮卡：很高兴为您服务！我带您到前台去结账。
Kevin: So what do I owe you?	凯　文：我该付你多少钱？
Monica: 12 dollars, please!	莫妮卡：12 美元！
Kevin: Here you go. Keep the change!	凯　文：给你钱，不要找零了！
Monica: Thanks! Have a great day!	莫妮卡：谢谢！祝您愉快！

❖ I won't bite. 我不会吃了你的。意思是不会趁机敲诈，此处 bite 是口语中一种

非正式的用法。

❖ I'll ring you out up front. 我带您到前台去结账。这句话乍一看难以理解，front 在此处的意思是"前台"。

❖ Keep the change. 不用找零。通常这些零钱就当作是小费了。

文化穿越

　　关于理发店，最有意思的是，留美的学生有很多人都养成了自己剪头的习惯，除了便宜外，更大一部分理由是因为美国的理发师经常无法剪出令中国学生满意的发型，因此大家便自己动手。美国城市不同，理发店的价格也会不同，从 15 美元到上百美元不等，另外还要付 15% ~ 20% 的小费。美国的便利店里都会卖很专业的理发套装，价格会比中国便宜很多。

Section 8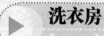
洗衣房
Laundromat

在美国，可能是为了节约资源或省钱，大家洗衣服差不多都是到洗衣房去洗，一周洗一次，每日换洗的东西都放在洗衣袋中，洗衣房有专门的洗衣机和烘干机。到周末统一到洗衣房清洗。周末你可以在任何地方看到很多美国人，拿个大布袋或推个小车，穿梭在街道中……去洗衣店洗衣。

1 Hey, I need to make change for laundry. 嘿，我要换点儿零钱洗衣服。

换零钱洗衣服：
- Hey dude, could I get some change to do my laundry? 嘿，伙计，我要洗衣服，能换些零钱吗？

给你零钱：
- No problem man, here you go. 没问题，老兄，给你。
- Sure, dude, here. 当然可以，老兄，给你。
- ❖ laundry ['lɔːndrɪ] n. 送洗的衣服，洗衣房

2 Man, I hate waiting for my clothes to dry! 老兄，我讨厌等着衣服烘干。

等衣服烘干的过程确实很无聊：
- Ugh, it's so boring waiting for clothes to dry. 啊，等着把衣服烘干真是无聊死了。

大家都认可这一点：
- I know man, I hate this shit. 我知道，老兄，我也讨厌这样。
- I hear ya dude, I hear ya. 没错，老兄，可不是嘛。
- ❖ I hear ya. 是啊，可不是嘛。表示认同对方的话，是口语中一种非正式的用法。

就这 900 句 玩转口语

3 This laundromat is overpriced! 这家自助洗衣店太贵了!

还可以这样牢骚一下:

- This is so expensive, just to clean your clothes! 只是洗一下衣服就这么贵。
- I hate how much this is, ugh. 我讨厌这东西这么贵,啊。

通常会有人附和:

- Yeah man, it's basically robbery! 是啊,简直就是打劫。
- ❖ laundromat ['lɔndrəmæt] *n.* 自助洗衣店
- ❖ overpriced ['ovɚ'praɪst] *adj.* 定价过高的

4 How do I work these laundry machines? 我怎么使用这些洗衣机?

还可以这样询问:

- How do I get this to run properly? 我怎样才能让这正常运转呢?

通常旁边人会很热心地告诉你:

- Just put your money in over here. 把钱从这里投进去就行。
- It's easy, dude. Just put the money in here. 很简单的,伙计,把钱从这里投进去就行。

5 Should I separate my colored clothes? 我该把有颜色的衣服分开吗?

不同颜色的衣服要分开洗:

- I should separate my colored clothes from the white ones, right? 我该把有颜色的衣服和白色的衣服分开,对吗?

当然要分开洗了,否则白色的衣服就要被染上颜色了:

- Yeah, use bleach with your white clothes and wash your colors separately. 是的,用漂白剂洗白色的衣服,有颜色的衣服分开洗。
- ❖ separate ['sɛpəˌret] *vt.* 分开,分离
- ❖ bleach [blitʃ] *n.* 漂白剂

6 I don't want to shrink this jacket, should I use hot or cold water? 我不想让这件夹克缩水,我该用热水还是冷水?

580

询问洗涤方式：

- What would work best for these jeans? Hot or cold water? 这些牛仔裤用什么洗最好？热水还是冷水？

洗涤说明：

- Hot water, for sure. 肯定是热水啊。
- I would use cold water for this. 这个该用冷水吧。

❖ shrink [ʃrɪŋk] *vt.* 收缩，缩水

Laundromat Conversation

Steve: Hey, do you know how much the new laundromat is?	史蒂夫：嘿，你知道那家新开的洗衣店要多少钱吗？
Kevin: Yeah I don't know about that new place, probably 2 or 3 bucks to do a load.	凯 文：我不知道那家新开的店要多少钱，可能洗一筐衣服两到三美元吧。
Steve: God damn it. Why does it have to cost so much? That's way too much for a poor college kid.	史蒂夫：天哪，怎么要那么多钱啊？对一个穷学生来说，那太贵了。
Kevin: Get a job! (laughs) Alright man, I used the after-hours box at the post office. Let's go do laundry.	凯 文：干点儿正经事啊！（笑）好了哥们儿，我还用过邮局的业余邮箱呢，咱们去洗衣房吧。
Steve: Alright man, I'll drive.	史蒂夫：好吧，我来开车。
(They drive to the laundromat)	（他们开车去洗衣房）
Kevin: Ugh, I hate doing laundry so much. So boring and expensive.	凯 文：啊，我讨厌洗这么多衣服。这么无聊还这么贵。
Steve: I hear you, I'm gonna have to start re-wearing clothes for a couple of weeks!	史蒂夫：可不是嘛，我打算把穿过的衣服再穿一两个星期。
Kevin: Gross! Hey do you have any detergent?	凯 文：真恶心！嘿，你有洗衣粉吗？
Steve: Sure, here.	史蒂夫：有，在这儿。

| Kevin: Thanks, man. Well, here's to waiting! | 凯　文：谢谢，伙计。好了，开始等吧！ |

❖ God damn it. 天哪，该死的
❖ Get a job! 干点儿正经事! 找份工作！
❖ after-hours 业余的，工作时间之外的
❖ gross [gros] *adj.* 恶心的，令人厌恶的（俚语）
❖ detergent [dɪˈtɜːdʒərɪd] *n.* 洗衣粉，洗涤剂

文化穿越

　　一般美国洗衣服与中国不同，很多地方的洗衣房都是洗衣机与烘干机分开，就像美国电影中那样。洗衣机是 1 美元左右，通常是 4 个 quarter (25 美分为 1 quarter)，30 分钟时间冲洗，之后是甩干机，1 个 quarter 10 分钟。另外，洗衣服时，要选择衣服的种类，普通衣服，衬衫，还有易变型的衣服有不同的按钮，同样，甩干机也分高温、中温和常温，根据衣服的种类选择温度。一般衣服高温即可。至于洗涤剂，要根据衣服量的大小，但要尽量少放，因为有可能会洗不净。

一笔在手，点遍振宇英语 MPR 有声读物

——振宇英语点读笔，随时点读随心学

- MPR 阅读器任意点读，即时发声，隐形老师随时随地为学习加 FUN。

- 高品质的 MP3，音质完美、娱乐、学习同步进行，还具有多种录音模式，随时随地记录下美好声音。

- 随身 U 盘，存储各种语音学习文件、歌曲等资料，实用方便。

- 外观小巧，携带方便，极富创意的设计，让大脑充满灵感。

与咨询

请访问：**zhenglish.taobao.com**
www.zhenglish.com

网上购笔，送笔上门
www.zhenglish.com

Only Click , Study Easily

只需一点，学习无障碍

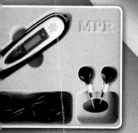